Masters of Illusion

Masters of Illusion

*The Supreme Court and the
Religion Clauses*

Frank S. Ravitch

NEW YORK UNIVERSITY PRESS
New York and London

NEW YORK UNIVERSITY PRESS
New York and London
www.nyupress.org

Library of Congress Cataloging-in-Publication Data
Ravitch, Frank S., 1966–
Masters of illusion : the Supreme Court and the religion clauses /
Frank S. Ravitch.
p.   cm.
Includes bibliographical references and index.
ISBN-13: 978-0-8147-7585-1 (cloth : alk. paper)
ISBN-10: 0-8147-7585-3 (cloth : alk. paper)
1. Freedom of religion—United States—Interpretation and
construction. 2. Church and state—United States—Interpretation
and construction. 3. United States. Constitution. 1st Amendment.
I. Title.
KF4783.R38 2007
342.7308'52—dc22   2006033973

Manufactured in the United States of America
10 9 8 7 6 5 4 3 2 1

*This book is dedicated to my wife, Jamie,
my daughters, Elysha and Ariana,
and my parents, Carl and Arline.
Thank you for all the love and support.
It adds perspective to everything I do.*

Contents

Preface

Law and religion scholarship relating to the First Amendment is broad and diverse. There are many wonderful and brilliant people engaged in this field, and as one might expect given the broad array of issues and concerns that arise under the religion clauses, there is a great deal of disagreement over any number of issues. It is remarkable, however, that so many divergent theorists and judges agree on one major premise. That premise is that religion clause jurisprudence is in a state of disarray and has been for some time. Most attribute this state of affairs to courts basing decisions on the wrong principles, using the wrong—or too many—legal tests, or favoring one side or the other in the debate.

My reason for writing this book is that I believe much of this disarray is a function of the interpretive presumptions and methodologies used by the courts in religion clause cases. Particularly, I will argue that both hard originalism and neutrality are illusory in the religion clause context, the first because it cannot live up to its promise for either side in the debate and the second because it is simply impossible in the religion clause context. Yet these two principles have been used in almost every Supreme Court decision addressing religion clause questions. This book is an attempt to look underneath these devices to find the other bases that may be driving the Court and commentators. Some of these bases such as liberty, equality, separation, and accommodation are openly discussed by courts and commentators, while others lie underneath the surface. Yet even the surface principles are generally justified based on the illusion of neutrality or arguments for determinate original intent.

My hope is to engage in a descriptive analysis of the various principles of religion clause interpretation and determine which ones are merely illusion and which ones actually add something of substance to the debate. The principles that add something will function as modes of religion clause interpretation that ebb and flow based on context. My assertion is simple: the use of various narrow principles that ebb and flow based on context will lead to more consistency and more interpretive transparency than reliance on broad but illusory principles. I realize that some may question this assertion and my belief that the descriptive is more important than the normative in framing religion clause jurisprudence, but I do not see how any normative framework can be expected to accomplish the goals of its advocates without a better descriptive understanding of the interpretive process. After discussing this process throughout the bulk of the book, I will propose a normative framework for religion clause cases, but I hope that readers will take the descriptive seriously regardless of whether they agree with my normative approach.

The illusion of objectivity has cast its power over religion clause cases and has led to a tortured jurisprudence. Supreme Court justices have often been the masters of this illusion. By exposing the illusion, we can hopefully foster a better jurisprudence and allow all sides in the debate to partake more of substance than shadow.

Acknowledgments

I owe a great debt to many of my colleagues both at Michigan State University and around the country for their support and comments. Most important, I am grateful to Deborah Gershenowitz, Despina Papazoglou Gimbel, and Salwa Jabado at NYU Press for their remarkably professional and efficient work on this book. I doubt it would have seen the light of day as quickly without Deborah's careful eye for interesting projects and wonderful disposition, and Despina and Salwa's incredible professionalism and efficiency during the production process. I would also like to thank Stephen Feldman, Brett Scharffs, Douglas Laycock, Mark Janis, Brian Kalt, Mae Kuykendall, Kevin Saunders, Steve Smith, Glen Staszewski, Bill Blatt, Donna Chirico, Elizabeth Dale, Rick Garnett, Steve Goldberg, Jessie Hill, Noga Morag-Levine, Tom Berg, Fred Gedicks, Steve Gey, Hazel Beh, Maurice Dyson, Lynn Daggett, Eric DeGroff, Robin Malloy, and Cynthia Starnes for their comments on this book or the articles that have been integrated in part into it, and/or for serving as co-panelists or discussants.

I am also grateful for helpful comments I received when I presented related papers at faculty workshops at the Syracuse University College of Law, Hofstra University School of Law, Michigan State University College of Law, and Penn State Dickinson School of Law. I am grateful to my co-panelists and audience members at the Association for Law, Culture, and Humanities Conferences at the University of Connecticut College of Law, the University of Texas, and the Syracuse University College of Law, the Association for the Sociology of Religion Annual Meeting, the Central States Law Schools Association Annual Meeting, the AALS Section on Law and Religion panel at the 2004 AALS annual meeting, the Section on Education Law panel at the 2006 AALS annual meeting, and the 2004 and 2005 Law and Society Association annual meetings. I would also like to thank Dean Terence Blackburn for his consistent support of this project. Thanks also to Charles Ten Brink, Jane Edwards, Hildur Hanna, and the staff of the MSU law library for their support; to Sara Belzer, Anna Graham, Kyle Reynolds, Elijah Milne, and Amy Anderson for excellent research assistance; and to my secretary, Jacklyn Beard, for her excellent work. Moreover, I would like to thank the three anonymous readers who reviewed the book proposal and lengthy articles attached to it for their helpful comments. Of course, any errors are mine alone.

This acknowledgments section would be vastly incomplete without thanking my wonderful family for their constant love and support. First, my wife, Jamie, who is always an inspiration and who is actually willing to read my work long before it goes to press. My wonderful daughters, Elysha and Ariana, who are a constant source of joy and wonder. They make life brighter and make me smile even on the busiest of days. My parents, Arline and Carl Ravitch, who are the best parents any child could hope for and are a constant source of support and inspiration. My late Bubby and Pop-Pop, who even after their passing continue to inspire me and to serve as examples of hard work, love, and kindness. To Barbara and Gerry Grosslicht, who defy the stereotypes of in-laws with their constant caring and support. My sisters, Elizabeth and Sharon, and my sister-in-law, Karen, and their wonderful families are not only supportive but also wonderful people. My grandmother-in-law, Hilda Sorhagen, who is fascinated by questions of religion in law and is always interested in what I am doing. Last, but not least, my Uncle Gary and Aunt Mindy and Aunt Jackie and Uncle Ken and their wonderful families, who are also interested in whatever I do.

As these acknowledgments suggest, I have incorporated modified sections of several articles into this book:

"A Funny Thing Happened on the Way to Neutrality: Broad Principles, Formalism, and the Establishment Clause," 38 *Georgia Law Review* 489 (2004).

"The Supreme Court's Rhetorical Hostility: What Is "Hostile" to Religion Under the Establishment Clause?" 2004 *Brigham Young University Law Review* 1031 (2004) (symposium).

"Religious Objects as Legal Subjects," 40 *Wake Forest Law Review* 1011 (2005).

"Some Thoughts on Religion, Abstinence Only, and Sex Education in the Public Schools," 26 *Children's Legal Rights Journal* 48 (2006) (symposium).

1

Building on Shadows

Interpreting the religion clauses is not an easy task. Courts and commentators have used a variety of devices to interpret the religion clauses. Some rely on historical arguments, others rely on broad principles such as neutrality, liberty or equality, and some rely on both history and these broad principles. Yet battle lines remain even if the tactics have changed over time. Few people find the totality of the jurisprudence in this area to be satisfying; although many people like one or another decision or approach. When one sets out to interpret the religion clauses or, for that matter, to write a book about them, it is helpful to ask, "What is the goal of this endeavor?" Is it to find a unifying theme, answer a specific question, glean some specific or broader meaning? Otherwise, how does one interpret clauses with vague text, contested history, and conflicted precedent?

The goal of this book is to gain a better understanding of what has really been going on in court cases in this area and what this means for a society caught in the grip of a "culture war."[1] Courts and commentators write of "neutrality" and the intent of the framers as though these things are capable of some sort of concrete definition.[2] As will be explained in later chapters, this is simply wrong. Concepts such as neutrality, liberty, and hostility are highly malleable, and they lend little more than rhetorical justifications for decisions based on other principles.[3] This does not mean that commentators who rely on such principles have nothing valuable to contribute, but rather that those contributions must be useful in their own right, divorced from any metaphysical claim to neutrality or historical claim regarding the intent of the framers. In fact, as will be seen, the mark of a valuable concept in this area is whether it retains usefulness when divorced from its rhetorical baggage—that is, there may be some value in the concept of "substantive neutrality," but not because it is actually neutral. The value lies elsewhere in the concept.

The discussion of neutrality will be mostly left to later chapters. This chapter will address the question of history and the intent of the framers, which has been tethered to every major principle the Court has used in the religion clause area. If the Court's claims regarding the history of the religion clauses are weak, then the jurisprudence based on such claims is called into question. As will be seen, this argument cuts both ways. Neither separationists nor accommodationists will necessarily agree with this point, but even without strong historical arguments both sides have plenty of ammunition to play with. After the discussion of original intent in the religion clause context, this chapter will provide an overview of the various religion clause principles courts and commentators have used. It will also provide an overview of the interpretive framework proposed in later chapters. This book asserts that multiple narrow principles of interpretation that ebb and flow based on context may work better than the broad, and often illusory, principles the Court has traditionally used in interpreting the religion clauses.

A. The Battle of the Framers

Historical arguments have been used by courts and commentators since the beginning of modern Establishment Clause jurisprudence. Early cases such as *Everson v. Bd. of Education*[4] and *State of Illinois ex rel. McCollum v. Board of Ed.*[5] rely heavily on historical arguments. The same is true of the Court's most recent cases.[6] Much of this jurisprudence relies on one or another interpretation of the "intent of the framers" as gleaned from contemporary practices, statements, or writings. Some of the historical jurisprudence relies on the "traditions" of the nation.[8] These arguments are sometimes linked,[9] but they are in a sense different arguments. One is an originalist approach and the other an approach based on long-standing tradition reaching well beyond the time of the framers or even the framers of the Fourteenth Amendment through which the religion clauses have been incorporated. Later chapters will address the "tradition" approach, which, as will be seen, suffers from serious interpretive flaws. For now, it is most helpful to look at the originalist approaches to the Establishment Clause, which have been used far more often and by every side in the debate.

It is fair to say that concepts of originalism, or, as I will sometimes refer to them in this book, "the battle of the framers," have driven much of religion clause jurisprudence. This is unfortunate because it is a debate that no one can really win. One should not interpret this to mean that historical analysis, or even some form of originalism, is irrelevant in understanding the religion clauses. Rather, those theories, whatever relevance they may have, cannot do the work they have been used to do by the Court and by many commentators. Interestingly, originalist approaches are useful in debunking other originalist approaches because presenting an alternative historical account with documentation can demonstrate at the very least that a given historical account is not the only one. The problem is that frequently when these alternative accounts are introduced to debunk another account, the justices or scholars introducing them assert that the alternative account is the correct one.[10] In reality, however, it simply proves that there is an alternative account, which—and this is quite important—demonstrates only that neither account can prevail without further, and often unstated, presumptions influencing the choice.

Neither the separationist historical account nor the historical account advocated by those who wish to see greater interaction between religion and the public sphere tells the whole story. In fact, given the large number of framers and people involved in the ratification process, it is impossible to claim that any single account is "the intent of the framers" in a specific sense.[11] An interesting exercise in this regard is to read back-to-back Leonard Levy's classic historical account of the framers' views on the religion clauses[12] and Philip Hamburger's historical account of the same.[13] Then read Justice Rutledge's concurring opinion in *Everson* and Justice Reed's dissenting opinion in *McCollum*.[14]

We may be able to determine some broad intent of the framers, but this intent is so broad that by itself it cannot answer specific questions that the framers never thought about. It becomes a factor in the interpretive process, but not necessarily a determinative factor. Thus, we know that a number of framers were concerned at a broad level about religious divisiveness and about financial support of religion by the federal government.[15] But can either of these broad concerns by itself, or the two concerns combined, answer the question of whether educational vouchers violate the Establishment Clause? Justices on all sides of these issues have relied on the intent of the framers. Some, such as Justices Scalia and Thomas, place an overt emphasis on originalism.[16] Others, such as Justices Souter and Stevens, rely on originalist arguments, even though they have criticized stringent reliance on such arguments.[17]

What we frequently end up with is a battle of the framers. *In this corner Justice Scalia's framers and in this corner Justice Souter's. . . .* We get to watch bouts between James Madison and John Adams, and even between Thomas Jefferson and more recent figures such as Abraham Lincoln.[18] Some bouts seem to be a case of internal struggle, such as James Madison versus James Madison.[19] And *the winner is . . .* confusion, subterfuge, and frequently, to quote Justice Jackson, the justices' own prepossessions.[20] Short of inventing a time machine and bringing a cadre of pollsters from Gallup back in time, it is unlikely that we will ever know what the framers intended about the wide array of specific issues confronting courts in the religion clause context, and while it is likely we can determine some broad intent, that intent only takes us so far in the analysis. Moreover, we filter our impressions of this intent through our own traditions and preconceptions in a way that may taint any application of such originalist data to current concerns.[21]

These criticisms of originalism in the religion clause context are aimed only at that context. The broader debates about the form and efficacy of originalism in constitutional interpretation are beyond the scope of this book. Still, given the problems with using originalism to answer specific questions in the religion clause context, it seems that relying on strict originalist approaches in this area is not terribly useful. You can choose the story that best suits your tastes (even if you do not realize you are doing so) and reason to a result. While this book avoids entering the broader debate over originalism, one concept from that debate is useful. It is the concept of "soft originalism" as proposed by Cass Sunstein.[22] It is useful because it looks at the broad concepts that many of the framers—including those who disagreed on narrower questions—agreed upon.[23] It may not answer specific questions, but it can help answer them by being a factor in the interpretive process if evidence of such broader agreement is available.[24] I will contrast "soft originalism" with "hard originalism,"[25] which is the type most often used by courts in the religion clause context. Hard originalism looks for a more concrete and unified intent on a broader range of issues than soft originalism, and hard originalism may also use original intent to answer specific questions that arise today.[26]

Ironically, the one area where hard originalist arguments might be realistic is the long-settled incorporation question. It does seem that the bulk of the original framers did not view the religion clauses as likely to become binding on the states at any future time.[27] Of course, this leaves the question of what the framers of the Fourteenth Amendment thought, and we might find ourselves back in the same conundrum.[28] Even if there were clear originalist evidence against incorporation (especially incorporation of the Establishment Clause), incorporation may still be justified on other grounds.[29] It simply begs a different question: whether originalism is the best interpretive device even where there is some clear evidence of specific original intent. Given the long history of incorporation and the useful constraint on interpretation provided by stare decisis, I would argue in this context that hard originalism is not the best interpretive device.[30] In fact, hard originalism may conflict with soft originalism as the narrower views of certain framers come into contact with the many changes to religious pluralism and to the nation over the last two centuries. Moreover, as H. Jefferson Powell has argued, there may be originalist arguments against using originalism—that is, the framers never expected their intent to govern future and potentially unforeseen constitutional questions.[31] This would make hard originalism an anachronism, but it might support —or at least not conflict with—soft originalism.

The bottom line when it comes to using historical arguments to support religion clause doctrine is that the historical arguments are a justification for decisions influenced by other factors, as the realists used to say.[32] Justices Scalia and Thomas have cast originalism as a sort of interpretive panacea in these cases.[33] If only we followed the framers' intent, we would have a clear answer to many questions that arise under the religion clauses. Of course, if the framers did not share any single set of assumptions, these arguments do not do what they claim—that is, they do not provide any "objective" concrete interpretive framework.[34] The various packages of framers' intent just sit on the shelf until a justice chooses which one(s) to use and uses it. Of course, in making the choice of which intent to use, the justice must be relying on something other than the history, and we are back to square one.[35] Justice Scalia's originalism in the religion clause context does not limit activism any more than Justice Stevens's originalism does. The question that needs answering is not which historical account is accurate, but rather what are the underlying bases for choosing a given historical account, and do any of these bases help obtain a better understanding and interpretation of the religion clauses regardless of the historical accounts?

More than forty years ago, Justice Brennan captured some of these concerns in his concurring opinion in *Abington Township v. Schempp*.[36] Addressing historical analysis of Bible reading and prayer at the beginning of the school day, Justice Brennan wrote of the futility of using hard originalism and the potential for using soft originalism:

A too literal quest for the advice of the Founding Fathers upon the issues of these cases seems to me futile and misdirected for several reasons: First, on our precise problem the historical record is at best ambiguous, and statements can readily be found to support either side of the proposition. The ambiguity of history is understandable if we recall the nature of the problems uppermost in the thinking of the statesmen who fashioned the religious guarantees; they were concerned with far more flagrant intrusions of government into the realm of religion than any that our century has witnessed. While it is clear to me that the Framers meant the Establishment Clause to prohibit more than the creation of an established federal church such as existed in England, I have no doubt that, in their preoccupation with the imminent question of established churches, they gave no distinct consideration to the particular question whether the clause also forbade devotional exercises in public institutions. . . .

Whatever Jefferson or Madison would have thought of Bible reading or the recital of the Lord's Prayer in what few public schools existed in their day, our use of the history of their time must limit itself to broad purposes, not specific practices.[37]

Of course, even in this concurring opinion rejecting strict original-ism, Justice Brennan elsewhere makes assumptions about the framers as though they were a unified group with unified motives. His recognition of the problems with originalist approaches, which were most likely appar-ent to him before *Schempp* because he was certainly familiar with the con-tradictions between the history set forth by the Court in *Everson* and *Mc-Collum* and that set forth by Justice Reed in his *McCollum* dissent,[38] is significant because as noted above Justice Brennan sometimes still relied on hard originalist approaches.[39] Reliance on the intent of the framers may be so ubiquitous in religion clause interpretation precisely because it is not objective or heavily constraining, but gives the appearance of being so. Since a supporting history can be found for most positions, it is a neat tool to pull out of the interpretive tool kit when it is unclear why a given result may be better than another. Of course, papering over the viability of multiple results with history does not change the possibility that there may be other ways to choose between them that are more useful in inter-preting the religion clauses.

B. Principles of Religion Clause Interpretation: Introduction to the Modal Approach

If we no longer rely on strong historical arguments as the primary source for justification of religion clause decisions, we are left with a number of broad principles the Court has used. Admittedly, the Court has often justi-fied reliance on these principles by reference to historical arguments. To the extent the historical arguments are of the "soft" originalist type, they may help choose between the competing principles, but in the end we must look at the principles themselves to see if they live up to their billings and if they are useful in interpreting and applying the religion clauses.

The major principles the court has used are neutrality, liberty, equality, separationism, accommodationism, traditionalism, and nonpreferential-ism (usually veiled). Sometimes these principles are used in coordination with each other, and sometimes they are used alone. Later chapters will address each of these principles, especially neutrality and liberty, which have occupied increasingly important roles within religion clause juris-prudence.

Two distinct problems are raised by the use of these principles. First, do they live up to their billing? For example, as will be discussed in the next chapter, is neutrality in its various incarnations really neutral, and if not, why should we use it as compared with any other principle? Second, assuming some or all of the principles live up to their billing, at least in part, how do we choose between the available principles? If we are able to use more than one principle, how do the applicable principles interact? These questions will be explored in greater detail in later chapters. For now, a brief overview may be helpful.

A useful way of viewing these principles is presented by Philip Bobbitt's concept of modalities of constitutional interpretation.[40] If each of these principles is equated to a mode of interpretation, we can see that some modes work better than others in a given situation, but in some situations more than one mode of interpretation (or principle) may be useful.[41] There are, of course, significant differences between Bobbitt's approach and the use of principles suggested in this book, but as will be seen in later chapters, the concept of principles ebbing and flowing based on the interpretive task at hand makes sense assuming the principles have some useful role in interpreting the religion clauses. Bobbitt's work provides a model for such a system of ebbing and flowing interpretive modes.[42]

Some may question the suggestion made in this book that greater consistency and transparency in religion clause interpretation may be achieved by relying on multiple principles that ebb and flow based on the context of a given case or issue than by the current reliance on one or two broad principles. Yet the current approach of relying on often unsubstantiated interpretive devices such as neutrality has not led to great clarity or a better understanding of religion clause interpretation.[43] Claiming that original intent or neutrality supports a position is not the same as proving it, and when one's evidence for these approaches can be easily countered by judges or commentators who hold a different perspective, the likelihood of confusion is greater than where, as suggested in this book, judges rely on narrow modes of religion clause interpretation that actually stand for something more than an illusion of objectivity. Most of the principles, such as separationism, accommodationism, liberty, and equality, have a strong pedigree in religion clause jurisprudence and are supportable without being justified by hard originalism or neutrality.

Interestingly, neutrality (see chapter 2) and hard originalism have no useful role in religion clause interpretation. These are the two most common methods used by the Court to support its choice of principles and outcomes in religion clause cases.[44] The consequences of this assertion are significant. I am arguing, in essence, that the two major interpretive devices used by the Court in religion clause cases are nothing more than legal illusions or rhetorical justifications. These illusions have been used to support specific results in cases,[45] to justify other principles,[46] and to support specific legal tests.[47] Peel away the illusion and the rhetorical bases for these decisions, and the other principles used to support them may become visible. Removing the rhetorical and historical fog from religion clause decisions is, in part, the goal of this book.

What this removal exposes from the early religion clause decisions to the most recent is a latent debate over the role of religious pluralism and religious freedom in American life. Many decisions seem to be based on a form of pragmatism covered over by originalist or neutrality-based arguments, and others seem to be more directly based on other principles they espouse, such as separationism or accommodationism, even if the use of those principles is justified by originalist or neutrality-based illusion.[48] Concerns about religious divisiveness, recognition of the religious traditions of the nation, protecting religion from state regulation, and protecting the state from religious influence also underlie a number of decisions.[49] Again, these concerns are often masked or justified based on hard originalist or neutrality-based arguments. The key question is whether any of the underlying principles or bases for these decisions can be legitimated without reliance on illusory historical or neutrality-based arguments. The answer to this question is yes. In fact, the bigger problem may be that a number of principles are applicable in religion clause interpretation, and thus an interpretive approach—in this case the modes of religion clause interpretation—must be devised to navigate the surf between these principles.

C. Justice Jackson and Hans-Georg Gadamer: Of Prepossessions and Preconceptions

Concurring in the *McCollum* case, Justice Jackson wrote: "It is idle to pretend that this task is one for which we can find in the Constitution one word to help as judges to decide where the secular ends and the sectarian begins in education. Nor can we find guidance in any other legal source. It is a matter on which we can find no law but our own prepossessions. . . ."[50]

Many scholars and judges have an uneasy response when assertions like Justice Jackson's arise. Yet, as will be discussed in chapter 6, the preceding quotation is a warning against unrestrained activism. Justice Jackson's statement is not a call for unrestrained judicial subjectivism. Rather, it is a warning that in such situations one ought to be careful to think through one's own preconceptions and to carefully consider any factors that may help restrain interpretive presumptions.[51] Without direct guidance from text or history, we must consider what modes of interpretation are valid in a given context and within a given interpretive framework. These modes offer a potential source of interpretive constraint.

In this context the philosophical hermeneutics of Hans-Georg Gadamer are useful. At the outset I should point out that Gadamer, who was a philosopher, not a law professor, is a highly misunderstood figure in the legal academy. Some folks simply shut down and stop listening when they hear a reference to him, or they confuse his theories with those of the deconstructionists (who Gadamer opposed in many ways).[52] He has been the subject of some crass and unsophisticated attacks in the legal academy.[53] Much of this ire seems to be the result of a perceived (but partially accurate) connection between philosophical hermeneutics and critical legal theory,[54] but Gadamer's approach can support any number of normative theories, and the fact that the critical theorists find support for their theory from Gadamer's descriptive point that we are all historically situated and influenced by our traditions says little about his broader theory.[55] In fact, Gadamer was not a great supporter of the Frankfurt school of philosophers upon whom many critical theorists rely, and the disagreements between Gadamer and Jürgen Habermas in particular are well documented,[56] even if they were adeptly mediated after the fact by Paul Ricoeur.[57] Critical theorists have simply used Gadamer's descriptive concept of interpretation, along with the work of other Continental philosophers, to support their normative positions. There is nothing wrong with this, but as noted above, Gadamer's theory can be used to support any number of normative positions.[58]

Given all this, why reference Gadamer's approach here? The reason is simple. It lends clarity to Justice Jackson's point, allows for a modal approach such as Bobbitt's where both text and interpreter are constrained but not led to automatic results, and explains just why it is that courts seem obsessed with justifying decisions with broad principles. Gadamer's theory at its base is mostly descriptive and not terribly controversial. In fact, any number of other theories such as Peirce's semiotics lead in similar directions.[59] Gadamer's approach has been heavily mystified in the academic context, but as used in the present context it is easily accessible to anyone once it is explained.

Gadamer asserts that there is no one proper methodology for interpretation (just as there is no single principle of religion clause interpretation).[60] This is because we are all situated in a historical and cultural context. The term for this is *dasein,* or being in the world.[61] What it means is that we are always projecting our preconceptions into the interpretive process, and those preconceptions are heavily influenced by the traditions into which we are enmeshed.[62] These preconceptions provide us with a horizon through which we view the world, and beyond which it is hard for us to see.[63] We may be able to confront our preconceptions when we interpret through the process of reflection, but it is hard to escape one's horizon.[64] The things we interpret (texts, facts, situations) provide a constraint on our interpretive presumptions because they also have horizons.[65] The goal of interpretation is the fusion of horizons, where the interpreter's horizon and that of the text are able to come to meaning. This may require the interpreter to throw out preconceptions that are inconsistent with the horizon of the text.[66]

In the legal context there are interpretive traditions that judges are acculturated to use.[67] In constitutional interpretation most of these are captured nicely by Bobbitt's modalities.[68] Judges may look for broad principles such as neutrality or interpretive devices such as original intent as a matter of course without necessarily having any strong ideological motive (of course, some judges do have such a motive). The problem in the religion clause context is that some of these traditional devices, such as hard originalism and neutrality, do not work and thus may be inconsistent with the horizon of the text, while other traditional modes may be more useful. Stare decisis may be both a blessing and a curse in the religion clause context. It clearly is part of the traditions of judging,[69] but in the religion clause context it has been sometimes ignored and frequently used to lock in decisions based on illusion.[70] Still, if we are able to create a better form of religion clause interpretation through the modalities approach, stare decisis may be a useful tool to support interpretations within the ebb and flow of religion clause jurisprudence.

Another key connection between Gadamerian hermeneutics and the approach discussed herein is that the fusion of horizons does not suggest that there is any one right answer in interpretation, but it also does not lead to nihilism. There is interpretive constraint, but there is a range of potentially "correct" answers to any interpretive dilemma, albeit a range constrained by the horizons of text and interpreter.[71] Similarly, Bobbitt argues that the modalities approach allows for legitimation of interpretation without "justifying" that interpretation.[72] The reason for this is that use of the modes can legitimate a decision without any claim that a given result is just, because "justice" claims are highly contestable.[73] Moreover, interpretive approaches based on a theory of justice can only be self-justifying and legitimating, while the modalities approach can legitimate results in cases without claiming any sort of metaphysical justice.[74] Significantly, Bobbitt's approach does not preclude the quest for justice or assume that there is one correct answer for a given issue because modes can conflict, and as long as one is acting within the modes, one can use moral arguments to reach what he, she, or a given theory characterizes as "just" results in such circumstances (I would suggest in such circumstances one is actually relying on the prudential mode).[75] From Bobbitt's perspective it is problematic to work backward from justice theories because they are hard to legitimate outside the theory.[76]

This gels nicely with Gadamerian hermeneutics because the modes may be considered a significant part of the horizon of the text that cannot be ignored. As will be demonstrated in later chapters, the modes of religion clause interpretation—or at least some of them—may also be imbedded in the horizons of most interpreters in religion clause jurisprudence, even if those horizons are often distorted by the haze of hard originalism or neutrality. The key is that far from being nihilistic, the approach suggested in this book offers real constraint in the interpretive process without pretending that a specific and superior normative outcome can be determined in every case.[77] There may be a number of possible outcomes depending on the facts of a case, the modes of religion clause interpretation, and the legal issues involved. Simply put, the approach herein provides more clarity and constraint on interpretation precisely because it does not pretend that there is some sort of objective and neutral basis for decisions that obviously could have come out more than one way. Rather than start with a normative presumption either up front or masked behind the illusion of supposedly objective criteria and work toward a legal justification, the approach in this book begins with a descriptive assertion about the nature of religion clause interpretation and works toward a normative solution without claiming historical or theoretical inerrancy.

This brings us back to Justice Jackson's assertion in regard to Establishment Clause jurisprudence. Jackson's claim is straightforward: neither constitutional text or history nor any other legal source can answer specific questions that arise under the Establishment Clause.[78] What Gadamer and Bobbitt add to this dynamic is quite important. Through the notion of interpretive constraint based on the need to fuse horizons or constraint based on the available modes of religion clause interpretation, one can heed Justice Jackson's implicit warning regarding unconstrained interpretation. The fact that no legal source by itself offers interpretive help does not foreclose the possibility that broader legal traditions or modes of constitutional interpretation might provide such constraint. The fact that there may be no clear objective answer to highly complex and fact-sensitive issues does not mean we must tread the path toward pure subjectivism or nihilism. Rather, such a dichotomy between the clearly "objective" and the purely "subjective" is a false construction, because one may still be constrained in interpretation even where no "objective" answer is available for a given issue.[79]

The remainder of this book will explore how all this works in the religion clause context by focusing first on the various principles of religion clause interpretation such as neutrality, liberty, equality, separation, and accommodation. The principles that actually serve any function beyond rhetorical justification will be considered modes of religion clause interpretation. In chapter 9, I set forth an interpretive approach based on the principles and modalities of religion clause interpretation.

The primary focus of this book is not normative. The goal is to understand what principles may drive the courts in religion clause cases and why some of them are hidden and others reified despite a lack of depth. Additionally, chapter 8 tackles the question of defining or recognizing religion in religion clause jurisprudence, a discussion that is essential to any detailed understanding of several major religion clause questions. I do not stake out a position in the broader culture wars or in the debate between various schools of legal thought, although I hope my conclusions in the religion clause context may be of use to a number of those schools. In chapter 10 I suggest a normative solution, the facilitation test, and apply it to a number of situations. One may reject my normative approach, however, without rejecting the descriptive observations and interpretive approach set forth in the first nine chapters of this book.

2

Neutrality

Neutrality, whether formal or substantive, does not exist in the religion clause context. Others have recognized this.[1] Still others have come partway to this conclusion by suggesting that neutrality is inherently dependent upon the baseline one chooses to use in describing it, and thus it does not exist apart from these baselines.[2] Yet claims of neutrality cannot be proven. There is no independent neutral truth or baseline to which they can be tethered.[3] This is important because it means that any baseline to which we attach neutrality is not neutral, and claims of neutrality built on these baselines are by their nature not neutral. This might seem circular—that is, since there is no independent state of neutrality from which to derive neutral rules or applications of rules, there can be no neutral results and no means by which one can prove a given baseline is neutral. Yet examples, even in Supreme Court opinions, are readily available.[4] The Court has used varying concepts or baselines of neutrality,[5] and in several cases justices in the majority and dissenting opinions claimed to be relying on the same or similar principles of neutrality, yet they reached opposite conclusions.[6]

This critique of neutrality applies to both the recent Court's use of formal neutrality (a concept explained further below) and to earlier Courts' substantive neutrality or separation as neutrality approaches (also explained further below). Much attention will be paid in this chapter to the concept of formal neutrality that seems most pervasive today, at least in cases involving aid to religious entities or individuals, equal access, and Free Exercise Clause exemptions. As will be seen, the critique of neutrality provided herein applies to any claim that a given approach is "neutral" in regard to the many highly contested questions arising when government and religion interact in our complex regulatory state. In the end, as with interpretive claims based on hard originalism, neutrality requires value choices that are often masked under the cloak of evenhandedness or other mostly rhetorical devices.

Steven Smith has explained:

[T]he quest for neutrality, despite its understandable appeal and the tenacity with which it has been pursued, is an attempt to grasp at an illusion. Upon reflection, this failure should not be surprising. The impossibility of a truly "neutral" theory of religious freedom is analogous to the impossibility, recognized by modern philosophers, of finding some outside Archimedean point . . . from which to look down on and describe reality. Descriptions of reality are always undertaken from a point within reality. In the same way, theories of religious freedom are always offered from the viewpoint of one of the competing positions that generate the need for such a theory; there is no neutral vantage point that can permit the theorist or judge to transcend these competing positions. Hence, insofar as a genuine and satisfactory theory of religious freedom would need to be "neutral" in this sense, rather than one that privileges one of the competing positions from the outset, a theory of religious freedom is as illusory as the ideal of neutrality it seeks to embody.[7]

Others have also acknowledged the elusive and malleable nature of neutrality.[8] The Court's use of the term until recently was often symbolic —not in the sense that William Marshall's fascinating work has used that term,[9] but rather in the sense that the Court was trying to send a message that it was being balanced in its resolution of the issues that it decided.[10] Of course, despite protestations otherwise, this was not always so. Still, the Court did not use neutrality as the be-all or end-all concept in actually deciding cases. Rather, it had to also rely on other principles because neutrality is so malleable, or parasitic, as Steven Smith has argued.[11] If there is no such thing as neutrality—or at least neutrality as more than a buzzword—this seems a logical state of affairs. The Court suggests that it is acting neutrally, but it can only define this neutrality by reference to other principles (which are not neutral).

The current Court, however, has begun to rely on neutrality more directly.[12] Neutrality is no longer a background principle that the Court sees no need to consistently define. Rather, it is an actuating principle that the Court apparently believes must be given a formalistic definition that can be rigidly applied.[13] As will be seen, the Court connects its formal neutrality with what appear to be arguments for formal equality between religion and "nonreligion."[14] Yet the current Court's neutrality is no more neutral than past Courts' neutrality. In fact, because of its formalistic nature it is potentially "less neutral"—if it is possible to be less than something that does not exist—because at least potentially if a government action or inaction meets the Court's definition of neutrality (and the element of individual choice discussed below), pesky things such as the effects of the program need not be considered.[15] This is particularly problematic because the Court does not explain why its formal neutrality is neutral given the competing views of neutrality, and the Court uses terms such as "entirely neutral"[16] and "neutral in all respects."[17] By relying on the term in this direct yet unsubstantiated manner, the Court gives it extra power.

Not to be outdone, the justices who reject the Court's formal neutrality have begun strenuously arguing for a return to substantive neutrality,[18] or sometimes to separation as neutrality, as the guiding principle.[19] The battle thus joined, the justices argue the meaning of neutrality, which as I have suggested is like arguing over the real location of Oz, and neither side is forced to confront in any serious way the interpretive presumptions that inform its chosen neutrality position, although the substantive neutrality wing often openly acknowledges its reliance on separation (without, of course, explaining how separation is in fact neutral). As will be seen, substantive neutrality—at least as envisioned by Douglas Laycock —has something important to lend to this debate, but not because it is neutral.

The current Court's formal neutrality approach requires a law or government policy to be facially neutral in regard to religion.[20] In the aid context there is an additional element to the formal neutrality approach.[21] Any benefit or funding that flows to religious entities must do so as the result of the choices of private individuals.[22] As will be seen below, this approach has not been applied in all aid cases, but to the extent it has been applied, the private choice element may have lost its substantive bite.[23]

The current version of neutrality that has become dominant in the aid, equal access, and free exercise contexts is intensely formalistic, and it appears to minimize the effects of government programs and actions.[24] Establishment Clause jurisprudence has traditionally been fact sensitive, but the Court's formal neutrality approach lacks the tools to enable it to deal with the many situations to which it will invariably be applied. The more flexible *Lemon* test[25] was much maligned because of the questionable distinctions drawn by the Court.[26] Thirty years from now the Court's apparent move toward a formal neutrality test might be viewed in the same way. Formalism does not necessarily beget clarity, and in the end when the issues that arise are complex and fact specific, the more formalistic the test, the less clarity it will likely bring in the long run, either because it must be contorted to fit the diversity of situations to which it will be applied or because it will ignore context and function somewhat like a bull in a china shop.

The Court's formal neutrality approach reminds me of a quotation from Professor Philip Kurland's classic 1961 article, *Of Church and State and the Supreme Court,*[27] which has influenced the Court's formal neutrality approach. In describing a "neutral principle" that would "give the most appropriate scope to the religion clauses," Kurland explained:[28]

> This "neutral principle" has been framed in reliance on the Aristotelian axiom that "it is the mark of an educated man to seek precision in each class of things just so far as the nature of the subject admits," rather than the Platonic precept that "a perfectly simple principle can never be applied to a state of things which is the reverse of simple."[29]

While it may at first seem an odd thing for a legal academic to state, I am inclined to favor the Platonic precept over the Aristotelian axiom upon which Professor Kurland relied, at least when it comes to formal neutrality. The vast web of factual scenarios involved in funding cases and equal access cases—situations where the Court has already and clearly applied formal neutrality—is indeed the reverse of simple, and formal neutrality is an intensely simple concept (although in no way perfect). While Professor Kurland may have advocated a version of formal neutrality, it is unlikely he was advocating the kind of acontextual neutrality toward which the Court has been headed.

Lurking underneath the Court's formal neutrality is the notion that religion has no special status, and thus there is no need to differentiate between religion and nonreligion if the government is acting "neutrally."[30] A corollary to this notion is the argument that by treating religion differently one is being hostile to religion. Thus, it is discrimination and hostility to religion if religious organizations are not given access to the same benefits as secular organizations,[31] and at the same time there is nothing wrong with failing to provide religious exemptions to "generally applicable" laws even if those laws interfere with core religious practices.[32] There would be significant problems with the Court's implicit presumptions even if neutrality were a real and attainable concept, but if neutrality is nothing more than an empty construction,[33] the Court's other presumptions are even more problematic.

To understand the Rehnquist Court's notion of neutrality, it is useful to explore several of the cases where the Court has used neutrality analysis in varying contexts. Thus, in this chapter we will look at three cases to see the formal neutrality doctrine in action. These are *Zelman v. Simmons-Harris,*[34] *Good News Club v. Milford Central School,*[35] and *Employment Division v. Smith.*[36] Each of these cases represents a major area where the Court has used a version of its neutrality concept: *Zelman* in the context of government aid to religious schools,[37] *Good News Club* in the context of equal access to government facilities by religious groups,[38] and *Smith* in the context of exemptions to "generally applicable" laws under the Free Exercise Clause.[39] Before analyzing these cases, however, it is useful to further answer the question of what is neutrality, or at least what does it pretend to be?

The answer to the question—"What is neutrality?"—is central to the discussion of neutrality's place in religion clause jurisprudence. Thus, the answer that neutrality, at least in the religion clause context, is a myth may seem wholly unsatisfying. Yet can there be some use for a concept that is impossible to achieve? Neutrality is nothing more than a variable social construction, and formal neutrality nothing more than a rigid judicial construction. Each relies on a baseline that is not provably neutral, but each has a value because people take solace in the notion of neutrality.[40] Even if objectivity does not exist in contested spaces, there may be value in the perception of objectivity.[41]

This sounds a bit odd at first, but it actually tracks much of what the pre-Rehnquist Court did with the concept of neutrality. Neutrality was mentioned quite a bit in numerous contexts; sometimes the Court used a vague adjective to describe it, such as "benevolent neutrality."[42] Yet the Court never relied exclusively on the principle, supplementing it with separationism or accommodationism.[43] For those who did not dig too deeply, there was always the reassuring tone of neutrality. For those who did dig, it was apparent that the Court could not substantiate its claim to neutrality, but the Court had the other principles to fall back on, and one could support or attack those other principles without focusing on whether they were neutral in application or effect.[44] It would not be a reach to read some of these cases and perceive that the Court was essentially saying, "We are following a separationist principle or an accommodationist principle that we think is more neutral than the alternatives in this context, but neutrality is only the lofty object of the religion clauses, not something we can prove with absolute certainty."

I do not defend the earlier Courts' use of the term. It was in a sense false advertising, because there is no way to prove that separationism or accommodationism is inherently more neutral than other principles.[45] Yet the implicit message that was at least potentially infused in these earlier decisions—that is, we know that neutrality is just a lofty principle and we are only using it to describe the outcome in this case vis-à-vis the alternatives—is less troubling than claims that both the mode of analysis and the results *are* neutral, and that the alternatives are not. The latter is the message of the formal neutrality approach. The current Court has converted neutrality from a lofty, albeit impossible, goal to both the means and ends of religion clause analysis.[46]

The Court's struggle with neutrality over the years reminds me of a conversation I had with my older daughter a few years ago when she was five years old and excited after realizing that her tooth was loose and would soon fall out. She realized that I might be the "tooth fairy" and asked if the tooth fairy was real or if I was the tooth fairy. Not wanting to burst her bubble or lie, I responded that the tooth fairy would leave her a present when she lost her tooth. She responded that she knew I was the tooth fairy, but that she wanted the tooth fairy to visit and leave her a present anyway.

This is akin to the struggle for neutrality. Like the tooth fairy, neutrality is just a myth, but like children who want the tooth fairy to visit, we want it to be real, or at least for something to stand in for it to make us believe it is real. Unlike my five-year-old daughter, however, the Rehnquist Court has strenuously argued in essence that the tooth fairy is real, and when confronted with the question of why, the answer seems to be "because we said so." The nuance of the stand-in concept—neutrality not as a real thing, but as a lofty principle that we try to emulate—seems lost.

Of course, even though neutrality as a lofty principle is less problematic than formal neutrality because it is not used to reach or empower outcomes, it is no more neutral. Moreover, in two contexts it has been used to, or argued to, empower results. These two contexts are substantive neutrality and separation as neutrality. As will be seen, one conception of substantive neutrality has some merit, but not because of the neutrality claim. This conception of neutrality is far more nuanced and sophisticated than other neutrality claims. It recognizes there is no agreement about what neutrality is. I am referring to Douglas Laycock's construction of substantive neutrality.[47] Laycock is not alone in arguing for substantive neutrality. Scholars,[48] as well as justices of the Supreme Court,[49] have argued for some form of substantive neutrality. Professor Laycock, however, provides the best and most succinct conception of substantive neutrality. His substantive neutrality has a lot to recommend it. In fact, it has had a strong influence on the facilitation approach I propose in later chapters. Still, as I hope to show, substantive neutrality may have a lot of substantive value, but no neutrality.[50] This might seem a bit nitpicky, since the approach has a lot to offer, but while Professor Laycock may have made a wise choice among potential baselines, his choice and the resulting baseline are no more neutral than the Court's formal neutrality.[51]

Professor Laycock's formulation of substantive neutrality is reflected in the following passage:

> My basic formulation of substantive neutrality is this: the religion clauses require government to minimize the extent to which it either encourages or discourages belief or disbelief, practice or nonpractice, observance or

nonobservance. If I have to stand or fall on a single formulation of neutrality, I will stand or fall on that one. But I must elaborate on what I mean by minimizing encouragement or discouragement. I mean that religion is to be left as wholly to private choice as anything can be. It should proceed as unaffected by government as possible. Government should not interfere with our beliefs about religion either by coercion or by persuasion. Religion may flourish or whither; it may change or stay the same. What happens to religion is up to the people acting severally and voluntarily; it is not up to the people acting collectively through government.[52]

Professor Laycock suggests that neutrality depends on the baseline one sets in defining it, and that there are varying baselines.[53] The baseline approach, however, is problematic because there is no superbaseline to determine whether a given baseline is neutral.[54] Yet the very term "neutrality" asserts an epistemic (in the sense that it suggests some theory or way to know something is neutral) and arguably a teleological claim. A given baseline might be a useful paradigm for Establishment Clause jurisprudence, but unless one can demonstrate the neutrality of the baseline itself, the baseline cannot support claims of neutrality.[55]

The *Zelman* case is a good example through which to view this. If the Court had held that vouchers are unconstitutional when given for attendance at religious schools, but that districts can maintain vouchers for secular private schools and of course can maintain the secularized public schools without any voucher program, would the result encourage secularism? Would such a limitation advance private choice, or would it place burdens only on the private choice of religious individuals because they must choose between a secular education free of charge and their values?[56] Yet, under the Court's holding that allows vouchers to be used at religious schools, there is a powerful argument that religion, and particularly more dominant and well-funded religions, will benefit from an infusion of government funds,[57] and that private choice will be skewed toward sending one's children to schools with whose faith mission one disagrees simply to keep them on a level playing field with other children in the area who may face no such conflict.[58]

Which of these options is neutral? Which encourages or discourages religion the most? These are actually two very different questions. The first is unanswerable in any objective way unless one has a magic key to demonstrate that a contested account of neutrality is actually neutral. Yet the second question is answerable, even if it is not precisely so. More important, even though the answer may be contestable, the contestability of the answer is more open to debate when it is not appended to the concept of neutrality. The answer must be debated on its merits, without regard to the unprovable claim that it is neutral,[59] and thus neutrality should have no power in the interpretive process. As Steven Smith has implied, calling a result neutral adds nothing of value to an argument.[60] I would add that doing so may obfuscate the nature and value of other principles that undergird an argument, or may unnecessarily prop up those principles.

Yet, as will be seen, this does not destroy the force of Laycock's principle.[61] Significantly, the fact that divorcing Laycock's substantive principle of religion clause jurisprudence from neutrality does not undermine that principle demonstrates the lack of import the neutrality concept has. As between formal neutrality and substantive neutrality, substantive neutrality is the better option, not because it is more neutral—neither option is neutral—but because it is still useful even when divorced from its neutrality claim. The Court's formal neutrality hinges too much on neutrality as a real concept, or at least on formal equality as neutrality,[62] and while a more sophisticated and consistently applied version of the equality principle could have independent value,[63] the formal equality as formal neutrality version has little to offer, since its claim to neutrality (and its implicit claim of equality) cannot be proven.

Separation as neutrality is another concept of neutrality that has at times been linked to substantive neutrality. The separation as neutrality approach was used in early cases such as *Everson, McCollum,* and *Schempp* and is currently favored by a minority of justices.[64] Of course, it is no more neutral than formal or substantive neutrality. Consider both arguments in *Everson.*[65] The majority held that funding the transportation of students to parochial schools did not violate the separation principle because the funding simply demonstrated neutrality between religion and nonreligion.[66] The dissenting opinions argued that neutrality mandated a separationist outcome, and thus the funding was unconstitutional.[67]

Assume the funding is constitutional as the majority held. How is it neutral? Putting aside for the moment that as Justice Jackson pointed out in his dissenting opinion the funding went only to Catholic school students and not to other parochial or secular private school students,[68] the bulk of the funds going into private hands for transportation will go to those attending religious schools. The Court noted that parochial schools were the primary venues for private school students in that area, and even if the program allowed transportation funding to all private schools,[69] the denominations with the largest number of schools would receive the largest benefit.

The reasons the Court gave for upholding the program, save one, make some sense. That one—that the funding regime and its practical outcome are neutral—is simply not true. The funding could provide additional encouragement for families to send their children to private school, and especially to parochial schools, which were the largest constituency of private schools in Ewing Township. Admittedly, this is not a huge windfall for religion, and in fact, it would be allowed under the facilitation test proposed later in this book, but speaking of neutrality simply covers over the real-world impact of such a funding regime given religious and private school demographics.

The dissents' position, however, would be no more neutral, because to deny funding under the facts in the case would give added encouragement to send one's children to the public schools. For those who chose not to do so because of their religious convictions, the denial of funding would impose an additional cost (in addition to property taxes to support the public schools and parochial school tuition) not borne by those who decide to send their children to the secularized world of the public schools. This *may* be justifiable under the separation principle, but it would end up discouraging religion. Neutrality talk adds nothing to the analysis except perhaps a rhetorical justification (as it did for the majority).

Issues surrounding government interaction with religious entities have become increasingly complex as over the last hundred years or so government, both state and federal, has grown and gotten involved in many areas of life where there was traditionally little or no government participation or regulation.[70] It is hard for government to act "neutrally" when its actions or failure to act in the same situation can have massive repercussions.[71] This creates problems for any "neutrality" test that must be applied to this massive web of government action and inaction. At the theoretical level such a test can make no absolute claim to neutrality because there is no principle of superneutrality that can be used to demonstrate its neutrality, and thus contested perspectives necessarily enter the process of developing such a test.[72] It would solve the problem if one could prove neutrality by looking at the effects of a court's approach, but as the above examples demonstrate, this is impossible to do without presuming that a certain baseline is neutral and using the presumed baseline to justify the neutrality of outcomes.[73]

Let us look at another example. A creation science advocate applies to the National Science Foundation (NSF) for a grant.[74] To make this hypothetical even more interesting, let us assume that the creation scientist is not an advocate of "intelligent design theory," which makes a greater attempt to assume the mantle of science,[75] but is a traditional advocate of creation science. Moreover, the creation scientist is applying on behalf of a creation science center, and not a specific church or religious organization, and the center has no direct connection to any religious entity. The applicant and members of his team all have doctoral degrees in biology or chemistry, some from Evangelical universities. Their proposed project consists of proving that spontaneous evolution in lower organisms proves that evolution could have happened in a much shorter period of time than is currently accepted, and that it is limited to certain organisms. They argue that the period of time would be between six and seven thousand years, and that humans are not among the organisms that have evolved. In fact, they suggest *Australopithecus, Homo erectus,* and *Homo habilis* were all simply spontaneous mutations from great ape species that never took hold and died out.

The NSF rejects their proposal because the creation scientists have not supported their hypothesis with adequate testable data. The scientists sue, claiming that the NSF's decision demonstrates hostility to religion in a program open to secular scientific debate and that the NSF undervalued their empirical data. How do we address this situation based on formal and substantive neutrality?

The natural answer is to say that the scientists were not qualified to participate in the program because they were unwilling or unable to produce adequate scientifically acceptable data to support their hypothesis, and their hypothesis was unscientific, yet the program from which they seek funding is a scientific program. This is of little help, however, because the creation scientists can simply charge that the whole selection process, including the reliance on secular scientific "theories" and "adequate scientific" data, is biased against faith-affected approaches, which are put at a disadvantage because they cannot compete for funding on an equal basis even if they engage in some empirical research. They would assert that the NSF's definition of science as requiring use of the scientific method is not neutral as between religion and irreligion.

Based on the formal neutrality approach, it would appear that the program discriminates against faith-based entities,[76] or at the very least against faith-based "scientific" viewpoints trying to compete with secular scientific theories in the marketplace of ideas.[77] To the extent it requires applicants to adhere to the scientific method preferred by secular science, it is not neutral as between religion and secularism. It prefers secular hypotheses and methods over religiously derived hypotheses, even when the "religious scientists" engage in some empirical research.

Perhaps the most obvious argument in the NSF's favor would be that in this case government is funding the research through a competitive process and on its own behalf, and by analogy to the free speech cases, government can "selectively fund a program to encourage activities that it believes are in the public interest."[78] The problem with the competitive process aspect of this argument is that the creation scientists are in essence arguing that the process is competitive only for those holding secular scientific views. It would be as if the NEA in *Nat'l. Endowment for the Arts v. Finley*[79] had said it would allow artists to compete only if their styles were influenced by secular art or artists. The problem with the government as speaker aspect of the argument is that the government does not necessarily endorse all the scientific research that arises from NSF grants, and indeed it seems to be creating a "funding forum" for the exploration of scientific ideas (thus it might be a designated public forum open to "scientists"). This might make the situation more like that in *Rosenberger v. Rector and Visitors of the Univ. of Va.*,[80] where the University of Virginia's system for funding student organizations was deemed a limited public forum,[81] although the competitive nature of NSF funding could still be a distinguishing factor. It is, of course, quite possible that a court would analyze the situation presented in this hypothetical under *Finley* or the government speech cases, but let us presume for the moment that as in *Rosenberger* it does not, and the applicable analysis is the Court's neutrality analysis. Would a decision favoring the creation scientists be neutral?

The answer to this question must be separated from the question of whether it would be good policy or good science. After all, neutrality, like objectivity, makes a universal claim that cannot be addressed based on one's policy preferences. One could argue that allowing creation scientists access to NSF funding is not neutral, because it gives religion a preferred status over other scientific theories that are not in the scientific mainstream. This begs the question for the other side, which could argue that not including religiously affected theories would give secularism and secular science preferred status and benefits over religiously affected theories.[82] The claim that the latter theories are not scientific or that the evaluators who make the scientific decisions reject those theories as unscientific is inadequate to address this concern under formal neutrality, because the creation scientists can argue that they included empirical data in their proposal and that the NSF policies and definition of science are hostile to religiously affected theories, and therefore the denial of funding puts those accounts at a disadvantage when compared with the secular scientific accounts.

Moreover, once this argument is made, other religious groups—for example, a UFO cult that believes humans were placed here by aliens from the planet Zermac—would also be able to challenge the use of secular scientific standards in the NSF selection process. To avoid discriminating against religion by favoring secular scientific standards in a government-funded program open to private applicants, the only "neutral" process for selection among those willing to include empirical data in their proposals might be a first come first serve system or a lottery system. The creation science scenario is not a huge leap under the Court's formal neutrality approach.[83]

How would the creation scientist fare under a substantive neutrality approach? One could argue that giving government funds to creation scientists certainly encourages religion, because of both the financial aid and the credibility that NSF funding might lend to creation scientists. One could also argue, however, that by funding only secular scientific theories, government increases the ability of secular science to replace religion-based theories and puts religion at a competitive disadvantage in the marketplace of ideas. Professor Laycock foresaw this tension between secular programs and religion, and recognized a caveat to his substantive neutrality approach, namely, that government is not encouraging or discouraging religion by funding secular social activities.[84] I do not disagree with his caveat, but with or without the caveat his substantive principles are not neutral. Either side could argue the result is not neutral if the other side wins. Thus, whatever the independent merits of the substantive neutrality approach, the term "neutrality" is a misnomer.

While Laycock's theory is highly useful in the religion clause context, the Court has unfortunately chosen to pursue the formal neutrality approach in regard to a number of issues. Let us turn, then, to some of these issues by exploring three landmark cases, each applying a version of the formal neutrality approach.

A. Zelman v. Simmons-Harris

Zelman is a significant case for several reasons. It is the first U.S. Supreme Court case to uphold a government-funded educational voucher program, and thus it is quite significant from the education policy perspective as well as the law and religion perspective. Additionally, a majority of the Court affirmed the use of formal neutrality, holding if a program is neutral on its face and functions through "true private choice," the program is constitutional.[85] Finally, while the majority opinion purports to consider whether private individuals who channel the government money to religious schools had real choices, the opinion expands the pool of "choices" to include public magnet and charter schools, leaving open the possibility that the comparison group could be further expanded to include all public schools, at least in districts that have open enrollment or public school choice programs.[86]

The Zelman Court ostensibly followed the Lemon test as modified in Agostini.[87] The Court first held that Zelman did not present a secular purpose issue, because the goal of providing a better education to students in the Cleveland School District was an adequate secular purpose[88]—indeed, at least in government aid and equal access cases, it is hard to imagine a situation where there would not be an adequate secular purpose. Thus, the case centered on the effects of the program,[89] as have several other funding cases.[90]

Yet there is a significant catch. The two factors that determine whether an indirect aid program meets the *Zelman* test are that the program must be neutral on its face and the money must flow through individuals who have "true individual choice" regarding where to direct the aid.[91] If a program is neutral on its face between religious and nonreligious entities, it is highly unlikely it would ever fail the secular purpose test, nor is there a significant distinction between direct and indirect aid, since so long as the government entity drafting the program relates the aid that flows to religious institutions to the number of individuals who choose to use the private service, it does not matter whether the check is written from the government directly to the religious institution.[92] It is not a stretch to say that at least in cases of government aid to religious institutions the test is one of facial neutrality plus a private "circuit breaker"—that is, the money ostensibly flows to the religious institution because of the choices of private individuals.[93] Significantly, the "circuit breaker" element is connected to the Court's broader neutrality analysis. It is the private individual "choice" that makes a facially neutral program "entirely neutral."[94]

This begs the question, however, of what constitutes "true private choice" under the Court's analysis. The Court's answer to this question is significant, because it involved a statistical sleight of hand that could potentially make all public schools the relevant comparison group to religious schools for purposes of government aid programs. This would be so even in areas with no secular private schools or where such private schools cannot afford to take voucher students, so long as secular private schools would be included in the program if they existed.[95] This makes the Court's new test an exercise in almost pure formalism.[96] If a program is neutral on its face—it does not specify religious entities as beneficiaries—and there is some government or nonreligious private entity that the recipients could conceivably choose to go to for service, the test is met because the program is neutral on its face and provides "true private choice,"[97] even if virtually all funding going to private organizations goes to religious organizations.[98]

If this really were neutral, and neutrality was an appropriate actuating principle under the Establishment Clause,[99] the Court's approach would be perfectly acceptable. Conversely, if the Court's approach is not neutral, calling it neutral should give it no further power, and it should be adequately supported by some other principle. In fact, if it is not neutral, having the Court pronounce its neutrality is especially dangerous, because the Court would simply be placing the label of neutrality on analysis that is neither neutral nor likely to lead to "neutral" results and using the label to validate its approach. The Court could call its undergirding principle "Ralph," and it would have the same descriptive accuracy.[100] In fact, Ralph might be more descriptively accurate because one would still have to determine what the essence of Ralphness is, and the nature of the term does not suggest that it has any extra power or reality until it is defined.

This might seem a bit tongue-in-cheek, and it is to a point, but it demonstrates the serious problems with claims to neutrality. Since there is no neutral foundation or baseline that can be used to prove that something is "truly" neutral, neutrality is nothing more than a buzzword, and a dangerous one at that, because it implies that the supposedly neutral approach should be taken more seriously because it is actually neutral.[101] Legal tests and definitions of neutrality do not make an approach neutral —they are simply tests or definitions, and neutrality is nothing but extra baggage.[102] As was explained above, this does not mean that conceptions of neutrality—such as Douglas Laycock's substantive neutrality[103]—are not useful tools, but it does mean that they are not neutral and should gain no additional validity from the use of that term.[104]

This suggests that the Court's formal neutrality approach is especially dangerous, because the formalistic approach leaves little room for introspection, and its very nature makes it less likely to account for nuances or context. Supporting such a rigid regime with a concept that cannot be proven is particularly dangerous, since once the formalistic test controls outcomes, there will be little opportunity to adapt to varied circumstances without sacrificing the clarity such formalistic tests are intended to create. Thus, courts applying the test must either rigidly apply a test that has never adequately justified itself because it is based on a nonexistent principle, attempt to modify the test in its application to varied circumstances without the help of a useful guiding principle, or in the case of the Supreme Court, abandon stare decisis and either overturn the decisions giving rise to the approach or apply the approach in a manner that goes against its underlying purpose.[105]

A response to this line of reasoning might be that none of this is relevant if the Court's approach is "truly" neutral. I will respond to this argument here. My response will proceed in three parts. First, I will look at whether the individual beneficiaries of the program in *Zelman* had "true private choice."[106] Second, I will examine whether the notion of a private circuit breaker can make a government funding program "neutral" where that program ultimately gives a disproportionate amount of public money meant for private entities to religious institutions. As will be seen, the answer to this question is related to the first question, even if one accepts the notion that neutrality exists and that it consists of treating both religious and nonreligious individuals and institutions the same. Finally, I will explore whether the "facial neutrality" of a law—the fact that a law does not distinguish between potential recipients within the broad class of recipients eligible for aid[107]—has anything to do with neutrality as an actuating principle for Establishment Clause jurisprudence.

In *Zelman,* the Court found that the parents of the students in the Cleveland School District, the private "circuit breakers," had real individual choice regarding where to send their children.[108] In finding this "true" choice, the Court went beyond the private school options the parents had and included several public school options.[109] Thus, government-run programs became part of the field of options the Court considered. Arguably, a program would be neutral, and parents would have "true" choices even if 100 percent of the money going to private entities went to religious entities or if the only private choices parents had were religious.[110] This would seemingly be so even if the resulting government-funded regime put nonreligious private programs at a competitive disadvantage and led to religious institutions funded by a single sect taking over a market for services.[111]

One argument in favor of so expanding the comparison group is that government is so pervasive that to exclude government-run programs—which are by their nature secular—from the comparison group would be to put religion at a disadvantage in the marketplace of ideas and programs.[112] Yet this argument is something of a red herring. For example, religious groups have not generally had equal access to compete to run police or fire services, nor would one have thought (prior to *Zelman*) that religious organizations could compete to take over road services or state-run children and family services. Moreover, religious organizations could not administer a public school or a charter school that relies on public funds for its existence. The relevant comparison group in the context of a voucher program is thus private schools.[113] Such schools are the only relevant entities that are not government run, wholly reliant on government funds, or subject to pervasive government regulation and oversight.

The relevant statistics regarding private schools in the Cleveland area were skewed such that the bulk of the money passing through the voucher program into private hands went to religious schools, and parents who participated in the voucher aspect of the Cleveland program had few nonreligious options.[114] More than 3,700 students participated in the voucher program, and of those, 96 percent enrolled in religious schools.[115] Forty-six of the fifty-six private schools participating in the program were religious schools.[116] Moreover, the nonreligious private schools were generally small and had fewer seats for voucher students.[117] These figures are not unusual because religious schools make up a significantly larger proportion of private schools nationally than do nonreligious schools.[118]

Rather than rehashing the debate regarding these data—a debate that played out between the various opinions in *Zelman* and in the law review literature—let us focus on the Court's characterization of the Cleveland program as an "entirely neutral" program of "true private choice."[119] Let us assume for the moment that the Court's statistical sleight of hand was a valid comparison of apples to apples, and thus in addition to the 3,765 voucher students in the program, we can consider the 1,400 students who stayed in public school and received subsidized tutorial aid, the 1,900 students enrolled in publicly funded community schools, and the 13,000 enrolled in public magnet schools.[120] The proportion of students attending religious schools drops to below 20 percent when the reference group shifts from 3,765 students to 20,000 students.[121] In fact, if we were to include the entire Cleveland school system in the comparison group using the *Zelman* majority's approximate figure of 75,000,[122] the proportion going to religious schools under the voucher program would be approximately 4.85 percent.[123] The 75,000 figure would represent all the "choices" parents in the Cleveland district had (or could have assuming open enrollment at all Cleveland public schools).[124]

Yet if parents choose to take advantage of the voucher program because of dissatisfaction with all public school options (including community schools), or the inability to get into a magnet school or failure to win a lottery slot at a community school,[125] the parent may have little choice but to send his or her children to religious schools or forgo the voucher option entirely.[126] If parents in the area do not subscribe to the faith of any participating religious school, as is likely for nonbelievers and many religious minorities, they can make the same "choice" as their neighbors who participate in the voucher program and who subscribe to one of the represented faiths, only by sending their children to a religious school that may indoctrinate them in a faith with which the family disagrees or at the very least does not believe in. This choice hardly seems neutral. Nor does the Court's assurance that the program is neutral, since it provides everyone with "true private choice" and does not discriminate on its face, provide much solace to a parent who desperately wants to provide the best education possible for her children but who is afraid that her children will be confronted daily with lessons and choices that are alien to the family's faith.[127]

This is the problem with neutrality. One person's neutrality is another's discrimination or favoritism, and if a court proclaims something to be neutral, there is no way of proving the proclamation to be true. The Rehnquist Court relies on "true private choice" and facial neutrality as the basis for demonstrating that a program is "entirely neutral,"[128] yet it is easy to dispute the availability of "true private choice," and the facial neutrality of a program does not mean that the program is neutral or even that it was not designed to discriminate against religious minorities or to favor dominant religious groups in a given area.[129]

Even if the Court were correct that parents had a choice of multiple, equally viable nonreligious options, the program is not neutral. The overwhelming amount of money flowing into private (i.e., not *initially* dependent on government for survival) hands flows to religious schools, as does the overwhelming number of students.[130] Unless the Court explains how the existence of "true private choice" under such circumstances is neutral, especially in light of the inequity in same-sect options between the denominational "haves" and "have-nots," there is no reason to take the Court's word for it. The Court's reasoning is circular—neutrality equals private choice and facial neutrality because if a program is facially neutral and provides private choice, it is neutral. The neutrality claim remains unsubstantiated, yet without the claim to neutrality the Court is left having to justify why religion is indistinct as a matter of constitutional law and why excluding only religion from the voucher program (as a contrary holding could require) might be unconstitutional. The claim that the program is neutral allows the Court to evade significant doctrinal and conceptual problems.

What if, on the other hand, a voucher program included a large number of nonreligious private schools?[131] Would this program be neutral? Where would the line be drawn if private choice is the sine qua non of neutrality so long as a program is neutral on its face? Seventy-five percent religious schools? Fifty percent? Forty percent? What if 70 percent of the 40 percent of participating schools that are religious belong to one denomination? What if 100 percent belong to one religion? As will be seen in later chapters, these questions can be answered—although not perfectly —but not by claiming the programs or the answers to the questions are neutral.[132] If there were a real range of choices available to parents within the voucher option, as was the case with the programs in *Zobrest v. Catalina Foothills Sch. Dist.,*[133] and *Witters v. Wash. Dept. of Servs. for the Blind,*[134] the program would be constitutional, not because the private choice makes an otherwise biased program neutral, but rather because the effects of such a program do not give religion a disproportionate and substantial benefit.[135]

B. *Good News Club v. Milford Central School*

Good News Club presents another version of the Court's formal neutrality, again grounded in the notion that treating religion differently would be hostile to religion.[136] *Good News Club* derives from a long line of equal access cases that at least arguably have a more consistent pedigree than the aid cases.[137] Equal access cases are those where a religious organization seeks access to government-owned facilities or government-funded forums to which nonreligious entities have access.[138] The primary difference in *Good News Club* is that the forum to which the religious group sought access was a central school that included an elementary school.[139]

I will note at the outset that I think all the equal access cases up to *Good News Club* were correctly decided, and that *Good News Club*, while a closer call, was also correctly decided, but not because the analysis or results were neutral or because religion should automatically be treated the same as nonreligion. In fact, by automatically connecting exclusion of the religious group with hostility to religion and thus nonneutrality,[140] the Court makes another leap that it fails to adequately support. The Court's use of the concept of hostility toward religion will be discussed in greater detail in chapter 3.

Good News Club is in many ways a straightforward speech case.[141] School district policy allowed a variety of noncurricular student groups access to school facilities when school was not in session.[142] Both parties agreed that the district provided a limited public forum for a variety of groups at the school.[143] The religious club was denied access because the religious character of its meetings was the equivalent of religious instruction.[144] The district argued that the denial of access under such circumstances was in compliance with New York law.[145] It was specifically the group's deeply religious mission, as well as its proselytizing nature, that gave the school district pause.[146] Thus, from a free speech perspective, the issue was one of viewpoint discrimination rather than content discrimination.[147]

Content discrimination occurs when government discriminates against or excludes an entire subject, but viewpoint discrimination occurs when the government discriminates against speech based on the specific viewpoint involved. Thus, it would be content discrimination to exclude all religious speech from a public forum, but it would be viewpoint discrimination to exclude only speech from a Jewish perspective. Claims of content discrimination in a public forum give rise to strict scrutiny,[148] and thus the district would need to demonstrate a compelling governmental interest and that its action was narrowly tailored to serve that compelling interest.[149] The Court has suggested that viewpoint discrimination in a public forum is presumed unconstitutional,[150] but the Court did not answer this question in *Good News Club*,[151] and there is some support for applying strict scrutiny to viewpoint discrimination, albeit especially strict scrutiny.[152] Regardless, the line between content and viewpoint discrimination is somewhat blurred.

The district argued that its compelling interest was compliance with the Establishment Clause, because the group was intensely religious, believed in proselytizing, was run by outside adults, and most important was geared for elementary school students who are young and impressionable.[153] Thus, this case had the potential to directly confront the issue of whether religion is constitutionally different from other aspects of life, but the majority passed on the opportunity to deeply analyze this question. Instead, the Court presumed that treating religion differently was hostile to religion, and would send a message of hostility to students in the same way the school feared the group's meetings would send a message of endorsement of religion to nonbelieving students.[154]

As the dissent points out, the group was connected to a national organization that focuses on getting a foothold with elementary-aged children precisely because they are young and impressionable.[155] The majority argued that religious organizations are the same as other organizations, and to deny them the same rights as other organizations is to discriminate against religion or religious viewpoints—that is, it is not neutral.[156] Differential treatment is not mandated by the Establishment Clause and indeed might violate that clause.[157]

Once again, the analysis boils down to formalism—this time with the aid of the Free Speech Clause. If religion is treated differently in a limited public forum, even in a sensitive context like an elementary school, this is viewpoint or content discrimination (depending on whether a specific viewpoint[s] or category of speech is focused upon).[158] Yet treating religion differently in a forum neutrally open to all student groups is never a compelling government interest, because such differential treatment is not required by the Establishment Clause, since that clause requires religion to be treated the same as nonreligion.[159] By assuming that religion must be treated the same as nonreligion, the Court both sets up the claim of viewpoint discrimination and answers the compelling interest defense to that claim.[160] Beyond asserting that differential treatment in this context is hostility to religion, the Court never explains why religion should be treated the same as nonreligion, and why differential treatment in this context is automatically hostile and nonneutral.[161] This is reminiscent of a long-standing critique of the Court's formal equality doctrine under the Fourteenth Amendment: Is treating differently situated groups the same equality?[162] The Court's formal neutrality-different treatment as hostility argument presumes that a differently situated (both textually and historically) classification—religion—is the same as every other classification for purposes of religion clause analysis.[163]

Yet I think the general result in *Good News Club* was correct. How is it possible to reach this conclusion without at least accepting the idea that government needs to treat religion the same as nonreligion in the equal access context? My reasoning, which will be explained in greater detail in later chapters, is that the policy allowing a variety of student groups to meet does not substantially facilitate religion as compared with nonreligion. If it did, it would be perfectly acceptable to treat religion differently because of Establishment Clause concerns. Additionally, the facilitation approach proposed in chapter 10 would not preclude the school from preventing completely equal access—that is, the school can limit the group's ability to advertise in the classroom (as opposed to bulletin boards) or could limit announcements over a generally available public address system to basic information about meeting times and locations, even if other groups are not so limited (and so long as all religious student groups have the same limitations).[164] Perhaps most important, if the group begins to interfere with the rights of other students through organized proselytization or by overreaching in recruitment efforts, the school can revoke access. Additionally, if the group were favored by the school, students (through parents) could bring an "as applied" challenge to the access policy.

The key is that the *Good News Club* result is correct not because it is inherently neutral—many religious minorities might not have the numbers or the desire to form such clubs, and thus the result may favor religions with greater numbers or a greater will to proselytize[165]—but because the free speech concerns cannot be rebutted under the facts of the case. Thus, precluding the group is not automatically hostile to religion and allowing it to meet does not automatically favor religion. The concepts of hostility and favoritism, like neutrality, are quite manipulable and can vary depending on who is evaluating the claim.

C. Employment Division v. Smith

Smith demonstrates the application of the formal neutrality principle in the Free Exercise Clause context. Two members of the Native American Church were denied unemployment benefits after being fired from their jobs at a substance abuse rehabilitation center.[166] They were fired because they had used peyote, an illegal substance under Oregon law, during religious rituals.[167] Oregon law stated that being fired for misconduct—which is how the firing was characterized—precludes the receipt of unemployment benefits.[168] Neither man had abused peyote, and there was no evidence that they used it other than in religious ceremonies.[169] In fact, it would violate the tenets of the Native American Church to use peyote outside of appropriate religious rituals because the substance has significant religious import for members of the faith.[170] Oregon, unlike many states and the federal government, did not have a religious exemption for Native American peyote use under its general drug laws.[171] Thus, the Court had to decide whether the two men denied unemployment benefits had a constitutional right to an exemption to the drug laws given the religious nature of their peyote use.[172] An exemption would preclude the denial of unemployment benefits based on misconduct.[173]

The backdrop of legal precedent seemed to favor the men, but that precedent—contrary to popular belief—was anything but clear or terribly helpful to religious minorities. The precedent many thought would be key to the decision was *Sherbert v. Verner,*[174] which held that a state must have a compelling governmental interest for denying unemployment benefits to a person who was fired for refusing to work on her Sabbath.[175] Relevant, but not decisive on my reading of the *Sherbert* opinion, was the fact that the state unemployment laws contained a number of exemptions for nonreligious reasons.[176]

Another decision, *Wisconsin v. Yoder,*[177] was also potentially relevant. In *Yoder* the Court held that Amish families with high school–aged children were entitled to exemptions from the state's compulsory education laws in the absence of a compelling state interest.[178] The court looked at the Amish community's track record of good citizenship, hard work, and the success of its young people within the community to demonstrate that the state had no compelling interest for denying the exemption.[179] There have been some serious criticisms of the Court's approach in *Yoder,*[180] but for present purposes this basic overview of the Court's holding is adequate.

Given this precedent, most people believed that the battle lines in *Smith* would be drawn over whether the state had an adequate compelling governmental interest.[181] In fact, Oregon's attorney general at that time later pointed out that the state never argued for disposing of the compelling interest test,[182] but rather argued that compliance with the state's drug laws satisfied the burden under that test, especially in light of post-*Sherbert* and post-*Yoder* case law.[183] As will be seen, that subsequent case law suggested that *Sherbert* and *Yoder* were primarily paper tigers, at least in the U.S. Supreme Court.[184]

Between *Yoder* and *Smith* the Court decided a string of free exercise exemption cases. With the exception of a few unemployment cases, the person seeking the exemption never won.[185] In some cases, the nature of the government institution, that is, the military or prisons, served as a basis for not applying the compelling interest test.[186] In others, the relief requested was decisive in not applying the compelling interest test, for example, cases where the government entity involved would have had to change its policies to grant an exemption.[187] Finally, there were cases where the court ostensibly applied the compelling interest test, but in a manner that made it anything but strict scrutiny.[188] It should be noted, however, that *Sherbert* and *Yoder* did influence the outcomes of some lower court cases.[189]

The *Smith* Court relied on the post-*Yoder* decisions, as well as some pre-*Sherbert* decisions, to hold that *Sherbert* is limited to the unemployment context where there are generally a variety of exemptions built into the unemployment laws.[190] Furthermore, the claim in *Smith* was different from earlier free exercise cases granting exemptions to unemployment laws because the claimants in *Smith* sought an exemption based on illegal conduct, whereas the claimants in the earlier cases sought an exemption based on religious conduct that was otherwise legal.[191] *Yoder* was harder to distinguish, but the Court created the concept of hybrid rights, cases in which the Free Exercise Clause right is connected to some other important right (in *Yoder* parental rights).[192] This theory works well to distinguish several earlier cases that involved freedom of expression as well as free exercise concerns,[193] but to characterize *Yoder* as a hybrid rights case was a stretch.

This stretch would be more troubling if the traditional story of Free Exercise Clause jurisprudence were accurate, but the reality is that *Sherbert* and *Yoder* were never the panacea they have been made out to be.[194] The idea of a compelling interest test held a lot of promise, but in the hands of shifting majorities on the Court that promise was never realized, although it was sometimes realized in the lower courts.[195] The relevance of the Court's failure to live up to the promise of *Sherbert* and *Yoder* for future attempts to interpret the Free Exercise Clause will be discussed in later chapters.[196] For now, I will focus on the implicit neutrality claim made by the *Smith* Court, and why that claim suffered the same flaws as other neutrality claims in the religion clause context.

Divorcing *Smith* from all the important—but for present purposes irrelevant—baggage regarding stare decisis and so forth, we are left with the basic notion that the Free Exercise Clause does not require exemptions to generally applicable (today the Court might say facially neutral) laws. The argument seems to be that because these laws are religion neutral, the Free Exercise Clause has no impact on them except through the political process.[197] This is, of course, a claim of formal neutrality. But how is formal neutrality "neutral" in this context. One might ask this in the language of *Smith*, how can a law be generally applicable in this context? The concurring and dissenting opinions essentially ask this question and answer that the laws are neither neutral nor generally applicable for free exercise purposes.[198]

Here there may be a dichotomy between claims of neutrality and general applicability. The law without religious exemptions is not neutral, whether viewed from the perspective of free exercise or from that of the legal regime as a whole. The Court admits as much in suggesting that no one is entitled to a religious exemption and religious minorities might be at a disadvantage when attempting to get exemptions through the political process.[199] Whatever baseline one sets for neutrality in this context, neither the result nor the baseline can be proven neutral. Yet one might set two different baselines for general applicability in this case: one that views general applicability without regard to the nature of the claim and one that views general applicability specifically in the free exercise context. From the latter perspective the law is not generally applicable because it places a significant burden on those whose religious practices require a violation of the law. From the former perspective the law is generally applicable because it applies to all citizens, even if it may have a differing impact on some. This, of course, simply begs the question.

How does one choose between these baselines? Certainly not based on the tortured use of precedent by both the majority and dissenting opinions. So what really allowed the justices to choose? We will, of course, never know for sure, but it seems the majority presumed that it is religion neutral to analyze the general applicability of the law without regard to the nature of the claim.[200] Otherwise, the Court's reasoning makes no sense. If the law was not religion neutral in the free exercise context, then it is not generally applicable because it would apply differently to different religious groups. The Court's approach is one of formal neutrality because it is concerned only with the facial neutrality of the law and not with its practical effects. The concurring and dissenting opinions seem to assume that the law is not generally applicable or religion neutral in the context of a free exercise claim.[201] Thus, for purposes of the present discussion, we will focus on the majority opinion.

Whether the decision in *Smith* is a valid interpretation of the Free Exercise Clause (I will suggest in later chapters that it is not) cannot be determined based on the implicit neutrality claim or on the presumption regarding the general applicability of the law. Rather, we must look elsewhere. The governing precedent was mixed; although it does seem the majority opinion took some liberties with precedent. In the end the Court had to answer the question, as the *Sherbert* Court tried to do, what does the Free Exercise Clause mean, and how should it be applied to exemptions from laws that are not directly aimed at religion? By relying on general applicability and facial neutrality, the Court never seriously engages this question. The answer is presumed—general applicability/neutrality is determinative because that is what the Free Exercise Clause requires. Why? Because generally applicable laws cannot burden free exercise in a constitutionally significant way. Why? Because we said so. The Court might be able to justify this approach with an appropriate mode of religion clause interpretation, but neutrality is not such a mode, and general applicability is used as a stand-in for neutrality. Even if one were to argue that general applicability has meaning separate from its implicit neutrality claim, one is left trying to determine if the laws of general applicability approach used by the Court is adequately supported by an appropriate mode of religion clause interpretation. Neutrality is used here to avoid carefully answering the tough question of what the Free Exercise Clause requires and why.

3

Hostility

Members of the Court have often, and especially recently, suggested that various government actions or decisions are "hostile" to religion. The use of the term "hostile" to describe the treatment of a person, idea, or entity generally implies that there is some negative intent or feeling involved—that is, that the treatment is actually hostile. Yet when that term has been used in connection with government entities' treatment of religion, the Court has failed to adequately explain what it means by "hostility."[1] Recent decisions indicate the Court has presumed the failure of government entities to follow the dictates of formal neutrality is sometimes hostile to religion,[2] although the Court has never seriously attempted to justify this characterization. The Supreme Court's use of the term in the Establishment Clause context thus appears to be only rhetorical. If the Court uses a powerful term such as "hostility," however, it should do so only when actual hostility is involved.

The Court's rhetorical use of "hostility" is consistent with its recent tendency toward formalism in religion clause analysis.[3] The problem, as was discussed in chapter 2, is that the trend has led to a doctrine that is based on unstated principles. Yet the Court attempts to substantiate this doctrine with concepts, such as "neutrality" and "hostility," which are mostly rhetorical. In several important contexts, the Court has begun to use bright-line tests that seem to depart from earlier precedent but which derive significant support from concepts and terminology that the Court never adequately justifies or explains.[4] The most significant of these concepts is neutrality, but hostility—which has been connected to the lack of neutrality by some justices and commentators—is also important.

In cases such as *Mitchell v. Helms,*[5] the Court (in *Mitchell,* a plurality of the Court) uses the term "hostility" without ever defining it or connecting it to hostile motives. It seems the Court applies the label of "hostility" to justify a result, but because the Court applies it to situations that may have little to do with "hostility" as commonly understood, the Court's rhetoric may turn into a blunt instrument to cast even mildly separationist doctrine and policies as hostile—and thus violative of the Court's new formal neutrality principle. This has an Alice-in-Wonderland-like impact, as justices use the term "hostility" in situations where there is no hostility and then, based on the term, find that the government action is not neutral, when the Court's neutrality concept is itself empty because neutrality is impossible in this context.[6] Interestingly, the Court's use of hostility in its most recent funding decision, *Locke v. Davey*,[7] suggests a limit to this trend, but its brief discussion of hostility in that case seems to conflict with the use of the same concept in other cases.

This chapter is not meant to address the long-standing debate over whether separationism and/or secularism is biased against religion.[8] That question will be taken up in later chapters. For now, it is enough to say that I disagree with those in the debate who automatically equate bias or bad effects with hostility toward religion. This, of course, suggests that those who automatically equate separationism with bias against religion should stick with the concept of bias (whatever its merits across issues) and use the concept of hostility only when there is evidence of actual hostility as discussed below. Still, hostility toward religion is sometimes a real concern that needs to be addressed. Significantly, the lack of formal neutrality should not be used as proof of actual hostility.

A. Background

In recent years the Court has used the concept of hostility toward religion primarily in cases involving equal access,[9] but the concept is also finding its way into the government aid context.[10] In both of these realms the Court (or a plurality of justices) has in essence said that failure to treat religious entities and individuals like all other entities and individuals is hostile toward religion. Thus, the Court seems poised to treat hostility and lack of formal neutrality as two sides of the same coin.[11]

I argued in chapter 2 that the current Court's notion of formal neutrality is an empty concept because neutrality does not and cannot exist, at least not in the Establishment Clause context.[12] In contrast, hostility toward religion can exist, and thus, it is a different kind of concept than neutrality. Whereas neutrality makes an untenable universal claim, hostility does not.[13] Of course, the fact that hostility can exist does not mean that the Court's use of the concept is accurate—this chapter will argue that it is not. Inaccuracy in the use of the term "hostility" was less problematic in earlier decisions in which the Court did not connect the term to formal neutrality, although a strong argument can be made that earlier Courts did not take hostility toward religion as seriously as they took religious favoritism.[14] Still, the Court has long held that "hostility" toward religion is prohibited by the First Amendment.[15] Yet the Court has done a poor job of defining "hostility," and the current Court's choice of definition has little to do with real hostility.[16] Since "hostility" has generally served as a tangential rhetorical justification for decisions, this concern has been little explored.

This is not simply a debate over semantics because terms such as "hostility" and "neutrality" represent concepts (however poorly defined) that the Court uses to justify its decisions. If the Court's "hostility" is not hostile and its "neutrality" is not neutral, the Court's approach must rest on some other footing. By failing to define and explain that footing, the Court forces those who question its approach to spar with shadows.

As noted in chapter 2, the oft-cited argument that the Court has simply chosen a baseline for neutrality does not solve the problem because there is no neutral place from which to create that baseline.[17] Thus, even though hostility toward religion can be real, the Court's evolving concept of hostility is problematic because the Court's apparent baseline for hostility is the lack of neutrality, which itself has no adequate baseline. Using a concept that itself has no adequate baseline as a baseline for hostility simply removes the problem by one degree; it does not solve it.

Recent cases supply examples of the Court's subtle but forceful use of the concept of hostility in the Establishment Clause context. The Court's use of the concept seems to be evolving (or devolving) over time. In *Mitchell v. Helms*,[18] a case involving a government program that loaned educational equipment to public and private schools, including religious schools, a plurality of the Court held:

> The pervasively sectarian recipient has not received any special favor, and it is most bizarre that the Court would, as the dissent seemingly does, reserve special hostility for those who take their religion seriously, who think that their religion should affect the whole of their lives, or who make the mistake of being effective in transmitting their views to children.[19]

The plurality simply assumed that the position of the respondents and the dissenting justices in *Mitchell* reserved "special hostility for those who take their religion seriously," without identifying any actual government hostility to religion.[20] There are, of course, many possible reasons for the position taken by the respondents and the dissenting justices short of hostility. It is one thing to challenge a doctrine—based on that doctrine's history—that was born of actual hostility toward a religion,[21] which as will be seen the plurality is easily able to do with the doctrine prohibiting any government aid to "pervasively sectarian" entities, but quite another to assert that those who adhere to a doctrine do so out of "special hostility" when that doctrine has evolved over the years to serve other purposes. Even if the "pervasively sectarian" doctrine was at least partially born out of hostility to Catholics as the *Mitchell* plurality argues (and there is a great deal of supporting evidence for this argument), current actors may not be aware of that history, and the doctrine has come to serve purposes that are divorced from its anti-Catholic history. That history may still render the doctrine invalid, but it says nothing about whether a given government actor or Justice is acting out of hostility to religion now.

More recently, in *Locke v. Davey*,[22] the Court suggested that not every government decision to deny funding based on the religious interests of funding recipients is hostile to religion. In *Locke*, the Court held that the State of Washington could deny funding under a facially neutral scholarship program to a student who planned to use that funding for ministerial training.[23] The state denied the funding because to provide it would have violated the state constitution's equivalent of the Establishment Clause, a clause that is broader than its federal counterpart.[24] The state did allow students under the program to use the scholarships at any accredited college or university, including religious institutions.[25] Thus, the state only precluded funding for training in devotional theology. Joshua Davey asserted that the denial of funding violated his rights under the Free Exercise Clause. The Court noted the tension between the two religion clauses in such cases but held both that there is some "play in the joints" between the two clauses and that a state decision not to fund training for the clergy fell within this play.[26] The holding was limited to training in devotional theology and thus did not address the broader question of whether a state could deny funding to religious institutions generally under a facially neutral funding program.

Interestingly, the *Locke* Court used the term "hostility" several times in the opinion.[27] For example, the Court noted: "That a State would deal differently with religious education for the ministry than with education for other callings is . . . not evidence of hostility toward religion."[28] The Court also noted that the fact that the state allowed the scholarships to be used at religious institutions, so long as the student is not training for the clergy, supports the argument that the denial of the scholarship in Davey's case was not evidence of hostility.[29] It is important to note that the *Locke* Court seemed to connect hostility with animus, as this chapter suggests is appropriate,[30] although the Court was not clear about this. Yet it is hard to gel the Court's approach to the concept of hostility in *Locke* with its use of that concept in other cases that did not involve proof of animus toward religion.[31] If *Locke* signals a move toward defining "hostility" in some concrete way that has something to do with actual hostility, this would be a welcomed development. This is unlikely, however, given the limited context and holding in *Locke* and the Court's general failure to clearly define the concept in other recent cases.

In *Good News Club v. Milford Central School*[32] and *Rosenberger v. Rector and Visitors of the University of Virginia*,[33] the Court held that the refusal to allow religious organizations to use public school property for meetings and the denial of funding for a religious student publication, respectively, were viewpoint discrimination. Neither of these cases is exceptional in the free speech context as there is ample support for the notion that the exclusion of religious entities from a public or limited public forum is content and/or viewpoint discrimination,[34] although both cases applied that concept to situations not addressed in prior opinions.[35] Interestingly, in both cases the government entities asserted that they were motivated by Establishment Clause (or related state law) concerns; the Court, however, treated their actions as hostile to religion.[36] In each case the Court cited *Board of Education of Westside Community Schools v. Mergens ex rel. Mergens*,[37] in which the plurality held, "if a State refused to let religious groups use facilities open to others, then it would demonstrate not neutrality but hostility toward religion."[38] The *Mergens* plurality, quoting Justice Brennan's concurring opinion in *McDaniel v. Paty*,[39] further defined what it meant by "hostility": "The Establishment Clause does not license government to treat religion and those who teach or practice it, simply by virtue of their status as such, as subversive of American ideals and therefore subject to unique disabilities."[40]

The *Mergens* plurality seems to have assumed that the exclusion of a religious student club would constitute such a government-imposed disability and, at least implicitly, that such would be the intent. Yet, there are many possible reasons for such treatment that have nothing to do with hostility toward religion.[41]

It is important to note that the Court has not used the concept of hostility in all its recent Establishment Clause decisions. The decisions in which it has used that concept, however, suggest that it is poised to use its rhetorical hostility in tandem with the doctrine of formal neutrality that it has developed in recent decisions.[42] Thus, the concept may come to occupy an important place in the Court's Establishment Clause jurisprudence.

B. The Supreme Court's Evolving Definition of Hostility

In recent cases where the Court has referred to "hostility," it may be suggesting that the effect of separationist policy is hostile to religion—that is, separationist policy has a disparate impact that negatively affects religion or a specific religion. This is ironic since the Court refused to consider the impact of the programs in question when defining "neutrality" in cases where policies had a positive impact on religion.[43] Is it possible that the Court will not consider the impact of government actions when those actions give religion, especially more dominant religions, a substantial benefit[44] and yet will consider the impact when the government attempts to prevent such disparate negative results?[45]

Another possibility is that the Court has equated disparate treatment with hostility.[46] This, too, is problematic because government entities engaged in disparate treatment, and parties who advocate for such treatment in Establishment Clause cases, may be motivated by many concerns that do not involve hostility toward religion.[47] In fact, in some cases they may be motivated by a belief that such treatment protects religion or that it recognizes religion's special place in our constitutional system.[48] Whether or not such assertions are accurate, they do not evince hostility toward religion.[49] Given that earlier Courts recognized valid reasons for treating religion differently, even "less favorably" in some contexts, the current Court's evolving notion of hostility may be quite different from that of earlier Courts.

If the Court's implication of hostility relates only to the negative effects of the government action or inaction in aid and equal access cases, rather than actual hostility on the part of government actors, the Court has created an interesting Establishment Clause doctrine indeed. The Court will overlook massive disparate favoritism of dominant religions (especially in the aid context),[50] yet easily overturn government action that has the effect of disfavoring religion.[51] If, on the other hand, the Court is relying on the idea that government entities are singling out religion for unfavorable treatment, then it needs to explain why that treatment is problematic in light of the Court's earlier decisions that relied on separationist principles. Ironically, the Court uses the concepts of neutrality and hostility to avoid doing so. The separationist approach, as used in some contexts, might be wrong, but it is not inherently hostile to religion.

The Rehnquist Court is certainly not the first to use the concept of hostility to describe the exclusion of religious entities from broad programs, but it is the first to place such immense faith in the concept of formal neutrality. It is the combination of the Court's use of formal neutrality and the potential expansion of the Court's use of hostility to undermine separation-driven arguments without directly confronting them that makes the Rehnquist Court's recent use of hostility troubling. It is not that modern separationist arguments or motivations are inherently correct, but rather that calling them hostile to religion, and dismissing them as a result, demonstrates a complete lack of legal or intellectual rigor and tells us nothing about the merits of those arguments. The Court's use of the term in *Locke* may be a step in the right direction because the Court appears to equate hostility with animus, but as was already explained, *Locke* is unclear about this and may be quite limited because of the facts involved.[52]

So what does the Court's evolving use of the concept of hostility tell us about the meaning of that term in the Establishment Clause context? First, it seems that hostile motives are certainly not a requirement for a claim that something is hostile toward religion. Second, much of what earlier Courts said about the Establishment Clause and its meaning—that is, favoring a separationist approach[53]—now apparently falls under the rubric of hostility toward religion.[54] Some scholars have long equated strong separationism with hostility,[55] and the current Court apparently agrees. Yet, did those who opposed the aid in *Mitchell*, or the officials at the University of Virginia in *Rosenberger*, act out of hostility toward religion, out of respect for the First Amendment, out of concern regarding some entirely different reason, or out of concern for some combination of these reasons? If the argument is simply that a facial distinction between religious and other entities is inherently hostile toward religion, using the term "hostility" seems to add little more than a rhetorical justification.

C. Actual Hostility and the Establishment Clause

The Court's failure to adequately define its notion of hostility does not mean that hostility toward religion does not exist. The question is how "hostility" should be defined under the Establishment Clause. Should purpose, effect, or both, be relevant to this question? The answer matters because the Court has been relatively consistent in suggesting that government cannot discourage religion (although it has been quite lax in defining what would discourage religion).[56] Scholars have also argued that discouragement of religion, not just encouragement, can violate the Establishment Clause.[57] Of course, the question remains as to what constitutes hostility, what constitutes discouragement, and whether the two are the same thing. This section asserts that hostility is a form of discouragement, but that discouragement is a broader concept.

I am generally suspicious of placing a great deal of weight in dictionaries when defining terms that have important legal meaning, but the power and impact of the term "hostility" when used to describe government action vis-à-vis religion suggest that the commonly understood meaning of that term—essentially hostile intent or general antagonism—is the best starting place for a workable definition under the Establishment Clause. When the Court uses the term "hostility" to justify its reasoning, people may draw on the commonly understood meaning of that term absent an alternative definition, which, as noted above, the Court has not provided.[58] *The Oxford Desk Dictionary* defines "hostility" as (1) "being hostile; enmity" and as (2) "acts of warfare."[59] It defines "hostile" as (1) "of an enemy" and as (2) "unfriendly; opposed."[60] Obviously, "hostility" suggests hostile intent or, at the very least, an antagonistic state of mind. This definition is consistent with the general use and understanding of the term in society at large.

Therefore, when the Court uses the term "hostility" to describe government action toward religion or a religious entity (or to describe the position of dissenting justices), the implication is that there is some hostile intent on the part of government or other actors. As noted above, such intent may be entirely absent in the contexts where the Court uses the term "hostility," unless one is willing to treat an intent to uphold perceived constitutional duties as hostile toward religion[61] or claim that disparate treatment not motivated by hostile intent is hostile toward religion.[62]

To be considered "hostile toward religion," a party's actions should involve some actual hostile intent or attitude toward religion qua religion or toward a specific religious entity. There are some obvious examples of this in recent Court decisions. For example, the actions of the city of Hialeah in *Church of the Lukumi Babalu Aye v. City of Hialeah* (a Free Exercise Clause case)[63] are an excellent example of actual hostility toward religion. The city set up a system of ordinances that were designed to affect only Santerian animal sacrifice.[64] The city's actions were taken against a backdrop of professed enmity toward the Santeria faith and its practice of animal sacrifice by some city residents, and even some city officials.[65] The ordinances were found to violate the Free Exercise Clause because they demonstrated discrimination against a particular religion,[66] but they might have also violated the Establishment Clause because the city seemingly engaged in hostile action designed to discourage religion (in this case a particular religion).[67]

The plurality opinion in *Mitchell v. Helms* provides another example of actual hostility toward religion when it discussed the anti-Catholic animus connected to the movement for baby Blaine amendments—state constitutional provisions modeled after a failed amendment to the U.S. Constitution that would have banned funding to religious schools.[68] There is little doubt that the movement behind these amendments and at least some of the motivation behind early separationism were highly influenced by anti-Catholic and, to a lesser extent, antiecclesiastical sentiment.[69] At that time, the so-called Blaine amendments were motivated, at least in part, by hostility toward religion, and they were certainly designed to discourage the growth of the Catholic school movement,[70] which itself evolved in part as a response to the Protestant domination of the common schools and ultimately the early public schools.[71]

Yet today there are other principles that may support the substance of the so-called Blaine amendments and separationism more generally.[72] The motivations of state officials who currently support such "no aid" amendments, and of parties who sue to prevent government funding of religious entities, may have nothing to do with enmity or hostility toward religion generally or a specific religion.[73] The Court's rationale in *Locke v. Davey* supports this. While the Court held that the state constitutional provision in question was not a baby Blaine amendment,[74] the Court acknowledged that the state's denial of funding for ministerial training was not hostile toward religion.[75] Given the definition of "hostility" above, however, it is hard to understand why the same conclusion would not apply to denials of funding or access in cases such as *Mitchell* and *Rosenberger,* even if the denial is unconstitutional for other reasons.

Of course, the above examples demonstrate hostility toward a specific religion or specific religions, but some have suggested that separationism leads to a purging of religious views more generally, and is thus hostile toward religion.[76] The broader relationship between religion and public life is complex and is discussed elsewhere in this book, but despite potentially valid concern that *strict* separationism may be unconstitutional and bad policy, it is not inherently hostile toward religion. In fact, some of its strongest supporters have been concerned with protecting religion.[77]

Thus, whether or not current separationist-oriented doctrines and principles are proper interpretations of the Establishment Clause, calling them hostile toward religion is nothing more than a rhetorical slap or verbal barb. The Court and some scholars derive support and power from using the term, but the term adds nothing of substance to their arguments. Unless the government entity denying funding or access or the party challenging government action demonstrates a negative intent or attitude toward religion generally or a specific religion, there is no proof of hostility toward religion. Disparate treatment in this context does not equate to hostility because those engaging in that treatment are often motivated by constitutional concerns or concerns for avoiding divisiveness in the community, rather than hostility toward religion.[78]

Moreover, in the absence of hostile intent, disparate impact must be analyzed as an effect of government action, rather than as its purpose. I strongly advocate an approach to the Establishment Clause that takes effects seriously, whether those effects favor religious entities or disfavor them.[79] The Court, however, writes off effects that seem to favor religion in cases like *Zelman,* yet puts great weight on effects that seem to disfavor religion in cases like *Mitchell* and *Rosenberger.*[80] It is possible that the

Court sees this apparent conflict but does not view it as such, thus intending its doctrine to require serious examination of effects when those effects harm religious entities, but not when they favor such entities.[81] However, this remains unclear.

The Court has not relied heavily on the concept of hostility in its recent Establishment Clause decisions, but the concept has had an impact. Given the Court's recent focus on formal neutrality in a number of contexts, such as government aid and equal access, the concept of hostility may take on more importance. When the Court has attempted to use the concept in recent years, it has done so only in a rhetorical sense: it presumes that the lack of formal neutrality is hostile toward religion. Yet this is not an adequate or accurate definition of "hostility." Disparate impact and even disparate treatment (depending on the motivation for that treatment) are not necessarily evidence of hostility toward religion. As with the concept of neutrality, the concept of hostility—at least as used recently by members of the Court—is illusory. It is a label slapped onto government decisions with which the Court disagrees. The question remains whether those specific decisions are hostile to religion, even if, as Justice Thomas has suggested,[82] some of the doctrines relied upon to make such decisions are historically tied to actual hostility.

4

Liberty

If neutrality and its potential mate hostility do not work as underlying principles for interpreting the religion clauses, what about other principles such as liberty and equality? These principles have sometimes been connected to neutrality, but they are capable of definition without being tethered to neutrality claims. This chapter will explore the concept of liberty, and the next chapter the concept of equality. The religious liberty principle has obvious relevance to Free Exercise Clause jurisprudence, but it can also be quite relevant in the Establishment Clause context.

The problem with religious liberty is defining it. As with neutrality, there are varying concepts of religious liberty, and the choice between these conceptions can effect outcomes under the religion clauses.[1] Neutrality asserts a claim of balance that is impossible to achieve regardless of the baseline one asserts. No conception of neutrality can be neutral in the religion clause area. Liberty suffers a similar, but somewhat different, problem. No one conception of religious liberty can claim to be the correct conception of liberty unless, as some contend, there is a clear historical understanding of religious liberty.[2] As will be seen, despite some excellent arguments to the contrary, there is no single concept of religious liberty that can claim historical preeminence. So any claim to liberty must operate from a context or baseline that is only self-justifying.

Yet, unlike neutrality claims which even when limited to a given approach or baseline suggest that some state of affairs is actually neutral, liberty claims do not inherently suggest any sort of absolute state of liberty.[3] Rather, they only suggest that a given approach may protect religious liberty in a given context or that a given conception of liberty is consistent with the intent of the framers. When one's suggested liberty approach infringes on the liberties of others, however, the concept of liberty loses much of its force because, as with neutrality, we end up with an explicit or implicit balancing of interests usually accompanied by the claim that one side of the balance fosters religious liberty more than the other.[4] This suggests that the liberty concept, to the extent it is useful, is likely to be more useful in the free exercise context than the establishment context because religious liberty claims are less likely to conflict in the former context.[5]

Scholars and judges seem to understand or at the very least intuit this, because most of the "liberty talk" in the religion clause context occurs in discussion of the Free Exercise Clause.[6] This does not mean that liberty has not been discussed in the Establishment Clause context,[7] only that discussion of the concept is less common in that context than it is in the free exercise context. When it is used in connection with the Establishment Clause, it is rarely used in a helpful way; although there are exceptions.[8] When a judge or scholar claims that separationism promotes religious liberty, one might question whose religious liberty and how. Conversely, when a judge or scholar claims that some form of governmental recognition of religion promotes religious liberty, one might ask the same questions. Each approach *may* promote the religious liberty of some, but only at the expense of others.[9] How are we to weigh whose religious liberty is more important and why without relying on some concept other than liberty?

In the free exercise context the liberty concept poses fewer problems assuming there is a sound basis for using it. When one seeks an exemption to a "generally applicable" law, the liberties of others will rarely be directly interfered with, although when the liberties of others are affected, such as when a seniority system is involved, the questions get harder. Thus, one can say that requiring exemptions to generally applicable laws, at least when such exemptions do not interfere with the rights of others, promotes religious liberty.[10] It may not be the only way to promote religious liberty, and, more important, saying that it promotes religious liberty does not mean that it is necessary to the existence of religious liberty generally or required under the Free Exercise Clause. Of course, if it creates more religious liberty for more people than the alternatives without interfering with the rights of others or conflicting with other valid religion clause principles, and especially if one can find support in other modes of religion clause interpretation, the use of religious liberty to justify exemptions to generally applicable laws under the Free Exercise Clause makes sense.[11] As will be seen, the only valid religion clause principle with which exemptions might be said to interfere is separation. In the free exercise context the ebb and flow of religion clause jurisprudence would favor what I will argue is a strong free exercise argument supported by liberty and several other principles over a weak separation argument.[12]

So we are left with a concept that is quite malleable but for which—at least in some contexts—a useful baseline may be found. This leaves the problem of determining what baseline(s) of liberty may be useful, why the arguments against neutrality baselines do not apply to these views of religious liberty, and in what contexts and to what extent liberty should be used in deciding questions under the religion clauses. This chapter will address each of these points except the last—to what extent liberty should be used. The last point, which relates to the ebb and flow of valid religion clause concepts, will be left to later chapters addressing the modes of religion clause jurisprudence. Of the remaining two questions, the second is easier to answer, and thus I will address it first.

A. Framing Religious Liberty

Given the argument in chapter 2 that there is no way to establish a neutral baseline for neutrality claims in the religion clause context, how can a baseline or baselines for a similarly malleable concept such as liberty be found? The difference lies in the concepts themselves. Neutrality suggests a state of balance between various interests that is simply impossible to achieve in the religion clause context given the religious diversity and massive role of government in the United States. Liberty is malleable like neutrality, but it does not suggest any universal epistemic claim. The problem with liberty is that there is no way to choose between conceptions of liberty from within the liberty principle itself. This it shares with neutrality. But unlike neutrality, government can act in a manner that promotes liberty.

To say X is neutral to a degree means that X is also not neutral to a degree, and in a complex area such as the religion clauses, one must be able to explain how X is then neutral. To say that X promotes religious liberty to a degree can be taken at face value and debated. If someone says that Y also promotes religious liberty, that too is possible. If X and Y conflict, we have no basis within the liberty principle to choose between them barring a clear historical argument (which as will be seen is lacking). Yet, unlike neutrality, which falls under its own weight and cannot be demonstrated by using any other principle, a given conception of liberty may be supported when other principles interact with it in the religion clause context. Thus, there may be more than one valid concept of religious liberty, and when and how these concepts can be used, and how they can be justified, will depend on other principles. This ebb and flow will be the subject of later chapters.

The difference between neutrality and liberty is that one is impossible to achieve in the religion clause context and the other may be achievable to a degree. Yet one might argue that we can achieve neutrality to a degree through concepts like formal neutrality or separation as neutrality, so how is that any different? The answer, as explained in chapter 2, is that the presumption is simply wrong. Formal neutrality does not create neutrality in any sense. It is only useful to those who already believe that formal neutrality is neutral. There are strong factual and theoretical arguments demonstrating that formal neutrality does not lead to neutral results. The same is true for separation as neutrality. If the "private choice" or separation arguments are to be supported, they must be supported by something more than the unprovable claim that they are neutral. Neutrality adds nothing of value to the discussion other than the illusion of an objective underlying principle—that is, a legal justification. To say that giving an exemption to a generally applicable law promotes religious liberty (at least for those getting the exemption) is a verifiable statement, even if it does not by itself answer the question of whether such exemptions are mandated under the Free Exercise Clause or how one would choose between that argument and one that suggests religious liberty may be promoted in the absence of such exemptions because everyone is still guaranteed the liberty of conscience to believe what they will, and the ability to practice their faiths to the extent that general laws are not infringed.

If there can be a baseline or baselines for religious liberty, what are they and how do we support them? These are tough questions. Yet because, as I have already stated, there is no way from within religious liberty to justify a given baseline, the questions are less important than which liberty concepts may be justified given the ebb and flow of other religion clause concepts. Still, several major theories of religious liberty have gained prominence in the literature and cases. Of the various conceptions of religious liberty, these are the most relevant and also the most likely to actually be considered in religion clause cases. Some of them work together, and others are in conflict with each other.

Professor (now judge) Michael McConnell is perhaps the leading advocate for using the liberty principle in interpreting the religion clauses.[13] His arguments based on the liberty principle are particularly compelling in the Free Exercise Clause area. He argues that the religion clauses are best understood as a means to protect religious liberty, and that when concepts such as formal neutrality conflict with the liberty principle—as occurred in *Smith*—the liberty principle should prevail.[14] The argument is that government should not place impediments to individuals' religious liberty without some sort of heightened scrutiny even when the impediment is caused by a law of general applicability.[15] This is a conception of religious liberty that strongly resonates with me, but that is the point. I like it because it maximizes religious liberty for both dominant and minority religious groups whose concerns may not be considered during the legislative process that led to the "generally applicable" law, and especially because it gives many religious minorities a chance to gain exemptions without having to go through the expense and sometimes impossible battles necessary to add exemptions to a law post hoc through the legislative process.

Yet, in *Smith,* the majority as per Justice Scalia argued that religious liberty consists of not being coerced in matters of religion or being discriminated against by government because of one's religion.[16] Belief is absolutely protected, but religious liberty under the U.S. Constitution does not mandate exemptions for religious practices that run afoul of generally applicable laws.[17] Such exemptions must be left to the political process.[18] I do not agree with this conception of religious liberty for the reasons explained below, but that is again beside the point for the present discussion. I have no means to prove that Professor McConnell's version of religious liberty is any more religious liberty than the *Smith* majority's.[19]

Recently, Professor Noah Feldman has argued that liberty of conscience is the proper principle to use in interpreting both the religion clauses.[20] He bases this claim, in part, on his reading of the views of the framers,[21] but eschews any sense of strong originalism—he views the intent of the framers as informative but not definitive.[22] His overall arguments echo some of the claims made by Professor McConnell and Professor Stephen Carter,[23] as well as others.[24] Feldman, however, argues that religion clause analysis has shifted from a paradigm of liberty of conscience to one of equality, often formal equality, of groups.[25] He argues that this shift, which was likely designed to increase religious protections for religious minorities under the Establishment Clause, has begun to backfire and lead to analysis that may expand the power of dominant religious groups, potentially at the expense of religious minorities.[26] Liberty might not provide some of the "protection" provided by equality principles, but in the long run he argues it will better serve both religious minorities and dominant religious groups and be more in keeping with the intent of the framers.[27]

Feldman's work is important and very well done, but it presumes too much clarity in the liberty concept and may create an artificial dualism between equality and liberty. Professor Feldman is almost certainly correct when he suggests that the framers would not have conceived of some of the uses to which the religion clauses have been put as the courts have increasingly used equality concerns to determine outcomes in cases.[28] They also would not have conceived of the massive regulatory state and incredible religious diversity in the United States today.[29] So the question remains what liberty of conscience or religious equality should mean today. What does it take to protect liberty of conscience—even if we agree on what it is—in such a pluralistic and heavily government regulated society?

Moreover, it is not clear that a belief in liberty of conscience in any way precludes the possibility that the framers may have also entertained equality concerns. Certainly, Madison, at least, was quite concerned about factions, religious and otherwise.[30] Whether he was concerned about a tyranny of majority factions or of minority factions, one might glean some equality principles from the broader concern. This is not meant to suggest that we rely on Madison or any specific framer in interpreting the religion clauses, but rather that even from an originalist perspective there is not necessarily a complete dichotomy between equality and liberty concerns. Feldman acknowledges that too strong a reliance on originalism is not required, but he is then left with his dichotomy between liberty and equality, and other than the intent of the framers one must buy into this dichotomy to accept his overall thesis.[31] Otherwise the lines between secularists and evangelicals he draws are far too porous because both sides may claim their liberty of conscience is being violated in the same situation depending on what the government does.[32]

Consider an example that Feldman writes about: the question of institutional separation—whether government funding should go to religious entities, and implicitly whether an individual should have to pay taxes to support such an entity.[33] This might be characterized as an establishment or free exercise problem, and from Feldman's perspective there is little difference in this context. Liberty of conscience would preclude the state from coercing someone to support an establishment or establishments, both because the coercion violates the Establishment Clause and because it interferes with a person's ability to support only those religious institutions he or she chooses.[34] Thus, if the religion clauses are incorporated, both an established church and nonpreferential aid to religion would violate the religion clauses.[35] This would be true for members of both religious minorities and the religious "majority."

Without endorsing Feldman's approach, it is worth noting that at the time this type of liberty of conscience thinking was influencing the framers, it was quite common to recognize only the liberty of conscience of the majority or dominant groups, and in fact this was done in many state charters.[36] Thus, the simple recognition that liberty of conscience applies to all, as Feldman correctly and readily suggests, has a rather strong equality component. After all, if the framers were not concerned about the freedoms of religious minorities, it would have been quite easy to protect the liberty of conscience of select groups. The fact that some framers would have strenuously opposed this only makes the argument that some notion of equality might have been animating the framers, or at least some of them, even more forceful.[37]

This is not to suggest that Feldman is wrong to assert that liberty of conscience is an important underlying principle for religion clause interpretation, or even that the Court slowly shifted from such a principle to one based in equality of groups, but rather that he overestimates the tension between these conceptions or at the very least gives liberty of conscience too much primacy when compared with other principles. Professor Steven Shiffrin in an indirect response to Professor Feldman—one that reflects the ebb and flow of principles suggested in this book—wrote:

> Many distinguished commentators have argued that the Court's focus on equality results in insufficient attention paid to the value of religious liberty. In my view, these commentators are right in contending that an equality emphasis misses much of importance in religion clause jurisprudence. But their emphasis on liberty or equal liberty is too narrow. Instead, I will suggest that understanding the proper place of equality in religion clause jurisprudence requires appreciation of a broader range of values with regard to both religion clauses, and a recognition that this appreciation is itself independently important.[38]

What Shiffrin captures in this passage is of twofold importance. First, he acknowledges that there can be tension between the equality and liberty concepts. Second, and far more important, he recognizes this tension as an artificial dualism and points out that there may be a number of values (this book uses the term "principles") that undergird the religion clauses and that complete allegiance to one works not only at the expense of the others but at the expense of religion clause jurisprudence itself. This latter point is very much the focus of this book and the modes of religion clause interpretation discussed in later chapters.

Professor Alan Brownstein, like Professor Shiffrin, argues that one need not choose between religious liberty and other constitutional principles such as equality. In an article where he criticizes neutrality theory Professor Brownstein writes:

> Religion is a multi-dimensional constitutional interest. In its varying aspects, it implicates personal liberty, group equality, and freedom of speech. In addition to protecting the freedom of religious individuals and the autonomy of religious institutions to follow the dictates of their faith, the constitution affirms the equal status and worth of religious groups and the faiths that sustain them. Further, it protects the rights of religious and secular individuals to espouse their beliefs on an equal basis with others and to influence personal and public policy in a competitive marketplace of

ideas. A theory for interpreting the religion clauses that concentrates exclusively on personal liberty and ignores these equality and speech values is inherently incomplete and will often be mistaken in its application.[39]

In all likelihood Professor Feldman would respond that this is only so if the shift toward equality principles in religion clause jurisprudence is itself justified, and Professor Feldman obviously believes this to be at the least highly questionable.[40] As noted above, however, his historical arguments in favor of a primary focus on liberty of conscience may not discount an equality focus, either because the framers may have had some broader view of equality implicit in their language and values or because the changes in society make the liberty of conscience concept and the equality concept complementary so that the latter may help support the former. None of this is meant to suggest that Professor Feldman is wrong that liberty of conscience was a value shared by many framers and that it remains a valuable concept today. Rather, the above discussion points out that liberty of conscience is not a self-defining concept, particularly given the unforeseen society and contexts to which it must be applied, and that accepting the vitality of liberty of conscience does not preclude the use of other principles.

There is no way from within the liberty principle to choose between Professor Feldman's, Professor McConnell's, or Professors Shiffrin and Brownstein's conceptions of religious liberty. Thus, other principles or preconceptions must in some way be driving—or at least effecting—the choice. In Professor Feldman's case historical analysis and concerns about social divisions seem to be driving the choice, but as explained in chapter 1, historical analysis is not self-justifying and often assumes a common historical worldview that may not be entirely accurate. Professor Feldman openly acknowledges this problem, but despite the excellence and meticulousness of his work, he is unable to escape it. In the end his answer to the social divisiveness problems must be accepted on either historical grounds, pragmatic grounds, and/or public policy grounds.[41] With history removed from the picture, one is left questioning whether his framing of the problem and focus on liberty of conscience is better than the alternatives discussed above and later in this book. Even if his approach is only influenced by historical analysis rather than completely dependent upon it, the flaws in that analytical methodology in the religion clause context detract from his approach.

One might view the problem through the Gadamerian lens discussed in chapter 1 and suggest that because we are all historically situated, when we go back in time to try to re-create historical views and then apply them to today's circumstances, we create a double conundrum.[42] In going back in time we bring our traditions and interpretive horizon with us, and in bringing the past forward to the present to use it in some normative way, we have most likely already been influenced by the normative values and interpretive traditions we are situated within.[43] Thus, in order to choose a conception of religious liberty to apply to religion clause issues—even if we base the choice on historical grounds—we must be relying on some principles or values outside of religious liberty.

Given all this and the malleability of the liberty concept, how can we pick any single conception of religious liberty for use in religion clause analysis? The answer is that we do not have to. What we need to do is understand how the liberty principle might interact with other modes of religion clause interpretation on given issues, and this engagement will help us understand when liberty is a helpful concept in addressing religion clause issues and if so what conception of liberty. The good news is that despite all the debate over the proper role of liberty in religion clause jurisprudence vis-à-vis other principles, most conceptions of liberty have a great deal in common in the Free Exercise context, the major exceptions being the approach espoused by the *Smith* Court and the strict separationist argument that free exercise exemptions violate the Establishment Clause.[44]

In the Establishment Clause context both the role and the meaning of religious liberty are more hotly contested. In chapters 9 and 10, I will address the potential role of the liberty concept in Establishment Clause analysis given the ebb and flow of religion clause principles. For now, the short answer is that the liberty concept should have little or no role in Establishment Clause cases, unless those cases involve questions of equal access or similar speech concerns as Professor Brownstein suggests.[45] Under the Free Exercise Clause the liberty principle has a more important role to play, and the arguments for robust free exercise protection supported by Professors McConnell, Feldman, Shiffrin, and Brownstein—albeit in somewhat different approaches—are favored by the ebb and flow of religion clause principles over either the *Smith* Court's approach or the strict separationist approach. As with the Establishment Clause analysis this will be addressed in greater detail in chapters 9 and 10, where the modes of religion clause interpretation, the ebb and flow of religion clause principles, and the facilitation test will be addressed.

B. To Whom Does Religious Liberty Apply?

A significant question remains regarding religious liberty. Assuming we can support the liberty principle in some contexts, to whom does it apply?

Does it apply only to individuals, or does it also apply to groups of people or religious entities? If it does apply to groups or religious entities, how might it do so? The implications of these questions are important because religious liberty of individuals is less likely to substantially conflict with other principles in the Establishment Clause context. Recognizing liberty in the contexts of groups or entities might lead to arguments that the majority has the right "to use the machinery of the state to practice its beliefs,"[46] because a dominant group could rightly assert that denying public recognition of their faith artificially separates their religious beliefs from the panoply of rights they can petition for in the public sphere and thus interferes with their religious liberty. I use the term "rightly" in the preceding sentence to point out that without some other principle to counterbalance it, the recognition of group-based religious liberty would potentially point out the inherent problems with the traditional separationist idea that religion is relegated to the private sphere.[47] For many people of faith, religion does not function that way. The ability to seek public recognition of religion is part of religious liberty for many people.[48] This does not mean the private sphere/public sphere dualism suggested by many separationists is not a useful pragmatic cutoff for such claims of religious liberty. It simply means that it is not an obvious or self-justifying cutoff if we recognize religious liberty for groups.

Religious liberty for religious entities poses a slightly different concern. Certainly, it would violate most baselines of religious liberty for a government entity to intentionally discriminate against a religious entity,[49] but would it violate religious liberty if a religious entity claimed that the government denied it access to a funding program to which nonreligious entities have access? Because of the approach to religion clause interpretation I argue for in this book, it would be possible for me to skirt the issue by arguing that other valid religion clause principles allow or preclude either of the above-mentioned concerns. The question of whether religious liberty applies only to individuals, to groups, and/or to religious entities, and why, is too important to be ignored. Thus, I will explore this question here.

Religious liberty would seem to obviously apply to individuals to the extent it applies at all, but from this simple statement one might assume that the reason for this is some notion from classical liberalism that religion and rights are individualistic.[50] Classic liberal theory, however, is not what drives this assertion. Rather, the assertion is driven by the pragmatic reality that free exercise rights at the least are often asserted by individuals and that state action that interferes with religious practices generally effects individuals at least. Additionally, as has been well stated, there is a textual basis for finding an individualized right under the Free Exercise

Clause, even without resort to originalist arguments.[51] This does not answer the question of whether there may also be group or institutional rights. The question of whether there is any sort of individual religious liberty right under the Establishment Clause will be severely limited by analysis later in this book suggesting that the liberty principle plays a minimal role in Establishment Clause analysis. It can be argued, however, that there could be an individualized right in the Equal Access context, but this may be as much a result of free speech concerns as establishment concerns. The very question of whether the Establishment Clause protects individual rights in the first place is a hotly contested issue taken up later in this book.

What about group and institutional liberty interests? It would be easy to write these off by stating that the free exercise concerns of groups or institutions are better analyzed under other modes of religion clause interpretation such as equality, but in some cases the burden on a group or institution may in fact be a relatively direct burden on the individuals involved in the group or institution. Yet allowing group or institutional rights in the Establishment Clause context might support factions "using the machinery of the state to practice their beliefs."[52] In fact, Justice Scalia suggested such a right in the school prayer context in his dissenting opinion in *Lee v. Weisman,* and Justice Stewart did the same based on group free exercise rights in his dissenting opinion in *School Dist. of Abington Township v. Schempp.*[53] This argument suggests that some segment of the population is denied free exercise rights when the government is denied the ability to sponsor organized prayer and so forth. This analysis enmeshes the question in the Court's Establishment Clause jurisprudence because if there is a group free exercise right to engage in religious practices using the machinery of the state, there are few governmentally sponsored religious ceremonies or symbols that could be precluded under the Establishment Clause. Of course, some have argued that such a result is precisely what is mandated by the interplay between the religion clauses.[54] As will be seen, the application of the facilitation test would provide robust individual free exercise rights but would not allow group free exercise claims to support governmental religious practices.

The above concerns militate against recognizing group or institutional liberty rights under the Free Exercise Clause, but other contexts may favor such rights. Consider the facts underlying the *City of Boerne* or *Lyng* cases.[55] In *Boerne* a church was denied the ability to meet the needs of its congregation because of local zoning regulations, and in *Lyng* sacred Native American lands were paved over for a highway project, thus effectively destroying the religious practices of several tribes.[56] While *Boerne* was a case about the constitutionality of the Religious Freedom

Restoration Act,[57] it, like *Lyng*, demonstrates how institutional or group free exercise concerns may be quite important and pose no conflict with the Establishment Clause.

The ebb and flow of religion clause principles allow the possibility of accounting for both concerns under the liberty principle. After all, if no one principle is consistently dominant in religion clause interpretation, but rather a set of valid modes of interpretation ebb and flow based on context, one need not choose between no recognition of group or institutional free exercise rights or always recognizing such rights. It is quite possible to argue that religious liberty principles should apply when a religious group or institution seeks an exemption to government action that does not violate the Establishment Clause. In other words, the liberty principle need not support groups or institutions using the machinery of the state—or combining with the machinery of the state—to facilitate their religions in society at large in order to allow groups or institutions to seek exemptions to government action that may substantially burden their ability to carry out their religious functions in a nongovernmental context. This, of course, presumes that such exemptions do not themselves violate the Establishment Clause, and as noted above this book asserts that the Establishment Clause is no bar to religious exemptions from generally applicable government laws or actions. Thus, like individuals, the Church in *Boerne* or the tribes in *Lyng* could use the liberty principle to help support arguments under the Free Exercise Clause, but the citizens in Abington Township or Santa Fe, Texas, could not claim a free exercise right to invoke public prayer at government-sponsored events.[58]

C. Conclusion

By now it should be clear that the liberty principle is quite malleable, but unlike neutrality it may have some force in the religion clause context. It should also be obvious that the approach in this book suggests that the liberty concept is likely to be most useful in the free exercise area and will play little role in the Establishment Clause context outside perhaps equal access issues. Since the liberty principle will combine with other modes of religion clause interpretation such as equality, separation, and accommodation in the ebb and flow of religion clause principles, this should not be surprising. As will be explained in chapters 9 and 10, certain modes or principles of religion clause interpretation will have more vitality in certain contexts, and in fact this ebb and flow can lead to more predictability and a more informed understanding of religion clause interpretation than the Court's current approaches.

5

Equality

Like liberty, equality is a useful concept in the religion clause area, but like liberty it is quite malleable.[1] Thus, before suggesting that equality is a valid principle to be used in the ebb and flow of religion clause principles, it is essential to define equality. This is no easy task. As in the Equal Protection area, there are some basic questions that cannot be easily answered. Does treating differently situated groups the same promote equality under the religion clauses? Does treating them differently promote equality? The answers to these questions have profound impact under both of the religion clauses. For example, the concept of formal neutrality suggests that the answer to the first question should be yes, and thus we get results like those in *Employment Division v. Smith*[2] and *Zelman v. Simmons-Harris*,[3] where the effects of the relevant government action seemed to favor more dominant religious groups over religious outsiders and dissenters. Of course, neither of the above-mentioned cases was couched directly in equality terms, but the analysis in those cases certainly has implications for the meaning of equality under the religion clauses.

As we saw in the last chapter, Noah Feldman has argued that analysis under the religion clauses has moved from a liberty of conscience model at the time of the framing to an equality of groups model in the twentieth century.[4] This raises yet another question, namely, whether equality principles should play any role in religion clause interpretation. As I noted in the last chapter, Feldman may overplay a false dichotomy between liberty and equality notions,[5] but his work forces us to consider whether equality should play a role—or at least a major role—in religion clause interpretation. This is a question for which most judges and scholars in recent years have presumed an affirmative answer.[6] Debate has centered more on what equality should mean.[7] If Feldman were correct, however, the meaning of equality would be mostly irrelevant in the religion clause context.[8] As was discussed in the previous chapter, there is a ready response to Feldman's argument in its broadest sense, but perhaps Feldman's observations may be relevant to understanding equality under the religion clauses even if his broader assertions can be rebutted.

Another important question in the equality context is the connection by many scholars and some judges between "neutrality" and equality.[9] Defining equality by reference to neutrality is like defining the structure of the galaxy by reference to astrology. You cannot define something that may have real bite by reference to something mythical, and as chapter 2 asserts, neutrality does not exist in the religion clause context. Simply put, any neutrality talk in the equality context is simply excess baggage that serves more to cloud the concept of equality than to help define it. It is an attempt to create equality with smoke and mirrors. If equality is itself simply a creation of smoke and mirrors, the solution is to exclude it from the modes of religion clause interpretation like neutrality, not to attach it to another mythical concept in the hopes that enough smoke might create something solid.

Despite the force of some of Noah Feldman's arguments and the problems with linking equality to neutrality, equality may still be a useful principle in the religion clause context. This chapter will first briefly address Feldman's arguments (which were also addressed in the previous chapter) and then the supposed link between equality and neutrality. This will be followed by a discussion of several conceptualizations of equality that avoid reliance on neutrality in any concrete way and that address the conceptual overlap between equality and liberty. These include Eisgruber and Sager's "equal regard" concept,[10] Alan Brownstein's approach to equality,[11] and Steve Shiffrin's approach to equality,[12] in addition to a few other conceptions. This discussion will also implicate questions of religious autonomy. Some might think autonomy concerns are better, or more naturally, addressed in the context of religious liberty, but this section will explain why they are more fruitfully discussed in the context of religious equality. Finally, this discussion will lead to a formulation of a principle of religious equality that may aid religion clause interpretation if it can be validated as a mode of religion clause interpretation as discussed in chapters 9 and 10.

A. Noah Feldman and the Leap from Liberty of Conscience to Equality

Noah Feldman asserts that the use of religious equality as a mechanism to interpret the religion clauses is primarily a creation of the mid-twentieth-century Court as expounded upon by later Courts.[13] As mentioned earlier, Feldman argues that the real core of religion clause principle lies with liberty of conscience and that the move toward equality is the result of an intellectual shift on the Court and in society more broadly.[14] Perhaps more important, he argues that this shift actually has a potentially negative impact on liberty of conscience and is also inconsistent with the intent and traditions of the framers.[15] If Feldman is correct, then defining religious equality is a mostly useless task because it has no place as a basic principle of religion clause interpretation. Feldman's argument is carefully reasoned and well written, but unfortunately it suffers from two flaws. First, it presumes an artificial dichotomy between liberty of conscience and religious equality.[16] Second, it relies too much on an originalist clarity that simply does not exist in the religion clause context.[17] Even though Feldman eschews complete reliance on original intent and historical analysis, it is obvious that it has had a major impact on his work.[18]

Both of these concerns were explained in chapter 4. For current purposes, however, Feldman's assertion that the focus on equality of groups is primarily a creation of middle and late twentieth-century Courts may have some implications for the usefulness and meaning of that concept in religion clause interpretation. How could this be so if Feldman's assertions are based on a problematic dichotomy between religious liberty and religious equality? Even if Feldman's assertions regarding the value of religious equality in light of religious liberty are problematic, his detailed discussion of the evolution of the equality of groups concept in Supreme Court jurisprudence still has a lot to teach us. Therefore, despite the problematic dichotomy it is essential to address the evolution of equality.

Principles of stare decisis would suggest that the Court should follow its own precedent, except when that precedent is itself a departure from settled doctrine or constitutional text.[19] If Feldman is correct, the equality-based doctrines that have arisen over the last sixty years or so may depart from constitutional meaning and earlier precedent.[20] The problem with this argument is the constitutional meaning he asserts is not based in constitutional text, but rather at least in part on a contestable historical argument, and the earlier precedent may be interpreted in a number of ways—that is, even if courts did not speak in terms of religious equality and in fact spoke in terms of liberty of conscience, their arguments may have incorporated both concerns.[21] Additionally, the intervention of the Fourteenth Amendment and the incorporation question may affect why and how this shift occurred.[22] If Feldman is correct, perhaps the Establishment Clause should not have been incorporated because it is not as clearly an individual rights provision as the Free Exercise Clause.[23] Of course, Feldman does not argue that the Establishment Clause should not have been incorporated.[24] Finally, there is the ever-looming question of whether the intent of the framers—in this case used to support Feldman's assertion that the focus of the religion clauses should be liberty of conscience— ought to be used to undo or question evolving constitutional doctrine that seems responsive to current social context while remaining within plausible interpretations of constitutional text,[25] as well as the related argument that perhaps the framers did not intend for their intent to be the basis for constitutional interpretation.[26]

These broader questions of stare decisis and originalism are beyond the scope of this book, but the point is that while Feldman asserts a plausible basis for reassessing the role of religious equality in religion clause interpretation, it is not necessary to ignore that principle based on his arguments. Rather, given the problems discussed in this section and in chapter 4, we should consider Feldman's work as an important warning not to presume too much about the inevitability or nature of religious equality as an interpretive principle. We should, in sum, not presume some interpretively predestined role for religious equality.

B. Equality and Neutrality

Court opinions and scholars alike have connected concepts of equality to neutrality.[27] In recent years the connection of formal equality to formal neutrality has been especially pronounced.[28] Chapter 2 explained why the "neutrality" in formal neutrality is a myth. Similar arguments could be made about the "equality" in formal equality, at least in the context of race, gender, and so forth.[29] But what about in the context of religion? Certainly in the sense that formal neutrality and formal equality have been used interchangeably, neither concept is of any use for the reasons explained in chapter 2,[30] but what about formal equality itself? If we reject formal equality, what about other concepts of equality that have been connected to neutrality?

Formal equality in the religion context essentially consists of either treating similarly situated groups and/or individuals similarly,[31] or treating all groups and/or individuals the same, at least to the extent that they are religiously affected.[32] The first version allows for differently situated groups to be treated differently, at least in a formal sense,[33] but the latter version requires all groups to be treated the same and has more in common with formal neutrality.[34] Therefore, the latter version can be rejected out of hand. What about the former version? Is it so encumbered by a connection to neutrality that it can be per se rejected? As the following discussion will demonstrate, the answer is yes.

To the extent that the first version would allow differently situated groups to be treated differently, it has promise because when it comes to religion not all groups are similarly situated either demographically or theologically. Understanding that equality might sometimes require differential treatment of differently situated religious groups avoids one of the major flaws of formal neutrality—its failure to consider effects of government action that are far from "neutral." Accepting relevant differences for religion clause purposes might lead to a rejection of the *Smith* doctrine and at least a serious consideration of the effects of programs such as those in *Zelman*.[35] Of course, it might not. The reason for rejecting this version of formal equality, however, is not the fact that it treats similarly situated groups the same and differently situated groups differently—an approach that will be advocated below. It is the formalism itself.

How does one determine what groups are similarly situated from a formal equality perspective? One of the vices of formalism is the tendency to ignore effects and social facts surrounding the legal question presented.[36] It is quite possible that this version of formal equality may end up edging toward or being interpreted in the same manner as the other form. Even if it does not, the tools available to a court using a formal equality approach may not enable it to draw the distinctions necessary to give effect to the more socially affected questions raised by similarity and difference. It should come as no surprise that this more nuanced form of formal equality is not the form favored by courts that have used the concept.[37] In fact, most courts that have considered relevant differences in the religion context have not used a formalistic approach.[38] Moreover, in such a pluralistic society it is quite hard to decipher, using formalistic tools, just who is similarly situated in the variety of contexts where issues arise. Such distinctions are highly contextual and reliant on variable social facts. Finally, there is the argument that this form of formal equality is not formal equality at all because—as noted above—it either morphs into the other form of formal equality in the interpretive process, treating all groups the same, or morphs into some form of substantive equality in the interpretive process, thus abandoning the "formal" in formal equality.[39]

This is not just a question of semantics. If a court were to apply the more nuanced form of formal equality, it would have to draw relatively rigid lines regarding similarity and difference and operate from there, treating similarly situated groups the same. This still sounds like formal neutrality, albeit a version based on less rigid categorizations. Substantive equality would potentially draw lines, but based more on a careful analysis of context and a balancing of information, interests, and the effects of state action.[40] Moreover, whether a given government action promoted equality would be scrutinized carefully under all the facts.[41]

I use the term "substantive equality" here to describe a group of religious equality theories that are concerned with important contextual issues such as the question of difference and similarity and the real-world effect of government action or inaction. While "substantive neutrality" has essentially taken on a specific meaning at least for justices and schol-ars who advocate for it,[42] substantive equality is really a bundle of theo-ries that are not mutually dependent and which in some cases may be mu-tually exclusive. I will explore these theories in the next section. To the ex-tent any of these theories make strong attempts to connect to neutrality—and few of them do—I will suggest that they must support themselves re-gardless of any neutrality claims in order to be helpful to religion clause interpretation.[43] The theories discussed below are not the only ones that might be categorized as theories of "substantive equality," but they are theories that may be particularly useful in understanding the principle of religious equality, and they also include concepts representative of a wide range of other religious equality theories.

C. Other Major Conceptions of Religious Equality and a Note on Religious Autonomy

In order to determine whether religious equality is a principle worth con-sidering in the ebb and flow of religion clause principles, it is useful to consider several views of religious equality that may have something to of-fer in framing the principle. Doubtless there are numerous other views of religious equality that might shed additional light on this question, but an exploration of all of them is beyond the scope of this book. The theories discussed herein have had some specific impact on the ultimate mode of religious equality that will be used in the ebb and flow of religion clause interpretation. It is a given that formal equality plays no role in defining that principle.

The first concept of religious equality we will explore is Christopher Eisgruber and Lawrence Sager's notion of "equal regard."[44] This concept has primarily been applied in the Free Exercise Clause context, but has implications for both religion clauses.[45] Eisgruber and Sager argue that the traditional justification for religious freedom—the special place of re-ligion in the constitutional order—has led to a notion of "unimpaired flourishing," where the paradigm for religious protection is one in which religion is allowed to flourish unimpaired by government restraints that may be placed on other deeply held values.[46] They argue that this model has been a failure as evidenced by the case law where it was never able to gain any substantial footing after cases such as *Sherbert* and *Yoder*.[47] The problem with "unimpaired flourishing," they argue, is that it is based on the notion that religion is special in and of itself for constitutional pur-poses.[48] They point out that religion has much in common with other deeply held bases for ordering one's life, and that what makes religion different is not anything inherent to religion, but rather the historical and contemporary tendency toward religious persecution and discrimination.[49] As a result, they propose an equality-based theory called "equal regard."[50]

Equal regard focuses on the ingroup-outgroup dynamics that can arise when it comes to religion, and it suggests that the goal of the religion clauses should be to treat all religious groups—minority and dominant—with equal regard.[51] This is not a formalistic construction of equal treatment because it heavily focuses on context and relevant differences, including the potential impact of "neutral" laws.[52] The goal is to prevent government from discriminating against or disparately impacting religious individuals or groups without an adequate basis.[53] To determine whether a government action disparately affects a religious individual or group, we must look to the way other religions are affected by the law and determine whether the complaining religious entity is treated equally "in fact" by the government action.[54]

The advantage to this approach is that it looks to the real-world effects of government action or inaction without predetermining a particular result. It also looks at difference and similarity among belief systems in a careful and informed fashion.[55] The vice of the approach is that it creates a clear dichotomy between religious liberty theories based on a special role for religion and those based on a theory of antidiscrimination and equal regard, although equal regard is not inconsistent with—and may promote—religious liberty.[56] I am not sure the two concepts are mutually exclusive, although the notion of unimpaired flourishing may well preclude the equal regard approach from being terribly effective. I would suggest, however, that there is a middle ground between unimpaired flourishing and treating religion the same as all other belief systems except where government action treats or affects it differently. The theories of Steve Shiffrin and Alan Brownstein discussed below represent examples of this middle ground.

The key is that religion can be considered different or special without—no pun intended—giving it exalted status. Eisgruber and Sager treat religion as though it is no different from other comprehensive value systems or even aesthetic views, save its unique history of discrimination.[57] The problem with this is the simple fact there are religion clauses in the Constitution, and like speech, it does seem that religion is somehow constitutionally different or special, whether in a favorable or unfavorable way.[58] Equal regard can coexist with this reality, however, because the fact that religion is special does not mean that it requires unimpaired flourishing, nor does it—as Eisgruber and Sager clearly acknowledge—prevent that difference or specialness from being based, at least in part, in the history of religious discrimination and persecution, although one must confront Noah Feldman's alternative views to assert this.[59]

So as a starting point for an equality principle it is useful to consider whether government action gives equal regard to various religious views and practices. This does not conflict with using religious liberty concepts in religion clause interpretation, but it does suggest that questions of religious discrimination, either intentional or in effects, are relevant in the application of the equality principle.[60] In other words, the current and historical situatedness of various religious groups in society is highly relevant.[61] This obviously has more impact in the free exercise context than the establishment context, but it is the starting point for crafting a broader notion of equality that may be useful under both clauses, although the greater relevance in the free exercise context will always be apparent.[62]

Alan Brownstein has argued that religious equality is a necessary principle in religion clause interpretation because liberty by itself is inadequate to address the broad and varied contexts that arise under the religion clauses.[63] He argues for the use of both religious liberty and religious equality in religion clause interpretation and sees the two principles as generally useful, although they can clearly be in tension with one another.[64] Eisgruber and Sager likewise suggest that liberty and equality are not mutually exclusive, assuming that the form of liberty is not unimpaired flourishing.[65] Brownstein's view of religious liberty would promote religious flourishing, but not unimpaired flourishing, and equality might serve as a check on liberty—that is, if someone's or a group's liberty interests would violate religious equality, religious liberty interests may need to give way.[66] Brownstein also sees free speech values as an essential part of the equation and a potential check on unfettered religious liberty arguments, but this part of his analysis is beyond the scope of this chapter.[67] Most important for present purposes is that Brownstein openly acknowledges that liberty and equality may not be adequate principles to cover the range of religion clause interpretation.[68] Given that he began pointing this out more than ten years ago, his views seem rather prescient today as we consider the inadequacy of any one principle of religion clause interpretation to cover the vast array of situations to which the religion clauses apply.[69]

Brownstein's views on religious equality are reflected, at least in part, in the following quote:

> The Constitution guarantees religious individuals and groups and the beliefs on which they base their identity an equality of standing very much like the racial and gender equality commanded by the Equal Protec-

tion Clause of the Fourteenth Amendment. While a constitutional theory designed to protect religious liberty will incidentally promote religious equality in many cases, the values at issue here are entirely independent. Because of this essential distinction, a liberty model cannot be an adequate substitute for a constitutional principle that recognizes the unique significance of equality as a constitutional value. Religious equality is not premised on the right to choose to be Jewish or Christian any more than racial equality is premised on the right to be black or Asian. Its focus is on group membership rather than belief, on religious status as opposed to religious practice. Religious and racial equality recognizes a person's racial and religious identity as a given characteristic and denies the state the power to favor or disfavor individuals on that basis. Discrimination is prohibited with regard to tangible benefits and burdens and more intangible inequalities related to stigma and status. Under equality principles, the government cannot promote a religious hierarchy by identifying people of a particular faith or their beliefs as superior or inferior to others—even if in doing so the government does not substantially burden the ability of a person to practice his or her faith. (footnotes omitted)[70]

Two additional points are important here. One, Brownstein clearly sees a difference between race and religion in that sometimes religious differences can be relevant.[71] He cites the example of a religious Christian child being given an excused absence on Good Friday or a Jewish child being given an excused absence on Yom Kippur.[72] Of course, in many situations drawing lines based on religious differences would violate the equality principle.[73] So for Brownstein government action based on religious difference and similarity is relevant and highly contextual. Two, he clearly acknowledges—as do Eisgruber and Sager—that disparate impact may violate principles of religious equality and/or liberty because unlike in the race context, where facially neutral laws allegedly do not impact groups differently because of race qua race, that is, they will not burden every person within a racial group,[74] facially neutral laws may affect every observant member of a given religion precisely because of the traits of that religious category,[75] for example, holding school on Saturday and its impact on Saturday Sabbatarians.[76]

Similarly, Steve Shiffrin has argued that religious equality and liberty are not mutually exclusive, and in fact, as this book argues, they are both part of a broader range of religion clause values.[77] Shiffrin's approach to framing and using those values is different from that taken in this book, but the fact that he recognizes the inadequacy of any single principle (or even a small set of principles) reinforces the broader theme herein. He promotes religious equality as part of a broader range of religion clause principles and notes that equality principles are often overshadowed by contrary concerns that are "deeply imbedded in the framework of government operations."[78] Contrary to Eisgruber and Sager, he openly states that religion is regarded as valuable in our constitutional framework and that this recognition has practical consequences.[79] He does not, however, advocate any sort of unimpaired flourishing, and in fact, in the Establishment Clause context points out that government favoritism toward religion must be limited to protect religion from being corrupted by government influence.[80] He proposes seven values in the Free Exercise Clause area and seven values in the Establishment Clause area that work together to frame how those clauses should be interpreted.[81] Equality is included under both, but it can clearly be effected or even circumscribed by the other principles in certain contexts.[82]

Shiffrin rejects formal equality as a useful principle of religion clause interpretation.[83] Like the position taken in this book, he is more concerned about the real-world effects of government action, and thus a form of substantive equality is a better approach in his view.[84] Moreover, for many of the reasons I reject neutrality theory, Shiffrin rejects formal equality's ability to ever achieve "equality." He argues equality is basically impossible in the varied factual contexts to which the religion clauses must be applied.[85] It can be a useful principle (at least the substantive version), however, when used along with other values to interpret the religion clauses. In his view both the courts and commentators have been far too obsessed with the concepts of equality and liberty—or equal liberty—to realize that these concepts are not capable of answering all the questions that arise under the religion clauses.[86] The primary role of the equality principle is to prohibit discrimination by government in favor of or against religion or religious individuals.[87]

Another value Shiffrin includes under both religion clauses is that of autonomy, which he links with religious liberty, but also discusses in the context of the equality principle.[88] We will not focus specifically on Shiffrin's conception of autonomy here, but rather on his broader suggestion that religious autonomy may itself be an independent value or principle of religion clause interpretation that may be linked with religious liberty, religious equality, and/or other principles. The notion that religious autonomy and liberty of conscience are central animating themes under the religion clauses has been a common theme in judicial opinions and scholarship.

For the reasons explained elsewhere in this book, but which I will summarize in this section, many of these discussions of religious autonomy presume an artificial self: human beings who are able to dissemble themselves from the community around them and the traditions that influence their preconceptions. Moreover, some autonomy talk—and the Court is far more guilty of this than many scholars—presumes that people can artificially dissemble portions of their being, such as religion, because some notion of civil society requires it.[89] Some of the scholarship addressing this issue is not so naive. For example, Noah Feldman argues for liberty of conscience without taking a classic liberalism position that requires an artificially autonomous notion of the self,[90] and Steve Shiffrin does the same.[91] Many others argue that religious autonomy requires a consideration of the whole self without artificially severing religious values and beliefs through the creation of a public/private distinction.[92] Most of these arguments have been made in the Free Exercise Clause area and may support what Eisgruber and Sager call unimpaired flourishing,[93] although the arguments have also been made in the Establishment Clause context, usually to criticize separationist court decisions.[94]

I will not take a side in this fascinating and intellectually enlightening debate. Rather, I reject the notion that religious autonomy is possible in relevant constitutional contexts due to the nature of human beings—our *dasein,* or being in the world[95]—and because of the pervasive nature of government interaction with society generally. The debate between classic liberalism and some forms of communitarianism can be recast in nonfoundationalist terms from a debate to different views of the mountain.[96] We are self, and we are community. We are our past as affected by our present because we are products of our traditions and yet historically situated.[97] Thus, we do not in a real sense operate autonomously, since we are always connected to others in our deepest beliefs and pursuits based on our being in the world. At the same time we are selves, because even those with shared traditions face different contexts every day that influence them.[98] Thus, classic liberalism's focus on autonomy is misplaced because people cannot easily be separated from their contexts.

This is where the pervasive nature of the modern state comes into play. The state plays such a major role in our daily lives that it would be impossible for it not to affect our contexts and thus our autonomy. If the state chooses to protect religious autonomy, the state will get to decide what counts and whose beliefs count for this protection as the Free Exercise Clause exemption cases demonstrate.[99] Therefore, in a constitutional sense religious autonomy is essentially a creation of the state, and thus to the extent that scholars and others argue for the protection of religious autonomy in the traditional liberalism sense, they are not arguing for religious autonomy at all, but for government recognition of a perception of autonomy.

This is why it makes sense to discuss autonomy here rather than in the chapter on religious liberty. Autonomy is a function of liberty theory, but religious liberty theory has enough power without reliance on religious autonomy. Yet if "religious autonomy" comes down to which religious identities the government is willing or able to recognize or protect, concerns about religious equality are invoked. In other words, as Steve Shiffrin and Alan Brownstein have noted, protecting religious individuals and groups—or what some perceive as individual or group autonomy—raises potentially important equality concerns.[100] Perhaps this is just a "potato-potaato" debate because whether we consider religious identity, as this book suggests, or religious autonomy is mostly a question of epistemology. In the end the question is by what mechanism do we protect or not protect various religious interests? But I think the distinction between religious identity and religious autonomy is important because autonomy carries a lot of baggage with it that, as Eisgruber and Sager have pointed out, can lead down problematic paths.[101]

D. The Meaning of Religious Equality

If religious equality is to serve as one of the principles that undergird religion clause interpretation, what form should it take, and can it be justified as a mode of religion clause interpretation? As with the other principles discussed herein, the latter question will be addressed in chapters 9 and 10. The first question will be discussed here.

At the start it is obvious that this book will not advocate formal equality, but rather a blending of the various principles of substantive equality discussed above. First, if religious equality is to be worth considering at all, it must consider the real-world impact of government actions. Thus, it would do more than protect religious entities and individuals from discrimination. It would suggest, like Douglas Laycock's substantive principle, that government neither encourage nor discourage religion or a specific religion(s).[102] This clearly allows for consideration of both intentional discrimination and disparate impact, because government can encourage or discourage religion as much through supposedly neutral incentives as by more direct means.[103] If the effect of a government action or inaction is to structure society or incentives in such a way as to favor or hinder religious choices or entities, the principle is violated. Of course, as with all the principles, equality is just one interpretive mode that may ebb and flow based on context, so there is no guarantee the equality principle would prevail in all circumstances where it conflicts with other valid principles of religion clause interpretation.[104] An example would be if treating religion and nonreligion the same substantially facilitates or discourages religion under the separation principle discussed in the next chapter or some other principle. Under such circumstances the equality principle might give way to the other principles, although given the ebb and flow of principles discussed in chapters 9 and 10, it may still affect the application of the other principles.

The key is that religious equality should include both intentional discrimination and disparate impact because religious differences matter and because religion is constitutionally special, even though that "specialness" need not lead to unimpaired flourishing or any particular notion of universal favoring or disfavoring. As noted elsewhere in this book, religion's special place in the constitutional order may sometimes be seen as favoring it and sometimes as disfavoring it, although such perceptions are based on the perceiver's preconceptions regarding what helps or harms religion. Most important, we should abandon any notion that religious equality is by itself, or combined with religious liberty, adequate to cover the range of interpretive situations that arise under the religion clauses.[105] None of this can predetermine answers under the religion clauses, but it suggests that equal regard or substantive equality is the best basis for an equality principle under the religion clauses. This does not preclude reliance on notions of religious liberty, separationism, accommodationism, or other principles. It simply adds another piece to the broader interpretive puzzle posed by the religion clauses.

6

Separationism

Separationism is not a single concept, but rather a group of concepts that must be unpacked to get at the core. Separationism and accommodationism (discussed in the next chapter) are a different variety of principle than neutrality or liberty, and equality. The latter concepts suggest, respectively, some sort of universal state of affairs or a connection to broader debates over what produces liberty or equality.[1] Without getting into any sort of metaphysical battle, one may assert that there can be degrees of separation (and accommodation).[2] We can speak of strict separationism, pragmatic separationism, or other limited degrees of separationism in a way that would be hard to do with neutrality, equality, or liberty—that is, imagine speaking of promoting partial neutrality (thus also promoting partial nonneutrality). Separationism's excess baggage lay entirely in the law and religion context. It may be good. It may be bad. It may be preferable. It may be hogwash. But in the end one need not engage it as a broad or grand principle like neutrality, liberty, or equality.[3]

This is a strength rather than a vice. As will be seen in the next chapter, it is also a strength of accommodationism, even though the two theories are often cast in opposition to each other.[4] In the law and religion area narrow principles may be more useful than broad principles because they do not hide their thrust behind unrealized rhetorical promises. These narrow principles become most problematic when they are attached to broad principles as the Court has sometimes done with separationism and neutrality and more recently between accommodationism and formal neutrality/equality. Let us now turn to the supposed connection between separation and neutrality.

A. Separation and Neutrality

In *Everson v. Board of Education*,[5] the Supreme Court asserted that the primary principle for interpreting the Establishment Clause is the "high and impregnable wall of separation between church and state."[6] Justice

Black's opinion for the Court also focused on neutrality, but connected separation to neutrality. The results in *Everson,* as opposed to the rhetoric, were not strictly separationist because New Jersey was allowed to fund bus fares for parochial school students.[7] The dissenting justices argued that separationism required the Court to strike down the bus fare program because it violated the wall of separation between church and state.[8] The dissenting opinions also spoke of separationism as neutrality.[9] Justice Black's opinion did the same, but the results in the case hinted that the form of separation may not be truly strict. Additionally, both Justice Black's opinion and the dissenting opinions, especially Justice Rutledge's, relied heavily on originalist arguments to support the wall of separation concept.[10]

A few years later, in *People of State of Illinois ex rel. McCollum v. Board of Education of Sch. Dist. No. 71,*[11] the Court solidified the notion that neutrality demanded strict separation,[12] a theme that was repeated often in cases until relatively recently.[13] Of course, the idea that separationism is neutral is as ridiculous as the claim that formal neutrality is neutral. Separationism is not, cannot, and never has been neutral. This does not mean that separationism is not a useful principle for other reasons. It simply states the obvious. Separationism will often put religious believers or entities in a different position than other actors in the private and/or public spheres, a position that some would view as disadvantageous for religion.[14] And, of course, as was explained in chapter 2, neutrality is itself impossible in the religion clause context whether tethered to separationism, formalism, or some other approach.

Of course, neutrality is not the only justification given by the Court for separation, and there are forms of separationism that do not rely at all on neutrality. The Court has also relied on historical arguments to justify separation, and while these arguments have sometimes been connected to neutrality talk, the historical justifications are not inherently based on neutrality. Moreover, there are pragmatic notions of separation that need not rely on neutrality or any claim to have found the "intent of the framers."[15] There are also religious arguments for separation such as those reflected in the writings of Roger Williams and mentioned by Alexis de Tocqueville when he wrote of his trip through the United States—of course most of the framers were unfamiliar with Williams's writings on this subject, and thus the fact that some had similar thoughts in Tocqueville's time suggests that the concept was wider than just in Williams's writings.[16] Finally, there are arguments for separation based in religious pluralism and a fear of religious divisiveness or competition that need not rely on the intent of the framers, but may overlap with pragmatic separationism.[17]

In the end the argument oft repeated by justices and some commentators that separation promotes neutrality in the government's relationship to religion suffers all the flaws of neutrality theory generally and then some.[18] A simple look at the many factual scenarios where separation as neutrality may apply demonstrates the flaws in this reasoning. If public and nonreligious private schools are able to get funding from government but religious schools are denied, the result clearly puts those schools at a disadvantage and is not neutral. This does not mean the government should provide aid to religious schools. It simply means that one cannot justify denying that aid on separationist grounds based on neutrality. There are better justifications for denying some forms of aid to religious entities, justifications that rely on other concepts of separation.

Consider also the current debate over intelligent design theory.[19] If a school teaches evolution but denies proponents of intelligent design the ability to introduce their theory because of separationist concerns, the results are not neutral. Secular scientific theory is placed at an advantage over religiously based theories.[20] There are solid separationist and other grounds for keeping intelligent design theory out of the schools—or at least the science curriculum[21]—but separation as neutrality is not one of them. In chapter 10 I will explain why intelligent design cannot be taught in public school science classes. While the separation principle plays a role in that analysis, neutrality does not.

If separationism is not neutral, what other justifications might there be for it? Significantly, as this book asserts, none of the other theories used in the religion clause context are neutral either. As we did with those theories, we must look at what separation actually does when divorced from its neutrality baggage. As will be seen, it does quite a lot, but not in its strictest form. Before discussing alternative forms of separationism, it is worth looking at the other primary justification the Court has used for separation, namely, originalism and/or historical arguments.

B. Separation and History

From the beginning of modern Establishment Clause jurisprudence, originalist arguments were used to support separationism. As noted above, in *Everson* both the majority and dissenting justices accepted the historical arguments for separation.[22] Moreover, from nearly the beginning of modern Establishment Clause jurisprudence, historical arguments were raised against separationism. In *McCollum,* Justice Reed's dissenting opinion offers a historical analysis that does not support separation and in fact supports strong accommodation of religion.[23] Both these historical strands have been apparent in both majority and dissenting opinions since that time.[24] In more recent years originalist arguments reflecting Justice Reed's position combined with arguments based on the "traditions" of the nation (rather than just original intent) have begun to prevail in decisions of the Court.[25]

Chapter 1 addresses the folly of this "battle of the framers" in the religion clause context. The "tradition" argument fairs little better than originalist arguments because it also uses selected excerpts from historical patterns and frequently gets even those wrong. For example, when the Court used the "traditions" approach to uphold a Nativity scene displayed by the city of Pawtucket, Rhode Island, in a park, it relied in part on the religious heritage and traditions of our nation.[26] Yet there is no long-standing history of displaying Nativity scenes on public property, even as part of larger Christmas displays, and in fact given the anti-Catholicism that was rampant through most of our "historical traditions," one would hardly expect to find such a tradition.[27] In fact, anti-Catholicism, anti-Mormonism, and anti-Semitism were long-standing "traditions" in our nation,[28] yet the Court certainly does not give these traditions weight. One would hardly expect the Court to allow a small Protestant-dominated town to include a display demeaning the "Bishop of Rome" as part of its celebration of a religious holiday on the ground that it is part of our nation's long-standing tradition of anti-Catholicism.

The point is that handpicking historical traditions to support an argument suffers a flaw that even hard originalism does not. There is no reason to presume those traditions are binding as society changes, although perhaps they may be one relevant factor to consider (hard originalism presumes the intent of the framers should be binding). Moreover, many unsavory traditions could be or have been used by the Court in similar ways, such as the tradition of segregation,[29] harsh corporal punishment in the schools,[30] and gender inequality.[31] These traditions are products of their time and place and have changed over time.[32] The Court uses the religious traditions argument based on statements of various political figures throughout U.S. history, but ignores the many contrary statements made by historical figures and the historical and sociological data that suggest these statements either had a different cultural meaning at different times or were not in sync with the everyday activities of most citizens.[33] So there is a dual problem of misinterpreting traditions and selectively applying them outside their cultural and historical context. Moreover, there is the overarching question of whether such traditions are even a valid basis for interpretation.[34] These questions may overlap a bit with the discussion of originalism in chapter 1, but although sometimes used in tandem with originalism, tradition arguments are not the same as originalist arguments because they lack the originalist self-justification that the intent of the framers should be binding.[35]

As pointed out in chapter 1, both sides have originalist arguments to support their positions, which at best proves the obvious: among the many framers and ratifiers of the Constitution there was no single view or set of assumptions on separation or specific questions of church-state law, whether contemporary or ones that might arise later. The problem here is that the early Establishment Clause decisions built separationism on the foundation of originalism, but that foundation was merely an illusion, which allowed later Courts (most notably the Rehnquist Court) to substitute its historical arguments, which are also merely an illusion. The illusion that historical arguments somehow ground decisions and make them more "objective" presumes the historical arguments are clear and decisive. If they are not—and they are not—they are merely justifications for decisions made on other bases, and later Courts can come along and discredit the principles built on these justifications, whether separationist or accommodationist, by discrediting the history without having to confront the other bases for decision, which may or may not independently support the principle advocated for.

In the case of separationism these independent bases do support some modicum of separation, but because the Court relied on flawed originalist arguments, separation was easier to attack when later Courts with different views and preconceptions on these issues came along. Because the later Courts rely heavily on equally weak arguments, their decisions may also be similarly easy to attack when some future Court chooses to do so. In the end, the Court's real interpretive presumptions get masked by an illusion of objective historicism.

One cannot get inside the heads of the justices in the early Establishment Clause cases, but even assuming some of them bought the historical arguments, which they certainly had to know were at least contestable,[36] one wonders what else may have motivated them. Possibilities include an increase in religious pluralism, a fear of religious divisiveness (which might be justified, in part, by soft originalist concerns),[37] a shift in legal and social thinking toward ingroup-outgroup dynamics and group equality concerns as pointed out by Noah Feldman,[38] a greater shift toward secularism on the Court and in public society,[39] anti-Catholicism,[40] or perhaps some combination of these concerns subsumed in a pragmatic approach.

There are hints in Court decisions between 1947 and the early 1980s that suggest each of these factors may have been relevant to the Court's separationist approach. Yet, if the Court's historical justification is countered, these factors never get considered on their own merits, and the doctrine of separation is put at risk of being subsumed in an all-or-nothing historical duel. This duel is reflected in the various opinions in the Court's recent Ten Commandment display decisions (discussed further in chapter 8).[41] Various justices took a strong separationist position based on historical and other grounds.[42] Others took a strong accommodationist position based on historical grounds.[43] Still others paid lip service to weak separation, but relied on historical arguments not to apply it,[44] while at least one justice relied on pragmatic concerns mixed with moderate historically influenced separationist arguments.[45] One can see many of the motivating factors discussed above under the surface of the historically influenced separationist opinions or sometimes on the surface of those opinions.[46]

1. Increased Religious Pluralism and/or Concern About Religious Divisiveness

There is little doubt that the early separationist decisions were influenced by the increased religious pluralism in the United States and the concern that religious divisiveness may be even more pronounced under such circumstances. The Court and various justices were explicit on this point in a number of opinions.[47] Rather than rely on these concerns to develop the doctrine given the vagaries of the religion clauses' text, the Court situated the pluralism and divisiveness concerns in a hard originalist argument.[48]

Certainly, concerns over divisiveness and religious pluralism in a broad sense might justify a soft originalist argument.[49] Yet to suggest that those concerns were shared by the framers and ratifiers of the Constitution in a manner that supported a wall of separation weakens the pluralism and divisiveness arguments. This is so because by overstating separationist history in the hard originalist account, the Court allows later Courts and critics to attack the history, not the underlying concerns. Had the Court relied directly on religious pluralism and divisiveness in an increasingly regulatory state, perhaps along with soft originalist arguments that the framers were concerned about minimizing religious conflict among sects,[50] the Court would have set a precedent that would be hard to attack, at least if one wants to adhere to principles of stare decisis.

Most likely, the Court chose to mask these arguments in the illusion of historical truth because originalism presented an easier—if not completely accurate—means to justify the wall of separation. The problem is that the wall may have been real, but the history used was at best half accurate and thus the wall built on that history was more illusion—or, as was later pronounced, metaphor[51]—than reality. Thus, the separationist position would have been stronger in the long run without reliance on hard originalist approaches.

Religious pluralism and potential religious divisiveness are important pragmatic concerns that cannot be ignored when interpreting constitutional provisions that apply to state action vis-à-vis religion in a massive regulatory state. For those with an originalist bent the history is anything but decisive,[52] but such individuals may take some solace from the fact that while the framers may have disagreed on specific interpretations and on future applications to circumstances they could have never foreseen, at least at a broad level it seems they shared a concern over minimizing religious conflict among the various sects in the union and in each state (mostly under state constitutions at that time).[53] This is a far cry from stating that they shared broad agreement on the specific methodologies for doing so, but it does lend some support for the notion that religious pluralism and religious divisiveness remain as potential bases for separationism. It simply is not decisive on that point.

Saying that religious pluralism and divisiveness in a massive regulatory state point toward some level of separation, and that such an approach might be consistent with at least the broad intent of the framers, leaves unanswered the key question of what level of separation. Religious pluralism can point in both directions. On the one hand, government favoritism for a religion, religions, or religion generally may cause divisiveness or competition by religious individuals and entities to win the favor of government entities.[54] On the other hand, strict separationism may fail to acknowledge the important and inseparable role religion plays in the lives of many believers.[55] Yet if separation is to operate as a principle under the religion clauses, we must have some mechanism for determining what kind of separation we are talking about. For the reasons mentioned earlier and in this paragraph, strict separation is too blunt a tool to be effective in the highly context-bound questions arising under the religion clauses, especially since the historical arguments for it are vastly overstated.[56] Yet as will be seen, this book calls for separation to be an important principle in religion clause interpretation.

The reasons separationism is important are precisely the fact that there is a middle ground—or rather broad middle area—between strict and no separation;[57] the fact that it helps navigate religious pluralism and limit religious divisiveness, at least when balanced with the other religion clause principles; and the factors discussed in the next few subsections. Separation plays a major role in the ebb and flow of religion clause principles discussed in chapters 9 and 10. This is precisely because it can be a somewhat flexible principle in the sense that it works in a number of contexts and that it is supported by a number of solid bases as discussed in this and the following sections. Yet like liberty and equality, defining separation is not an easy task. Fortunately, the bases for separation and the balance with accommodation, especially in the free exercise context, allow us to usefully define separation. Respecting religious pluralism and minimizing religious divisiveness facilitated by government action play an important role in that mix. The other bases for separationism will help determine what level of separation serves these goals.

2. The Shift Toward Group Equality and Increased Secularism on the Court and in Public Life

It is hard to contest the point that in the twentieth century, society and the courts increasingly used concepts of group equality in defining social and legal issues.[58] As noted earlier, Noah Feldman has done a nice job of demonstrating this shift in the religion clause area even if one can question his claim that the shift is inconsistent with historical notions of liberty of conscience.[59] This shift was very much a product of the aftermath of the Civil War and the courts' attempts to grapple with issues of race, and to a lesser extent gender, as well as the increased ethnic and religious diversity that occurred as the result of immigration patterns in the latter half of the nineteenth century and the early part of the twentieth century.[60] This manner of thinking entered the discourse on religious freedom and certainly had an impact on the development of separationist doctrine.[61] In a pluralistic society, managing religious diversity in the public realm might best be served by minimizing government's interaction with religion.[62]

This shift toward group equality-based thinking occurred roughly contemporaneously with an increase in secularism in society at large,[63] although this does not mean that such a secular shift was pervasive in all parts of society or walks of life. Still, the slow shift from premodernism to modernism had more firmly taken hold.[64] This confluence of group equality concerns and secularism fit nicely with the strict separationist language of *Everson* and its progeny, but the results in *Everson* and some subsequent cases such as *Zorach v. Clausen*,[65] demonstrate that these social trends were not as pervasive as some might have thought and that religion continued and continues to play a major role in our pluralistic society.[66]

As a justification for separation, equality concerns may be more persuasive than secularization. The same arguments that make pluralism an important part of the analysis support equality concerns. Government activities are pervasive, reaching almost every aspect of life.[67] At the same time, we are an incredibly religiously diverse and increasingly mobile society,[68] a trend that began even before the early separationist decisions.[69] Moreover, for the reasons stated in chapter 5, equality itself has some utility as a principle of religion clause interpretation.

The key is to view equality in the separationism context as a mechanism for navigating religious pluralism in a manner that minimizes government-facilitated religious tension or favoritism. Separation is a mechanism for doing this, but for the same reasons strict separation is highly problematic. A large portion of our polity are religious, and many are deeply religious, so strict separation would do exactly what the equality justification for separation seeks to avoid—strict separation may increase religious tension by making the devout feel unwelcome in the public sphere and may disfavor religion.[70] It is the wedding of equality with secularization that has been used, along with historical arguments, to support strict separation. Strict separation promotes secularization but not religious equality.

Thus, we see attacks from many fronts on "separation" (meaning strict separation), but such attacks are really focused on a straw man, because the Court has never consistently adopted strict separation, and other than a few radical separationists, most separationists do not support strict separation.[71] Concepts such as equal access for religious groups to public or limited public forums on government property are not of great concern to many separationists.[72] Since strict separation does not serve to navigate pluralism in a diverse society or serve any of the other underlying bases for separation—except perhaps secularization—it is an easy target. Still, secularization may be a valid basis for separation to the extent that it helps navigate religious pluralism in a manner that does not discriminate against people of faith.

The argument here is precisely the opposite of that posited by those who believe government should be able to display patently religious symbols and engage in religious ceremonies.[73] Preventing such symbolism by government or on government property except in a public forum, where free speech and expression are allowed regardless of the content, helps prevent government from facilitating one religion or religion generally.[74] In such a circumstance secularism along with the other bases support a separationist approach (which will still have to be balanced with the other religion clause principles). Yet keeping religious voices and views out of public debate or preventing religious expression in a public forum disfavors religion in the same way that government displays of religious symbols would facilitate religion—by skewing the expression of religious ideas via government largesse or negativity.[75] This result might be supported by strict separation relying primarily on secularization grounds.

Religious equality is a useful basis for separationism, and it is pretty clear that equality concerns underlay the Court's early separationist decisions.[76] Conversely, secularization by itself is not terribly helpful in supporting separationism unless one wants to support strict separationism. It may, however, retain some potential when considered with the other bases the Court seems to have been using in the separationist decisions. For now it is enough to say that religious pluralism, concerns over divisiveness, religious equality, and secularization all factored into the Court's early separationist decisions, even if the illusion of historical truth was used to justify the decisions.

One other factor that some have argued motivated the Court is anti-Catholicism.[77] The more accurate statement may be that anti-Catholicism most likely was a motivating factor for some of the justices.[78] It is possible that this is true at least in the decisions between *Everson* and *Engel*, but *Engel* and *Abington* (the school prayer cases) do not evince a strong anti-Catholic motivation, nor does *Zorach*.[79] Suffice it to say that to the extent that anti-Catholicism motivated any of the justices in these cases, such a reason is not a valid basis for separationism, and the doctrine must stand or fall on the other bases. Of all of the bases that seem to underlay the Court's early separationist decisions, anti-Catholicism is the lone one that is per se invalid. Some will argue that whether it is per se invalid as a basis for separation today is irrelevant because it may have influenced the justices' thinking on other issues.[80] This may be true—at least among the justices who harbored anti-Catholic sentiments—but the other bases may have motivated them with or without anti-Catholic sentiments. The key is whether the other bases can stand or fall on their own. Of course, even though separation may be defined and used as a valid mode of religion clause interpretation, it is still part of an ebb and flow with other principles of religion clause interpretation.

3. Protecting the State from Religion and Religion from the State: The Wall, the Garden and the Wilderness

According to the Court, the primary basis for supporting the wall of separation was the Jeffersonian notion that the wall protects government from religious influences. The Court used Jefferson's and Madison's writings, as well as some other historical arguments, to stake out its originalist claim for separation.[81] As pointed out above, while some of this history seems accurate, there is also a counterhistory, and certainly not all the framers and ratifiers of the Constitution shared Jefferson's vision.[82] The beauty to the approach taken here is that the best the counterhistory can do is offset the separationist history. It cannot supplant it because the separationist history counters it back. The reality is that we do not know what the bulk of the framers and ratifiers thought about separation, and certainly not in the contexts that we speak of today.

If one were to resurrect Jefferson and ask what he thought about prayer at public school football games or the display of Nativity scenes on public property, one might envision a response along these lines: "There are public schools? That is wonderful. Ben Rush and I had always hoped one day that might happen. And you say they are all around the nation? This is great. Our youth will be educated and make the nation stronger. What's this football you speak of and why do people want to pray for it? And why would someone want to display a Nativity scene on public property? Isn't the Nativity scene mostly a Catholic symbol? I would think many would object to such a symbol being displayed by government. I am not sure about the constitutionality of such things, but could you please explain how the First Amendment applies to the states? A few of us wanted such a result, but James warned us it wouldn't work at the constitutional convention because John [Adams] and his ilk like their state establishments. What's this frozen yogurt I keep seeing people eating? It looks interesting . . ."

The point is, from a hard originalist perspective neither Jefferson's wall nor some accommodationists' rejection of separation can be proven. There were simply too many framers and ratifiers, and many may have had multiple feelings about such issues. Moreover, few of them would have foreseen the scope of government activities, the breadth of the nation, or the religious diversity we have today. This does not mean that the belief in protecting government from religion is invalid. It simply means that it must be justified on grounds other than hard originalism. One of those grounds, pragmatic concerns in a diverse society, will be addressed in the next subsection. The others will be discussed here along with the concept of protecting religion from the corrupting influence of secular government.

The first argument one might use to support the notion that government should be protected from religion is the concept of soft originalism.[83] We do know that some framers, such as Jefferson, were suspicious of religion's influence on government.[84] We also know that many framers were concerned about the confluence of religion with governmental power based on recent European history; although we have no way to find out what this meant to the bulk of the framers and ratifiers.[85] Significantly, we do know that at least when it came to the federal government, many framers had a broad concern about the commingling of the national government and a church because of their experiences with the commingling of church and Crown in England.[86] Whether this could be readily transferable to the states is more a question of the methods and meaning of incorporation and is beyond the scope of this chapter. The key is that many framers shared a broad concern about the national government being too closely affiliated with religion.[87] From a soft originalist perspective this may be a gloss that is helpful in supporting the notion that one basis for separation is protecting the government from religion.[88] It is certainly not decisive, and plainly any such concern at the time of the framers would have been primarily in regard to the national government, but the broader concern could be extrapolated for today's circumstances.[89] This issue is further addressed below in the discussion on protecting religion from the state.

The next argument one may use to support this proposition has already been raised in this chapter, namely, concerns over religious pluralism and divisiveness. If government is too closely affiliated with any one religion or religion generally in such a pluralistic society filled with believers in many faiths and those who believe in no faith or no deity, there is a risk of religious conflict to gain the largesse or approval of government. This may be particularly acute at times when the government-funded pie is at its smallest.[90] Moreover, at the local level too close a relationship between church and state may lead to a form of religious gerrymandering because people may be afraid to send their children to schools that openly promote alien faiths for fear that the indicia of the state may influence the children's religious views or that the children's classmates may persecute them.[91] These concerns combined with the soft originalist arguments make protecting the state from religion a viable concern underlying separation, although as will be seen, the strongest arguments in this regard are pragmatic.

A related concern is protecting religion from government. Perhaps the most famous metaphor for this is Roger Williams's garden and wilderness.[92] Williams likened religion to a beautiful garden and the secular state and secular world to the wilderness, and warned that lest there be a strong hedge wall to protect the garden, the wilderness might overgrow it.[93] The idea of course is that government can have a corrupting influence on religion. Today, in response to the increase in charitable choice and the school voucher movement, we see legal arguments based in Williams's reasoning. There frequently are strings attached to government funding, and religious entities may be forced or induced to compromise their religious values in order to take the biggest (or any) share of the government-funded—and government-regulated—pie.[94]

The reality is that most of the framers were completely unaware of Williams's writings on this subject, and those writings have primarily become relevant to the debate in the twentieth century. Still, as noted earlier, when Tocqueville toured the United States, he heard similar sentiments from a number of people, and certainly some of the framers may have held such views.[95] Of course, there is no way to poll them to demonstrate that a hard originalist approach on this issue could be supported, so we must look to the soft originalist concerns mentioned above, and it is at least plausible that the concern about the church influencing the state may have also been connected to fears of the state corrupting the church. One of the best soft originalist arguments to this effect is often used by antisepara-tionists. The framers at a broad level did seem quite concerned about the national government interfering with and influencing state establishments —that is, protecting state-established religion from national government influence.[96] After incorporation, this argument could be extrapolated to state and local government as well. Thus, unless one rejects incorporation, this argument can be turned on its head to support separation in the manner that Roger Williams suggested.

Additionally, arguments based on religious pluralism and divisiveness are useful here. If government plays favorites among religions or induces religious entities to take advantage of government funding or other support, there is a risk that some religions will be favored over others and that religious divisiveness will be fostered.[97] Moreover, religious gerrymandering might result at the state or local level as government entities favoring one sect or religion alienate those of other faiths.[98] This mixing of G-d and Caesar may violate some of the tenets of the very faiths engaged in the governmental favoritism[99]

4. Pragmatism

In the end, it seems that the early separationist decisions may have had a strong pragmatic component hiding underneath originalist and neutrality claims. All of the above justifications for separation (except hard originalism and neutrality) have a basis with or without pragmatic concerns, but the combination of these justifications as applied to an increasingly pluralistic and mobile society in which government has become pervasive suggests that pragmatic concerns may have driven the Court. Additionally, the legal realist leanings of some of the justices also suggest a pragmatic concern about the effects of state action in the religion context.[100]

In fact, pragmatic concerns may underlie most religion clause jurisprudence from the early cases to the present cases. This is bolstered by the dramatic reality set forth in this book that both of the major interpretive methods used by almost every Court to address religion clause issues over the years from the Stone and Vinson Courts to the Burger and Rehnquist Courts—originalism and neutrality—are basically nothing more than illusions masking other interpretive methodologies and preconceptions. This certainly may explain the shifting jurisprudence in religion clause decisions as different justices with different preconceptions and pragmatic concerns face new and old issues alike. As we saw in chapter 1 Justice Jackson once captured this quagmire in a now famous statement regarding Establishment Clause interpretation in tough cases. In his concurring opinion in the *McCollum* case, Justice Jackson wrote:

> It is idle to pretend that this task is one for which we can find in the Constitution one word to help us as judges to decide where the secular ends and the sectarian begins in education. Nor can we find guidance in any other legal source. It is a matter on which we can find no law but our own prepossessions. . . ."[101]

Justice Jackson suggests in the remainder of the excerpt that judicial restraint or perhaps the passive virtues might have a role in limiting how much "business of the sort" the Court is faced with, although he is not explicit about this.[102]

Many scholars and judges have an uneasy response when the subject of pragmatism comes up. First, there are problems of definition. Richard Rorty's view of pragmatism is quite different from Judge Richard Posner's.[103] I make no pretense to having any great background in the niceties of various theories of pragmatism. I am using the term in a much less theoretical way and really as a corollary to the theory I do rely on, nonfoundationalism, and specifically a descriptive brand of philosophical hermeneutics.[104] Thus, when I argue that the Court's decisions have most likely relied on pragmatic concerns masked by the justifications of originalism and neutrality, I mean simply what Justice Jackson suggested. Sometimes neither the text nor the history of a constitutional provision provides the clarity needed to interpret that provision in light of the facts presented. In such circumstances, one may have little to go on but one's own prepossessions.[105]

Significantly, contrary to popular belief, this is a warning against unrestrained activism. Justice Jackson's statement is not a call for unrestrained judicial subjectivism. Rather, it is a warning that in such situations one ought to be careful to think through one's own preconceptions and any factors that may help restrain interpretative presumptions.[106] Without direct guidance from text or history, we must consider what modes of interpretation are valid in a given context (the subject of chapter 9) and within a given interpretive framework (the subject of this and the next chapter).

Thus, in the context Justice Jackson primarily refers to, namely, the text and history of the Constitution, judges may be left to choose between competing conceptions based on often unstated preconceptions and principles. In slight contradiction to Justice Jackson's statement, however, there may be legal guidance. That guidance may come from soft originalism, stare decisis, and a balance of other social and legal factors, such as those discussed in the previous three sections of this chapter. Engaging in this balance when none of the factors can be shown to offer firm guidance may lead to a pragmatic choice based on legal and social facts, but a restrained pragmatic choice.

C. Conclusion

The Court has made unstated choices for years in the religion clause context, but because it has chosen to do so behind the illusion of original intent and neutrality, it is hard to pin down how the Court balances the various factors it mentions in its decisions (or ones it may have relied on but did not mention). If the Court had openly confronted the "real" bases for its decisions in the early separationist cases, separation would have stood on stronger footing in the long run because later Courts would have had to confront and reject these bases head-on without the ability to discredit them by discrediting the illusion of neutrality or original intent. Balancing all the factors, from a pragmatic perspective or not, separationism makes a great deal of sense, especially when it is simply one of several modes of religion clause interpretation to be balanced in the ebb and flow of religion clause principles. Of course, the separation suggested in this chapter is not strict separation, but rather separation designed to minimize government's ability to play favorites among religions, facilitate or discourage religious pluralism, facilitate religious divisiveness or battles over the governmental aid pie, or interfere with the workings of religion or religious entities. Most of these factors are supported by soft originalist arguments and social reality, but they cannot be clearly justified in concrete situations based on hard originalist arguments. As a practical matter, pragmatic concerns may play an important role in how judges use these factors, but it should be clear that such pragmatic concerns may serve to restrain interpretation rather than leading to purely unrestrained interpretation.

7

Accommodationism

As with separationism, accommodationism raises questions of definition because it is not a single concept, but rather a group of concepts. The "easiest" context for accommodationist arguments is the Free Exercise Clause area, but such arguments also may have application in the Establishment Clause area under the ebb and flow of religion clause principles. What is accommodationism, and how can it function as a principle of religion clause interpretation?

At its base, accommodationism suggests that religion, religious individuals, and/or religious entities may be accommodated by government in regard to such things as free exercise rights, access to government programs and facilities, and religious expression. Just what should be accommodated, how, and how much, however, are harder questions, and just as there is no one separationist perspective on all issues, there is no one accommodationist perspective. At one end of the accommodationist spectrum are the nonpreferentialists who believe government should be able to facilitate and promote religion generally so long as it does not engage in sectarian favoritism.[1] Some prominent figures such as Justice Scalia would even allow the latter in the context of promoting monotheism over other religious views.[2] At the other end of the spectrum are what I will call the "free exercise accommodationists." Free exercise accommodationists are generally more separationist in the establishment context, but support accommodating religion through exemptions to generally applicable laws under the Free Exercise Clause.[3]

There are also religious voluntarists who are frequently accommodationist in approach. While they believe that government should not thrust religion onto people, government also should not inhibit citizens' ability to take part in public life or programs based on religion.[4] Additionally, there are what I will term "mild accommodationists." Mild accommodationists support equal access to public and limited public forums for religious entities, equal access to some governmental programs, and strong free exercise rights.[5] Some balance accommodationist and separationist approaches in an often contextual and unstated ebb and flow of principles, much as I suggest in this book.[6] There are also pragmatic accommo-dationists who share much in common with pragmatic separationists and sometimes overlap with the latter group.[7] These are just rough groupings of various accommodationist perspectives, and it should be understood that as is true with separationism, there is great diversity within each per-spective and also between perspectives. Also, like separationists, accom-modationists may rely on other principles in addressing religion clause issues.

Separation and accommodation are often perceived as antithetical, or at the very least not highly complementary. This may be true for the ex-treme forms of both, but in reality these principles need not be in conflict with each other. The key is to take a contextual approach such as the one suggested in chapters 9 and 10 and/or like Douglas Laycock's substantive principle discussed in chapter 2. Thus, in some contexts separationism may be more relevant than accommodationism and vice versa. An obvi-ous means to see this possibility is to contrast the role of accommodation-ism under the two religion clauses. It has a role under both clauses, but it seems an especially relevant principle in the Free Exercise Clause context. Therefore, we will explore the principle under the Free Exercise Clause and then under the Establishment Clause.

A. The Free Exercise Clause

Most, but certainly not all, accommodationists support broad free exer-cise rights.[8] This seems a natural extension of a core accommodationist concern, namely, minimizing government interference with religious belief and practice through government accommodation of believers.[9] On free exercise issues accommodationists have strong company from many sepa-rationists and others.[10] Moreover, the principles of religious liberty and religious equality overlap with accommodation nicely here, especially reli-gious liberty.[11]

The primary issue of relevance is the question of providing exemptions to generally applicable laws. The question of affirmative religious discrim-ination is not really a question of accommodation, but rather one of sheer government discrimination against a religion or religions.[12] One need not accommodate religion to prevent discrimination; one must instead stop and remedy the discrimination. Exemptions, however, directly implicate questions about the nature and boundaries of religious accommodation.

From most accommodationist perspectives religious exemptions should be granted from laws that interfere with religious practices because those laws place a burden on religion. Government may be able to deny an exemption, but only if it meets the appropriate standard, usually the compelling interest test.[13] That test requires government to accommodate religious exercise, but not if doing so is overbalanced by a government interest of the highest order and there are no other practical means to achieve that interest without interfering with the religious exercise in question.[14] Many who do not consider themselves "accommodationists" also take this position, but regardless of their views on other issues, this is essentially an accommodationist position. In fact, a strong argument can be made that the Free Exercise Clause is itself an accommodationist provision, and thus it is not at all hypocritical to promote accommodation under that clause but not the Establishment Clause.[15] This may lead to a game of rock, paper, scissors when the two clauses seem to collide, but that is only so if one views each or both clauses through the narrow lens of a specific principle or principles. The ebb and flow of principles argued for in this book would allow accommodationism and separationism to coexist under the religion clauses based on the relevant context to which those clauses are being applied.

Still, accommodationism must be justified by more than the assertion that it makes sense in the Free Exercise Clause context. Originalist arguments have been made to support this approach, but while there is some evidence that some framers would have supported religious accommodation even under laws of general applicability,[16] others expressed a fear that if such were the case, each person would become a law unto himself.[17] Moreover, it is unclear whether the framers would have supported exemptions for the vast array of religions in the United States today. This increased pluralism may have made exemptions more appealing or less so. There is no way to be sure.

Soft originalism may be useful here because we do know that the framers agreed at a broad level that liberty of conscience and religious freedom mattered,[18] even if they disagreed over the definition of that liberty and freedom and their application to real-world circumstances.[19] One can extrapolate from this a broad view that religious freedom should be protected against government encroachment when practicable, but to get an answer to the exemption question we must look beyond soft originalism.[20]

Concerns about religious freedom girded, but not completely reliant upon, soft originalism are relevant to the debate over exemptions. Textualism may also lend some support here, but while the text may be a bit less vague than the Establishment Clause, the text hardly answers the exemption question by itself.[21] Navigating religious pluralism and treating diverse religions the same vis-à-vis government regulation are also relevant concerns. Finally, pragmatic concerns are relevant to this analysis. Each of these will be discussed below.

1. Free Exercise, Religious Freedom, and Religious Liberty

Judge and Professor Michael McConnell has strenuously argued that religious liberty concerns embodied in the Free Exercise Clause require accommodation of religious practices that may conflict with generally applicable laws.[22] He acknowledges that even under the compelling interest test the Court rarely protected religious liberty in an adequate fashion,[23] but implies that an approach based on accommodation of religious practices would help to increase religious liberty.[24] In a nutshell, he argues that religious liberty and religious accommodation go hand in hand, at least in the free exercise context. He is not alone in this assertion.[25] Moreover, he is joined by many scholars who assert that religious liberty demands exemptions, but who do not directly speak in the language of accommodation.[26]

It makes sense to link religious accommodation with religious liberty in the Free Exercise Clause context because both principles seem naturally relevant to free exercise questions.[27] But as Justice Scalia argued in *Employment Division v. Smith*,[28] providing exemptions to generally applicable laws may not be a necessary predicate for religious liberty. Justice Scalia argues that liberty of belief is absolutely protected, but accommodation through exemptions to protect religious practices that run afoul of generally applicable laws is not required under the Free Exercise Clause (although it is allowed).[29] This reasoning is much criticized, and rightly so, but it may provide a means to explore just how much religious liberty concepts and accommodationism inherently overlap. As noted in chapter 4, religious liberty is a relatively malleable concept, and while some conceptions of it, including that advocated in this book, are consistent with mandatory exemptions, not all conceptions of it are.

As Justice Scalia acknowledges, his view of religious liberty will primarily promote accommodation only for those whose religious needs are considered in the legislative process (usually more dominant faiths) or those powerful or intrepid enough to be granted exemptions through state or political judicial processes.[30] Many have argued this is inconsistent with religious liberty.[31] The critics would appear to be correct if one views liberty from the perspective of the real-world impact of state action. From that perspective Justice Scalia asked the "general applicability" question from the wrong perspective. He asked the question from outside the Free Exercise framework, while many critics ask it from within that framework—is this law generally applicable as it applies to religious practitioners? Given that the cases involved are free exercise cases and that formal neutrality is a baseless concept, the latter question seems better, but the key is that in the ebb and flow of religion clause principles Justice

Scalia's answer works poorly if accommodation is a valid principle of religion clause interpretation because accommodation may limit the conceptions of liberty applicable in a given context.

As I have written elsewhere, I like the lofty concept of religious liberty.[32] It sounds good. But then again, it is my concept of religious liberty that I like, and I doubt that Justice Scalia shares my concept of religious liberty. Yet I have no means to prove that my view of religious liberty is any more correct than his view from within the religious liberty principle because both views promote liberty to an extent. I can argue based on other principles that his view of religious liberty is wrong, but I cannot prove that it is any less or any more religious liberty than my view without some ultimate conception of religious liberty or perhaps an absolutely decisive historical record, which does not exist. For present purposes it should be enough to note that many concepts of religious liberty work well within an accommodationist framework, but that religious accommodation can stand on its own even without the bulwark of religious liberty to support it. Yet in the ebb and flow of religion clause principles, accommodation can help define and apply the liberty principle in certain contexts and vice versa.

There is no doubt that an accommodationist perspective in the Free Exercise Clause context may expand the view of religious liberty and provide maximum liberty for the maximum number of believers regardless of faith. This does not justify accommodation by itself, but it acknowledges at least that accommodation is consistent with the liberty principle. This will play out further in chapters 9 and 10. In this chapter, however, we can view the connection between religious liberty and accommodation, along with the other concepts that support accommodation in the free exercise context, in a manner that reinforces accommodation and helps us define it.

2. Free Exercise and Textualism

The religion clauses read as follows: "Congress shall make no law respecting an establishment of religion, or prohibiting the free exercise thereof. . . ." While some have made textual arguments for interpreting the Establishment Clause,[33] most scholars and many judges agree that at best that clause provides some clues as to its meaning in the variety of situations to which it has been applied.[34] Similar arguments have been made for and against textual approaches to the Free Exercise Clause.[35] The text of the Free Exercise Clause may be useful, however, in determining whether the clause supports accommodation of religion.

It is certainly not clear or decisive, but as some scholars have noted, "exercise" of religion implies more than simply belief.[36] The question must still be raised whether failure to grant an exemption to a generally applicable law "prohibits" free exercise and how broad a scope that term should have,[37] but the text certainly lends support to the notion that government should not affirmatively interfere with or coerce individuals to act in a manner that goes against their religious beliefs (or aggressively foster citizens to reject their own beliefs or accept alien beliefs).[38] This suggests that government should engage in some level of accommodation, but just what that level is remains open to interpretation.

Folks have long tried to read greater detail into the text of the religion clauses than is plausibly there.[39] When they do so, they are really interpreting the text based on their preconceptions and the principles they may already believe underlie that text.[40] Yet the text of the Free Exercise Clause suggests that accommodation is at least consistent with the First Amendment, just as the Establishment Clause suggests that some level of separation is consistent with the First Amendment.[41] In the end, however, the text cannot demonstrate the degree of accommodation and even less so the degree of separation.[42] For now, however, we can say that there is some level of textual support for accommodation, albeit vague support. The other bases for accommodation help to solidify its meaning.

3. Free Exercise, Religious Pluralism, and Religious Equality

Accommodation in the free exercise realm also accounts for the impact that laws may have on various groups in a religiously pluralistic society in a manner that will tend to minimize the disparate effects of generally applicable laws on less dominant religions. Of course, Justice Scalia's argument against mandatory accommodation might counter that it is precisely this religious pluralism that makes mandatory exemptions so problematic because there may eventually be a patchwork of religious exemptions from almost every law, making it hard to enforce these laws.[43] As a practical matter the evidence goes against this view, because both before and after (under state Religious Freedom Restoration Acts [RFRAs] and constitutions) *Smith* there have been few problems with enforcement of laws because of mandatory exemptions.[44] This is as true in the states that stringently enforce the compelling interest test as it was under the post-*Yoder* federal regime where that test was barely enforced outside the unemployment compensation area.[45] Moreover, even the most ardent supporters of mandatory exemptions would allow government some leeway when a truly compelling interest is involved and there are no practical means to meet that interest while granting a religious exemption.[46] This book is less concerned with the nature of the test in this context than it is with the principles used to apply it because as the post-*Yoder* cases demonstrate, even a stringent test is of little use if the principles underlying its application are underexplored.[47]

So how should religious pluralism play into the discussion of accommodation? Rebutting Justice Scalia's view of the issue does little more than suggest that accommodating religious pluralism will not necessarily lead to legal mayhem. It does not answer how, if at all, religious pluralism should connect with accommodation or how it may affect the meaning of religious accommodation. As was explained in chapter 5, Professors Steve Shiffrin and Alan Brownstein argue that the principle of religious equality supports free exercise exemptions precisely because of the religious diversity in our society and the fact that the failure to exempt would place many religious minorities at a disadvantage when their religious liberty is threatened by laws of general applicability.[48]

Similarly, Professors Eisgruber and Sager argue that under the principle of "equal regard," free exercise exemptions would often be mandated, but they are a bit less committal on a broad rule in this regard.[49] Of course, they would also reject the liberty-based arguments for accommodation because they may lead to the problematic concept of unimpaired flourishing.[50] Still, they would support some degree of religious accommodation when the principle of equal regard requires such accommodation.[51] Brownstein and Shiffrin base their support for free exercise accommodation in both equality and liberty concerns,[52] while Eisgruber and Sager do so solely under the principle of equality. The key for present purposes is that all four recognize the relevance of religious equality and religious pluralism to the accommodation question under the Free Exercise Clause.

In a pluralistic society such as ours it is problematic when basic freedoms are allocated or protected in an unequal fashion.[53] This, of course, begs the question of whether leaving exemptions to the political process fails to protect various religious individuals and groups equally and whether failure to exempt means such basic freedoms are not being equally protected. This is relevant to the way in which we view questions under the religion clauses. If one looks to the real-world effects of government action, as suggested in this book, it would seem that mandatory exemptions would be necessary to protect various religions in a pluralistic society because the political process will not adequately protect many religions.[54] Under this view you take the world as you found it and look at the effects of government action in society as it really exists.[55] Justice Scalia's approach is representative of a more formalistic view of the question that connects with formal neutrality.[56] It looks at laws on their face to see whether religious distinctions are drawn, and if not, presumes those laws are neutral and any disparate—even greatly disparate—impact they have on religious practice is not of constitutional importance.[57]

For the reasons discussed in chapter 2, the approach advocated in this book rejects neutrality, and especially formal neutrality, as a valid principle of religion clause interpretation. It is also worth noting that in a discussion well worth reading, but beyond the scope of this chapter, Alan Brownstein explains why disparate impact in the free exercise context should require exemptions despite the fact that such impact is not recognized as actionable in the equal protection context.[58] He focuses heavily on the fact that race and religion may function differently in the disparate impact context.[59]

The failure to accommodate in some cases may lead to real-world effects that deny religious individuals the ability to practice their religion or that put them to the choice of engaging in religious practices or losing significant opportunities that would otherwise exist.[60] Moreover, dominant religious groups will rarely have to deal with such choices because they will generally be considered in the legislative process and will likely have an easier time getting exemptions after the fact.[61] Thus, religious pluralism would seem to support accommodationism in the Free Exercise Clause context because failure to accommodate would create equality concerns as well as concerns about religious liberty or, more specifically, equal liberty—the ability to freely practice one's faith regardless of whether one is a member of a dominant faith in a given locale.

4. Free Exercise and Pragmatism

Unlike in the separationist context where pragmatic concerns suggest some level of separation may help navigate religious diversity in a society where government activity is pervasive, pragmatic concerns by themselves point in both directions when it comes to free exercise exemptions. On the one hand, it makes sense to accommodate diverse religions in a diverse society to the greatest extent possible because this would lead to effects that promote strong free exercise protections. On the other hand, one might argue, as Justice Scalia did for the *Smith* majority, that religious diversity militates against mandatory accommodation because the results would be potentially devastating to an orderly society.[62] As was explained above, however, the facts do not seem to back up this slippery slope toward anarchy.

The best that can be said from a pragmatic point of view is that pragmatic concerns may support strong free exercise accommodation in a diverse society assuming there are other good reasons for doing so—perhaps liberty and equality concerns. It is also possible to argue against such accommodation from a pragmatic perspective, but if one looks at the effects on the ground, as it were, this argument seems weaker than the former. In the end pragmatism can lend mild support to free exercise accommodation, but other bases are necessary to undergird accommodation.

It seems that religious liberty, religious pluralism, religious equality, and soft originalist concerns are the strongest bases for accommodationism in the Free Exercise Clause context. Accommodationism also gains some mild support from textual and pragmatic concerns. Given that religious accommodation would seem to further both liberty and equality concerns, and that both those principles play a role in the ebb and flow of religion clause principles, it would seem that accommodation, which can be more narrowly defined and more usefully applied, is a solid mode of Free Exercise Clause interpretation. Moreover, at least in the free exercise context it need not conflict with separationism unless one advocates strict separation in the free exercise as well as the establishment context.[63] Many separationists do not advocate such a result.[64]

B. The Establishment Clause

Under the Establishment Clause, accommodationism raises a number of important questions. It is here where accommodationist approaches may conflict the most with separationism.[65] It is also here where the nonpreferentialist brand of accommodationism lurks, either directly or through the guise of formal neutrality, as will be explained below.[66] Still, accommodationism and separationism may be able to coexist peacefully in some Establishment Clause situations such as equal access and moment of silence cases. In other areas the ebb and flow of principles as affected by the context of the relevant cases will determine whether accommodationism should play any significant role in the analysis. More on that in chapters 9 and 10. For now it is important to discuss when, why, and how accommodationism may play a role in Establishment Clause analysis. As will be seen, with a few exceptions it is a concept that fits better under the Free Exercise Clause, but it may also have some relevance to the Establishment Clause.

1. Equal Access and Moment of Silence Laws: Accommodationism's Establishment Clause Homes

Equal access cases involve access by religious groups or individuals to government property or facilities that are open to other groups on a nondiscriminatory basis.[67] The most common example of this is equal access to school facilities, and there have been a number of cases.[68] The general rule is that when the government creates a public forum or limited public forum, religious or other groups may not be excluded from that forum based on religious content or viewpoints.[69] In the school context this means that if a school lets non-curriculum-related groups meet during noninstructional time, it cannot deny equal access to its facilities to religious groups.[70] The only way to overcome this presumption is where government can show that its regulation is narrowly tailored to serve a compelling governmental interest.[71]

The Supreme Court has held that there is no Establishment Clause interest in denying a religious group access to a limited public forum because government would not be responsible for any religious activity and denying access would put religious entities at a disadvantage in what is otherwise an open forum.[72] This constitutional analysis is also supported by the federal Equal Access Act, which requires equal access in the types of situations described above in all public secondary schools.[73] The act uses slightly different language than the constitutional cases, and it provides more detail regarding the proper role of school officials and so forth.[74] Recently, however, the Court has held that equal access is mandated even for an avowedly proselytizing group aimed at the elementary school level, so the constitutional doctrine is in many ways broader than the Equal Access Act.[75]

The key to analyzing accommodation in the equal access doctrine is to understand that the doctrine is primarily based in free speech analysis, not religion clause analysis. However, when the Court holds that the Establishment Clause is not a bar to such religious activity on government—and especially school—property, strict separationism is clearly checked. It is not necessary to view this as inherently accommodationist because it is easy enough to argue that it is just a basic application of free speech doctrine and "accommodating" religion is not the issue, but rather the issue is concern over content or viewpoint discrimination.[76] This is a sensible enough way to view the doctrine. Those of us who support equal access do not necessarily view it through an accommodationist lens, and in fact many separationists support equal access.[77] Where this becomes more of an issue, and where a lot of the consensus about equal access begins to fall apart, is in cases like *Good News Club v. Milford Central School*.[78]

What happens when a group that is designed to proselytize and influence young children seeks access to an elementary school (or a building housing one) shortly after the school day ends or before it begins? Does the government now have a valid enough Establishment Clause interest to prohibit the group from meeting or require it to meet at a time more remote from regular instructional hours? Also, what may the school do about distribution or posting of the group's literature or meeting notices where other groups have the ability to distribute literature or post notices? In *Good News Club* the Court answered the first two questions as follows: Religious clubs can meet on the same terms and the same times as other non-curriculum-related groups even in elementary schools and even if they are focused on evangelizing.[79] Moreover, there is no valid Establishment Clause argument to deny equal access because in a limited public forum the conduct is not attributable to government.[80] The implicit answer to the third question is that equal access means equal access and that religious clubs may use the same channels of communication as other non-curriculum-related groups, although the Court never explicitly addresses this issue, which was not before it. Lower courts, however, have answered this question in the way just suggested.[81]

Several justices, including Justices O'Connor and Breyer, who joined the majority and concurred in *Good News Club,* respectively, have suggested that there may be circumstances where endorsement of religion can occur even in a limited public forum, and thus there may be situations where there is a valid Establishment Clause interest to prevent equal access.[82] Justices Stevens, Souter, and Ginsburg believed that the situation in *Good News Club* was just such a situation.[83] While the arguments against equal access are stronger in *Good News Club* given the age of the students and the nature of the religious group, the Court seems inclined not to explore such real-world distinctions when a public forum or limited public forum is present.[84] The fact that the Court barely explored these concerns in *Good News Club* is evidence that while the Court has acknowledged that Establishment Clause concerns may provide a compelling governmental interest in some access cases,[85] this is little more than lip service, because if there ever were such an interest, it would have been in *Good News Club.*[86]

What does all this have to do with accommodation? The answer is that this formalistic solicitousness for religious groups in equal access cases can be seen as a form of religious accommodation for religious viewpoints in the marketplace of ideas.[87] The argument need not be couched in accommodationist terms, but the formalistic mechanisms used in these cases may signal a willingness to accommodate religious speech even in the face of potentially strong Establishment Clause concerns. While I do not support the formalistic approach because there may be some cases where the facts on the ground support an even stronger Establishment Clause issue than that in *Good News Club,* I do support the accommodation or protection, depending on how you view it, of religious perspectives in public forums and limited public forums.[88] The doctrinal reasons for this will be discussed in greater detail in chapter 10. The reason for supporting it in the ebb and flow of religion clause principles, as will be further discussed in chapter 9, is the combination of accommodationist and equality-based concerns that preclude placing religion at a disadvantage in the expressive context. The limitation of this argument to the expressive context also suggests, and correctly so, that accommodation takes a stronger place in the ebb and flow because of the free speech (and equality) concerns.[89]

Moment of silence laws are another area where accommodationism may play a valuable role in the religion clause context and for reasons similar to those discussed in the equal access area. Barring a purposeful attempt to promote religion through a moment of silence law as the Alabama legislature did in *Wallace v. Jaffree*,[90] or application of such laws in a manner that favors religion,[91] these laws are generally constitutional even if they mention prayer among the options for silent reflection.[92] The question is why?

At one level this makes perfect sense because these laws do not generally take a position on religion and leave it to the individual children what to reflect upon during the moment of silence.[93] Students may think about the school day, a party over the weekend, a TV show, or the state of the world, or they may silently pray.[94] There is no outright religious favoritism, and the moment of silence constitutes a sort of short limited public forum for silent expression by students.[95] As a practical matter, moment of silence laws may function to accommodate students who want to silently pray without placing the imprimatur of the school on the prayer.

Moment of silence laws—to the extent they allow students to silently pray—seem a good compromise between separationist and accommodationist concerns in a religiously diverse society with a large population of devout believers. These laws are certainly not a panacea from either perspective. Some believers would prefer to pray collectively, and thus the individual silent prayer may not be enough.[96] Others may need to pray in a group, such as the Jewish minyan (ten or more men or men and women, depending on the tradition).[97] Yet here, too, there is balance because both concerns can be accommodated. The believers who want to worship together may do so outside of instructional time under an equal access policy, and schools can and do accommodate ritual concerns through a variety of accommodation methods, including making a nonpublic area available for Jewish or Muslim prayer services, which are required to be held three times a day and five times a day, respectively (obviously only the morning through afternoon services would be relevant).[98] Of course, schools are not required to do this under the Free Exercise Clause as things currently stand,[99] but to the extent they do, such accommodation could be consistent with the Establishment Clause as long as there is no favoritism.

Moment of silence laws are a means to accommodate religion in a manner that minimizes separationist concerns because religion is not the primary focus of such laws. If religion were the primary focus or purpose, the law would be unconstitutional.[100] Like equal access, moment of silence laws are a means to balance separationist concerns with the reality that many students are religious and are essentially captive during the school day. These laws allow religious students the opportunity to connect with their faith during (moments of silence) or shortly before or after their school day (equal access) without fostering government support for religion or a particular religion.[101]

2. Vouchers, Aid, and Nonpreferentialism: Separation Versus Accommodation

As explained in chapter 2, arguments for government-sponsored financial and other support for religious entities can be characterized in accommodationist terms. For example, those who advocate tuition vouchers can argue that religious families who do not feel the public schools are an appropriate venue for their children's education must pay property taxes to support the public schools and private school tuition. Therefore, tuition vouchers may be a means of accommodating religion. Of course, the *Zelman* Court did not explicitly make this argument in accommodationist terms, relying instead on the concept of formal neutrality.[102] Had the Court relied on accommodationism rather than neutrality, it would have had to balance the accommodationist principle against equality and separation concerns regarding the real-world effects of the program. By hiding behind the illusion of neutrality the Court avoided this challenging task.[103] Perhaps the reason for this—other than a misguided reliance on neutrality—was that under the facts in *Zelman* it would have been hard to overcome the strong separationist concerns and the unequal effects of the program.[104] Thus, the accommodationist argument, which might be successfully balanced with separationist concerns in other aid cases,[105] would not have been up to the task. The illusion of formal neutrality permits far more, at least as the Court has used it.

In fact, the Court's formal neutrality approach leads to a form of de facto nonpreferentialism in some cases. This, too, might be argued to serve accommodationist ends. However, the fact that it may serve a mode of religion clause interpretation does not by itself support this sort of de facto nonpreferentialism. The reasoning and results in these cases must still consider other modalities of religion clause interpretation. Again, separationism and equality may, and most likely will, overbalance any form of accommodationism that leads to substantial government facilitation of religion. Of course, the facts matter. In cases where government aid is distributed to a wide range of entities serving a valid governmental purpose, the accommodationist argument is stronger because government is most likely not substantially facilitating religion.[106] When, however, the aid disproportionately benefits religion or serves to promote proselytization through government funds, separationist concerns may take on even greater importance.[107] Moreover, it is hard to argue that such scenarios accommodate religion because they do more than that—they favor or facilitate it.

This is exactly the point. Without the illusion of neutrality to hide behind, arguments for government aid that provides significant and disproportionate benefits to religious entities can not be said to accommodate religion. Rather, such aid facilitates religion.

From a nonpreferentialist perspective this is not problematic because government may favor religion over nonreligion so long as it does not favor a specific religion (under the facts in *Zelman* even this concern may not have been met).[108] The approach advocated in this book rejects nonpreferentialism for two primary reasons, one theoretical and the other practical. First, nonpreferentialism raises significant concerns under the separation principle (whether viewed from the Jeffersonian or Williamsonian perspective), and when real-world effects are considered in light of demographics and social reality, it may also raise concerns under the equality and liberty principles. Unless one subscribes to one side in the battle of the framers or has an unusual faith in government's ability to avoid playing favorites among various faiths, even when one or two faiths are more dominant in a given area, nonpreferentialism has little to recommend it.[109] Second, the Court has never accepted nonpreferentialism directly as a guiding principle and has specifically rejected it on a number of occasions,[110] although as I have argued, the reasoning in *Zelman* may constitute a form of de facto nonpreferentialism.[111]

Still, accommodationism may be relevant in the aid context. Consider cases such as *Agostini* and its predecessor *Aguilar*, where special education services mandated under federal law were first offered at parochial schools on the same terms as at other schools, were then forced into nearby trailers because the situation was found to be unconstitutional in *Aguilar*, and were ultimately allowed back on campus when the Court overturned *Aguilar* in *Agostini*.[112] Doctrinal reasoning aside, *Agostini* is an excellent example of accommodation in the aid context. The students at the religious schools were entitled to the services regardless of whether those services were provided in the school building or in nearby trailers or public schools.[113] No schools other than religious schools were forced to offer such services off campus, and doing so was quite costly, disruptive of the general school day, and perhaps stigmatizing for the students.[114] Allowing the courses to be taught on school grounds seems a reasonable accommodation absent evidence that the government-funded teachers were involved in religious education or religious entities were otherwise being favored.[115] Some of the other cases discussed in chapter 2, such as *Witters* and *Zobrest*,[116] are also good examples of accommodationism in the aid context. Such programs would be subject to the ebb and flow of religion clause principles, and thus there may be no one clear answer for all programs, but it is at least possible that accommodation can nicely coexist with the other principles of religion clause interpretation in these types of cases.

3. Ceremonial Deism: Pragmatic Accommodation and Theoretical Gymnastics

The broad topic of ceremonial deism is beyond the scope of this chapter, but a brief word on the topic is appropriate here because accommodationism has played an important role in the ceremonial deism debate. First, it is necessary to define ceremonial deism. There is no one conclusive definition for the term, and what is and is not included in the concept has been the subject of debate.[117] The specifics of the debate are, like the broader topic, beyond the scope of this chapter. As used here ceremonial deism refers to a long-standing public recognition of G-d, religion, or the divine in a nonsectarian, nonproselytizing context.[118] This definition is not perfect, but for present purposes it will do. It would tend to include things such as patriotic songs with references to the divine, "In God We Trust" on currency, and perhaps Christmas trees on government property.[119] For purposes of this book it clearly does not include legislative prayer or the display of Nativity scenes or other religious objects with a strong theological connection.[120] Some have labeled the latter "ceremonial deism,"[121] but as will be discussed in chapter 8, this only demeans the religious nature of such activities.[122] The "under God" language in the Pledge of Allegiance has been included as ceremonial deism by some,[123] but not by others.[124] Given the discussion in this section, there is no need to classify the pledge one way or the other here.

The approval of ceremonial deism is often couched in accommodationist or traditionalist terms.[125] This could only be the result of mental gymnastics because most ceremonial deism does more than accommodate religion, and at least for things such as the display of crèches, which some have labeled ceremonial deism, there is no long-standing tradition to rely on.[126] What is really going on is a form of pragmatic accommodation that recognizes the religious heritage and nature of our society, or at least many people in it.[127] If one wants to be consistent with established doctrine, either most ceremonial deism would be unconstitutional or much of what the Court has found unconstitutional would be constitutional.[128] Of course, the whole notion of pragmatic accommodationism is that there are certain areas where the normal doctrines do not apply. This makes a certain amount of sense given the religious nature of much of our populace.[129] After all, to protect religious freedom in the broad range of cases there may be some areas that must be left untouched lest public backlash lead to the destruction of Establishment Clause values through amendment or less direct (and perhaps unconstitutional) means. This reflects the pragmatic notion that it may be unwise to fight a particular battle that may be winnable, but which could weaken broader Establishment Clause concerns, and thus lose the "war."[130]

The problem, of course, is in defining what is part of the battle and what part of the broader war. A broad notion of ceremonial deism could swallow much of the Establishment Clause as it is currently understood.[131] On the other hand, too narrow a definition may increase angst among the competing sides in the culture wars.[132] Here the principle of accommodation is useful.

The line between accommodating the religiosity and heritage of the nation and substantially facilitating religion is not a clear one, but several things help us when we apply accommodationist principles to the question. First, the display of certain theologically charged religious objects and organized theistic prayer (such as legislative prayer) do more than simply accommodate religion.[133] They promote it, and they tend to promote Christianity in particular.[134] As the next chapter will explain, when such things are written off as forms of ceremonial deism, the nature, value, and power of religion are often overlooked and religion may end up being demeaned by the very courts attempting to accommodate it.[135] Whether such activities are constitutional must be answered using the same principles and approaches used for other religious activities rather than simply labeling them ceremonial deism and upholding them. It is the very power and nature of the religious activity that helps remove it from the concept of ceremonial deism and makes government sponsorship or support more than simply accommodation of religion.[136] Obviously, activities that do not rise to the level of religiosity discussed here and in the next chapter may also be religious, but accommodating them may be less problematic on pragmatic grounds when pragmatic concerns are balanced with the principles of religion clause interpretation as has often been the case in the ceremonial deism context.[137]

This is the ultimate question when it comes to ceremonial deism. How should we, if at all, justify the constitutionality of whatever it is we label ceremonial deism or the unconstitutionality of similar activities we do not so label? Some brilliant work has been done attempting to justify this on historical, doctrinal, and/or theoretical grounds.[138] In the end, however, it all ends up being a form of mental gymnastics unless one is willing to argue that organized school prayer and the like are constitutional or that the singing of patriotic songs with religious references is unconstitutional. The reality is that maintaining intellectual consistency in this area requires an honest acceptance of doctrinal inconsistency and the fact that this inconsistency is driven by pragmatic concerns. What we basically have is a form of religious accommodation that is almost entirely driven by pragmatism even if it is sometimes justified on other grounds such as selective use of the "traditions" of our nation.[139]

Here there is a choice. We can either accept this pragmatic compromise and essentially except ceremonial deism from competing principles in the ebb and flow of religion clause principles or we can challenge it. Were the definition of ceremonial deism herein not so narrow and the approach to religion clause interpretation herein not so flexible, this book might argue in support of the latter approach (of course, some ceremonial deism would survive the challenge). However, because the definition of religion in the next chapter substantially narrows the range of what may be called ceremonial deism and because the approach to interpretation proposed in this book is not so rigid as to preclude closer examination of situations that do not clearly involve ceremonial deism, I support the pragmatic compromise for what it is, a pragmatic accommodation of a small number of activities that might otherwise be unconstitutional. This can be done by giving the principle of accommodation some prominence in these cases and by acknowledging the pragmatic nature of this solution.

4. School Prayer and Religious Symbolism: The Unbearable Weakness of Accommodationist Arguments

Two areas where accommodationist arguments are especially weak are the school prayer context and government display of what I argue in the next chapter are "pure religious objects." The reason accommodationist arguments are so weak in these contexts is because neither context would seem to involve accommodation of religion, but rather they both involve affirmative support for religion in a theologically charged context.[140] Any time religion is accommodated there may be some benefit to religion.[141] Unless that benefit, however, substantially facilitates religion, accommodation may have a role to play in the interpretive process. As will be seen in the next chapter and chapter 10, school prayer and the display of "pure religious objects" do substantially facilitate religion, and thus calling the government sponsorship of such activities "accommodation" is to read into that term the ability to promote religion. It should be obvious that promotion goes further than accommodation even if there is no neat line between the concepts.[142] Such a neat line is unnecessary in the school prayer and symbolism contexts because allowing these practices involves significant promotion of religion generally or a specific religion or religions.[143]

In the landmark school prayer decisions of the early 1960s, Justice Stewart argued in dissent that organized, collective Bible reading and prayer may be a means for the majority of students to express their faiths.[144] He implied that such collective exercises may provide benefits that more individualistic religious exercises do not.[145] While Justice Stewart certainly had a point regarding the differences between collective and individualized religious expression for some,[146] his broader point sounds like a form of majoritarian accommodation, perhaps tweaked with a perception of collective free exercise rights. In more recent cases other dissenting justices have expressed similar points.[147] To the extent that Justice Stewart and the others rely on accommodationism, the arguments are either strained or based in nonpreferentialism.

Any sort of organized school prayer does more than accommodate religion; it promotes religion to some degree.[148] Whether or not school prayer is constitutional can not be determined by relying solely on accommodationist principles. These exercises also raise serious concerns from the equality and separationist perspectives.[149] The liberty principle may point in both directions in such situations (it would most likely be connected to accommodationism where it supported religious exercises).[150] The debate over whether such exercises can ever be constitutional will be left to later chapters, when the ebb and flow of religion clause principles is addressed. For now it is essential to point out that when government promotes or facilitates organized religious exercises it does more than accommodate religion. This does not mean that such exercises may not be perceived as accommodating religion. It simply means that they go well beyond accommodation to promotion. The nonpreferentialist view might support promotion of religion over irreligion,[151] but for the reasons discussed above nonpreferentialism is not a viable form of accommodation that will find its way into the ebb and flow of religion clause principles.

Similarly, when government displays "pure religious objects" as defined in the next chapter, the theologically charged nature of these objects leads to similar concerns.[152] Such displays go well beyond accommodation of religion. Outside a few limited contexts such as museums, the display of these objects cannot be justified on accommodationist grounds.[153] In fact, these objects may present problems even for some nonpreferentialists because they tend to be sectarian, and thus displaying them takes sides among religions.

With the advent of moment of silence laws, equal access policies, and public forums for private religious speech, there are ample opportunities to accommodate religious expression in the public sphere without government promotion of that expression. It is within these types of policies that accommodationism works best in the Establishment Clause context. Otherwise, its primary value is under the Free Exercise Clause. The ebb and flow of accommodationism with other principles of religion clause interpretation will be discussed further in chapter 9. The beauty to the ebb and flow of principles is that accommodationism need not be inherently in tension with separation or any other principle, even in the Establishment Clause context.

8

The Meaning and Recognition of Religion Under the Religion Clauses

The first seven chapters explored the various principles used to interpret the religion clauses. Chapters 9 and 10 will use this analysis to determine valid modes of religion clause interpretation and attempt to craft a workable test based on those modes of interpretation. The purpose of this chapter is to explore a question that is at the heart of the religion clauses, yet is often overlooked or for which an answer is assumed, namely, what is religion? Or, more specifically, what is religion for purposes of interpreting the religion clauses in the First Amendment to the U.S. Constitution? While the question is often overlooked or the answers assumed, there has been quite a bit of excellent writing on this subject.[1]

Several themes emerge from this writing. First, some scholars assert that the definition of religion under the religion clauses should be the same for both the Free Exercise Clause and the Establishment Clause.[2] This group often includes those who view the clauses as a unitary clause.[3] Second, some scholars assert that the definition of religion should be different for the two clauses given their asserted purposes and/or natures.[4] Third, some scholars assert that it is unnecessary or unwise for the courts to attempt to define religion under either or both of the religion clauses because to do so would entangle the courts in the business of determining what is or is not a valid religion.[5] Fourth, some scholars have argued that the definition of religion should vary even within a given clause because of the varied circumstances to which each of the religion clauses must be applied.[6]

With the exception of the third group, most of these scholars either directly accept or reject the Supreme Court's definition of religion, which has often been called the *Welsh/Seeger* test based on the two cases that gave rise to it.[7] Of course, this test was limited to the Free Exercise context, and specifically to the question of conscientious objectors under a statute governing the military.[8] Thus, the Court has never directly defined religion under the Establishment Clause,[9] has done so only in a limited context under the Free Exercise Clause,[10] and has shown a general reticence to get involved in the question of defining religion even though that question often seems highly relevant to outcomes in specific cases.[11] Many scholars have argued for very broad definitions of religion as in *Welsh/Seeger* or narrower definitions that would limit religion to belief in a higher power or even to monotheism specifically.[12]

At a certain level the most persuasive argument is that the courts should not attempt to define religion because they are ill qualified to do so and because of potential religious freedom issues that might result from the attempt.[13] As the examples below will show, however, the question of "what religion is" must be answered in order to address issues that are likely to continue coming before the courts, and eschewing the task can lead to more mischief in religion clause doctrine and theory than engaging the task. The question, What is religion? does not matter in a large number of religion clause cases where it seems obvious the courts are dealing with "religion,"[14] but the answer to that question does matter in a sizable minority of cases, and paying it short shrift creates more problems than it solves. After discussing a potential definition, or set of definitions, for religion, this chapter will look at three areas where the definitions matter quite a bit: (1) religious symbolism cases, (2) cases involving sex education or teaching morality in the public schools, and (3) Free Exercise Clause exemption cases.

A. Defining Religion Under the Religion Clauses

As the preceding discussion should make clear, there are a number of subquestions that arise when one tries to define religion under the religion clauses. In this section I will endeavor to craft a workable definition—or more precisely a set of definitions—of religion while remaining cognizant of these subissues. There will certainly be flaws in this analysis, as the temptation to create a useful framework for courts overwhelms what many theologians understand religion to be. At the same time I will not ignore the lessons of theology in an attempt to unduly simplify religion or create a one-size-fits-all definition that may be pleasing to one side or another in the broader culture wars.

Religion should generally be defined differently under the Free Exercise Clause and the Establishment Clause. In fact, even if one reads the religion clauses as a unitary clause, the definition should still be different in the free exercise and establishment contexts, although the underlying purpose of the establishment and free exercise contexts might be seen as more uniform under the unitary clause approach.[15] The nature and contexts of the two clauses suggest that a single definition is unworkable unless one adopts a definition that includes only organized, deity-focused religions. There are strong arguments for this latter approach if for no other reason its simplicity,[16] but it is far too underinclusive.

Moreover, textual arguments based on the single appearance of the word "religion" in the religion "clauses"[17] do not answer the question unless one reads the clauses in an overly simplistic fashion. Textual arguments usually suggest that because the word appears only once in connection with both clauses, the term must have the same meaning for both clauses. This, of course, ignores the operation of the clauses themselves. If I say, "You shall not make a game or interfere with the ability of others to play," we may know that we are speaking of a "game," but the single use tells us nothing about what games are included or whether the games I might make are the same as the games others might play. The single use of the term "game" tells us little about what it may mean in the context of the two clauses. It could be that the same games are relevant to both or that context changes what games may be affected.

When addressing the religion clauses, an organized, deity-centered approach to defining religion would, for example, exclude Buddhism and some adherents to Reconstructionist Judaism, and in the free exercise context it could lead to questions about whether members of a given faith actually believe in G-d, even if they "follow the tenets" of their faith. A focus on organized, deity-centered religions might also exclude those who believe in a deity, but subscribe to no organized faith. This might exclude many agnostics, but could also exclude those who have deeply held beliefs in an organized set of religious values but no organized venue or co-believers. Ironically, under this definition the religious tenets of Abraham, Jesus, and Muhammad would have been unprotected under the religion clauses until they at least had organized followers.

Thus, a dilemma is posed. If a definition of religion that focuses on organized, theistic traditions is rejected, how can we know what constitutes religion and what constitutes a deeply held belief that is not religious? Where can we draw the line between the religious and the secular?

One option is to follow the Court's approach in *Welsh* and *Seeger*. We would focus on whether a given belief holds the same place in the life of the claimant as traditional religious beliefs would,[18] but this raises problems of its own. It may make some sense in the Free Exercise Clause context, where a broader definition of religion is less likely to exclude free exercise claimants, even if the definition seems a bit overinclusive. Yet the alternative of a deity-focused approach creates an artificial dualism and would exclude a number of traditions widely recognized as religion, even if they share little common theology with theistic religions.[19] Not focusing on a deity, however, can blur the line between core philosophies and religion.[20] The key is that the line is blurred to begin with and any definition adopted may create an artificial dualism that is underinclusive, such as the theistic approach, or overinclusive, such as the *Welsh/Seeger* approach—unless, of course, we recognize the blurry line and try to adopt a set of definitions that are responsive to the various contexts to which the religion clauses are applied.

The fact that the line between deeply held philosophies and religion can be so blurry may account for the courts' general reluctance to define religion. Doing so risks establishing dominant religious views at the expense of less recognized religious views or defining religion in such an expansive way that the definition seems far too broad and alien to most religious believers. This is especially true in the Establishment Clause context, where too broad a definition may include generally accepted secular principles and too narrow a view may itself promote a form of establishment. Yet when one looks at the religious symbolism cases, which are consistently criticized, for example, one of the great flaws is the failure to confront the "religion" question.[21] On the other hand, when one confronts the religion question in cases involving teaching morality or "loaded" secular theories such as human origins in the schools, the temptation to dance around the religion question, or presume an answer to it that is pleasing to dominant preconceptions, is almost too much for courts and commentators to resist.

If one defines religion broadly, it is hard to avoid the argument that secular concepts may occupy a role similar to that of religious belief.[22] Some who have made this argument have bordered on the ridiculous by arguing that the government has established a religion of "secular humanism."[23] Ironically, what is ridiculous about this is not the broader assertion, but rather the conceptual confusion that underlies the assertion. There actually is a group of "secular humanists."[24] They follow documents called the humanist manifestos, often the second one, which eschews any claim to be a religion, but which could certainly be argued to be a religion under the *Welsh/Seeger* test, and perhaps under narrower definitions as well.[25] Their numbers as an organized movement are relatively small.

Two groups are at the forefront of organized "secular humanism" in the United States. The American Humanist Association is the group most directly connected to the humanist manifestos.[26] The second group is the Council on Secular Humanism, which split off from the American Humanist Association in the 1980s.[27] The problem with the claim that "secular humanism" has been established is that it confuses and intertwines "secularism" with "humanism." Certainly some secularists are humanists in a broad sense, but so are many religious folks. In fact, Jesus was arguably a humanist, at least based on many of his teachings, as were many other great religious figures such as Rabbi Hillel.

Secularism and humanism are not necessarily the same thing. While many aspects of classic liberalism—frequently the focus of assertions that there is an established secular humanistic bias—are both secular and humanistic, many aspects of major religions are also humanistic. Moreover, many who buy into the tenets and broader theoretical underpinnings of classic liberalism are religious, while many who reject the theoretical underpinnings of classic liberalism (although not necessarily some of the end principles it leads to) are secular.

Therefore, those who rail against the supposed establishment of "secular humanism" are often really opposing the establishment of secularism, unless of course a government entity attempts to establish the tenets of atheism or the humanist manifestos.[28] The argument that the government is establishing secularism is, however, much weaker conceptually than the straw man of established secular humanism.

Of course, if someone tried to establish atheism in the sense that the former Soviet Union did—that is, to counter religion, which is seen as the "opiate of the people,"[29] there is little doubt that this would easily be considered an establishment of religion, especially because it relates to the ultimate belief in a deity.[30] Another problem would occur if a school district decided to teach the Humanist Manifestos as the ultimate moral truth. The key is that secular humanism implies some underlying organizing philosophy that may occupy a similar place in the life of adherents as religion, and which may in some ways supplant religion.[31] Secularism, on the other hand, especially when practiced by government, may coexist quite nicely with religion.[32] Justice O'Connor pointed this out in her concurring opinion in *ACLU v. McCreary County,* one of the Court's recent "Ten Commandments" cases.[33]

The establishment of a secular state, in the sense that the government is secular, is not by itself inherently antireligious. Religious thinkers from Thomas Aquinas to Roger Williams have recognized this.[34] The real problem is a perceived failure of the courts and government generally to recognize the holistic nature of religion in the life of many believers,[35] but this failure, while often real, is not inherently antireligious.[36] Surely government often acts in a manner that for lack of a better term "establishes" secularism, but this is somewhat question begging because unless secularism itself can be defined as religion, and I suggest above that it can't, the fact that government is establishing secularism is not itself unconstitutional, and we are back to square one.

So how should we define religion under the religion clauses? The answer is that it depends on context. In the free exercise context a broader definition makes a good deal of sense, and given that in most cases courts will be clearly dealing with "religion," any test developed will be primarily used in the harder cases such as *Welsh* and *Seeger.*[37] The crux of the *Welsh/Seeger* test is that there must be a belief system that occupies a place in the life of the adherent similar to that of traditional religion, and that no belief in a higher power in the traditional sense is necessary.[38] This seems useful enough in the conscientious objector cases, but what about other exemption cases? What about political-ethical beliefs that may be said to take on such a role for adherents? For that matter what about a scientist who claims an ordered belief in the scientific method and the "laws of nature"? Or a mathematician who seeks inherent order and higher planes of meaning through math and logic? What about a philosophy like that of the Vulcans in *Star Trek* to act on logic and suppress emotion, which in the *Star Trek* saga was based on the teachings of Surak, a great Vulcan philosopher?[39] Would this be religion or philosophy? If it is religion, how do you differentiate it from those who follow the teachings of John Rawls or those who follow the teachings of Aristotle? If it is not a religion, how do you differentiate it from those who follow the teachings of the Buddha?

The key seems to be to capture the notion that religion must occupy a central role in adherents' understanding of the universe and/or create an ordered set of principles that guide adherents' beliefs and/or behavior, but somehow separate this from general or personal philosophical belief systems. Some have argued that there is no need to separate out such belief systems because there is no reason to privilege "religious" belief systems.[40] This is a respectable argument, but if, as this book suggests, religion is constitutionally important and the Free Exercise Clause is to have any meaning separate from the Free Speech Clause, one must reject this argument.[41] Under the rejected argument, religion and philosophy would be the same thing, and any significant free exercise protection for religion would be dangerous because virtually any belief system might be protected under the Free Exercise Clause. As has been often noted, the broader the definition of religion under the Free Exercise Clause, the less likely courts will be to provide broader protections for it.[42] On the other hand, too narrow a definition risks providing no protection to those whose belief systems fall outside the definition.[43]

The definition proposed in this chapter for the Free Exercise Clause context will undoubtedly raise concern among those on both sides of the debate because it is both broad and narrow, and is an attempt to maximize those who may assert free exercise protection while still maintaining some coherent notion of religion. It takes from the *Welsh/Seeger* test, but is not as broad. Religion under the Free Exercise Clause should include belief systems that are organized around a belief in a deity or deities (or a central belief that there is no deity); other supernatural forces that provide a guiding set of principles or beliefs (this would also include nature-based belief systems that see nature or aspects of nature as holding power beyond that perceived by most people); or a universal or transcendent set of principles, traditions, or truths that guide belief and behavior. The specifics of this approach will be spelled out in section D of this chapter and in later chapters.

The Establishment Clause is an even harder context for defining religion, and in most circumstances doing so is unnecessary as government entities are unlikely to establish more iconoclastic or individual religious beliefs and practices. This may be why the Court has never directly defined religion under the Establishment Clause. Yet in some cases a definition, or at least recognition, of what religion is would aid courts. In the Establishment Clause area the definition of religion could be affected by the context of each case. Thus, the meaning of religion in the context of a religious symbolism case may be different than in a government aid case.

The one thing that the definition should include in all Establishment Clause cases is some core of theological principles or beliefs. These do not necessarily need to be deity related, but they should relate to questions that may be expressed as ultimate truths or goals. Under such an approach Buddhism would be included, as would atheism. The practical reality is that the most likely religions to be involved in Establishment Clause cases are the more dominant religions in American culture, especially Christianity. Demographic shifts may affect this over time and in specific geographic areas as Islam, Buddhism, Hinduism, and Sikhism continue to grow in prominence, but the dominant religions in a given area are likely to be well recognized as religion.

Still, the need to understand and define religion remains in certain contexts. Is a crèche a religious representation, and if so what might this mean for analysis of a government display that includes one? Is an abstinence-only sex education program a representation of religion or something else? Is the highly secularized public school curriculum somehow establishing a religion of secularism? Are the beliefs espoused by intelligent design theorists religion? Those espoused by evolutionists?

The next two sections will attempt to answer the first two of these questions, and in so doing demonstrate how the broad definition above might work. What is involved is really more of a *recognition* of religion than a *definition,* but this is unproblematic in the Establishment Clause context. The other questions will be addressed in chapter 10. The last section of this chapter will be devoted to the definition of religion under the

Free Exercise Clause, and specifically the question of exemptions to laws of general applicability.

B. Religious Symbolism Cases

Imagine that you enter a public park and a theater troupe is performing a version of *The Passion of the Christ* in the center square. A number of signs nearby advertise various products and services, and several street artists perform near the theater troupe. Depending on your background, you may find the story consistent with your religious beliefs, you may be ambivalent, or you may be offended. In any event, you know what the play is about. Is your understanding of the religious significance of the play altered by the presence of the advertisements and the street performers?

Now imagine that instead of a play there is a large Nativity scene, cross, menorah, or Ten Commandments monument and that instead of being in a public park you are on the lawn or in the courtyard or entrance of a municipal building or at the state capitol. Courts have repeatedly struggled with issues raised when the government displays religious objects and symbols or such objects are displayed by others on government property. Cases have involved objects such as Ten Commandments displays,[44] crèches (Nativity scenes),[45] Latin crosses,[46] menorahs,[47] and Christmas trees.[48] The results in these cases, especially in cases decided by the U.S. Supreme Court, have been the subject of a great deal of criticism.[49] The criticism has often focused on the desacralization of religious objects or on the failure to evaluate the impact such objects have on religious outsiders.[50] The courts and those criticizing them have generally overlooked or undervalued the significance of treating religious objects as legal subjects in the first place. In sum, they have ignored or underanalyzed the religion question in religious symbolism cases.

Religious objects and religious symbolism generally do not lend themselves well to analysis under any of the legal tests developed by the Supreme Court,[51] but of course, courts do not have the luxury of ignoring issues related to religious symbolism when such issues are appropriately raised by parties. Nor should they.[52] Both the courts and their critics would face an easier and more fruitful task if they more carefully considered the objects addressed in religious symbolism cases.

This task involves significant interpretive difficulties.[53] When a court evaluates a case involving religious objects, it must subject those objects to the prevailing legal rules, norms, and analysis. It thus makes them legal subjects.[54] This creates interpretive problems because of the potentially varied symbolic meaning of many religious objects and the various messages such objects can hold for various groups.[55] It also raises questions regarding the nature of "religious objects," since many symbolism cases involve objects that courts suggest exude varying levels of religiosity depending on their context,[56] and which some critics suggest may or may not be perceived as religious depending on the perceiver's interpretive presumptions.[57]

Thus, religious symbolism cases raise questions that implicate semiotics and hermeneutics. The symbolic meaning of the objects must be determined and analyzed within an interpretive framework where judges' preconceptions interact with the objects being interpreted.[58] Unfortunately, the semiotic and hermeneutic concerns have been addressed by courts in a reflexive way. This has led to a general failure to adequately explore the power of religious objects and a strong tendency to characterize them in a manner that reinforces a secularized, yet majoritarian, view of religion in public life. By failing to squarely address the religion question, courts frequently reinforce their own preconceptions in religious symbolism cases or, as Justice Jackson has explained, their own prepossessions.[59]

The Supreme Court has tended to focus on the message sent to observers by religious objects.[60] This is a problematic undertaking, however, since the Court has failed to adequately consider the objects "carrying" the message. The Court's approach to religious objects is akin to evaluating a text based on the message it conveys to readers without ever seriously considering the words or structure of the text. It is not that the text has a fixed meaning, but rather that any evaluation of the text would be aided by interacting with the horizon of the text (the range of information that can be seen from the "vantage point" of the text).[61]

This is not to say that extant judicial and academic discourse is useless. Some justices (and commentators) have asked good questions, such as what impact a given religious object has on believers,[62] and what impact it has on religious outsiders.[63] Yet there are even more basic questions that need to be asked in order to adequately analyze the impact of religious objects on believers and nonbelievers alike. What is a religious object? Is there a difference between religious "objects" and religious "symbols"? This section begins by asking and answering some of the threshold questions that have been all but ignored by the Court, but which have a major impact on the issues the Court grapples with in religious symbolism cases.

1. What Is a Religious Object?

Religious objects are powerful representations that may connect to deeply held beliefs.[64] For believers they may be symbols of, and conduits to, transcendent and very real truths.[65] This may have an impact on how such objects are perceived by nonbelievers who are aware of the power such objects have for believers.[66] For others, such objects may retain some of the power they have for believers, or they may simply be things to look at.

Of course, not all religious symbols are religious objects.[67] In fact, behavior, words, events, or ideas may reflect deep religious symbolism.[68] This chapter concerns itself primarily with tangible religious objects because these are what the courts most often grapple with in religious symbolism cases and these cases raise strong questions about the nature and meaning of religion. Still, the question of what constitutes a religious object remains. Courts have dealt with such disparate objects as crosses, crèches, Ten Commandments monuments, menorahs, and Christmas trees. Are all these items "religious objects"? If so, are all religious objects equally "religious," and what do we mean by "religious"?

This subsection will provide a definition of religious objects, or rather a set of definitions. This is necessary to be able to analyze such objects as legal subjects in a nonreflexive way. Before doing this, however, it is essential to get a glimpse of how the Court and some commentators have characterized these objects. The Court's characterization will be discussed in much greater depth below.

In *Lynch v. Donnelly*,[69] Justice Burger writing for the Court described a crèche (Nativity scene) as follows: "The crèche, like a painting is passive; admittedly it is a reminder of the origins of Christmas. Even the traditional, purely secular displays extant at Christmas, with or without a crèche, would inevitably recall the religious nature of the holiday."[70] Putting aside for the moment the highly questionable assertions that a painting is "passive" and that any Christmas display can be "purely secular," the idea that a crèche is "passive" is simply out of touch with well-accepted theological thought regarding religious symbols,[71] as well as at least some anthropological thought.[72] Interestingly, Justice Rehnquist writing for the plurality in *Van Orden v. Perry* referred to the Ten Commandments monument involved in that case as "passive," both before and after acknowledging its religious significance.[73]

A number of commentators have suggested that Justice Burger's description of the holiday display in *Lynch*, which included the crèche, was the result of a reflexive application of his and the other justices' preconceptions regarding such objects. These preconceptions, the argument goes, were both highly secularized and Christocentric.[74] This is a valid critique. One might think that Justice O'Connor's endorsement test would have helped to resolve such concerns given its focus on the message sent by objects,[75] but her concurring opinion in *Lynch* did little to suggest that she viewed the crèche all that differently from the majority.[76] In *Van Orden*, Justice Rehnquist acknowledges that the Ten Commandments are religiously significant, but he does so while attempting to show how they can also have secular relevance[77]—that is, he acknowledges the "religious significance" of the Commandments, but he does not adequately analyze the significance of that "significance." Legal tests in this area seem to operate to reinforce the apparent preconceptions of the justices regarding the nature of specific religious objects or religious objects generally.

Any legal approach to religious objects should account for the fact that they are not just passive "things," but rather powerful conduits for religious meaning and cultural meaning, at least for believers. The *Lynch* Court did not adequately analyze the nature of the crèche. Moreover, to the extent the Court did evaluate the object, it failed to look at what theologians have long understood about the power of religious symbolism.[78] This is also true of the plurality opinion in *Van Orden* and the Court's opinion in *County of Allegheny v. ACLU of Greater Pittsburgh,* where the Court analyzed several religious objects in different settings.[79]

While *Lynch* and *Allegheny* framed the point differently, both Courts were quite focused on the potential message sent by the relevant religious objects in their given setting. This, however, is the wrong inquiry. An object does not send messages as though it were some sort of informational strobe light. Rather, objects hold a range of messages to be discovered by those who interact with them.[80] The observer brings his or her preconceptions to the interaction, and the object holds a range of possible messages for the observer that can be fleshed out as the observer's preconceptions interact with the object.[81] Depending on how reflective the observer is, this process can be instantaneous or play out as the observer interacts with the object.[82] Still, the object holds meaning based on the tradition(s) to which it relates (including its history, religious significance, and cultural significance), and assuming the observer shares or is aware of this tradition, the horizon of the object acts as a constraining force on interpretation.[83]

The theologian Paul Tillich characterized religious symbols as pointing beyond themselves to important religious meaning, while simultaneously participating "in the reality to which [they] point."[84] More specifically, in the context of a broader discussion of religious symbols Tillich wrote: "Religious symbols are double-edged. They are directed toward the infinite which they symbolize *and* toward the finite through which they symbolize it. They force the infinite down to finitude and the finite up to infinity. They open the divine for the human and the human for the divine."[85]

Similarly, anthropologist Clifford Geertz has written that religious symbols "function to synthesize people's ethos—the tone, character, and quality of their life, its moral and aesthetic style and mood—and their world view—the picture they have of the way things in sheer actuality are, their most comprehensive ideas of order."[86] Far from being the passive "things" depicted by the Court, religious symbols, including objects, can point to transcendental truth and are constitutive for the believer. Any attempt to define religious objects, then, must determine what objects possess such traits and what objects do not, as well as how one would define objects that fall in between. Again, the purpose for undertaking this task is simply that courts must treat religious objects as legal subjects, and thus determining the "nature" of these objects to the greatest extent possible is important. One cannot effectively grapple with religious symbolism unless one grapples with the "religion" question.

Tillich and Geertz are from quite different disciplines, yet they both wrote of the power of religious symbols. Of course, while both have been highly influential in their fields, each has been controversial within his respective field. Significantly, their views on religious symbols have generally met with agreement, although that agreement is not universal. The prominent theologian Abraham Joshua Heschel disagreed with Tillich regarding his definition of religious symbols.[87] For present purposes, however, it is significant that Heschel's disagreement with Tillich was over the potential theological pitfalls of symbols rather than the power they hold for believers.[88] While Heschel suggests that religious symbols reduce God to a fiction and demean religion,[89] and thus he rejects Tillich's notion that symbols have any real connection to the divine or the infinite, Heschel acknowledges the power religious symbols have.[90] Thus, his critique of Tillich does not undermine the idea that religious symbols are powerful. Rather, it suggests that power is dangerous rather than wondrous.[91] Moreover, aspects of Catholic theology may be in tension with Tillich's dichotomy between the infinite and the divine, but if anything these differences enhance the theological power of religious objects rather than diminish it.[92]

I refer to Tillich and Geertz here because it seems logical to focus on the religious and cultural impact of religious symbols in an attempt to define if, why, and how they are "religious" for purposes of this chapter. Moreover, Tillich's and Geertz's views of religious symbols are consistent with a wide range of semiotic theory.[93] The key is to understand the power that religious objects have for believers and the potential impact this power may have on believers and nonbelievers when these objects are displayed by government or on government property—that is, are they religious in these contexts?

In order to address the issues raised herein, it is essential to discuss the various types of objects that courts have addressed. These objects generally fall into three categories: (1) pure religious objects, (2) multifaceted religious objects, and (3) secularized religious objects. A deeper analysis of each category will be set forth later after a review of several significant religious symbolism cases. Significantly, the courts intuit, but they generally do not analyze, the different categories into which religious objects fall. In fact, because courts often fail to consider the nature of the religious objects they analyze, they sometimes end up treating "pure religious objects" the same as "secularized religious objects,"[94] and this has created a great deal of mischief in the relevant legal doctrine. As will be seen, paying more attention to the religious objects themselves would make it harder for courts, and specifically the Supreme Court, to reflexively act on preconceptions when analyzing religious objects as legal subjects.

A. PURE RELIGIOUS OBJECTS

Objects of veneration and objects used in religious ritual (as well as some objects that represent core religious principles such as a crèche) can easily be defined as religious objects. This chapter refers to these as "pure religious objects."[95] These objects raise immediate concerns when displayed by government. While a more detailed discussion will be provided later, it is important to note that objects such as crèches, crosses, and menorahs fall into this category. Pure religious objects relate to the rituals or represent the central stories of a given religion as understood by any of the traditions within a religion, or they are venerated.[96] They do not by themselves hold much, if any, secular meaning. They, to use Tillich's conceptualization, point to the infinite.[97] What religious symbols symbolize for a believer is often profound and transcendent, yet the Court's doctrine in the religious symbolism cases does not reflect this.

B. MULTIFACETED RELIGIOUS OBJECTS

Multifaceted religious objects share traits with pure religious objects in that they are relevant to the theology of a given religion or religious tradition. They are not, however, objects used in rituals or objects that are generally venerated.[98] Most important, they are objects that may symbolize deeper religious meaning for believers and nonbelievers, but they may hold widely varying messages even for believers.

Thus, for example, a pure religious symbol like a crèche symbolizes a sacred moment for most devout Christians, and even if theological interpretations and personal and emotional responses vary, the power of the story represented in the crèche is still there for believers.[99] A Ten Commandments monument may or may not elicit the same type of response, especially when it includes other secular symbols or writings. Many believers may respond to the object's symbolism and the powerful religious message that potentially inheres in the Ten Commandments. Others, however, may not. For example, some believers may see it as a political statement (as might many nonbelievers). In fact, other than in synagogues, one rarely sees the depiction of the Ten Commandments in houses of worship, and the Jewish community has not generally been associated with attempts to display the Ten Commandments on government property.

There is more of a disjunction between the symbol and the symbolized with a Ten Commandments monument accompanied by other texts than with a crèche.[100] The former suggests that the Ten Commandments are important, but there is no automatic latent suggestion as to why, whereas the latter represents a more direct and more purely religious message. This might be so even if the Ten Commandments monument does not include other symbols or texts. As will be discussed below, however, this does not mean that Ten Commandments monuments displayed by government are automatically constitutional. In the religious symbolism context, the messages an object may hold for observers are often varied, but the power inhering in the object may crosscut the variety of messages it holds. In the end, multifaceted religious objects may or may not be "religious" for Establishment Clause purposes, but the answer to whether they are or not is not to be found in any formalistic test or formalistic definition of religion.

C. SECULARIZED RELIGIOUS OBJECTS

The final category of religious objects is "secularized religious objects." These are objects generally associated with a particular religion and/or its holidays, but which do not themselves have a specific theological base or which have lost association with any such base even for most believers. These objects are not "religious objects" in the same sense that pure and multifaceted religious objects are, but because courts must sometimes address them, they are included in the present discussion. Secularized religious objects may symbolize a religious holiday or be connected to a religion, but they are not themselves imbued with theological relevance or they have lost their theological relevance over time. Perhaps the best examples of such objects are Christmas trees and Santas. There are significant differences between these objects and "pure religious objects" or "multifaceted religious objects."[101] Yet, as will be seen, the display of secularized religious objects is not always constitutional. The next section will consider how courts have addressed various religious objects. This will help frame a deeper discussion of the various types of religious objects in the legal context.

2. The Religious Symbolism Cases

The U.S. Supreme Court has decided six cases involving the display of religious objects or symbols by government entities or on public property. In *Lynch v. Donnelly*,[102] and in *County of Allegheny v. ACLU*,[103] the Court addressed the display of Nativity scenes—crèches—by government entities. *County of Allegheny* also involved the display of a large menorah next to an even larger Christmas tree accompanied by a sign saluting liberty.[104] In *Stone v. Graham*,[105] the Court addressed a Kentucky statute that required a copy of the Ten Commandments to be placed on a wall in all public school classrooms in the state. More recently, in *McCreary County v. ACLU of Kentucky*,[106] the Court struck down courthouse displays in two Kentucky counties that included the Ten Commandments. And in *Van Orden v. Perry*,[107] the Court upheld the display of a Ten Commandments monument on the grounds of the Texas state capitol. Finally, in *Capitol Square Review and Advisory Board v. Pinette*,[108] the Court addressed the placement of a large cross on government property that was deemed a public forum. In *Capitol Square,* the public forum issue was dispositive of the outcome. In addition, a number of lower court decisions have addressed everything from large Latin crosses[109] to Ten Commandments monuments.

This section will set forth the ways in which courts have approached a variety of religious objects and symbols. The section will be organized around the objects themselves, with separate subsections devoted to crèches, crosses, menorahs, Ten Commandments displays, Christmas trees, and other holiday displays. Naturally, some of these objects overlap in a given display, and this too will be discussed. A major focus, however, will be Ten Commandments displays because of some of the unique and important questions they raise.

A. CRÈCHES

In *Lynch,* the Court considered whether a crèche (a Nativity scene) that was placed in a park in Pawtucket, Rhode Island, as part of a larger Christmas display that included such things as a Santa Claus house and plastic reindeer, violated the Establishment Clause.[110] The city owned the display and clearly supported and sponsored its erection in the park.[111] Thus, this was a case involving a government-supported display. The Court held the display was constitutional, ostensibly applying the *Lemon* test, which was the then prevailing test for Establishment Clause claims.[112] In applying that test, the Court utilized analysis similar to that it had used in *Marsh v. Chambers*[113] to uphold the practice of legislative prayer. The Court noted the long history of various forms of government interaction with religion, such as legislative chaplains. The Court acknowledged the religious meaning of the crèche, yet held that holiday displays like that in Pawtucket are part of a long tradition connected to the winter holiday season and that Christmas has a secular aspect in addition to its religious aspects.[114]

The Court focused heavily on the importance of the broader context of the display, which included "a Santa Claus house, reindeer pulling a sleigh, candy-striped poles, a Christmas tree, carolers, cutout figures" of a "clown, an elephant, and a teddy bear, hundreds of colored lights, [and] a large banner that [read] 'Seasons Greetings'. . . ."[115] It also noted the display's connection to the secular and commercial aspects of the holiday. In this context the display as a whole represented the secular aspects of Christmas.[116] Thus, while the crèche is a religious symbol,[117] it did not foster a government establishment of religion in the context of the broader display and the holiday season because that context demonstrated both a secular purpose and a primary effect that neither advanced nor inhibited religion.[118] In a passage that has particular import, the Court referred to the crèche as "passive."[119] The Court also found no entanglement because of the low cost of the display and held that political divisiveness, which was an element of entanglement at that time, was insufficient by itself to support an Establishment Clause claim.[120] In short, the Court acknowledged that a crèche is a religious symbol but essentially ignored or minimized any significant discussion of the challenged object or its religious relevance.

In a concurring opinion, Justice O'Connor introduced the "endorsement test."[121] While many people have questioned Justice O'Connor's application of that test in *Lynch*,[122] the test itself has become highly influential, especially in cases involving government-supported or government-endorsed religious symbols.[123] Justice O'Connor wrote:

The Establishment Clause prohibits government from making adherence to a religion relevant in any way to a person's standing in the political community. Government can run afoul of that prohibition in two principal ways. One is excessive entanglement with religious institutions, which may interfere with the independence of the institutions, give the institutions access to government or governmental powers not fully shared by nonadherents of the religion, and foster the creation of political constituencies defined along religious lines (citation omitted). The second and more direct infringement is government endorsement or disapproval of religion. Endorsement sends a message to nonadherents that they are outsiders, not full members of the political community, and an accompanying message to adherents that they are insiders, favored members of the political community. Disapproval sends the opposite message.[124]

Later in her concurring opinion she characterized the inquiry into the display as follows:

> The central issue in this case is whether Pawtucket has endorsed Christianity by its display of the crèche. To answer that question, we must examine both what Pawtucket intended to communicate in displaying the crèche and what message the City's display actually conveyed. The purpose and effect prongs of the *Lemon* test represent these two aspects of the meaning of the City's action.[125]

As has been pointed out repeatedly in the scholarly literature, Justice O'Connor's application of this test—a test that was at least ostensibly concerned with religious ingroup/outgroup dynamics in the political realm —seemed to betray the words of the test.[126] This is especially vivid when one learns in the dissenting opinions that the city and mayor supported keeping "Christ in Christmas."[127] Justice O'Connor found that the city's purpose was not to endorse Christianity, but rather to celebrate the secular aspects of a public holiday that has "cultural significance."[128] Her discussion of effects follows a similar line of reasoning:

> Pawtucket's display of its crèche, I believe, does not communicate a message that the government intends to endorse the Christian beliefs represented by the crèche. Although the religious and indeed sectarian significance of the crèche, as the district court found, is not neutralized by the setting, the overall holiday setting changes what viewers may fairly understand to be the purpose of the display—as a typical museum setting, though not neutralizing the religious content of a religious painting, negates any message of endorsement of that content. The display celebrates a public holiday, and no one contends that declaration of that holiday is understood to be an endorsement of religion. The holiday itself has very strong secular components and traditions. . . ."[129]

Thus, while Justice O'Connor would have applied a different test than the *Lynch* majority, her analysis under that test is quite similar to the majority's approach. In fact, she acknowledges this in her concurring opinion.[130] The physical context of the crèche figures prominently in her analysis, as does the privileging or desacralization, depending on one's perspective, of Christmas.[131] Justice Brennan filed a dissenting opinion joined by Justices Blackman, Marshall, and Stevens,[132] and Justice Blackman filed a dissenting opinion joined by Justice Stevens.[133] The dissenting opinions pointed out that had the Court applied the *Lemon* test in the manner it had in other cases under the Establishment Clause, the government-sponsored crèche would not have survived scrutiny.[134] Justice Brennan's dissenting opinion also pointed out that placing a patently religious symbol representing an event central to Christian theology in the context of a broader display of items connected to the Christmas holiday is likely to favor the dominant Christian tradition, and thus could not be saved by relying on the commercialized aspects of the holiday.[135] Such government action favoring one religion would violate the *Lemon* test.[136] Moreover, both dissents argued that by minimizing the religious import of the crèche in the context of the display, the Court both degraded the religious meaning of the symbol and the holiday, and failed to address the exclusionary message the display sent to non-Christians.[137] Thus, the dissents at least attempted to grapple with the "religion" question.

In *Allegheny,* the Court also addressed a crèche display.[138] As will be discussed below, that case also involved the display of a menorah and a Christmas tree. The Court's analysis of the crèche utilized the endorsement approach set forth by Justice O'Connor in *Lynch*.[139] As in *Lynch,* the physical context of the crèche display was central to the Court's decision.[140] The crèche was owned by the Holy Name Society, a Roman Catholic organization, and was located on the grand staircase of the county courthouse. It was not surrounded by sundry plastic figures and other "secular" symbols of the "holiday season" as had been the crèche in *Lynch*.[141] Instead, it was surrounded on three sides by a wooden fence, and red and white poinsettia plants were placed around the crèche.[142] There was a sign denoting that the crèche was donated by the Holy Name Society, and there were also two small evergreen trees decorated with red bows, but these basically blended into the manger scene depicted in the crèche.

Justice Blackmun, writing for the Court, held that the display of the crèche violated the Establishment Clause because unlike the crèche in *Lynch,* the one in the Allegheny County courthouse sent a message endorsing Christianity, and "nothing in the crèche's setting detract[ed] from that message."[143] Government may "acknowledge Christmas as a cultural phenomenon," but may not celebrate it as a "Christian holy day."[144] The crèche, which has an obvious religious message, is a celebration of the religious aspects of the holiday.[145] Interestingly, *Lynch* and *Allegheny* together stand for the proposition that a patently religious symbol, the crèche, can somehow become adequately secularized if part of a larger holiday display celebrating the "secular aspects" of Christmas.[146] The

Court does not hold that the crèche loses its religious nature based on its context, but rather that in some contexts its religious message is appropriately secularized such that government may display it.[147] This argument is inconsistent with the general understanding of religious objects and symbols.

B. CROSSES

Perhaps the most famous case involving the display of a cross on government property is *Capitol Square Review Board v. Pinette*,[148] which involved the display of a large cross on the grounds of the Ohio state capitol. The cross was placed there by the Ku Klux Klan, a notorious hate group.[149] The Court held that the square was a public forum for speech purposes.[150] Because the government wanted to exclude the cross from the square and the square was a public forum, the state needed to show a compelling governmental interest to support the exclusion of the religious message.[151] This is because the state's actions in attempting to exclude the cross constituted content discrimination. The state's reason for excluding the cross was compliance with the Establishment Clause. The Court acknowledged that compliance with the Establishment Clause could constitute a compelling government interest,[152] but the state's action in this case was not mandated by the Establishment Clause because the Establishment Clause does not prohibit private religious expression in a public forum.[153] Thus, the state could not exclude the cross without violating the Free Speech Clause.[154] The question of the cross's religious nature was irrelevant given the free speech basis for the Court's conclusion.[155] Thus, the debates between the plurality and the concurring and dissenting justices will not be addressed here.

While *Capitol Square* is the only U.S. Supreme Court case involving the display of a cross on government property, there are a number of cases in the lower courts. Significantly, many of these cases involve government display of crosses rather than private displays in a public forum. For example, in *Separation of Church and State Committee v. City of Eugene*,[156] the U.S. Court of Appeals for the Ninth Circuit held that a fifty-one-foot-tall concrete Latin cross that had been erected in a public park and subsequently designated a war memorial violated the Establishment Clause.[157] The cross was illuminated on certain holidays.[158] In a per curiam opinion the court held that the display endorsed Christianity:

> There is no question that the Latin cross is a symbol of Christianity, and that its placement on public land by the City of Eugene violates the Establishment Clause. Because the cross may reasonably be perceived as government endorsement of Christianity, the City of Eugene has impermissi-

bly breached the First Amendment's "wall of separation" between church and state. (footnote omitted)[159]

Thus, the court acknowledged in unequivocal terms that the cross is a religious symbol. There have been a surprising number of similar cases decided under the federal Constitution and several state constitutions. Most of these cases seem to treat crosses as pure religious symbols.

C. MENORAHS

As noted earlier, the *Allegheny* decision also addressed the placement of a menorah outside the city-county building.[160] The menorah was owned by Chabad-Lubavich, a Hasidic Jewish group,[161] and was placed near a large Christmas tree and a sign saluting liberty.[162] The Court acknowledged the religious nature and history of the menorah and the holiday of Hanukkah,[163] to which the menorah is related.[164] Yet the Court held that the context of the menorah—situated near the Christmas tree and a sign saluting liberty—did not endorse Judaism or religion generally.[165] Rather, the Court held the display sent a message recognizing religious pluralism and cultural diversity.[166] The Court viewed the display as representing the winter holiday season rather than a specific religion or holiday.[167] In her concurring opinion, Justice O'Connor stressed that the message sent by the display to a reasonable observer was a message of tolerance and good tidings for the holiday season.[168] Even though the majority opinion contained a rather detailed discussion of the theological and historical relevance of the menorah, the Court's approach demonstrates that there is an important difference between explaining the history of a religious object, or even discussing its role in ritual or theology, and carefully considering what an object's theological or ritualistic role says about the object.

Justices Brennan and Stevens authored opinions dissenting from the Court's holding regarding the menorah.[169] Justice Brennan, joined by Justices Marshall and Stevens, agreed with the majority that Hanukkah and the menorah are religious, but they disagreed that the context of the display could adequately secularize the menorah.[170] Interestingly, Justice Brennan also questioned the notion that the Christmas tree was necessarily a secular symbol even if it could be in some contexts,[171] but ultimately he focused primarily on the meaning and message of the menorah. In his view the menorah was purely a religious object.[172] Justice Stevens, in an opinion joined by Justices Brennan and Marshall, argued that "the Establishment Clause should be construed to create a strong presumption against the display of religious symbols on public property."[173] Both Justice Brennan and Justice Stevens were concerned that the Court's decision would offend both believers and nonbelievers by minimizing the religious meaning of the object involved—in this case a menorah—and by minimizing the impact such displays have on religious outsiders and nonbelievers.[174] A number of lower courts have followed the *Allegheny* Court's analysis.

D. TEN COMMANDMENTS DISPLAYS

In *Stone v. Graham*,[175] the Court held that a Kentucky law requiring the posting of the Ten Commandments in every public school classroom in the state violated the Establishment Clause. The law required the inclusion of a notation "concerning the purpose of the display," which focused on the "secular application of the Ten Commandments" in legal codes.[176] *Stone* is a short per curium opinion,[177] but it is notable for purposes of the discussion herein. Specifically, the Court stated, "The Ten Commandments are undeniably a sacred text in the Jewish and Christian faith, and no legislative recitation of a supposed secular purpose can blind us to that fact."[178] As this passage suggests, the Court held that the law failed the secular purpose prong of the *Lemon* test because there was no valid secular purpose for mandating the posting of a sacred text on the walls of every public school classroom in the state.[179]

Whatever potential this language from *Stone* had to get the Court to seriously consider the impact of the religious nature of religious objects was never realized. In subsequent cases the Court paid lip service to the historical or theological relevance of religious objects, but any serious consideration of the power these objects hold ended there.[180] This trend continued in the Court's most recent Ten Commandments decisions, which also added confusion regarding the principles and legal tests applicable in religious symbolism cases.[181]

In *ACLU v. McCreary County*,[182] the Court held that Ten Commandments displays in two separate county courthouses were unconstitutional. The Court relied on the secular purpose prong of the *Lemon* and endorsement tests. The history of the displays in question played a significant role in the Court's analysis. Each of the displays originally consisted of a framed copy of the Ten Commandments taken from the King James Version of the Bible.[183] The courthouse displays were readily visible to those using the courthouse. In response to a lawsuit aimed at forcing the counties to remove the displays, the counties modified the displays to include a variety of other documents, including "an excerpt from the Declaration of Independence . . . the Preamble to the Kentucky constitution . . . the national motto of 'In God We Trust' . . . [and] a page from the Congressional Record" declaring 1983 the year of the Bible.[184] Each of the documents mentioned G-d, and some documents were edited to include only the religious references contained in them.[185] The district court granted the plaintiffs' request for a preliminary injunction despite these modifications to the displays.

In response, the counties posted a third version of the displays that included fuller versions of some of the same documents contained in the second version, but also included some additional documents that did not reference G-d.[186] The new displays also included a "prefatory document" that claimed the displays contained "documents that played a significant role in the foundation of our system of law and government."[187] This document suggested that the Ten Commandments influenced the Declaration of Independence but made no attempt to connect the Ten Commandments to the other items in the display.[188] This unsubstantiated connection was highly relevant to the Court of Appeals and also played a role in the Supreme Court's decision.

The majority opinion was authored by Justice Souter.[189] The opinion focused heavily on the history of the display and the lack of a secular purpose evinced by that history. The Court's analysis begins with a promising quotation from *Stone* recognizing that the Ten Commandments "are undeniably a sacred text in the Jewish and Christian faiths,"[190] but rather than analyze that point or what it might mean under the Establishment Clause, the Court moves into its secular purpose analysis, recognizing that the *Stone* Court found the religious nature of the text relevant in determining that there was no secular purpose.[191] The Court's secular purpose analysis utilizes the *Lemon* test, but explains that the purpose analysis in that test is meant to assure government neutrality between religions "and between religion and nonreligion."[192] The Court then applies endorsement analysis, explaining that when government favors religion or a particular religion, it sends a message to "nonadherents 'that they are outsiders, not full members of the political community, and an accompanying message to adherents that they are insiders, favored members" of the political community.[193]

The majority rejects the counties' invitation to reject or minimize the secular purpose test. Explaining why analysis of secular purpose is possible and not simply an exercise in getting into government actors' heads, Justice Souter writes: "The eyes that look to purpose belong to an 'objective observer,' one who takes account of the traditional external signs that show up in the 'text, legislative history, and implementation of the statute,' or comparable official act."[194] According to the Court, if an objective observer would perceive the predominant purpose behind a government action as religious, the government is "taking religious sides."[195] In determining what an objective observer would perceive, the history and context of the display—of which the observer is presumed to be aware—are quite important.[196]

The Court recognized that the *Stone* Court had found the Commandments to be an "instrument of religion," and that this was decisive under the facts in that case.[197] Still, the Court held that there is no per se rule against displaying the Ten Commandments under all circumstances.[198] At this point in the opinion the analysis gets quite interesting, at least in relation to the points made here. Justice Souter acknowledges the theological significance of the Commandments and the impact of their divine origin.[199] In so doing, he points out that the text of the Commandments is a powerful indication of their religious nature and the likely religious purpose in displaying them. The opinion notes that where the text is absent, it is less likely that an observer will perceive the depiction of tablets, and so forth, as religious; conversely, when the text is present, "the insistence of the religious message is hard to avoid" absent a context that suggests "a message going beyond an excuse to promote [a] religious point of view."[200] As a result, when the government places the text of the Commandments "alone in public view"—as the counties did in the first of the three displays—the religious purpose is obvious.[201] Moreover, surrounding the text with other historical documents, whose main connection is that they contain religious references, would only make a reasonable observer more likely to perceive a religious purpose.[202]

The counties' third display, which included a number of secular documents and the text of the Ten Commandments, was ostensibly intended to represent the foundations of American law.[203] The Court recognized that in a vacuum such a display might have a secular purpose,[204] but in light of the history of the courthouse displays and the odd choices of historical documents—that is, including the Magna Carta and Declaration of Independence but not the Constitution or the Fourteenth Amendment—the displays could not survive secular purpose analysis.[205] The Court found especially odd attempts to link the Ten Commandments, with their divine origin, and the Declaration of Independence, which derives governmental power from the people.[206]

The Court held that neutrality, although an elusive and variable concept, is an important focus of the religion clauses because the framers were concerned about the civic divisiveness that can be caused when the government takes sides in religious debates.[207] This militates against the constitutionality of government displays that evince a religious purpose.[208] The Court rejects the dissent's brand of strict originalism because there are historical arguments that support both sides. Additionally, given the long line of precedent recognizing neutrality as a guiding principle, the Court does not find the dissent's reading of history persuasive.[209]

Justice O'Connor, who joined the majority, filed a concurring opinion.[210] She argued that given the religious divisiveness in nations without some level of separation and given the success of the American experiment with separation—both for religion and for society more generally—it makes little sense to reject core Establishment Clause principles and allow the government to favor one religion or set of religions over others or over nonreligion.[211] She cited the American tradition of religious voluntarism, and wrote that when government endorses one religious tradition or another it can distort the marketplace of ideas and foster divisiveness.[212]

Justice Scalia filed a strongly worded dissent, which was joined by Justice Thomas and Chief Justice Rehnquist, and in part by Justice Kennedy.[213] Justice Scalia relied on originalist arguments to assert that the government can endorse monotheistic religious traditions so long as it does not discriminate against other religious views or play favorites when it comes to funding or other aid.[214] Justice Scalia pointed to a number of statements and actions by various framers endorsing monotheism, as well as to a number of historical practices that do the same.[215] As Justice Souter points out, Justice Scalia's history is quite selective, and it leaves out other historical information that may suggest support for a broader separation or that may suggest a favoring not of monotheism as a broader concept, but rather of specific Protestant religious views.[216] Justice Kennedy did not join this portion of the dissenting opinion. Justice Scalia also criticizes the majority for its focus on secular purpose, arguing that determining legislative purpose is not a fruitful task for the judiciary and that purpose analysis can cause a great deal of mischief.[217] Justice Scalia looks to legal coercion or disparagement as the appropriate test, and he finds both lacking in this case and in all cases involving "passive" religious displays.

Interestingly, Justice Scalia does acknowledge the religious nature of the Ten Commandments, but he morphs them into some sort of nonsectarian, monotheistic acknowledgment of a common heritage.[218] This ignores the fact that the text involved in this case came from the King James Version of the Bible and it ignores the power involved in that choice, but at least Justice Scalia is forthright about the religious nature of the Commandments themselves. Unfortunately, like the majority, he does little to openly discuss the implications of the religious nature of the object. In fact, and interestingly given his rejection of endorsement-type analysis, Justice Scalia argues that the context of the displays dispel any argument that they lack a secular purpose. Rather, he argues the displays manifests a purpose to recognize the influence of the Commandments on American law and the long-standing and common practices of the nation.[219]

Van Orden v. Perry[220] and *McCreary County,* though decided the same day, seem to conflict with each other. *Van Orden* is a split decision. Justice Rehnquist wrote the opinion for a plurality of justices. Significantly, there are four justices in the plurality and four dissenting justices. Thus, Justice Breyer's opinion concurring in the judgment seems to be the key opinion. This is quite similar to the famous *Bakke* case,[221] where the Court was split four to four and Justice Powell's concurring opinion became the key precedent.[222] Unfortunately, Justice Breyer's opinion seems more a policy compromise than a guidepost for future Courts, albeit a reasonable policy compromise.[223] Before addressing Justice Breyer's concurrence, however, it is useful to address the plurality opinion.

The case involved the display of a Ten Commandments monument on the ground between the Texas state capitol building and the state supreme court building.[224] The monument was one of a number of monuments scattered around the grounds of the capitol. Its location did not call any special attention to it. The monument was donated in 1961 by the Fraternal Order of Eagles, which paid the cost of erecting it.[225] There was little evidence of the legislative intent behind accepting the monument, and there was no evidence of the sort of religiously motivated purpose evident in *McCreary County.*[226]

The plurality opinion begins by asserting that the Establishment Clause has a dual nature. It recognizes "the strong role played by religion and religious traditions throughout our nation's history," and at the same time it recognizes that "governmental intervention in religious matters can itself endanger religious freedom."[227] The plurality applies analysis quite similar to that applied in *Lynch*; it does not apply either the *Lemon* or endorsement tests.[228] Thus, the plurality focuses on the "unbroken history of official acknowledgments by all three branches of government of the role of religion in American life . . ." as asserted in *Lynch.*[229] The plurality also discusses the religious monuments and sculptures adorning federal buildings in the District of Columbia, including the Supreme Court. This is all used as evidence that the Ten Commandments can have a secular meaning as well as a religious meaning, namely, the Decalogue's historical role in American law and culture.[230] Significantly, this seems to conflict with the Court's earlier holding in *Stone,*[231] but the plurality distinguishes *Stone,* arguing *Stone* involved the public schools, where heightened Establishment Clause analysis has generally been applied.[232]

From the perspective of this chapter, there are two especially significant aspects of the plurality opinion. First, it repeats the argument from *Lynch* that religious objects can be "passive."[233] Second, it creates an artificial dualism like that in *Lynch,* which suggests that monuments such as the one in Texas can have "a dual significance, partaking of both religion and government."[234] The argument seems to be that so long as the monument "partakes" of an appropriate secular "significance," the religious "significance," while still there, is somehow sterilized for Establishment Clause purposes.[235] As is explained elsewhere in this book, that argument is flawed. The dual nature suggested by the plurality may, however, be a recognition of the fact that Ten Commandments displays are multifaceted.

Justice Thomas wrote a concurring opinion repeating his call in earlier cases to reevaluate incorporation of the Establishment Clause,[236] and arguing that to the extent that clause is incorporated, the touchstone of Establishment Clause analysis should be legal coercion.[237] A refreshing aspect of Justice Thomas's opinion is that he openly acknowledges and engages with the religious nature of religious objects,[238] even if the conclusions he draws from that engagement are questionable.[239] In relation to the *Newdow* (Pledge of Allegiance) case[240] and the religious objects cases Justice Thomas wrote:

> Telling either nonbelievers or believers that the words "under God" have no meaning contradicts what they know to be true. Moreover, repetition does not deprive religious words or symbols of their traditional meaning. . . .
>
> Even when this Court's precedents recognize the religious meaning of symbols or words, that recognition fails to respect fully religious belief or disbelief. . . .[241]

Justice Thomas goes on to point out that the Court's endorsement approach "either gives insufficient weight to the views of nonadherents and adherents alike, or it provides no principled way to choose between those views."[242] Unfortunately, rather than analyze what the nature of religious symbols might have to say about their constitutionality from the perspective of the objects themselves, Justice Thomas ends up relying on his view of the intent of the framers to find that displaying such objects is constitutional.[243] Thus, while he comes close to seriously engaging the power of these objects, he, like the other justices, falls back into a contested doctrinal argument, in this case one based on history.

Several themes emerge in Justice Breyer's concurring opinion. First, Justice Breyer views this as a "borderline" case to which no legal test can be appropriately applied.[244] This leaves only the "exercise of legal judgment" for determining the outcome.[245] Justice Breyer stresses, however, that such legal judgment is "not a personal judgment: "Rather . . . it must reflect and remain faithful to the underlying purposes of the clauses, and it must take account of context and consequences measured in light of those purposes."[246] Second, Justice Breyer, like the plurality, writes that the purpose of the Establishment Clause is maintaining some level of separation between church and state while avoiding hostility to religion, although it seems clear that Justice Breyer weighs these factors differently than the plurality.[247] Third, Justice Breyer asserts that avoiding religious divisiveness is a major goal of the Establishment Clause, but this can cut both ways.[248] Therefore, the type of religious purpose evidenced in *McCreary County* is unconstitutional, but so would be attempts by the "government to purge from the public sphere all that in any way partakes of the religious."[249] Fourth, Justice Breyer argues that long-standing religious displays do not generally raise the same Establishment Clause concerns as new attempts to display religious objects, because the long-standing displays are less likely to be divisive, assuming their context and purpose adequately secularize them.[250] This seems to be an attempt to protect against Establishment Clause challenge most long-standing government displays that include religious themes—recognition of a form of symbolic ceremonial deism, if you will.

Unfortunately, like the plurality—in fact, even more so than the plurality—Justice Breyer argues for a dualistic (or triadic) analysis of the symbolic meaning of the Ten Commandments. He argues that the Commandments, while religious, can also represent "a secular moral message" and in some contexts "a historical message."[251] He uses these potential secular messages, in light of the physical and historical context of the monument, to argue that the display in this case was meant to reflect Texas's moral and historical traditions and not the religious aspects of the display.[252] Thus, like the plurality, Justice Breyer seems to recognize the Ten Commandments' multifaceted nature without seriously considering the impact of the religious facets of the monument. Like the plurality, he essentially argues that the religious aspects of the monument, while there, are appropriately desacralized. Unlike the plurality, however, Justice Breyer engages in an endorsement-like analysis even as he argues that no legal test can be applied to borderline cases.[253] Justice Breyer rejects most of the plurality's reasoning and seems to carve out a narrow group of cases involving long-standing religious monuments or displays whose physical and historical context make them appear less divisive than they might appear in other historical or physical settings.

Justice Stevens wrote a dissenting opinion that focuses heavily on the religious nature of the Ten Commandments and, more important, takes the question of the Commandments' religiosity seriously.[254] He, like Justice Thomas, does not believe that context can detract from the religious meaning of the Commandments, at least not when the full text of the

Commandments is displayed.[255] He also points out the intense theological disputes that can arise in relation to the choice of text for the Commandments. Like the majority in *McCreary County,* Justice Stevens focuses heavily on the concepts of neutrality and separation.[256] He expresses great concern about the potential divisiveness of a display with such obvious theological significance. In light of that theological significance, he distinguishes displays of the Ten Commandments that focus on the Commandments' text from other displays with religious content the Court has upheld.[257] In his view, such displays inherently create religious insiders and outsiders and thus violate the neutrality and separation principles.[258]

Justice Stevens also attacks the plurality and Justice Scalia (in his *McCreary County* dissent) for relying on isolated statements of the framers and on the framers' contemporary practices. He notes that persuasive evidence exists to counter that history with a more separationist version and that the sectarian nature of a Ten Commandments display has little to do with the practices supported by history and the nation's long-standing traditions regarding public acknowledgment of religion.[259] Essentially, he rejects the hard originalist approach as being indeterminate and the tradition approach as being irrelevant under these facts. He also notes that if one wanted to take a true hard originalist approach, it would be possible to support religious discrimination and favoritism by the states against non-Protestants (and against many Protestant groups as well).[260] Justice Stevens comes closest to taking the "religious" in religious objects seriously, but his analysis remains external to the objects, and thus it differs from that suggested in this book.[261]

Justice Souter wrote a dissenting opinion in which he argues that the context of the Texas display, especially the fact that the full text of the Commandments appears on the monument, demonstrates a form of religious favoritism that violates the neutrality principle (and implicitly endorses religion).[262] He argues that unless context alters the message, government cannot display "an obviously religious text" consistently with the neutrality principle. Justice Souter looks at the purposes of the Fraternal Order of Eagles in donating the monument and the state's purpose for placing it on the capitol grounds, as well as the physical attributes of the monument—which included sizing and capitalizing words that reinforce the most religious aspects of the text—and concludes that the state was clearly sending a religious message by displaying the monument.[263] Justice Souter specifically notes that the Ten Commandments are a divine injunction to follow the laws stated therein and that the monument was designed so as to accentuate the divine.[264]

The physical setting on the twenty-two-acre capitol grounds along with sixteen other monuments does not alter the message sent by the

Commandments because there is no common theme among the monuments.[265] Justice Souter does argue, however, that Ten Commandments displays—especially those not including the text of the Commandments—would be constitutional if they are appropriately contextualized by other objects to suggest that the total display is about the historical role of the Commandments in Western law.[266] He chides the plurality for relying on generalities in earlier cases rather than on more relevant cases such as *Stone*,[267] and he argues the plurality's attempt to limit *Stone* to the classroom setting was against the lessons of that case and other precedent.[268]

In addition to the Supreme Court opinions there have been a number of lower court opinions involving Ten Commandments displays in recent years.[269] These cases are a mixed bag when it comes to analyzing the religious aspects of religious objects. Because these courts are bound by the Supreme Court's doctrine, which generally fails to seriously address the religion question, most of these opinions do not do so either.[270] The important thing for present purposes is that Ten Commandments displays have been characterized in different ways by different courts (and sometimes in different ways by the same court). Thus, they have been characterized as purely religious, as multifaceted, and as secularized by their context. Most Ten Commandments monuments are multifaceted, and the various characterizations of such monuments are evidence of their multifaceted nature.

E. CHRISTMAS TREES AND OTHER HOLIDAY DISPLAYS

The constitutionality of the display of Christmas trees and other similar holiday displays by government was essentially resolved by the Court's reasoning in *Lynch* and *Allegheny*, where the Court presumed such displays were constitutional.[271] The opinions of the Court in both cases scarcely questioned the constitutionality of Christmas trees and objects such as Santas, elves, and plastic reindeer. Even Justice Brennan's opinion concurring in part and dissenting in part in *Allegheny*, which suggests that a Christmas tree can have significant religious meaning in some contexts, seems to assume that a Christmas tree by itself is not a religious object.[272] Lower courts have followed suit. As will be seen, such analysis—or lack thereof—is problematic.

The next section will address some common critiques of the legal doctrine in religious symbolism cases. This doctrine has generally been considered a morass by all sides in the debate. This will be followed by a section on the problems inherent in treating religious objects as legal subjects. That section directly confronts the implications of the preceding discussion for the definition or recognition of religion in the religious object cases.

3. Critiques of the Prevailing Legal Doctrines

The doctrine developed by the Court in religious symbolism cases has been the subject of intense criticism. While this criticism is quite rich and diverse, it generally falls into one (or more) of four broad categories. I have labeled these the artificial secularization critique, the majoritarian dominance critique, the contextual critique, and the traditionalism critique. Moreover, scholars have questioned the efficacy of the "endorsement test" and looking at the "message(s) sent" by a given government action more broadly.[273] The discussion in this section is very basic, but the fact that so many scholars (and judges) have criticized the Court's religious symbolism cases from so many perspectives is evidence of the doctrine's failure to address the nature of religion in religious object cases, even if many of the critics do not recognize this. The problems that arise in religious symbolism cases are inherent to reflexively treating religious objects as legal subjects. The following critiques are not necessarily separate, and many commentators have used a combination of some or all of them. The following is a brief description of each of the critiques.

The artificial secularization critique suggests that the Court's doctrine in religious symbolism cases leads to an artificial characterization of religious objects that eviscerates, ignores, or minimizes their religious nature and messages.[274] One might also refer to it as the "desacralization critique." As Steven Smith has pointed out, the Court never held in *Lynch* that the crèche lost its religious nature by inclusion in a broader holiday display.[275] Yet those who have criticized the Court for its desacralization of religious objects in the religious symbolism cases have a valid concern.

While the Court never held that the crèche in *Lynch* and the menorah in *Allegheny* were any less religious objects because of their inclusion in broader displays, the Court did hold that the religious message sent by the objects was appropriately secularized.[276] The idea that sacred objects can be robbed of their sacred meaning by placement in a broader display is not in keeping with the general understanding of the nature of religious objects and symbols. The plurality opinion in *Van Orden,* which asserts that objects can maintain their religious nature while also having a nonreligious nature,[277] does not alleviate this critique both because the plurality relies on *Lynch*-like reasoning and because the plurality uses the dual nature of the object in a manner that essentially desacralizes the Commandments. Moreover, the fact that some people may not perceive a religious message in these contexts is not all that surprising because it is unlikely that everyone will fully perceive the religious power of the objects even without the added context of the broader display.

The critique naturally addresses the serious problems with the Court's attempt to use physical or thematic context to desacralize a religious object or symbol.[278] Religious objects and symbols hold powerful meaning for believers. They are not, contrary to the Court's assertion in *Lynch,* passive.[279] Physical or thematic context cannot take away the deeply spiritual meaning many devout Christians perceive when viewing a crèche.[280] At most the believer might feel that the broader context of a crèche demeans its sacred meaning when that context includes other objects, but that does not minimize the sacred meaning of the crèche itself. The artificial secularization critique recognizes this fact and suggests that viewing religious displays through the "lowest"—secularized—common denominator demeans the religious nature of the objects displayed.

The majoritarian dominance critique suggests that the Court's doctrine in religious symbolism cases minimizes the impact and message sent to religious outsiders and nonbelievers by government display of religious objects.[281] The displays almost always represent objects of dominant or at least less marginalized religious groups, and thus the failure to find such displays unconstitutional in many circumstances amounts to a de facto establishment of majority religious preferences. A corollary of this critique suggests that it is not so much larger religious groups that benefit from the Court's approach, but rather the dominant secularized religious culture.[282] This critique can be used in tandem with the artificial secularization critique, and it is not uncommon to read articles (or dissenting opinions) which suggest that the Court's approach in religious symbolism cases both demeans the religious nature of the symbols and disregards the message such symbols send to nonbelievers and religious outsiders.[283]

Interestingly, the concern underlying this critique, namely, that the Court further marginalizes religious outsiders and nonbelievers by suggesting government displays of religious objects from the dominant faiths in a given area are constitutional, is played out in the Court's battles over the endorsement test. As some commentators have suggested, the phrasing of that test held the initial promise of sensitivity to the impact of government religious activities on religious minorities, but the Court's subsequent application of the test—at least in the religious symbolism cases—has not lived up to that promise.[284] Critics frequently blame Justice O'Connor's adoption of the reasonable observer standard because her reasonable observer appears a lot like a member of the dominant religious group in a given area, since the reasonable observer is charged with knowledge of local customs and settings.[285]

This critique is reflected in the dispute between Justice O'Connor and Justice Stevens in their respective opinions in *Capitol Square Review Board v. Pinette,*[286] where they debate the perspective of the "reasonable observer" under the endorsement test.[287] Justice Stevens would have made

the reasonable observer a member of a religious outgroup or a nonbe-
liever, while Justice O'Connor would have used a more general reasonable
observer standard that did not as clearly consider outsider perspectives.[288]
Those espousing the majoritarian dominance critique generally reject the
use of the endorsement test or advocate an approach more in keeping
with Justice Stevens's application of the endorsement test.[289]

Of course, this critique is not limited to the Court's application of the
endorsement test. In fact, the critique has even more compelling application in relation to the "long-standing tradition" approach.[290] After all,
long-standing traditions rarely reflect the practices and beliefs of religious
outsiders,[291] and the fact that they have not been challenged may say more
about the subordinated role of religious outsiders than it does about long-
standing "community" acceptance of a given practice.[292]

Finally, one of the most salient features of this critique is that in cases
like *Lynch* the physical and thematic context of the display, far from
evincing a celebration of a secular holiday, reflects even further Christian
dominance.[293] This should seem an obvious critique, since Christmas,
or "Christ's Mass," in any of its forms is not celebrated by most non-
Christians, some smaller Christian groups, and many atheists.[294] Far from
sending a nonreligious message, the placement of Santas, reindeer, elves,
and Christmas trees near a crèche sends a message that Christianity is the
preferred religion.[295] Rather than detracting from the religious meaning of
the crèche, these other figures reinforce that the display is about Christmas, which is not "our" holiday.[296] The same message may be sent to
Muslims, Buddhists, or atheists by a large Christmas tree, a menorah, and
a sign saluting liberty—that is, some outsiders might question whose liberty is being saluted by this display.[297] Thus, the context of religious objects does not cure, and in fact may exacerbate, the concerns raised by this
critique.

The contextual critique suggests that the Court's focus on the physical,
historical, and/or thematic context of religious objects in religious symbolism cases downplays the message sent by the objects themselves,[298] and
often ignores the fact that the "nonreligious objects" in a given context
may reinforce the religious message sent to outsiders by the "religious objects." This latter point is shared with the majoritarian dominance critique. Thus, the message sent to non-Christians by the display of a crèche
with Santa and his reindeer is relevant to this critique.[299]

In many ways this critique is a natural corollary to the first two critiques, since both of those assert that physical context cannot alter aspects
of the message sent by a religious object. Yet the contextual critique can
stand on its own as well. Central to this critique is the idea that the physical context or setting of a patently religious object cannot generally alter

its meaning for constitutional purposes when it is displayed by govern-ment.[300] Neither can its thematic context—that is, the fact that it is con-nected to the holiday season.[301] It is either constitutional to display the object or not, but that answer may not be dependent on the physical or thematic context of the object except in the rarest of circumstances (such as a museum setting).[302]

Finally, the traditionalism critique questions the Court's use of "long-standing tradition" to uphold religious displays by government or on gov-ernment property.[303] The critique asserts the Court has never adequately explained why such long-standing tradition should affect results in rele-vant cases. Nor has the Court adequately explained the seeming discrep-ancies between situations where the Court allows such tradition to affect outcomes and those where it does not.[304]

If the display of a purely religious object would otherwise be unconsti-tutional, could a long-standing tradition of displaying the object make it constitutional? The answer would appear to be no if the object is a cross, so why should the answer be any different if the object is a crèche?[305] This critique asserts that tradition is at most a factor to be considered in deter-mining the context of a display. At worst, it is an excuse for upholding displays that would never pass constitutional muster otherwise.[306] The critique is consistent with this book's treatment of the long-standing tradi-tion approach.

4. The Problem with Treating Religious Objects as Legal Subjects

As the above critiques demonstrate, the Court's approach to religious objects is devoid of the tools necessary to analyze these diverse and often deeply powerful symbols. Contrary to the assertions of many of the crit-ics, however, the answer does not lie in simply finding a better version of the endorsement test or in instituting some other test. The Court has failed in its semiotic task so completely that any test used without serious consideration of the religious and cultural power often held by religious objects would create problems similar to those created by the current doc-trine. Yet because these objects do not have a fixed meaning for all observ-ers, the task of deriving meaning from such objects may seem impossi-ble.[307] However, it is not the "meaning" of the object that matters most—since meaning is variable—but rather its power.

It must be recalled that the Court has essentially analyzed religious ob-jects without paying much attention to what counts as a religious object or how such objects operate in the lives of believers and nonbelievers. Moreover, once the Court developed its reflexive approach to religious objects, it applied it in a reflexive way that was heavily affected by the preconceptions of the justices[308]—preconceptions that were both secularized and Christocentric. Of course, there is no set meaning for religious symbols, and the Court could never create a test that would show what a given object "means" in any general sense. This is exactly the problem, since that is precisely what the Court has attempted to do.[309]

While religious objects hold no fixed meaning for the general public, we do know that they hold powerful and profound—even if varied—meaning for believers.[310] This points to a problem inherent in treating religious objects as legal subjects. In order to craft a coherent doctrine, the Court is tempted to create a general meaning for these objects, but religious objects may hold vastly different meaning for both believers and nonbelievers.[311] By relying on a more secularized meaning as it did in *Lynch* and *Allegheny,* the Court minimizes the power these objects hold and fails to distinguish between objects that are sacred and those that are secularized.[312]

The simple reality of treating religious objects as legal subjects is that short of a bright-line test either prohibiting or permitting government to display religious objects, the objects will be distorted through the legal lens simply by being subject to the process of legal reasoning. The only question is how much distortion should be tolerated. Yet, as I have written elsewhere, a bright-line test in these cases is quite undesirable.[313] Such bright-line tests are blunt instruments for dealing with a complex phenomenon. This is why a middle ground is better. The problem is that while the Court was correct to consider the context of religious displays as a variable through which to analyze specific religious objects in those displays, it never adequately analyzed the objects themselves, in essence making context a determinative variable regardless of what was supposedly being contextualized by the physical setting. This is highly problematic and not a terribly well-informed middle ground. The ebb and flow of religion clause principles and the facilitation test will help provide a middle ground, but this can only be done if one takes the religion question seriously. Otherwise, religious objects analysis is devoid of the tools to address the questions religious symbolism cases raise.

Given the seeming dominance of both secularized and Christocentric traditions among the justices and judges engaging in this analysis, it would be useful if the applicable approach includes elements that rein in the justices' own prepossessions, to use Justice Jackson's famous terminology,[314] or their own preconceptions, to use Hans George Gadamer's.[315] By carefully considering the nature of the object being analyzed, the impact of judicial preconceptions can be countered as they come into contact with the horizon of the object, to use Gadamer's terminology, even if these preconceptions do ultimately play into the analysis under a given legal test.[316] If a court first decides that an object is a pure religious object because it is used in ritual, represents an important theological meaning, or is an object of veneration, it would be much harder to justify government display of the object in terms that suggest it is passive and desacralized by its context.[317] A justice or judge confronting such a situation would have to explain why or why not government display of such an object is constitutional given its religious and cultural power. The context of the object would still be relevant, but the Court, having acknowledged the power and role of the object for believers, would have to carefully explain how the context of the object could desacralize it adequately so that its display by government does not facilitate religion. A purely reflexive jurisprudence such as that in *Lynch* would work poorly here, although perhaps it is to be expected.

It is important to clarify the role of meaning and context in this analysis. Both context and meaning are relevant to the equation, but neither can dictate outcomes because both are inherently indeterminate. Context can involve a number of factors such as physical proximity, and so forth, and the framing and interpretation of the context of religious objects are not terribly useful without considering the objects themselves. The meaning of a religious object is also variable depending on who is perceiving it. Yet we do know that religious objects have powerful—even if varied—meaning for believers, and it is this power that makes government interaction with the objects so problematic. While the context of an object may limit this power vis-à-vis government—for example, where a religious painting is displayed in a public museum or a Buddhist bell donated by Japan is displayed in a town that was involved in the development of nuclear weapons[318]—the context does not operate in a vacuum. The object itself must be analyzed to see what is being contextualized. Thus, while the context and meaning held by an object may be relevant variables, it is the power of the religious object that is key.

An obvious retort to this approach would be that by choosing the power an object may hold for believers as an important reference point, the approach does make meaning somewhat determinative. The response to this is "absolutely." The reason these objects are so highly contested is precisely because they are "religious" or argued to be so. Thus, looking at the religious aspects of religious objects—even if they vary—seems a logical first step in evaluating the constitutionality of displaying such objects. This does not require an assertion that objects have specific meaning that is fixed, but rather that some religious objects are imbued for believers with a great deal of spiritual meaning and power. The specific "meaning" of the object may vary even for believers depending on their preconceptions, but the connection between the real world and the divine inheres in the object for the believer. Once the religious aspects of the object are addressed, the context of the object can be considered. Determining the religious nature of an activity is relevant to the issue in the next section, namely, teaching abstinence-only and sex education in the public schools.

C. Teaching Morality and Sex Education in Public Schools

This issue actually involves both Establishment Clause and Free Exercise Clause concerns. The free exercise concerns arise when parents seek exemptions to sex education instruction or other similar programs, or even to remove such programs from the general curriculum.[319] The establishment issues arise when schools teach abstinence-only programs that have an uncanny resemblance to the religious views of certain groups and sometimes a direct connection to religious entities that developed the curricula.[320] Another area where establishment issues arise is when schools seek to teach morality directly in the curriculum or through school-sponsored programs.[321] Most such programs are secularly based and do not run afoul of the Establishment Clause, but some either have a theological connection to a given religion or religions or use clergy in a manner that raises establishment clause concerns.[322] At the core of some of the Establishment Clause analysis is the meaning of religion. Thus, this section will focus heavily on the establishment issues. The Free Exercise issues raise the religion question in a more traditional way and thus will be addressed after discussing the establishment questions.

1. The Establishment Clause

Abstinence-only programs present a number of interesting questions. Few of these programs advertise themselves as religious, but are they "religion" for purposes of the Establishment Clause. Some scholars have certainly argued that they are.[323] The reasoning is that while most sex education programs teach abstinence in addition to other forms of protection, some abstinence-only programs ignore or misstate information on contraception that would help prevent the spread of sexually transmitted diseases (STDs) and teenage pregnancies.[324] Thus, the argument goes, such programs cannot serve the goals of promoting children's health and welfare, and in fact may promote greater spread of STDs.[325] Moreover, some of these programs openly demean homosexuality or discuss it only in the context of AIDS or other STDs.[326] This also can have a negative impact on the mental health of gay youth and on the perceptions of their classmates.[327] These are powerful arguments for the shortsightedness and naïveté of most abstinence-only programs, but these arguments do not necessarily show that such programs are religious without more.

The "more" comes in the form of the organizations and interests that promote abstinence-only programs and sometimes the statements of school boards that adopt them and school officials who carry them out.[328] In some cases, the program's treatment of homosexuality and other sexual issues seems to directly reflect conservative Christian theology.[329] The problem with defining "religion" in this context is that despite the evidence that some, if not most, of these programs are religiously motivated, religious motivation does not necessarily make a given program religious. If every policy that had some religious motivation were an establishment of religion, religious motivation would render everything that stems from it religion.[330] The Court has wisely trod carefully on this question, distinguishing situations where religious purpose was obvious and those where religion may have been one of a number of motivating factors.[331] Under this analysis the abstinence-only programs that are easily connected to religious entities or purposes would be unconstitutional for that reason, but the underlying question of whether such programs constitute "religion" remains in the other cases. Moreover, even in the clear purpose cases the underlying question is unanswered, but rather religious purpose becomes a substitute for "religion" in such cases.[332]

Perhaps the best analogy to this situation comes from Justice Stevens's opinion concurring in part and dissenting in part in *Webster v. Reproductive Health Services*.[333] In the opinion he discusses the nature of the preamble to a Missouri statute regulating abortion, which stated that life begins at conception and that conception occurs at fertilization.[334] While his discussion focuses on the purpose for this statement and thus is consistent with a long line of legislative purpose analysis in the Establishment Clause context, Justice Stevens ultimately concludes that even without evidence of legislative purpose the correlation between the legislative statement in the preamble and the tenets of certain religious doctrines, and the lack of any other plausible secular basis for the statement are enough to render the preamble unconstitutional under the Establishment Clause[335]—that is, he implies that the preamble's assertion is religious despite the lack of any express citation to religious sources. The definition of religion set forth herein would support Justice Stevens's conclusion and suggest that some of the abstinence-only programs are also inherently religion, even though they may not clearly explain why. The natural questions are how are these things "religion" for establishment clause purposes and how is the definition of religion affected by secular purpose analysis? The second question can be answered easily. The answer is that while there may be some factual, or even conceptual, overlap in the definition of religion and secular purpose analysis, the recognition that something is religion is not based on secular purpose analysis. This will become more clear in the following analysis.

Assume that the public schools in a small town dominated by conservative Christian values teach a form of abstinence sex education that favors abstinence over the alternatives, but also teaches about contraception and abortion because of fear that lack of such teaching might lead to STDs or unwanted pregnancies among those who stray from "community values." Moreover, homosexuality is barely mentioned in the program, but homosexuals are not disparaged. Community members and school board members discussed the form of the program in open meetings. Many expressed a preference for a religiously based abstinence-only program, and all expressed their support for the community religious values. In the end, however, the voices favoring a broader abstinence program including the above-mentioned factors won out. There would seem to be a religious purpose on the part of the schools for choosing even the broader abstinence program over general sex education curricula, and a court might conclude there was no secular purpose (although a court might also conclude that religion was just one factor and that concern for the health and safety of the students was an overriding factor given the end result of the community discussion).

Before reaching the purpose question, however, it would need to be determined if the program could even be considered religion or religious. If not, there is no Establishment Clause issue in the first place. The program does seem to have some theological connection to the dominant faith community in the area given its focus on abstinence, but at the same time it teaches material that would seem to go against that same theology. Is some theological connection enough to make this program subject to Establishment Clause scrutiny? Keep in mind that the answer to this question is simply a gatekeeping answer, because even if the program were considered within the realm of religion for Establishment Clause purposes, it may yet be found constitutional. The problem with this context is that finding the program is religiously affected may affect the Establishment Clause analysis in a way that a similar finding may not in other contexts. Under these facts it is a close call, but the fact that the program has some connection to core theology is not enough to make it "religion" given the other factors. Yet, most abstinence-only programs do not share the mitigating factors with this hypothetical, and thus many could be subject to Establishment Clause scrutiny. There may be a "chicken-and-egg" element here. The hypothetical situation would probably survive Establishment Clause scrutiny under the facilitation test proposed later in this book (and under the Court's current tests). Conversely, many abstinence-only programs would fail the facilitation test because they have too close a theological connection and facilitate certain religious views at the expense of student health interests.

In the end, the question of whether abstinence-only programs violate the Establishment Clause cannot sensibly be answered without addressing the question of what constitutes religion under that clause. The substitute question used by the courts as to whether there is a secular purpose for the program may lead to results that are both underinclusive and overinclusive unless the "religion" question is addressed first. Once that question is addressed (assuming the answer is that the program could constitute religion), we can move on to the Establishment Clause inquiry relating to secular purpose—a question that may have already been partially answered in the analysis of whether the program is itself religion or religious.

One might view this issue as implicating the debate over publicly accessible reasons (PARs).[336] The PAR debate is long-standing and far beyond the scope of this chapter. In a nutshell, it involves the question as to whether government action that is religiously motivated should be supported by a publicly accessible reason or reasons that nonbelievers might accept as a valid basis for the law.[337] There are many sophisticated arguments from all sides in the debate. Some argue that PARs are unnecessary because religious motivation should not condemn a law that has secular benefits.[338] Others argue that such reasons are necessary because when the government acts based on religious beliefs (or other comprehensive belief systems), political discourse becomes inaccessible to those who do not subscribe to the comprehensive belief system or systems (and some may understand all too well the reasons for the law and thus be made to feel like outsiders in the political discourse).[339] Still others argue that such reasons—if used to cover over religious reasons—are problematic because they allow government to establish religious tenets without providing those who may challenge those tenets with the means to challenge the government actors' real reasons.[340] Finally, some argue that the whole debate is somewhat moot because at least when dealing with legislative action there may be no way to glean the various motivations of government actors or purposes for given actions, and of course even an individual legislator may be motivated by more than one factor. Therefore, PARs could exist for almost any government action depending on how it is viewed. Thus, the search for PARs or for religious motivation is a search into a tangled web of motivation that may be supported by little proof.

This, of course, is a vast oversimplification of the many sophisticated positions in the debate, but for present purposes it will do because the abstinence-only question exists in a realm where in many cases there will be ostensible PARs, but at the same time many will reject that these reasons are publicly accessible because they make no sense in the current state of reality and thus must be motivated by religion. In other words, the very question of whether there are PARs in this context is so highly contestable by both sides of the debate that one need not take a position in the broader PAR debate to address this issue.

Moreover, given the facilitation test's primary focus on the effects of government action, a law that was supported by PARs may still be religious and may still violate the Establishment Clause. It is conceivable, but less likely, that a law with no PARs may still be found constitutional given the way it actually functions. Still, if one views abstinence-only programs as irrational and naive responses to current trends among teens, it may be impossible to convince that person that there is any plausible PAR for such a policy, especially in light of the demographics of those who usually support such programs. At the same time, if one views abstinence as the only and best option for preventing teenage pregnancy and the spread of STDs, it would be hard to convince such a person—even if he were motivated by religious concerns—that there are no PARs for such a policy. So, for now, we will leave the PAR debate aside and focus on the basic question of whether abstinence-only programs violate the Establishment Clause.

In the Establishment Clause area the definition of religion should be affected by the context of the given case. Thus, the meaning of religion in the context of a religious symbolism case may be different than in a government aid case. The one thing that the definition should include in all establishment clause cases is some core of theological principles or beliefs. These do not necessarily need to be deity related, but they should relate to questions that may best be expressed as ultimate truths or goals. The abstinence-only context is a particularly tough one to address because of the variety of programs and circumstances underlying them, the seemingly obvious connection to religious beliefs, groups, and values, and the reality that this connection may not always be easy to prove even where it exists. It is no secret that the biggest proponents of abstinence-only programs are certain faith groups.[341] It is also no secret that some of these groups have had a role in funding or developing some abstinence-only curricula and in lobbying the federal and state governments to support such programs.[342] Moreover, abstinence-only programs reflect the theological and social views of these groups regarding sex and sexual activity.[343] The problem is that such programs may also be supported by people or groups with no religious affiliation or those who support such programs based on reasons other than their faith. This means that for such programs to qualify as religion under the Establishment Clause, there must be some more direct link to religious theology or religious entities.

This link can take several forms. First, there are programs that define life as beginning at conception or make other primarily theological claims regarding sexuality. Similar to Justice Stevens's argument in *Webster,* there is no serious secular reason to make the claim that life begins at conception or to disparage homosexuality in order to teach an abstinence-only program.[344] Second, there are programs or curricula developed by an entity or individual with close connections to a religious entity or entities, which connections might include substantial funding. Third, there are programs that include direct religious references in the materials. Fourth, there are programs enacted or administered against a background or context where it is apparent religion is being taught or favored (this analysis may cross over heavily with secular purpose and effects analysis).

If any or all of these links exist, it is likely that the program will be "religious" and thus subject to challenge under the Establishment Clause. This is so because these factors all point to a theologically or otherwise religiously infused curriculum. Whether any one of these factors is met would be a question of fact and for some of them a question of degree. Of course, even if a program is religious for purposes of the Establishment Clause, it must still be analyzed under that clause to determine whether it violates the Constitution.

Under the Court's traditional tests, programs that involve links one, three, or four would most likely be found unconstitutional under an endorsement or *Lemon* analysis because direct religious references or a curriculum that makes theologically charged claims about sexuality will have a primary effect that advances religion, especially if the program could be run without those connections.[345] Depending on the facts, such a program may also lack a secular purpose. Similarly, programs enacted or administered against a background or context where it is apparent religion is being taught or favored would most likely violate the secular purpose prong of *Lemon.*[346] Such a program may also violate the effects prong of *Lemon.* Significantly, recent decisions by the Court suggest that outside of the aid context, divisiveness—traditionally an element of the entanglement prong of *Lemon*—remains a factor in some cases.[347] Thus, these programs may also involve entanglement based on divisiveness as well as institutional entanglement, depending on how they are structured and administered. Programs that involve the second link may be found unconstitutional under the secular purpose or entanglement prongs, but this would be a particularly fact-sensitive analysis. Moreover, if such a program developed or funded by a religious entity has religious content, it would most likely also fall under the other three links. If not, the program is more likely to be constitutional.

Endorsement analysis would likely lead to similar conclusions because a reasonable observer would most likely view any of the above links as favoring the religious sect or sects that support the program and treating as outsiders those who do not share the "community values" reflected in the program.[348] Thus, the purpose and/or effect of such programs would be to endorse religion.[349] This is, of course, a highly fact-sensitive analysis, and some programs with similar content to constitutional programs may be found unconstitutional depending on the differences between the programs and the facts surrounding the creation, institution, and administration of the programs.

Interestingly, under a coercion analysis the fact that a given program constitutes "religion" and that these classes are generally mandatory may support a claim for coercion. The classes would in essence be a formal religious exercise (or event) that dissenting students would in a real sense feel compelled (or literally be compelled) to attend.[350] It is possible that an opt-out option would save some programs under a coercion analysis, because students would not feel compelled to attend, but even with such a provision students may feel coerced to attend due to peer pressure.[351] Thus, the specific facts of a given case and the court interpreting those facts would have a major impact on the coercion analysis where an opt-out provision exists. Still, the fact that the program would likely violate the *Lemon* and endorsement tests would ordinarily be enough to deem it unconstitutional.[352]

The facilitation test proposed in this book would lead to many, but not all, of these programs being found unconstitutional. The details of the test are spelled out in greater detail in later chapters. For now it is enough to note that a program that takes a theological position, is developed by a religious entity, includes religious content, and/or was created, enacted, or administered under circumstances favoring religion or specific religions would substantially facilitate religion. Such a program would be using the public schools to promote a religiously based ideology, while at the same time denying students information that may help protect them from STDs or unwanted pregnancies because of that religious ideology.[353] Certainly, not all abstinence-only programs will involve the above-mentioned factors. Those programs that do not substantially facilitate religion may be unwise and naive, but they would not be unconstitutional. The effects of the program would be key to this analysis, but the nature and creation of the program would also be relevant.

2. The Free Exercise Clause

The question that arises under the Free Exercise Clause is whether religious parents or students can demand an exemption to all or part of a general sex education curriculum based on religious objections to the content of such programs. This is often referred to as the ability to "opt out" of such programs.[354] Schools, of course, have the ability to grant opt-out exemptions to religious students if they choose,[355] but the harder question is whether the Free Exercise Clause mandates such exemptions. Given the Court's decision in *Employment Division v. Smith*,[356] many have assumed that opt-out exemptions are not mandated by the Free Exercise Clause. *Smith* held that when the government enacts and applies a law of general applicability—a school curriculum would be considered generally applicable—there is no duty to provide an exemption to that law under the Free Exercise Clause even if the failure to exempt places a substantial burden on the complaining party.

However, the *Smith* Court created the concept of hybrid rights, situations where the free exercise right combines with other fundamental rights such as free speech or parental rights to mandate an exemption unless the government meets a higher burden, most likely a compelling government interest and narrow tailoring.[357] Many scholars, including this author, believe that the hybrid rights idea was a means for the *Smith* Court to get around inconvenient precedent, namely, *Wisconsin v. Yoder*[358] and *West Virginia Bd. of Educ. v. Barnette*.[359] As will be discussed in later chapters, the hybrid rights concept seems odd because the Court seems to be saying an otherwise inadequate free exercise claim can become adequate if mixed with another fundamental right, but this leaves two options. First, the independent fundamental right is also inadequate by itself to support relief, in which case it is hard to understand how two inadequate constitutional claims can render each other adequate. Second, the hybrid right is itself adequate to grant relief, in which case the free exercise claim is unnecessary.[360] As this book suggests, the *Smith* analysis is itself problematic, and the hybrid rights concept seems to be an attempt by conservative judicial activists to cover their activist tracks just as an earlier liberal activist Court attempted to do in *Sherbert v. Verner* when it failed to adequately address *Braunfeld v. Brown*.[361] Whatever its purpose, the hybrids rights concept has been used inconsistently by lower courts.[362]

The hybrid rights concept may have significant import in the context of requests for opt-out exemptions from sex education curricula. This question is still an open one, and the suggestions herein are simply that, suggestions as to how such a scenario might play out. Simply put, in many cases schools will have a duty to provide exemptions to allow students to opt out of sex education courses or portions of those courses. The basis for this assertion is the hybrid rights concept (as well as state RFRAs and constitutional provisions discussed below).

The question regarding the definition of religion that arises in these cases is whether the asserted religious concern is religious or simply social. In most cases, it will obviously be religious (or both), and in cases where it is less clear, courts have generally given great deference to complainants' assertions that a given concern is religious, and as asserted earlier in this chapter, such deference is appropriate in the free exercise clause context where the definition of religion should be broader. Thus, there is at least a plausible free exercise concern in most cases involving a denial of an opt-out exemption to a sex education curriculum.

The quintessential hybrid rights in *Smith* were freedom of expression and, more relevant here, parental rights.[363] As mentioned above, the hybrid rights concept was used as a means by the *Smith* Court to distinguish *Yoder*, which itself involved a parental rights element;[364] although the *Smith* Court greatly overstated the relevance of that element to the outcome in *Yoder*.[365] Thus, if a parent asserts the right to direct the upbringing of his or her child combined with a free exercise right, courts may find a hybrid right exists and require the application of a higher burden on the government such as the compelling interest test.[366] Of course, from a children's rights perspective such a recognition of parental will is not necessarily a good social outcome, but that question is beyond the scope of this chapter. In fact, even if a student sought the exemption on behalf of herself, there is a plausible hybrid rights claim based on freedom of expression and/or association, although absent a hybrid-rights claim such claims will generally fail in the public school context (and such claims may very well fail even when hybrid rights are asserted).[367] If a hybrid right is found, courts may apply the compelling interest test as developed in *Sherbert v. Verner* and its progeny.[368] Thus, courts will look to see whether the failure to provide an exemption places a burden on the religious practices/faith of the complainant, whether the government has a compelling interest for denying the exemption, and whether the denial is narrowly tailored to meet that interest.[369]

Courts tend to be deferential to complainants' claims that their religious beliefs or practices are being burdened by a given governmental action.[370] In the case of opt-out exemptions the parents could assert that sex education curricula undermine the religious values regarding family life, sex, and sexuality required by their faith and central to their family life, and that exposure to sex education might cause the child to act against his or her faith or question the values taught at home and by the faith.[371] This is a tricky argument because it may be hard to distinguish sex education from other portions of the secular curriculum here, and courts may fear a slippery slope.[372] Still, other than perhaps the teaching of evolution, sex education is the only area where there is likely to be a viable claim that the lessons so directly conflict with family values and religious beliefs so as to substantially burden religious freedom.

Next the government would need to demonstrate a compelling interest for denying the exemption. This is key. The government obviously has a compelling interest in teaching sex education—that is, the health and safety of students—but does that interest translate into one supporting the denial of an exemption? As in *Yoder*, this may be harder to show, especially if the parents or student can show that the religious values relating to such issues are being inculcated at home and that at the very least the student is being taught about abstinence. It would be harder still if the family can show that the rates of STD transmission and unwanted pregnancies are significantly lower in their faith community than among the general school population.[373] Still, the government could argue that exempting any child from sex education potentially exposes that child to health risks that could be passed to other children and that portions of the curriculum are not likely to be objectionable to the family.[374] This will be a tough call for a court, but if the family can show, as the families in *Yoder* did, that the risk is minimal in their faith community and that alternative approaches are being taught at home, the school may lose on this element.[375]

Assuming the school does have a compelling interest in denying an exemption, the question remains whether denying the exemption is narrowly tailored to meet that interest. It is possible that the student might be exempted only from the objectionable portions of the course or that the school could require the family to demonstrate that alternative, but religiously acceptable, lessons are being given to the child such as training in the risks of STDs in the absence of abstinence. If the parents can demonstrate that the state's interest is not served by denying the exemption to their child because of the low risk that the child would be involved in the types of activities the school is concerned about, the school would likely lose this argument. In sum, there are many ways for parents to win under the compelling interest test and fewer ways for the school to win. Schools may want to consider simply exempting students when requested to avoid a protracted legal battle. The strongest argument for schools that do enter the legal fray is that there is no hybrid right involved under the facts of the given case.[376]

Hybrid rights claims are not the only basis for reviewing the denial of an opt-out exemption under the compelling interest standard. Many states have RFRAs, which require that the compelling interest test be applied in all cases involving the denial of an exemption from a generally applicable state or local law.[377] Still other states provide for such a requirement under their state constitutions.[378] So there may be many circumstances where the compelling interest test discussed above could be applied to the denial of an opt-out exemption. As will be seen in chapter 10, the facilitation test would require an exemption in most of these cases because a failure to provide one would substantially interfere with religion. The issue of whether parents should have such rights as a matter of policy is irrelevant to the religion clause question under the facilitation test except where the student objects to the parents' choices, in which case a court would have to determine under state law who has the right to make curricular decisions for the student. Additionally, arguments from outside the religion clauses might be made to dispute the parental rights in such cases, but these are beyond the scope of this book.

D. Defining Religion in the Context of Mandatory Exemptions Under the Free Exercise Clause

As you read this section, you might find it odd that it is so short in relation to the two examples under the Establishment Clause given the importance of the exemption issue under the Free Exercise Clause. Aside from the fact that the exemption issue was discussed a bit in the previous section, however, there are some obvious reasons for the disparity. Under the Establishment Clause, defining religion is a dual task involving both definition and recognition of religion in contexts where the Court has traditionally paid little attention to either. In the Free Exercise Clause context there is a stronger tradition of at least grappling with the nature of religion,[379] even if that tradition has borne little fruit beyond the tests mentioned in the introduction to this chapter.

Moreover, a definition of religion was proposed for the free exercise context earlier in this chapter, and that definition can be applied to the question of religious exemptions. As you may recall that definition is as follows:

> Religion under the Free Exercise Clause should include belief systems that are organized around a belief in a deity or deities (or a central belief that there is no deity); other supernatural forces that provide a guiding set of principles or beliefs (this would also include nature-based belief systems that see nature or aspects of nature as holding power beyond that perceived by most people); or a universal or transcendent set of principles, traditions, or truths that guide belief and behavior.

As noted earlier, in many if not most free exercise cases, resort to this definition would be unnecessary because it would be obvious that the case involves religion. Still, there will be hard cases, and the Free Exercise Clause context lends itself better to a broad definition of religion than does the Establishment Clause context. Any individual who meets the above definition would be entitled to an exemption under the Free Exercise Clause wherever that clause mandates an exemption be given. Whether the Free Exercise Clause mandates religious exemptions will be addressed in chapters 9 and 10 and was also addressed a bit earlier.

Obviously, all theistic religions would be covered under the above definition, as would atheism and agnosticism. Moreover, most nontheistic religions such as Buddhism would be included because they involve a "universal or transcendent set of principles, traditions or truths that guide belief and behavior." Internal theological disputes, such as those between Mahayana and Hinayana Buddhism,[380] Sunni and Shiite Islam,[381] or conservative and liberal Presbyterianism,[382] would not affect a court's use of the definition. Thus, the fact that some sect within a faith tradition considers other sects or individuals not to be of that faith would be irrelevant. The fact that differences between sects may imply a specific claimant's belief system is not universal would also be irrelevant. The key is that for adherents of the given sect the belief system is universal or transcendent.

The definition suggested herein would deny protection—and thus free exercise exemptions—to those who simply hold profound philosophical positions. Thus, it would exclude some individuals or groups that might be included under the *Welsh/Seeger* test. As suggested earlier in this chapter, the proposed definition of religion under the Free Exercise Clause does take sides in the debate over whether religious comprehensive viewpoints should be protected even in contexts where secular or philosophical ones are not. The ebb and flow of religion clause principles supports this added protection for religion, as does the existence and text of the Free Exercise Clause.[383] Thus, those who fit the definition of religion herein will receive exemptions if warranted under free exercise analysis, while those with equally strong, but nonreligious, philosophies or worldviews would be excluded. As explained above, those who take a position on the existence of a deity, such as atheists and agnostics, would be considered religious under the definition, as odd as that terminology may seem in reference to atheists (it should be remembered that it is definitional terminology, and therefore the label should not be seen by atheists as implying that atheism is religion in the same sense that Christianity is). The discussion of when and why exemptions may be mandated under the Free Exercise Clause will follow in chapters 9 and 10.

9

The Ebb and Flow of
Religion Clause Principles

Steve Smith has lamented the seeming obsession of jurists and constitutional scholars with the development of a "principle" of religion clause interpretation.[1] While Smith and I may proceed in different directions with our response to this obsession, I wholeheartedly agree with Smith's assertion that the quest is doomed to fail. As Smith has eloquently pointed out, no single principle or theory of religion clause interpretation is up to the task of making sense of the religion clauses.[2] This book asserts, however, that multiple principles that ebb and flow based on context may be up to the task. As counterintuitive as it may seem, my assertion is that multiple narrow principles of interpretation can lead to more clarity, consistency, and coherence in religion clause interpretation than can any single broad principle or theory.

Of course, the incoherence created by reliance on broad principles of interpretation in religion clause jurisprudence is well documented.[3] I have asserted elsewhere in this book that part of the problem is that the courts, and even many scholars, assert that neutrality, original intent, or some other comprehensive "interpretive" theory can determine the meaning of the religion clauses while relying on an unstated principle or set of principles. The mark of a useful principle of religion clause interpretation is whether it actually performs some work in the process of interpretation aside from rhetorical justification and whether one can substantiate the claims made in the name of that principle.

Ironically, as will be seen, this inquiry eliminates the two principles of interpretation most relied upon by the Court and commentators: originalism (at least in its "hard" form) and neutrality. The approach proposed herein raises many questions. How does one determine which principles perform work in the religion clause context? How does one validate the use of these principles? How does one engage the ebb and flow of multiple principles in various situations? How might one address cases where principles that seem relevant to a given situation conflict with each other or seem to do so?

It is helpful to address these questions, and, in fact, the entire notion of the ebb and flow of religion clause principles, through the lens of modalities of interpretation. Specifically, it is helpful to look at Philip Bobbitt's discussion of the modalities of constitutional interpretation.[4] Ultimately, an exploration of Bobbitt's work leads me to propose the notion that there are modalities of religion clause interpretation. These modalities most likely fit well within Bobbitt's modalities, but quite honestly such a fit is less relevant to the approach proposed herein than Bobbitt's broader assertions about the benefits of a modal approach and his understanding of legal justification and legitimation, most clearly discussed in one of his seminal works, *Constitutional Interpretation*.[5]

Bobbitt argues that the focus on theories attempting to generate "right" answers creates interpretive problems because those theories tend to focus on concepts of justice that they can never satisfy.[6] There is a certain irony here. Theories that focus on obtaining justice must themselves define justice, and thus they are in a way self-fulfilling, but not self-justifying.[7] There is no way to justify one of these theories except from within the theory.[8] Bobbitt argues that rather than focus on the normative quest for justice, constitutional interpretation would be better served by looking at the range of interpretive principles that are generally accepted in constitutional law.[9] Thus, he proposes six modes of constitutional interpretation, each of which can be said to be a valid interpretive principle in constitutional law.[10] These modalities are not mutually exclusive and can work together in the interpretive process.[11] To Bobbitt, it is the use of these modes of interpretation that may lead to justice, because in the end they allow for prudential concerns to affect interpretation.[12] Rather than relying on theories that attempt to mask the role our preconceptions play in the interpretive process, he argues that we should rely on the modalities of interpretation and then openly rely on our normative views when choosing between the modes or when the modes must be applied in hard cases.[13] This approach would lead to more interpretive openness without excessive reliance on contested normative theories.

Significantly, Bobbitt draws a distinction between justification and legitimation.[14] He argues that one can legitimate a mode of interpretation without justifying the results it may lead to.[15] His is not a teleological approach. This fact makes his approach particularly useful in the present context. The possibility of a more descriptive, less results-driven, approach to religion clause interpretation is exciting. The reality is that whatever normative approach one wishes to take in the religion clause context, such approaches are less likely to serve whatever ends one wants them to unless one understands what is really going on in the interpretive process.[16] Thus, for a court to justify a decision based on hard originalism or neutrality, when that decision was more likely affected by pragmatic or other concerns, can lead to inconsistencies in later cases as courts take the earlier decision at face value or use the same illusory tools to reach different results. In the end, understanding religion clause interpretation as best we can is a necessary precursor to any normative approach, and it may be that the descriptive approach discussed in this chapter could support a variety of normative approaches. In fact, as I will explain in chapter 10, one can reject my proposed facilitation test, but still benefit from the discussion in the rest of this book.

In earlier chapters we discussed the modes of religion clause interpretation: separationism, accommodationism, liberty, equality, soft originalism, and pragmatism. As will be seen, these will function as narrow principles rather than broad ones, and they will ebb and flow based on the context of the case. This is consistent with Bobbitt's approach.[17] This is not to say that Bobbitt would approve of the modes suggested in this book or my use of the modalities approach in the narrow context of the religion clauses, although each of the modes of religion clause interpretation is consistent with one or more of Bobbitt's modalities of constitutional interpretation.[18] It simply means that the idea of modes of interpretation that ebb and flow based on context and do not dictate a specific outcome in all cases is consistent with his approach.[19] The fact that use of these modes legitimates a decision is also consistent with his approach.[20]

It should be noted, however, that there are possible differences in how Bobbitt and I legitimate the modes themselves. Bobbitt's modes are well entrenched in constitutional interpretation, and one would be hardpressed to argue that courts have not relied on each of his six modes in various cases.[21] So far so good for the theory in this book because the same could be said of the modes of religion clause interpretation. But the same might also be said of hard originalism and neutrality, which I reject as valid modes of religion clause interpretation. This is because in the specific context of religion clause jurisprudence these two interpretive principles do nothing but mask the real bases for decisions—that is, they are useless or, as Steve Smith has suggested in regard to neutrality, parasitic.[22] As was explained in detail in earlier chapters, the hard originalist approach defeats itself in the religion clause context because of the competing historical accounts, and, of course, neutrality is impossible to achieve in any form. Thus, I add one essential factor to legitimate the modes of religion clause interpretation. It is one that Bobbitt's approach does not directly address, namely, that any valid mode of religion clause interpretation must do something more than provide an illusion to mask decisions made using other modes of interpretation or sheer judicial will.

A. The Ebb and Flow of Interpretive Principles

In earlier chapters we learned that separationism and accommodationism are useful concepts because they are both capable of existing in varying degrees outside of a specific metaphysical claim. Significantly, unless one claims to rely solely on separation or accommodation, the suggested inherent tension between these concepts is a false antinomy. These concepts can coexist in an ebb and flow of interpretive principles even though they will sometimes conflict.

Religious liberty and religious equality are potentially broad and malleable concepts. Thus, we need to understand of what we speak when we use these terms. Earlier chapters helped provide this specificity.

Soft originalism—understood to mean the broad intent of the framers as Cass Sunstein has used that term—may also be useful. Although it will not answer many questions by itself, it may provide a constraint or gloss on interpretation. Finally, pragmatism—which may be consistent with Bobbitt's prudential mode—has clearly had an effect in any number of religion clause cases, and it may provide a helpful bridge between the various modes of interpretation and the facts in a given case.

We are still left with the question of how to validate these modes. Chapter 1 and chapters 4 through 7 provide a significant part of the answer. More important, we are left with the question of how to engage in the ebb and flow of religion clause principles—that is, how do we know when to use a particular mode or modes, and what do we do if they conflict? The answers in this chapter are a first bite at the apple, if you will. This is an early attempt to seriously frame this approach. Still, the discussion herein should provide more than enough information to both support the modal approach proposed in this book and explain how it might work.

When one asserts that multiple principles of interpretation that ebb and flow based on context should be used to engage in legal interpretation, one runs straight into a variety of theories and approaches that see such a concept as antithetical to sound legal reasoning and perhaps even as inviting nihilism. As to the first concern, I will explain why this approach—as limited to the religion clause context—not only is a sound approach to legal reasoning, but actually leads to better, or at least more realistic, legal reasoning. Regarding the concern about nihilism, I will explain why it is completely out of place in connection with the theory proposed herein and why the approach proposed herein may actually lead to greater clarity and consistency than more traditional methods of religion clause interpretation.

A number of legal schools of thought suggest that constitutional interpretation should be based on one or a small number of approaches such as originalism,[23] the quest for justice,[24] or textualism.[25] Some of the scholars and judges advocating these approaches would suggest that any interpretive approach that is not so limited is an invitation to judicial anarchy or an invitation for judges to judge unjustly.[26] Some of these theories seek the "best" answer or presume that there is an obviously correct answer if only we would use the "correct" approach to reach it.[27] Most of these theories suppose an artificial dualism in judging—that a judge behaves either objectively or subjectively and the relevant interpretive theory will help the judge behave more objectively.[28] Some suppose that there is a clear notion of justice and that judges are capable of serving justice if they adopt the correct interpretive strategy.[29]

The first supposition presumes that the choices are judicial objectivity or subjectivity, that there is some clear line between the two, and that they are opposites. The opposite of objectivity, however, is not subjectivity, but rather context. To presume that a judge who rejects a supposedly objective framework such as originalism is behaving in an unconstrained and subjective fashion is naive. First, it presumes that the supposedly objective framework is actually objective. As earlier chapters pointed out, originalism is hardly objective in the religion clause context. Yet there is interpretive constraint even when a firm method of interpretation is lacking—that is, the available methods simply cannot answer the question or cannot be justified as *the* correct approach to interpretation.[30]

When "objective" methodologies fail to provide broad-ranging answers, the context of the case—i.e., the fact that the relevant case is a school prayer case under the Establishment Clause—may provide some constraint. The interpreter is aware of the potential principles of interpretation and the context of the case. Stare decisis may provide further constraint. The context of the case helps the interpreter navigate the interpretive process and reach a result. Far from being nihilistic, this more open method of interpretation constrains the judge to using the modes of religion clause interpretation and denies the judge the ability to hide behind a supposedly objective legal justification.[31] Interpretation is more out in the open, and judges must openly grapple with the question of whether a given approach actually does anything of value because judges will be aware there are other potential principles available and there is no need to rely exclusively on one method of interpretation.[32]

The view of religion clause principles as modes of interpretation constrains the interpreter to the modes of interpretation and forces her to grapple with the application of those modes to the case or situation at hand. At the same time it allows for pragmatic decisions within a given mode or modes, but pragmatic decisions that cannot hide behind the illusion of neutrality or hard originalism. Multiple narrow principles that ebb and flow may not provide complete constraint on interpretation—especially when one of the modes is pragmatism—but they provide more constraint than highly manipulable concepts such as neutrality and (in the religion clause context) hard originalism. Rather than mask decisions as the latter concepts do, judges will be forced to explain how and why they use certain principles in certain contexts. In the long run this should lead to more consistency and transparency in interpretation.

Although it seems counterintuitive at first, one can readily see, I hope, how the approach suggested herein can lead to more consistency (given the state of religion clause jurisprudence it would be hard to lead to less), but what about transparency? Why couldn't a judge use one or more of the principles to justify seemingly predetermined results much as the originalists and some neutrality folks have done? The answer comes from the way in which modes of interpretation function. Bobbitt points out that one may choose among the modes, but one should apply the relevant mode or modes openly with the prudential bases for decision laid bare.[33] This does not mean that Bobbitt's approach requires judges to express their inner motivations when deciding cases, so long as the judges act consistently with the modes.[34] The process of working one's preconceptions out in light of the modes could, however, force judges to confront some of their biases at least some of the time.[35]

In the religion clause context, where there are limited modes and potentially strong contextual constraints, the prudential or pragmatic aspects of a decision sometimes may play a less pronounced role because of the constraint in the modal approach. When one must explain the mode one is relying on given the potential applicability of other modes, it is hard to make conclusive assertions along the lines of the "framers said so" or this approach or result is "neutral." A judge would at least need to explain what mode or modes are being used, why other potentially applicable modes are not, and how the chosen modes apply given the facts of the case. In chapter 10 I will set forth a legal test that allows judges to do this in a useful manner while maintaining some flexibility for new and unforeseen situations. For now it is useful to look at the principles (modes) of religion clause interpretation, how they may interact, where each is most useful (establishment, free exercise, or both), and why they may lead to decisions that are both consistent with some prior precedent and more realistic about the underlying reasons for some of that precedent.

B. The Modes/Principles of Religion Clause Interpretation

The notion that there is tension between the broad principles traditionally used in Establishment Clause cases and the results in those cases is not new.[36] Moreover, the relationship between broad principles and the tests used under the Establishment Clause has been well explored. As was explained in earlier chapters, none of the broad principles traditionally discussed in the religion clause context work as broad principles. Thus, separation, accommodation, equality, and liberty all may be valuable in some contexts, but some of these concepts are too vague to be of great use beyond platitudes and buzzwords without some functional definition.

The following sections will briefly explore each of the principles/modes of religion clause interpretation. Of course, these principles were narrowed in chapters 4 through 7, but the following sections are not meant to rehash the discussion there. Rather, the principles discussed in those chapters will be discussed as modes of interpretation. This will be helpful for the application of the modes through the facilitation test proposed in chapter 10.

1. Separation

Because separation works well as a narrow principle of interpretation, it is highly useful in the ebb and flow of religion clause principles. One possibility is to use a given principle such as separation as a guiding principle in some contexts, but not others.[37] Thus, separation would be used in the school prayer context, the public school curriculum context, and perhaps the direct aid context, but not in equal access or indirect aid cases. This is not too far from the current situation,[38] but this is more a result of the positions of the swing voters on the Court, none of whom take a consistent separationist position, than of a dedication to separation on these issues. The modal approach would suggest that separation may be applied in some contexts and not others, but that these contexts cannot be set forth prior to the open application of the modes; although once the Court has begun to use separation in a given context, stare decisis would suggest that it is a guiding mode in that context.

As noted in chapter 6, separation can function as a narrow principle in given contexts, a broad principle that urges as much separation between the government and religion as possible, or somewhere in between. Separation is less problematic than neutrality because some degree of separation may be achieved, but separation is still problematic at the practical level because one must still choose where and how to implement it, and short of a draconian absolute separation, which is hard to implement, troubling from a policy perspective, and contrary to several other modes of interpretation, separation must function in some narrower form.

The fact that separation can be used as a narrow principle based on the factors set forth in chapter 6 provides some basis for determining the scenarios where it will most likely function as the, or a, major mode of interpretation. These are situations where government acts in a manner that raises concerns over religious diversity and pluralism by picking sides in a religious context or, as will be seen in chapter 10, by substantially facilitating religion. Other situations where separation may play a primary role are where government activity or regulation poses a real threat to the "garden" of religion, or where it substantially discourages religion, as will be explained in chapter 10. Additionally, situations where religion poses some sort of threat to the state would also be a prime opportunity for the application of the separation principle, but most such situations are subsumed in situations involving substantial facilitation of religion or questions of religious pluralism and diversity.

Separationism would not seem to have a major role in the context of the Free Exercise Clause because, as explained elsewhere, that clause is primarily an accommodationist clause, to which both liberty and equality principles may be relevant. Yet, even in the free exercise context one could imagine cases where separationist concepts may be relevant. For example, separation and equality might combine to preclude a government entity from favoring or disfavoring particular groups in regard to exemptions from generally applicable laws, or where, as in *Church of the Lukumi Babalu Aye v. City of Hialeah,*[39] a government entity engages in religious gerrymandering based on a religious individual's or group's religious practices. The test proposed in the next chapter will address in greater detail the particulars of the various situations to which the modes may be applied.

2. Accommodation

Like separation, accommodation can arguably function both at the level of a broad principle and as a narrow principle, or as a facet of a doctrinal test.[40] Accommodationist arguments are most common under the Free Exercise Clause.[41] In that context, accommodationism would support exemptions from laws of general applicability.[42] However, accommodationism can also be used in the Establishment Clause context.[43] When accommodationism functions in the Establishment Clause context as a broad principle of strict accommodationism, for lack of a better term, it becomes hard to distinguish from nonpreferentialism.[44]

Accommodationism does not work well by itself in the Establishment Clause context. This is not because it is not feasible—nonpreferentialism is feasible—but because short of moving toward nonpreferentialism, accommodationism requires distinctions to be made that allow government to engage in or foster religious activities while somehow denouncing the religious nature or impact of those activities. An example is turning religious symbols or rituals into a form of ceremonial deism in order to accommodate them without acknowledging that government is sponsoring or performing a religious function.

To the extent that accommodationism is connected to notions of formal equality between religion and nonreligion, it may be a more plausible approach than neutrality. However, it would not by itself solve the concern that the formal equality approach ignores the disparities between more dominant and minority religions, thus giving dominant religions in given areas a competitive edge and a preferred status.[45] Still, accommodationism has a role to play under the Establishment Clause, and a potentially important role to play in the Free Exercise Clause context.[46] Yet, overreliance on accommodationism under the Establishment Clause might force the big square peg of religion into narrow round holes in order to maintain some minimal level of separation. As will be seen, however, a narrow view of accommodationism together with a narrow view of separationism may be useful. Perhaps the best examples of this are the equal access cases.[47]

Under the Free Exercise Clause, accommodation has the potential to be a major mode of interpretation, especially when connected to religious liberty and perhaps equality. By its nature the Free Exercise Clause is an accommodationist clause. This does not answer the question of what it means or how it should be applied in specific contexts such as exemption cases, but the fact that it prohibits government from interfering with the free exercise of religion[48]—whatever that means—requires that government accommodate religious interests at some level.[49] The modes of interpretation help us to understand how and why. When liberty, equality, and accommodation are combined, they suggest that mandatory accommodation of religious practices is appropriate because otherwise government could deny individuals the ability to practice their religions simply because they were not recognized and/or are unable to be recognized or understood in the legislative process.[50] Any of the three—accommodation, liberty, or equality—might lead to this conclusion, but it is the combination of the three that makes the argument more salient because of the potentially varied meaning of each, that is, they help constrain each other. Soft originalism may also support this conclusion,[51] as might pragmatism, although pragmatism might point the other way as well. The details of these interactions will be worked out below.

3. Religious Liberty

The concept of religious liberty must struggle with its underlying epistemic claim—that is, that there is some way of knowing what religious liberty is. Yet every school of thought that has addressed the religion clauses claims to be promoting religious liberty at some level, and some view their approach as synonymous with religious liberty. At its broadest, religious liberty is more a platitude than a principle. Thus, religious liberty must either be tied to some baseline or viewed simply as an aspiration to be fulfilled by the doctrine or theory du jour. Yet, whatever baseline or results one argues are consistent with religious liberty, there can be a competing baseline. Thus, in chapter 4 I attempted—hopefully successfully—to create a narrower definition of religious liberty based on the varying underlying bases for that principle. That definition is what I refer to here as "religious liberty."

The principle of religious liberty, linked with accommodation, operates best in the Free Exercise Clause context. The concept may also have a role to play under the Establishment Clause, but this role is less clear, and a judge using the principle in that context would need to explain how accepting or denying the constitutionality of an alleged government establishment of religion is supported by the liberty principle. Certainly, in the equal access context such an argument would be plausible, and there may be other contexts as well. The modal approach does not predetermine answers; it simply provides some interpretive constraint and requires interpretive transparency to the greatest extent possible. For example, a judge might link liberty and separation to suggest that paying tax dollars to support a religious institution is unconstitutional, but the judge would have to confront the fact that such an approach—at least if taken to an extreme—could discourage religion in violation of the equality principle, the accommodation principle, the soft originalist principle, and a potentially different use of the liberty principle.

In the next chapter I will argue that the liberty principle, combined with other modes, supports both mandatory accommodation under the Free Exercise Clause and equal access under the Establishment Clause. Yet tax-supported government aid to religious entities cannot be deemed constitutional or unconstitutional based on the liberty principle. Separation, accommodation, equality, and pragmatism may be more useful modes in this context. Of course, one can reject my normative conclusions and still use the modal approach. One should not confuse my application of the modal approach with the descriptive argument that the modal approach better captures what is really going on in religion clause jurisprudence, and does so in a more open fashion.

4. Religious Equality

Like religious liberty, an approach to religion clause analysis grounded in the quest for equality sounds good. If it could be delivered, all religions would be treated equally, and religion would be treated equally with nonreligion. Scholars who have advocated an equality-based approach to the religion clauses are not naive enough to think that such a state of perfect equality could exist,[52] just as scholars who have advocated a neutrality-based approach are not naive enough to think that perfect and incontestable neutrality could exist.[53] Yet, as with neutrality, one person's equality is another's hostility. As was discussed in chapter 5, many questions arise regarding the equality principle. Do we measure equality by government purpose? By the facial equality of government action? By the effects of government action? Is treating similarly situated groups the same equality, even if doing so has a disparate impact based on social factors? Is treating differently situated groups the same equality?

The important point here is that equality, like religious liberty, can function as a broad amorphous principle that is never clearly definable or reachable, but it cannot do the work of answering questions in a variety of contexts without some functional definition as set forth in chapter 5 or the help of some other narrow principle.[54] To the extent the Court has tied formal equality to formal neutrality in its more recent cases, the results have hardly been equal for many religious minorities and nonbelievers.[55] Using neutrality and equality in the way the Court recently has only masks the fact that it is relying on other principles.

Equality does have a role to play in religion clause jurisprudence. That role is the opposite of the role equality plays in the Court's formal neutrality approach. Equality comes into play because we should consider the results of even facially neutral government actions (including those that utilize private intermediaries) in order to determine whether those actions give substantial benefits to some religions over others or to religion over nonreligion.[56]

Needless to say, this focuses a great deal more on the effects of government activity than the current Court seems willing to do in the government aid and free exercise contexts.[57] To the extent the approach herein (and the test in chapter 10) uses equality, it does not do so in an absolute way, and it acknowledges that any claim to equality is simply based on a construction of that term that deals with significant disparities in the effects of government actions.[58] The specifics are set forth in chapter 5.

5. Soft Originalism

Soft originalism—in the sense of broad concepts the framers might have agreed upon even if they would not have agreed upon specific applications of those concepts—is an additional mode of religion clause jurisprudence.[59] This mode does not provide specific answers to specific questions, but rather may provide support for the choice between different modes in certain contexts and an added tool in constraining interpretation. At the least controversial level we know the framers were opposed to direct religious control of government.[60] A more controversial but strongly supportable position is that the framers were concerned with religious divisiveness,[61] although there were significant differences among the framers on the specifics and application of this concern.[62]

One of the problems with this mode is that it can only function where there is adequate evidence of a broad intent of the framers.[63] Thus, where even at a broad level the framers disagreed, this is not a useful mode. The idea is to avoid the mistakes of hard originalism in this area, where competing histories that are quite incomplete (or even inaccurate) vie for interpretive supremacy and where those advocating them claim the framers' intent can answer specific questions about which the framers never thought.[64] The soft originalist mode could function under both the religion clauses, but in many situations it will be hard to glean even a broad intent of the framers because of the many practical and philosophical differences between the many framers and ratifiers of the Constitution.[65]

This mode could come into play in almost any situation where the broad intent of the framers was somewhat consistent and can be adequately substantiated. Yet, even when it does come into play, it does not provide specific answers to questions, and thus it functions more like a background principle. In other words, this mode must operate along with other modes to be of any practical use. It may support the choice or rejection of another mode or modes, and it may constrain a judge from using modes in a manner that would conflict with the broad intent of the framers, but they don't call it "broad intent" for no reason; one can frequently support any number of approaches with broad intent so the other modes remain the key.[66]

6. Pragmatism

When reading the Supreme Court's decisions under the religion clauses, especially in the Establishment Clause context, it is apparent that justices of all stripes have relied on pragmatic concerns masked behind other principles, but often not too far from the surface.[67] The use of unconstrained pragmatism in judicial interpretation has the potential to lead to judicial chaos, especially in a field as highly fact sensitive and hotly contested as the religion clauses. When pragmatism is recognized, however, as a valid mode of religion clause interpretation, it comes into the open and is also constrained by the other modes in most circumstances. Judges will use pragmatism, or what Bobbitt refers to as prudentialism—essentially pragmatism driven by a concern for balancing relevant factors, which may be affected by a judge's moral views, moral theory, or sense of justice— anyway.[68]

The role pragmatism plays in religion clause interpretation is not unlike Bobbitt's mode of prudentialism.[69] Pragmatic concerns can help a judge make decisions consistent with concerns about justice in the "hard" cases where the modes, precedent, and facts do not suggest an answer or answers without more.[70] Such concerns may also help a judge make choices even in easier cases so long as the choices are consistent with the other relevant modes of interpretation, and yes pragmatism may even help determine what other modes are applicable in situations where that question cannot be answered using the modes or other legitimate approaches to interpretation.[71] It is essential to point out, however, that judges should not rely on pragmatism alone so long as other modes apply. Pragmatism in this context should not be seen as synonymous with "subjectivism." Pragmatism, in the sense used here, means reasoning that helps reach a conclusion given the various modes, facts of the case, and relevant legal tests (I will suggest the facilitation test in the next chapter).[72] It may reflect a given judge's sense of justice, but in the religion clause context judges using the pragmatic mode should be mindful of Justice Jackson's implicit warning that even when one is left only with his or her own prepossessions in interpreting a clause, one should be vigilant in one's interpretive methods.[73]

Pragmatism and soft originalism might be viewed as secondary or background modes when viewed in light of the four other modes of religion clause interpretation. It would be naive, however, to assume that pragmatic concerns will not enter the interpretive process in hard cases that take place in contested areas such as the religion clauses. Such concerns have clearly affected the Court in many religion clause decisions, but because the justices were unwilling to acknowledge this in most cases and thus hid behind the illusion of neutrality and/or original intent, religion clause jurisprudence has become something of a mess.[74] Better to directly confront the interpretive reality at hand and constrain interpretation with modes that actually do something than to ignore the interpretive reality at hand and hide behind illusory broad principles that mask other interpretive presumptions.[75]

7. Principles and Tests

It should be clear by now that this book does not advocate reliance on specific broad principles, especially for purposes of developing legal doctrine, but various principles can inform the development of useful doctrine. For this to happen, the principles must be honestly confronted. This requires acknowledgment that some principles are simply social or judicial constructions that have no claim to accuracy or truth. Thus, narrower principles that do not suggest universal truth, and which are readily subject to degrees of implementation without undermining their meaning, are more useful in developing a normative approach such as a legal test.

At the base, though, legal tests themselves are central to the practical meaning of the religion clauses, even if that meaning has become quite confused as a result of the application of such tests. For example, whether a court uses the *Lemon/Agostini* test,[76] the endorsement test,[77] the coercion test,[78] the tradition test,[79] or the Court's new formal neutrality test (ostensibly part of the *Agostini* test)[80] can have a significant impact on the meaning of the Establishment Clause. Yet how a given test is applied may be more important than the doctrinal approach used,[81] and each of these choices can be affected by the principles one believes undergird the Establishment Clause (or subconsciously assumes undergird that clause).[82]

This interplay between principles and tests is important and complex, but where does it leave us if we accept the idea that most broad principles are impossible to pin down and that there is no superprinciple that enables us to correctly choose between competing narrow principles because there is no way to gauge "correctness" in this context? It leaves us with the modes of religion clause interpretation and the normative approaches (doctrinal tests) they support; normative approaches that will generally be divorced from any one principle because of the near impossibility of absolutely realizing any given principle, but which can be informed by multiple principles once we realize and acknowledge the limitations inherent in those principles.

In the next chapter I will propose a normative approach based on the ebb and flow of principles discussed in this chapter. It should be obvious based on the first nine chapters of this book that one can accept or reject my normative approach without rejecting the descriptive and interpretive claims in this book. The approach proposed in the next chapter is similar to Douglas Laycock's theory of substantive neutrality tweaked with aspects of separationism and accommodationism, but divorced from the term "neutrality" and wary of any such claim. His approach gels aspects of liberty, equality, separation, and accommodation, because each of these principles has a role to play in minimizing government encouragement or discouragement of religion. Yet in a massive regulatory state, how one minimizes government encouragement of religion without discouraging religion is a complex problem.[83] The facilitation test discussed in the next chapter is an attempt to avoid government encouragement of religion without unduly discouraging religion.

10

The Facilitation Test

It should be clear by now that multiple principles can inform the development of useful doctrine. For this to happen, the principles must be honestly confronted. This requires acknowledgment that some principles, such as neutrality, are simply social or judicial constructions that have no claim to accuracy or truth. Thus, narrower principles that do not suggest universal truth, and which are readily subject to degrees of implementation without undermining their meaning, are more useful in developing legal tests. The ebb and flow of such principles might be used to justify any number of legal tests. The test proposed in this chapter, however, may do the best job of integrating the various modes of religion clause interpretation into a legal test that has some promise to increase consistency in religion clause interpretation while acknowledging the heavily context-bound—both legally and factually—nature of such interpretation.

This chapter will first set forth the basic structure and nature of the facilitation test. Following this will be a discussion of the interaction between the test and the modes of religion clause interpretation. Next, the reasons for choosing the facilitation test over alternative legal tests will be discussed. Finally, the facilitation test will be applied to a variety of situations that arise under the religion clauses. It is essential to note here that even if one disagrees with the normative approach embodied in the facilitation test, it is possible to reject that approach while seriously considering the discussion in earlier chapters.

A. *The Facilitation Test: The Basics*

The facilitation test is essentially this: government action that substantially facilitates or discourages religion violates the Establishment Clause. The definitions of "government action" and substantial facilitation or discouragement of religion are essential to understanding this test. Before addressing these two issues, it is useful to note that the test is very much focused on the effects of government action, and as will be seen, purpose is relevant only when there is relatively clear evidence of an intent to favor or discriminate against religion. Focusing on effects is certainly not a new idea.[1] The effects prong of the *Lemon* test is a good example,[2] and the endorsement test also focuses on effects.[3] Additionally, a number of scholars have proposed effects-oriented tests, often based on the *Lemon* effects prong.

For purposes of the facilitation test, government action consists of any program, activity, or decision supported by government entities or officials (in their official capacity). Additionally, whether the actions or decisions of private individuals can cut off the government's role in facilitating religion depends on the nature of the government action and the role of the private individual or individuals. This is a clear rejection of the formalistic "true private choice" doctrine espoused in *Zelman v. Simmons-Harris* and *Mitchell v. Helms,*[4] but it allows for private choice to play a role in the analysis in certain contexts. This will be demonstrated below when the test is applied to a variety of situations.

Defining substantial facilitation or discouragement of religion is both hard and easy. Facilitation is not the same thing as support. One can provide attenuated support for something without facilitating it.[5] Facilitation is about furthering the religious activities of a program or entity, or about furthering religious practice or the stature of a given religion or of religion generally.[6] For example, in the aid context the facilitation test does not rely on bright-line distinctions such as direct or indirect aid, because it is the effect of the aid that determines whether it facilitates religion under the test. While it is more likely that direct aid to a religious organization will facilitate religion than will indirect aid (although indirect aid can facilitate religion as well), it is not automatically so.

Discouragement of religion is especially relevant in the Free Exercise Clause context. Significantly, discouragement relates more to religious adherents than to religious organizations. Thus, for example, government cannot facilitate the religious work of religious organizations, nor can it prevent individuals from using public funds at religious institutions under truly broad and open government programs.[7] These two concepts would dramatically conflict with each other were it not for the substantiality requirement. Discouragement will be addressed in a few of the examples in section D of this chapter.

Substantial facilitation is more than simply giving some minor support to a religious institution—it is not a strict separationist concept. It is a balancing approach that looks to the real-world impact of government action. Significantly, substantiality is tied to the government action—that is, whether a substantial effect of the action is to facilitate religion. Thus, in some contexts such as government-sponsored prayer it is always violated, while in the context of government aid programs the total amount of aid going to religious entities matters, as does the proportion of program funds that goes to religious entities.

The facilitation test will not provide bright-line answers in some contexts, but it might in others. Bright-line answers, however, are not the primary goal of the facilitation test. Rather, reasonable consistency is the most that can be expected. Reasonable consistency is possible under the test even in aid cases where context has the largest impact on its application. The goal is to provide reasonable consistency while remaining sensitive to the variety of principles that are at play in religion clause cases.

While the test is not perfect, it has the potential to be useful as an alternative to current formalistic approaches without sacrificing a reasonable level of consistency. The test attempts to effectuate various principles, especially separationism, accommodationism, liberty, and equality. Through its application the false antinomy between separation and accommodation will hopefully be reduced. The next subsection will explain in greater detail the connection between facilitation and the modes of religion clause interpretation. The subsection after that attempts to answer the question, "Why base the test on facilitation as opposed to other possibilities?" Finally, the test will be applied to a variety of situations that have arisen under the religion clauses.

B. Facilitation and the Modes of Religion Clause Interpretation

Any test that can flourish in the ebb and flow of religion clause principles must be capable of surfing the various principles of religion clause interpretation and the many factual scenarios to which these modes may be applied. The test must be flexible enough to apply to the vast web of religion clause scenarios yet concrete enough to give some semblance of consistency in its application.[8] Ironically, the fact that the various modes may ebb and flow in various contexts allows for some consistency within those contexts and may lead to a jurisprudence that is more consistent over time precisely because of its internal variations in different contexts.[9] The facilitation test is geared to do just this.

The test clearly connects to the separation mode because the test forbids government from substantially facilitating or discouraging religion. This places some level of separation between government and religion, although unlike strict separation the level of separation will depend on the given facts and issues in a given case.[10] Thus, separation may play a greater role in school prayer cases than it does in equal access cases (as is already the case), and this is perfectly acceptable because no one mode governs all situations, and using a strong level of separation in the latter context might conflict with several other modes.[11] The preclusion of substantial facilitation by government suggests a strong separationist component, but clearly does not require anything near strict separation.

Substantial facilitation also leaves room for accommodation because of the substantiality requirement. Government may accommodate religion, and even facilitate it, so long as it does not substantially facilitate it.[12] This will be seen when the test is applied to a number of issues in section D, and it explains why organized school prayer is problematic but equal access for prayer groups where a school has created a public forum is not. Moreover, accommodation is reflected in the facilitation test's prohibition on substantially discouraging religion.[13] As will be seen, this aspect of the test supports exemptions to generally applicable laws under the Free Exercise Clause under certain circumstances.

Equality is also promoted by the facilitation test. If government cannot substantially facilitate or discourage religion, it will be prevented from giving any particular religion or religions substantial benefits or inflicting harms on one group as compared with others.[14] The same would be true were government to substantially facilitate religion over nonreligion.[15] This is reflected in both the Establishment Clause and the Free Exercise Clause examples in section D.

Liberty may be fostered by the facilitation test, especially under the Free Exercise Clause. While religious liberty is the most malleable of the modes, the test may further it in a number of ways.[16] By prohibiting government from substantially facilitating religion, the liberty interests of those who do not wish their tax dollars or symbolic support to go toward such facilitation will be furthered.[17] Because the test requires substantiality, those religious individuals and institutions that simply gain some minor benefit from government will not be denied such benefits so long as the test is met.[18] Of course, the biggest connection between the facilitation test and liberty arises in the context of free exercise exemptions when such exemptions are necessary to prevent government entities from substantially discouraging religion.[19]

From a soft originalist perspective the facilitation test makes sense.[20] It precludes government from taking sides directly or indirectly (through substantial actions) in religious disputes or favoring religion generally or a given religion. At the same time, it allows for the flexibility to accommodate the reality that many in our nation are religious and may wish to express themselves religiously or have the freedom to practice their faiths free from unnecessary government interference.[21] The framers may not have foreseen the vast web of government activities we have today or the incredible religious pluralism, but at a general level they were concerned about navigating religious pluralism to avoid social upheaval and about preserving religious liberty at some level.[22] While the facilitation test is consistent with soft originalist concerns, it is certainly not mandated by them, and any number of legal tests may also be consistent with those concerns.

Finally, pragmatic concerns allow the facilitation test to function in a manner that minimizes encouragement or discouragement of religion, to use Douglas Laycock's language.[23] Pragmatism helps support the ebb and flow of the other modes and may help navigate the tension between them when such tension arises. The examples later in this chapter will help demonstrate this in action. While some may fear the pragmatic mode leaves the door open for subjective application of the other modes to support a given application of the facilitation test or that it increases the potential for doctrinal inconsistency, such concerns are misguided. Chapter 9 explains why, but for present purposes it is worth noting that pragmatism could not be used to undermine all the other modes of religion clause jurisprudence just because a judge wants a result inconsistent with those modes. The other modes would bind the judge to at least consider them, and the judge might use pragmatism to apply the facilitation test given the other modes or to choose which modes to apply.[24] As time goes on, stare decisis will lock many of these decisions into the case law, leading to greater consistency than under the current system, which has been anything but consistent.[25] Under the current approach judges use the modes along with illusory principles, often without openly confronting them, and this leads to inconsistency as different judges with different perspectives apply the same tests or principles in different ways.[26]

C. Why Facilitation?

Given the many possible tests that could be based on the various narrow principles that undergird the Establishment Clause, why should facilitation be the preferred test? There are several reasons for focusing on facilitation. First, facilitation resonates better with both separation and accommodation when they are construed as narrow principles. Moreover, it resonates with broad notions of liberty and equality, even considering the malleability of those concepts. Second, as will be seen, facilitation works well across the varied issues that arise under the Establishment Clause.[27] Third, the facilitation test is designed to minimize the real-world encouragement or discouragement of religion by government, and thus embodies

Professor Laycock's substantive principle (minus its claim of neutrality), which this book has suggested is quite valuable in analyzing Establishment Clause claims.[28] Finally, the facilitation test melds aspects of a variety of tests the Court has used in the past, and thus is not a completely new test. Its reliance on a variety of narrowly construed principles is new,[29] as is its attempt to avoid the tension between principles and tests that has been inherent in much of the court's doctrine, but the test is not alien to that doctrine, even if it is not perfectly consistent with it.[30]

Any test that arises in the religion clause context must function in a space where thousands of religious traditions thrive among hundreds of millions of people in a complex regulatory state. It must grapple with the constitutional command that religion, like speech, is special,[31] and it must do so in the context of a diverse array of issues.[32] The current Court seems to believe that the way to approach religion in the constitutional realm is to treat it the same as everything else in some contexts, yet recognize that it is different in other contexts.[33] While there is a plausible distinction between the contexts in which the Court has treated religion the same as other considerations and where it treats religion differently, the likely reason for the dichotomy is the vastly different alignment of justices in the various cases.

From the time of *Everson* until recently the Court seemed to understand that religion is different.[34] The early cases, animated as they were by notions of separation, clearly did not see religion the same as other considerations.[35] Yet even in those cases it was understood that religion could not be discouraged or discriminated against by government.[36] Ironically, the distinction seemed to be based on the real-world functioning and effects of programs in the aid context, a distinction that was later reflected in cases like *Zobrest* and *Witters*.

The facilitation test attempts to maintain fidelity to this distinction, and its focus is on the real-world impact of the government action or program in question—a necessary focus given the massive web of government programs in the modern regulatory state. It also tries to maintain consistency across issues so that the same test, relying on ebbing and flowing narrowly construed principles, can function in the aid context, the equal access context, the school prayer context, the religious symbolism context, and so on. Inconsistency in the treatment of claims between (and within) these various contexts has been a hallmark of Establishment Clause jurisprudence, because none of the tests works well in this diverse array of contexts without betraying the (often broad) principle(s) said to undergird them. The facilitation test can be applied across these contexts without betraying the narrow principles that undergird it. This can only be done by recognizing that religion is indeed constitutionally special or different, and that therefore religious entities and exercises should be treated the same as others only when treating them differently would discourage religion *and* when treating them the same would not cause government to substantially facilitate religion. To strike this balance the context and real-world impact of government action is of central importance. As a corollary, formalism is not the friend of consistency, and indeed consistency across the many issues that arise can only be achieved by carefully analyzing government actions in their context and by maintaining a connection to the narrowly construed principles that govern Establishment Clause analysis under the facilitation test.

I make no suggestion that the facilitation test is determinate in the sense that notions of formal neutrality or strict separation claim determinacy. There is no universal principle of facilitation that can be automatically applied to varied factual contexts to yield consistent results. Context matters. Yet, as was explained above, underlying the test is a narrow view of separation, which requires that government not facilitate the religious mission of religious institutions or enhance the stature of religion vis-à-vis irreligion or of a specific religion(s), and a narrow view of accommodation, which requires that government not discourage religion. There is potential tension between separation and accommodation, even when they operate as narrow principles. The facilitation test attempts to balance the competing aspects of these, and the other, principles.

In doing so it attempts to maintain equality as a narrow concept, but not by always treating religion the same as other factors. Rather, the test requires that religion be treated the same where doing so does not substantially facilitate religion, but the latter qualification recognizes that religion need not always be treated the same, and in fact that sometimes treating religion the same as nonreligion will give dominant religions an advantage over less dominant religions, and would therefore foster "inequality." Thus, facial evenhandedness is not the animating force behind this narrow view of equality. Equality, in this context, can only be judged by looking at the effects of a government policy/action and determining whether religion or a religious entity (or irreligion or an antireligious entity) or a specific religion(s) is receiving a symbolic benefit not received by others or a material benefit not practically available to others. Even then, it is not claimed that this is equality in any universally recognized sense, and it must be considered in light of the narrow versions of separationism and accommodationism. No approach to Establishment Clause cases would result in absolute and universal equality given the vast number of religions and potential government interactions with religion in the

United States, but the facilitation test attempts to make sure government actions do not make some religions "more equal" than others, or religion "more equal" than irreligion (and vice versa).

As was explained above, the test attempts to protect religious liberty to the greatest extent possible given the amorphous nature of that concept. It does so by attempting to minimize government interference in religious affairs and institutions. This is, of course, consistent with Douglas Laycock's notion of substantive neutrality.[37] Thus, it views religious liberty in the narrow sense of noninterference, but is cognizant of the fact that in a massive regulatory state noninterference by itself may not always promote what many people think of as religious liberty and that such a formulation is one of many said to further religious liberty.

In attempting to minimize government encouragement or discouragement of religion, the facilitation test recognizes that as a practical matter any choice will to some extent encourage or discourage religion, but as Laycock has argued, the goal must be to minimize the encouragement and discouragement of religion, not to make it nonexistent.[38] The substantiality requirement in the facilitation test is meant to help provide balance here. If the government action in question substantially facilitates the religious mission or status of a religion, religious individual, or religious organization, it encourages religion and conflicts with the separation principle. Moreover, allowing such substantial facilitation cannot be said to simply accommodate religion because religion would be receiving an important benefit from government be it material or symbolic. Conversely, if the facilitation is not substantial, it is more likely that religion is not being encouraged, and thus allowing the government action is less likely to conflict with the separation principle. Failing to provide the benefit to religion in these contexts might discourage religion, and thus allowing the benefit would be consistent with the accommodation principle.

The facilitation test is somewhat (although not completely) consistent with Court doctrine, both past and present. Its focus upon real world effects has much in common with the effects prong of the *Lemon* test. Yet the substantiality requirement would likely have allowed the programs at issue in *Meek v. Pittenger*,[39] *Wolman v. Walter*,[40] and *Aguilar v. Felton*,[41] to survive, while the programs upheld in *Mueller v. Allen*,[42] *Zelman v. Simmons-Harris*,[43] and *Bowen v. Kendrick*,[44] would have been struck down.

As will be seen, it is a given that government-sponsored or government-fostered prayer substantially facilitates religion,[45] but the display of religious symbols is very much connected to the question of whether a given display is a private display in a public forum or something else.[46] As will be seen, *Marsh v. Chambers,*[47] *Lynch v. Donnelly,*[48] and *County of Allegheny v. ACLU*[49] would have come out differently under the facilitation test, but every other symbolism, school prayer, and equal access case would most likely have come out the same way, albeit for reasons different than the Court's. Yet the facilitation test retains aspects of the endorsement test. For example, while the facilitation test generally rejects looking at legislative purposes given the problems with determining the purpose of a broad group of individuals acting as a legislative body, it does allow a purpose analysis in situations where a government actor, including a legislature, demonstrates an overwhelming purpose to endorse religion.[50] An example of such a situation is provided by the actions of two Kentucky counties in the *McCreary County v. ACLU* case, which involved the posting of Ten Commandments displays in county courthouses.[51] Another example is the well-publicized behavior of the former chief justice of the Alabama Supreme Court, Roy Moore.[52] Moreover, while the facilitation test is not directly concerned with the effect of government actors on reasonable observers, a government action that substantially facilitates religion is likely to result in a perception of endorsement by a reasonable observer; although whether it does or does not do so does not alter the conclusion that such an action would be unconstitutional.[53]

Additionally, an act that coerces participation in a religious event or program would ordinarily be one that substantially facilitates religion,[54] but the facilitation test is concerned with far more than coercion. Of the Court's three major tests, the facilitation test probably has the least in common with the coercion test, but as a practical matter the results in cases involving religious exercises (where that test has been most clearly used by the Court) would likely be the same. What coerces an individual to participate or remain silent while the government endorses or engages in a religious ceremony will substantially facilitate religion, but coercion is not necessary for the facilitation test to be violated.[55]

None of this adequately answers the question why the facilitation test should be preferred over these other tests. Even if one accepts the modal approach to religion clause interpretation and the value of ebbing and flowing narrow principles, such an approach might be used to support any or all of the current legal tests, or some other test. As was noted earlier, I do not suggest that the facilitation test is the only possible test under the interpretive approach suggested herein. Rather, I propose it because it does a good job of balancing and responding to the concerns addressed in this book and because it can lead to greater consistency both with the modes of religion clause interpretation and in the cases themselves. None of the existing tests has done this. Perhaps some other new test might, but such a test would be for others to propose, and then the merits of that test versus the facilitation test could be debated. For now, I will contrast the facilitation test with each of the Court's current tests.

1. The *Lemon* Test

The *Lemon* test has been oft criticized, and there is no need to rehash that criticism here.[56] The strength of the *Lemon* test is its flexibility and potential for considering real-world effects. Its extreme flexibility has also been considered a significant weakness of the test.[57] I do not see flexibility as a weakness unless that flexibility is not attached to some helpful mechanism for navigating it. This is the weakness of the *Lemon* test, which appears to be based on the concept of separation as neutrality, and further supported by originalism.[58] The problem is that other than separation none of these bases has anything to offer in supporting or applying the test. Moreover, because the test has often been equated with strict separation and formal devices such as the distinction between "pervasively sectarian" institutions and others or the distinction between direct and indirect aid, it has come to be known for both its strictness and its malleability.[59] Thus, it has drawn criticism from a number of quarters.[60]

The weakness of the *Lemon* test—its failure to adequately link up with legitimate interpretive principles—is absent in the facilitation test. The strength of the *Lemon* test, namely, its ability to consider and balance the real-world effects of government action, is shared by the facilitation test. Moreover, the tripartite nature of *Lemon*, where in order to avoid violating the effects prong in some contexts a government might be forced to violate the entanglement prong, is not present in the facilitation test.[61] The original goal of the *Lemon* test may have been to consider the facts on the ground as it were and make sure that government does not substantially further religious ends.[62] If so, this goal is consistent with the facilitation test, but the facilitation test accomplishes the goal without *Lemon*'s baggage, its failure to connect to helpful interpretive principles, and its sometime reliance on formal distinctions.

2. The "Formal Neutrality" Test

The Court has cast its formal neutrality test in the aid context as an application of the *Lemon* test as modified in *Agostini v. Felton*.[63] As you saw in chapter 2, this is a serious mischaracterization of the test, and formal neutrality is for all practical purposes a separate test used by the Court in the "indirect" aid, equal access, and free exercise exemption areas.[64] Given that this test was the subject of an entire chapter, there is no need to rehash the criticism of it here. Obviously, the facilitation test does not rely on the illusion of neutrality. Nor does it use formalism as a mechanism to avoid grappling with the real-world impact of government action. Perhaps most significantly, the facilitation test is openly based and applied under the principles that support it, and it does not make a metaphysical or purely rhetorical claim as does neutrality.

3. The Endorsement Test

The endorsement test has gained a great deal of support since it was first introduced by Justice O'Connor in her concurring opinion in *Lynch v. Donnelly*.[65] The problem with the test, as was suggested in chapter 8, is that it does not adequately grapple with what appears to be its focus—the perception of those who observe government action. This failure is potentially at two levels. The first level is who the reasonable observer should be under the test.[66] This has been much debated. It is unclear that the disagreement over this issue is evidence of the test's failure or of a good faith disagreement over the application of the "objective observer" standard in the test.[67] The bigger flaw in the endorsement test—and the one that may have quietly led to much of the dissatisfaction with it—is that the test does not accurately characterize the way people interpret.[68] The test treats religious symbolism or government action as though it sends messages to human receivers who are hit with the message and either perceive endorsement or do not.[69]

As was explained elsewhere in this book, the interpretive process is more complex and interactive than the endorsement test suggests. The meaning of various government actions may not be consistent even for reasonable observers, because of the way in which text (including situations) and interpreter interact.[70] Thus, trying to determine what message a given government actions sends is problematic.

Still, the endorsement test's potential focus on the impact of state action for both religious insiders and outsiders is quite important. The facilitation test asks similar questions, but rather than answer them based on the messages sent by state action, the test answers these questions based on the practical effect of the given government action. Part of that effect may be its impact on observers, and in such cases it makes sense to consider the effect the state action has on observers, but that is just part of the inquiry under the facilitation test.[71] In making that inquiry, the test does not treat the state action as though it were an informational strobe light hitting people with messages, but rather the test would require exploration of the perceptions of observers who have interacted with the text or situation.[72]

Given the way in which people interpret meaning, the endorsement test, at least as used by Justice O'Connor, has the potential to be quite indeterminate and to function as a mask for judicial preconceptions.[73] Justice Stevens's suggestion to view endorsement through the lens of a reasonable outsider or religious minority makes a great deal of sense if the focus of the test is to be whether state action makes outsiders feel like outsiders and insiders like insiders,[74] but these concerns can also be subsumed in the real-world focus of the facilitation test. That test may consider the perceptions of those actually affected by a given government action, but those perceptions will simply be part of the broader array of effects of the state action.[75]

4. The Coercion Test

This section compares the facilitation test to Justice Kennedy's indirect coercion test as set forth in *Lee v. Weisman*.[76] First, this test would be hard to apply in the aid context due to the lack of a "formal religious exercise" and seems best suited to situations where government speaks religiously.[77] Even in these circumstances the test has been used more as a floor below which government cannot go, while many actions that do not violate this test may still violate the Establishment Clause.[78] Moreover, Justice Scalia has criticized the test as not really being about coercion, but rather psychological pressure.[79] This seems an accurate description. Any coercion is not direct, but rather the result of a response to the situation involved.[80] Thus, it seems the indirect coercion test is not nearly as different from the endorsement test as Justice Kennedy suggests.

Certainly legal or indirect coercion to participate in a religious exercise would substantially facilitate religion, but such coercion is not necessary for substantial facilitation.[81] What if, for example, a student does not feel coerced to participate in prayers at graduation or a public school football game, but rather is highly offended by the prayer and sees it as just another way of promoting the dominant faith(s) in the area? What if the student feels neither coerced nor offended, but is moved toward a religious position because of hearing the prayer? In both cases government may have substantially facilitated religion without coercion. Moreover, as noted above, without a religious exercise the test seems harder to apply, and thus in the aid context, and possibly the equal access context, coercion is not terribly useful.[82] The best that can be said about coercion is that it is a relevant factor in considering the effects of state action, but by itself it is not up to the task of answering the many questions that arise in the religion clause context without first relying on unstated principles.

5. The "Tradition" Test

The "tradition" test was discussed in chapters 1 and 8. The earlier discussion raises the many flaws with this approach. It is worth noting, however, that long-standing traditions may be one factor to consider in analyzing state action under the facilitation test. The difference between this and the so-called tradition test is that these traditions are inadequate by themselves to demonstrate that religion is or is not being substantially facilitated.[83] Therefore, long-standing tradition is just a piece of evidence under the facilitation test, but may be of little use or may prove too much (i.e., that people did not complain about the tradition because of a sense of being powerless or at risk if they did so). For the reasons stated earlier in this book, the tradition test (when used by itself to reach results) is not a useful approach even as compared with the other tests used by the Court.

C. Applying the Facilitation Test

Perhaps the best way to understand the above discussion is to see the facilitation test applied to some of the common situations that arise under the Establishment Clause. The following subsections will apply the facilitation test to such situations.[84] As with any test in this area, there may be a tendency for those predisposed toward the results reached by the test to like it and those not so predisposed to reject it. Of course, this may not bode well for the facilitation test as folks on all sides of the Establishment Clause debate will like some of the results reached and dislike others. I see this as a strength of the test, because by considering context and rejecting either formalistic extreme (formal neutrality or strict separation), the test is able to reach results that resonate better with the narrow principles undergirding it and many of the Court's holdings (although certainly not all of them).

1. School and Legislative Prayer Cases

School prayer is perhaps the easiest scenario for the facilitation test. When government sponsors school prayer or other quintessentially religious exercises such as Bible reading, whether nonsectarian or not, it substantially facilitates religion.[85] The separation principle is clearly implicated here, as is the equality principle because of the effect school prayer can have on religious minorities and dissenters.[86] The liberty principle might also support this, but could go the other way as discussed below. Given the availability of private prayer anytime during the school day and equal access before and after school, the separationist concerns would outweigh any asserted group right to pray based on accommodation and/or liberty.

The question gets trickier when someone claims that the prayer is not government sponsored.[87] If the prayer occurs at a government-sponsored event, it generally violates the test because the government controls the forum and thus facilitates the prayer,[88] but what if the government-sponsored forum is a public forum? In this limited case, government is not substantially facilitating religion. Contrary to the odd ruling of the U.S. Court of Appeals for the Eleventh Circuit in *Chandler v. Siegelman*,[89] however, events such as graduation ceremonies are not public forums unless the government opens them up to counterspeech.[90] Even in a limited or designated public forum, the forum would have to be open to other speech by those appropriately using the forum.[91]

Thus, the results in *Engel v. Vitale*,[92] *Abington School Dist. v. Schempp*,[93] *Lee v. Weisman*,[94] and *Santa Fe Independent School District v. Doe*[95] were all correct under the facilitation test. On the other hand, *Marsh v. Chambers*,[96] which dealt with legislative prayer, was wrongly decided, because maintaining the chaplaincy and having the daily prayers in the Nebraska legislature substantially facilitated religion, both because the most substantial aspect of the prayer is religious[97] and because a formal daily prayer substantially provides religion with significant ceremonial recognition.[98] Moreover, under the facts in *Marsh* the special recognition went primarily to a single religion.[99]

Interestingly, *Wallace v. Jaffree*[100] is a questionable decision under the facilitation test. The legislative purpose to favor religion would violate the test if that purpose were clear, but given the large number of legislators involved in passing a state statute, such clarity can be hard to come by.[101] The evidence relied upon by the Court, including statements by the bill's sponsor, might not reflect the overall legislative purpose (assuming that such a purpose could be determined), and the facilitation test might not be violated. Under that test a moment of silence law that allows for silent meditation, prayer, or any other silent reflection a student may wish to engage in is not facially invalid.[102] In this context, prayer may be a small portion of the effect of such a moment of silence, and to the extent the moment of silence does allow prayer, the prayer remains personal to the student who chooses to silently pray.[103] If a statute were written in such a way that prayer was the primary option, or if prayer were encouraged under the statute as may have been the case in *Wallace*, the statute would be unconstitutional for the same reasons that *Marsh* would fail the facilitation test. More important, if a moment of silence law were applied in a manner that encouraged prayer, it would be unconstitutional as applied.[104]

2. School Vouchers

The Cleveland program upheld in *Zelman*[105] would violate the facilitation test. Yet not all voucher programs would automatically violate the test. There is little doubt that the Cleveland voucher program substantially facilitated religion even if one uses the comparison group the Court used in its analysis. As explained in chapter 2, the Court's choice of comparison schools is highly questionable.[106] The facilitation test is clearly and significantly violated if we remove the public school programs the Court relied upon to dilute the choice statistics.

Assuming that the Court was correct to include magnet schools, community schools, and tutoring stipends for public school students in the comparison group with private schools,[107] the voucher program still substantially facilitates religious entities. The fact that 3,637 students were given tuition vouchers to attend religious schools,[108] and that those vouchers were more than enough to cover full tuition for many of the students,[109] would have a substantial impact on enrollment at religious schools. Those schools are benefiting from thousands of students they would otherwise not get; as a result, the sponsoring religious institutions will have substantially increased ability to meet budgetary needs and further their religious missions, and thousands of students will worship and receive religious training at taxpayer expense.[110] Perhaps more significantly, since nearly two-thirds of those "choosing" to go to religious schools had inadequate religious school options within their own faiths, more than two thousand students are attending schools outside of their own faiths.[111] This gives those religious sects that believe in proselytization a captive audience, and even if students are excused from religious worship and religious training, they are still a captive audience in a potentially religiously infused environment with peers and teachers who may overwhelmingly share the sponsoring religion.[112]

While the largest group of religious schools in Cleveland consists of Catholic schools, which have a solid track record of tolerance toward those of other faiths in many areas,[113] the reasoning in *Zelman* is not limited to Cleveland. For those who live in areas of the country where the dominant religious schools are Evangelical, the likelihood that students will be regularly witnessed to by peers and others even if they are excused from religion classes is higher. Even in a religious school environment where there is extreme sensitivity to nonbelievers, the impact of spending one's elementary and secondary school years in an environment dominated by a religious faith different from one's own is bound to cause many voucher students to be more open to the school's faith. All of this on the government's dollar.

The above scenarios—increased student bodies with full tuition paid at government expense and impressionable students who may face serious challenges to their core beliefs or be influenced to adopt the core beliefs of the religious schools they attend—are indications of substantial facilitation of religion. The percentage of students in the Cleveland schools is irrelevant from this perspective. One could expand the comparison group to include the entire Cleveland school system, and the fact that more than 3,637 students are giving up to $2,250 each at religious schools (or $1,592—the average Catholic School tuition),[114] for a total of approximately $8,200,000 in the 1999–2000 school year based on use of the full $2,250 by all students,[115] or a total of $5,790,104 if one uses the lower Catholic school tuition rate, is enough to substantially facilitate religion.

When one excludes the public school options that the Court included in the comparison group, the facilitation is even more obvious. A total of 3,637 out of 3,765 students,[116] or 96.6 percent of students receiving private school vouchers, used them at religious schools.[117] Moreover, almost five times as many religious private schools as secular private schools participated in the program,[118] and on average the secular schools had fewer seats per school than the religious schools.[119] This is in addition to the millions of public dollars flowing to religious entities and the possibility of indoctrination mentioned above. Yet under the facilitation test voucher programs are not inherently unconstitutional just because a substantial amount of money may flow to religious entities and indoctrination may occur.

Ironically, since the facilitation test is not a rigid formalistic test, if there were a program of "real private choice" the program would be constitutional even if money flowed to religion through such a program. The reason for this is similar to the Court's reasoning in *Zobrest*,[120] because in a situation where government gives money to a large number of individuals to spend as they choose on a particular service, and there really are a wide array of comparable choices, both religious and nonreligious, it is no longer government that facilitates religion.[121] Moreover, the amount and percentage of funds in such programs that flow to religious schools are likely to be relatively small.[122] Yet if a large amount of funding in a given program flowed to religious institutions, the program might be subject to an as applied challenge under the facilitation test, because the test focuses on the effects of government action.

Of course, the Court used each of these points (except the last one) to support its ruling in *Zelman*.[123] The difference under the facilitation test is how seriously one looks at the effects of the government program and what counts as an effect that facilitates religion as compared to the Court's formalistic neutrality plus private choice approach. Under the facilitation test, the neutrality of a program on its face is only relevant to the extent that a program openly discriminates between religions or between religion and antireligion. The individual choice/circuit breaker concept is essentially a defense to claims that the effects of a government action substantially facilitate religion. Still, a program that provides "true individual choice"—something that did not exist in Zelman[124]—is not completely immune from constitutional scrutiny. Moreover, whether a program provides such choice is dependent on the way that program actually functions and the effects it has. As noted above, the Cleveland voucher program in Zelman did not provide such choice, and even if we use the Court's expanded comparison group, thus expanding the choice between private schools and certain types of publicly supported schools (but still not expanding the choice within the private school subset), the effects of the program substantially facilitate religion.

This approach is consistent with several modes of religion clause interpretation, especially separation and equality, because the real-world effects of some voucher programs will be to vastly favor religion or specific religions, putting nonbelievers in an untenable position.[125] The liberty principle may also come into play here because if the program is skewed toward religious schools as was the program in Zelman, the students may be proselytized by alien faiths in a captive audience situation on the government's dime.[126] Moreover, in some cases voucher programs will cross from accommodation to favoritism, and in such cases the accommodation principle is of little help, but in cases where there are really broad options a program may be upheld under the facilitation test and religion would be accommodated. Finally, the use of tax dollars going to support religious indoctrination at religious institutions may violate the principle of soft originalism,[127] and thus this mode, too, may be consistent with the above discussion. Of course, while many voucher programs may share the flaws of the program in Zelman, not all will. The next section looks at situations where government aid programs may survive the facilitation test.

3. General Educational Aid Programs

For purposes of this chapter, "general educational aid programs" are programs that provide money to individuals to be used at an educational institution for a specified service or services. Cases like Zobrest[128] and Witters[129] provide excellent examples of such programs, both of which involved funding for disability-related services. Other examples would be the GI Bill and Pell grants. These programs give a specified amount of funding to an individual based on legislatively or administratively determined factors. The funding is to be used for a given purpose at a qualifying educational institution.[130] A variety of secular and religious institutions qualify,[131] and there is generally breadth in the level of religiosity and religious affiliation of such institutions.[132]

Such programs do not substantially facilitate religious institutions as compared to nonreligious institutions, because there are generally a large number of qualifying institutions and a wide range of program beneficiaries from across a given state or the entire nation. To the extent that they funnel money to religious institutions, these programs generally fund only a particular service such as a sign language interpreter or other accommodation,[133] or tuition for only a small proportion of students attending a given institution.[134] Thus, these programs do not provide the disproportionate and/or substantial benefit to religious institutions that the Cleveland voucher program did in *Zelman*.[135] Still, by enabling students to attend religious institutions that they otherwise might not be able to attend, these programs might allow a substantial amount of money to flow to religious institutions over time. This is where the private choice defense comes into play.

If there really is a wide range of comparable alternatives for program participants to choose from under a government program, government is no longer facilitating religion unless the program consistently and disproportionately funds religious institutions as applied. Thus, the private choice of the individual recipient really does act like a circuit breaker, but the defense only comes into play where a program that does not disproportionately support religion provides a substantial sum of funds to a religious institution or institutions. Where a program does not disproportionately support religion and substantial funds do not go to religious institutions, the facilitation test is not violated. When the former is true but not the latter, the private choice defense can come into play to demonstrate that the government is not substantially facilitating religion, but rather individuals choose from a wide array of options to go to a religious institution.[136]

Two significant definitional problems arise here: first what constitutes "disproportionate support of religion," and second what would constitute a "substantial sum" of money. Both of these questions would be answered on a case-by-case basis based on the dynamics of the programs involved. Still, some guidance is in order. The most obvious examples of disproportionate funding would be where most of the funding in a given program went to religious institutions, or where one particular religious organization or a variety of entities from a specific religion or sect get the bulk of the funding that goes to religious institutions. In the second situation, so long as the program does not disproportionately support religion over nonreligion, the individual choice defense would be available.

What constitutes a substantial sum of money depends on the breadth of the program and the benefit the money gives religious institutions. Thus, in a statewide or national program, $8.2 million split among hundreds or thousands of participating religious entities would not be a substantial sum, but that same amount when applied to fewer than fifty private schools in one city would be substantial. The benefits allegedly garnered by the high school in *Zobrest* and the university in *Witters*[137] were not substantial even if one considers other students who might use the funds at religious schools under the relevant programs.[138]

An aspect of this is also tied to the substantiality of the funding to the religious institutions themselves. Thus, there is a huge difference in substantiality between a program that may enable a few disabled individuals to attend a religiously affiliated university or a religious high school (not even on a full tuition subsidy)[139] and a program that pays full tuition for many students at a given religious school or schools.[140] The latter program substantially facilitates the religious institution in its mission, but the former simply provides an incidental benefit to the religious institution while not limiting the educational choices of the program beneficiaries (who have a wide range of choices). To use Douglas Laycock's terminology, the former program does not significantly encourage or discourage religion, but the latter encourages religion.[141]

This is consistent with both separationist and accommodationist concerns. These modes need not be in total opposition to each other. By looking at the real effects of the programs at issue, the facilitation test effectuates the separation mode without conflicting with the accommodation mode. The reasoning also seems consistent with equality and liberty, which one might expect when separation and accommodation can be balanced (at least in part) based on the real-world effects of state action.

4. The Debate over Evolution and Intelligent Design in the Public Schools

The intelligent design issue is complex and promises to become even more complex over time. This section presents only a brief overview of how this issue might be addressed under the facilitation test. As a result, the complexity of the issue may be oversimplified here. The real question regarding intelligent design theory under the facilitation test is whether it is religion.

Recently, in *Kitzmiller v. Dover Area School Dist.*,[142] a federal district court found intelligent design theory is religion after hearing substantial expert testimony on both sides. Given the history of that theory, including its seeming evolution from the creation science movement and the fact that much of the funding supporting the intelligent design movement comes from religious entities, this would seem to be a fair assessment.[143] The evidence connecting intelligent design to religion is overwhelming.[144]

Intelligent design is really more of an antitheory than a theory. Its primary reason for existence seems to be to poke holes in evolutionary theory or fill any gaps in that theory with the notion of an intelligent designer.[145] Intelligent design theorists argue that some organisms are so complex that those organisms could not have evolved via natural selection and thus their existence must be the work of an intelligent designer.[146] These theorists use a good deal of scientific-sounding lingo, but in the end they do not subject their ultimate hypothesis, that an intelligent designer explains complex life and fills gaps in evolutionary theory, to the scientific method.[147]

One might use the work of Thomas Kuhn to argue that the scientific method is just a paradigm, that theories which presume an outcome are simply an alternative paradigm, and in the absence of some superparadigm to choose between them, one should not be privileged over the other.[148] The problem with this is that the same argument could be made by ufologists who believe aliens placed life on earth or astrologers who want astrology taught in astronomy and physics classes. In the end the broader scientific community accepts evolution and the scientific method, and it is that community that usually has the largest role in fostering the substance of the science curriculum in schools.[149]

Thus, the question becomes whether intelligent design is a generally accepted scientific theory, and if not, is it a religious theory? If the answer to the first question is no, which obviously seems to be the case,[150] the second question becomes key. If the answer to the second question is no, there is no religion clause problem, and teaching intelligent design in the science curriculum would simply reflect a questionable curricular and pedagogical choice on the part of school officials. If the answer to the second question is yes, then teaching that theory in science class would substantially facilitate religion because as the federal district court in the *Kitzmiller* case held, the theory is consistent with the beliefs of particular religious denominations and not based in good science.[151] Thus, teaching intelligent design as fact or potential fact would be like teaching theology as fact or potential fact. This would substantially facilitate religion in the most direct way possible, by using the machinery of the state to indoctrinate a captive audience of children with a religious message.[152]

In situations where intelligent design is not taught directly, but is mentioned as *the* alternative to evolution, the same problems would arise, albeit to a smaller degree.[153] Even mentioning intelligent design as *the* alternative to evolution will substantially facilitate religion by inculcating the religious values of certain faiths in students or at the very least greatly increasing the possibility that such values may be inculcated.[154] If the school also taught astrology, ufology, and so forth, this may be less of a problem. Clearly the teaching of intelligent design implicates the separation principle in a major way, and it cannot be justified by accommodation any more than organized school sponsored prayer could be.[155] Equality or liberty might go either way in this context, but pragmatism would seem to favor the separationist mode here given what is at stake when intelligent design is taught in the science curriculum.[156] As courts and commentators have noted, it may be possible to teach intelligent design or even creationism as part of a world religions or philosophy of science course so long as it is taught "objectively."[157] Such a course would not inherently facilitate religion unless there is evidence that religious theories generally, or specific religious theories, are being favored.

5. Government Display of Religious Symbols

This topic was discussed in depth in chapter 8 and thus will only be touched on here to show how the facilitation test might apply. Justices have used a variety of tests to evaluate government displays of religious symbols, including the *Lemon* test (perhaps now the *Lemon/Agostini* test), the endorsement test, and an apparent version of the "tradition" test.[158] This has led to some highly criticized decisions by the Court.[159] Under the facilitation test any government display of a religious symbol that gives special attention or recognition to a religious holiday or religion substantially facilitates religion because through such expression government gives the specified religion or religion in general a special place in the public conscience. The effect of such a display inherently has a significant religious component.[160] Of course what counts as a religious symbol is highly relevant here, as is whether it gives special attention or recognition to a religious holiday or religion generally.

The latter point is easier to address. The situation presented in *Lynch v. Donnelly* is an easy one to analyze under the facilitation test.[161] The crèche at issue in *Lynch* is inherently a religious symbol, and to a non-Christian as well as to devout Christians a few plastic reindeer and other plastic figures—most of which reflect the Christmas holiday—can not adequately (if at all) dilute the special recognition given to Christmas and the birth of Jesus which that holiday celebrates.[162] Christmas, whether celebrated in its commercialized form or as the religious holiday it is, is simply not a holiday celebrated by many non-Christians. Thus, the government display of a crèche during the Christmas season, regardless of the placement of that religious symbol, inherently gives special attention and recognition to the holiday and beliefs of a single religion, and in doing so it substantially facilitates religion.

The special attention or recognition requirement would not be met, however, by a religious painting in a museum because in such a setting the recognition given to religion is reduced by the context of the display. Religion is not substantially facilitated. Yet if the same painting were hung (not as part of a larger exhibit) in the main hall of the state capitol building the situation might be different.[163]

The symbol question determines how far this analysis would go. After all, a Christmas tree is also a symbol of Christmas. Yet a Christmas tree is not a cross, or for that matter a crèche The facilitation test would consider anything that is associated with a specific religion or religions a religious symbol. Thus, a Christmas tree, which is associated only with the Christian holiday of Christmas, cannot be considered non-Christian just because that holiday has taken on a commercial aspect as well. It is, however, a secularized religious symbols as used in chapter 8. Thus, erecting a Christmas tree even on government property without more would facilitate religion, but not substantially. The question becomes harder when official Christmas tree lighting ceremonies are involved.

Does this mean that the president publicly lighting the White House Christmas tree violates the facilitation test? The short answer is yes. The presidential lighting of the White House Christmas tree consists of the leader of the nation formally lighting a symbol that represents a major holiday of the dominant religion in the nation. This gives special attention or recognition to that holiday in a significant way. Imagine what would happen if a non-Christian president refused to have or light the White House Christmas tree. Of course, while the presidential lighting of the tree violates the facilitation test, it is a battle one might wisely abstain from engaging in.[164]

The point here is that the government should not be in the business of favoring religious symbols.[165] Doing so calls special attention to, or gives special recognition of, a religious holiday or a specific religion or religions. Unlike the endorsement test, however, the facilitation test rejects the notion that government posting of a religious symbol in situations like that in *Lynch* can ever be constitutional, because by their very nature such postings reinforce the religion(s) whose symbols are posted. This is not meant to minimize the potential conclusion under the endorsement test that the posting of such symbols may reinforce those whose faith is favored, or alienate those whose faith is left out.[166] It simply acknowledges that such feelings are the likely by-product of government engaging in actions that support a specific religion or religions. It is the support that violates the facilitation test, not the response of those who view the support to the extent the two can be detached.[167]

One final note here. This section does not address the private posting of religious symbols on government property when that property is a traditional or limited public forum. That issue would be dealt with under the facilitation test in a manner consistent with the equal access situations addressed in the next section. The distinction between government speaking religiously and private entities speaking religiously in public forums helps balance the separationist and accommodationist modes.

6. Equal Access

If organized school prayer is the activity most obviously prohibited under the facilitation test, equal access to generally available government forums is the situation most obviously allowed—in fact mandated. When government opens a forum to general access by a variety of groups, it cannot keep religious groups from accessing that forum. To do so would discourage religion, by putting religious groups at a disadvantage when compared with other non-government-affiliated groups.[168] This would violate the accommodation, equality, and liberty principles. So long as a forum is really open to all groups that are able to use that forum consistent with reasonable and generally applicable use guidelines, allowing a religious group to meet there does not substantially facilitate religion as compared with nonreligion. In fact, denying the religious group equal access puts it at a disadvantage when compared with other groups.[169] The same would be true of equal access to a public forum for expressive purposes.[170] Given the existence of a public forum, separationist concerns are not present, or at the very least they do not outweigh the other modes.

Equal access is something of a balancing act because one could argue that opening such forums to religious groups does give them a substantial benefit, even if it does not do so in a fashion that is disproportionate to nonreligious groups.[171] Yet this benefit, which probably would not meet the substantiality test in many situations, must be balanced against the discouragement that would occur if such groups were denied access on an equal basis.[172] When these concerns are balanced, providing equal access is more consistent with the facilitation test than denying access. Still, if a government entity administered an access policy in a manner that favored religion over nonreligion, or a specific religion over others, that policy would be unconstitutional as applied.

7. The Free Exercise Clause

This section will briefly address the implications of the facilitation test under the Free Exercise Clause. Free exercise concerns have been addressed throughout this book. As will be seen, the facilitation test need not be substantially modified to fit the free exercise context.

The primary issue in the free exercise context is that of exemptions to generally applicable laws. To the extent that government intentionally discriminates against a specific religion or religions, the test is automatically violated because such targeting substantially discourages religion in violation of all the major modes of religion clause interpretation. This is generally consistent with *Church of the Lukumi Babalu Aye v. City of Hialeah*.[173] On the more contentious issue of exemptions to generally applicable laws, there is a tension within the facilitation test that is not all that different from that which has arisen under other religion clause tests, namely, the tension between government action that interferes with religious practice (and for facilitation test analysis discourages it) and exemptions (which might encourage religious practice). This might be couched as a tension between separation and accommodation.

The facilitation test would mandate exemptions unless the government demonstrates a compelling government interest for not providing an exemption. Because the test is concerned with effects, the impact of a generally applicable law on religious practice would be taken seriously, since the effect of the law would be different as between the burdened religion and other religions and nonbelievers. The formal neutrality approach in *Smith* would preclude a mandatory exemption, thus discouraging the religious practice of the burdened religion,[174] but mandating an exemption would remove an impediment to the burdened religion and make the impact of the law more balanced between the potentially burdened religion and other religions. This is supportable under an equality approach, but not formal equality.[175] Moreover, as explained in chapters 4 and 7, the liberty and accommodation modes are especially well geared for the free exercise context, and mandatory exemptions are consistent with both modes, although without the equality concerns mentioned above, arguments could be more easily made for exemptions based on legislative discretion rather than those that are judicially mandated.

When exemptions are viewed in light of the burden a law places on the exempted religion, the encouragement an exemption provides is balanced against the discouragement resulting from failure to provide an exemption. When a "generally applicable law" substantially burdens a religious practice, the resulting discouragement is presumed to outweigh any encouragement. Thus, accommodation and liberty concerns outweigh separationist concerns in this context. The government still has the opportunity to demonstrate a compelling governmental interest, and may be able to do so.[176] The "compelling interest" requirement under the facilitation test allows for government concerns to be considered in weighing the practical effects of a law. It should be clear by now, however, that the compelling interest test proposed herein is openly based on accommodationist and liberty principles, and thus would be a more serious test than the compelling interest approach the Court inconsistently used post-*Sherbert*.[177] Open interaction with, and application of, the principles is more important than the wording of the test, even if the principles inform that wording.

D. Conclusion

This book suggests that the major tools of religion clause interpretation used by courts to justify religion clause principles and results in specific cases—neutrality and hard originalism—are illusions that serve no useful purpose. Yet, other principles of religion clause interpretation often underlie claims of neutrality or originalism. These bases—separation, accommodation, liberty, equality, soft originalism, and pragmatism—can be viewed as modes of religion clause interpretation. These principles can be interpreted narrowly and applied in a manner that allows them to ebb and flow based on context. Although it may seem counterintuitive, this book asserts that the use of multiple modes of religion clause interpretation that ebb and flow based on factual and legal context can lead to greater consistency in religion clause jurisprudence than reliance on broad, amorphous, and illusory principles such as neutrality. Moreover, the book suggests that those interpreting the religion clauses must better grapple with the meaning of religion broadly and its meaning for believers and nonbelievers. In the end, the book proposes a test that addresses these various concerns and applies that test to a variety of religion clause questions. Whether one accepts or rejects this normative approach, however, the description of religion clause interpretation and the discussion of the modes of religion clause interpretation can lead to a better understanding of the religion clauses.

Notes

1. *See* JAMES DAVISON HUNTER, CULTURE WARS: THE STRUGGLE TO DEFINE AMERICA (Basic Books 1991); *see also* NOAH FELDMAN, DIVIDED BY GOD: AMERICA'S CHURCH-STATE PROBLEM — AND WHAT WE SHOULD DO ABOUT IT (Farrar, Straus & Giroux 2005).

2. *See generally* Frank S. Ravitch, *A Funny Thing Happened on the Way to Neutrality: Broad Principles, Formalism, and the Establishment Clause,* 38 GA. L. REV. 489 (2004) (reviewing and criticizing the various forms of neutrality asserted by courts and commentators); Steven D. Smith, *Symbols, Perceptions, and Doctrinal Illusions: Establishment Neutrality and the "No Endorsement" Test,* 86 MICH. L. REV. 266 (1987) (same).

3. *See generally* Ravitch, *supra* note 2.

4. U.S. 1 (1947).

5. U.S. 203 (1948).

6. McCreary County v. ACLU of Kentucky, ___ U.S. ___, 125 S. Ct. 2722 (2005); Van Orden v. Perry, ___ U.S. ___, 125 S. Ct. 2854 (2005) (plurality opinion).

7. *See, e.g., supra* notes 4–6; Engel v. Vitale, 370 U.S 421 (1962); Abington Tp. v. Schempp, 374 U.S. 203 (1963); Lynch v. Donnelly, 465 U.S. 668 (1984); Zelman v. Simmons-Harris, 536 U.S. 369 (2002).

8. *Van Orden,* 125 S. Ct. 2854 (plurality opinion); *Lynch,* 465 U.S. 668; Marsh v. Chambers, 463 U.S. 783 (1983).

9. *Van Orden,* 125 S. Ct. 2854 (plurality opinion); *Marsh,* 463 U.S. 783.

10. The recent Ten Commandments cases provide an excellent example of this. Various justices claim originalist arguments support their positions, only to be countered by other justices who demonstrate some flaw with the first approach and claim historical support for their own. Perhaps the most interesting of these is the interaction between Justice Stevens's dissent in the Texas case and Justice Scalia's dissent in the Kentucky case. *See generally* the various opinions in *McCreary County,* 125 S. Ct. 2722; *Van Orden,* 125 S. Ct. 2854 (plurality opinion).

11. *Schempp,* 374 U.S. at 237–41 (Brennan, J., concurring).

12. LEONARD W. LEVY, THE ESTABLISHMENT CLAUSE: RELIGION AND THE FIRST AMENDMENT (Macmillan 1986).

13. PHILIP HAMBURGER, SEPARATION OF CHURCH AND STATE (Harvard 2002).

14. *Everson,* 330 U.S. at 28 (Rutledge, J., concurring); *McCollum,* 333 U.S. at 238 (Reed, J., dissenting).

15. *See* ISAAC KRAMNICK & R. LAURENCE MOORE, THE GODLESS CONSTITUTION: THE CASE AGAINST RELIGIOUS CORRECTNESS 31 (1996); Marci A. Hamilton, *Religion and the Law in the Clinton Era: An Anti-Madisonian Legacy,* 63-SPG LAW & CONTEMP. PROBS. 359, 361–63 (2000).

16. *See, e.g., McCreary County,* 125 S. Ct. at 2755–56 (Scalia, J., dissenting); *Van Orden,* 125 S. Ct. at 2865 (Thomas, J., dissenting).

17. *See, e.g., McCreary County,* 125 S. Ct. at 2743–45 (Souter, J., majority opinion); *Van Orden,* 125 S. Ct. at 2882–88 (Stevens, J., dissenting).

18. *See, e.g., McCreary County,* 125 S. Ct. at 2729 (Souter, J., majority opinion), 2763 n.13 (Scalia, J., dissenting); *Van Orden,* 125 S. Ct. at 2859, 2863 nn.9 & 14 (plurality opinion), 2883–84 (Stevens, J., dissenting).

19. *See, e.g.,* Wallace v. Jaffree, 472 U.S. 38, 53–54 n.38 (1985) (Stevens, J., majority opinion), 92 (Rehnquist, J., dissenting).

20. *McCollum,* 333 U.S. at 237–38 (Jackson, J., concurring).

21. Gadamerian hermeneutics (the philosophical hermeneutics of Hans-Georg Gadamer) provides an excellent framework for understanding this process. For more on philosophical hermeneutics, there are a number of useful primary and secondary texts. Perhaps most important is Gadamer's magnum opus, TRUTH AND METHOD (Joel Weinsheimer & Donald G. Marshall trans., Continuum, 2d rev. ed. 1989); *see also* HANS-GEORG GADAMER, PHILOSOPHICAL HERMENEUTICS (David E. Linge ed. & trans., 1976); HANS-GEORG GADAMER, REASON IN THE AGE OF SCIENCE (Frederick G. Lawrence trans., 1981). In addition to Gadamer's work, there are a number of good books that can serve as introductions to the subject. *See, e.g.,* JOSEF BLEICHER, CONTEMPORARY HERMENEUTICS: HERMENEUTICS AS METHOD, PHILOSOPHY AND CRITIQUE (1980); JEAN GRONDIN, INTRODUCTION TO PHILOSOPHICAL HERMENEUTICS (Joel Wein-

sheimer trans., 1994). Examples of sources addressing legal hermeneutics include LEGAL HERMENEUTICS: HISTORY, THEORY, AND PRACTICE (Gregory Leyh ed., 1992); William N. Eskridge, Jr., *Gadamer/Statutory Interpretation*, 90 COLUM. L. REV. 609 (1990); Francis J. Mootz, *The Ontological Basis of Legal Hermeneutics: A Proposed Model of Inquiry Based on the Work of Gadamer, Habermas, and Ricoeur*, 68 B.U. L. REV. 523 (1988); *see also Symposium on Philosophical Hermeneutics and Critical Legal Theory*, 76 CHI.-KENT L. REV. 719 (2000).

22. *See* Cass R. Sunstein, *Five Theses on Originalism*, 19 HARV. J.L. & PUB. POL'Y 311, 312–15 (1995).

23. *Id.* at 313.

24. *Id.* at 313–14.

25. *Id.* at 312–13.

26. *Id.*

27. *See, e.g.,* Mary Ann Glendon & Raul F. Yanes, *Structural Free Exercise*, 90 MICH. L. REV. 477, 481–84, 91–92 (arguing that incorporation of the Establishment Clause was done somewhat reflexively, in conflict with its original purpose as a restraint on the federal government's ability to interfere with state establishments, and that this has led to an unnecessary tension between the Establishment Clause and the Free Exercise Clause).

28. See sources cited in Robert J. Kaczorowski, *The Supreme Court and Congress's Power to Enforce Constitutional Rights: An Overlooked Moral Anomaly*, 73 FORDHAM L. REV. 153, 213–14 n.276 (2004).

29. *See, e.g.,* Clifton B. Kruse, Jr., *The Historical Meaning and Judicial Construction of the Establishment Clause of the First Amendment*, 2 WASHBURN L.J. 65, 66 (1962); Richard A. Posner, *Bork and Beethoven*, 42 STAN. L. REV. 1365, 1373–74 (1990).

30. *Cf.* Ravitch, *supra* note 2 at 556–58.

31. H. Jefferson Powell, *The Original Understanding of Original Intent*, 98 HARV. L. REV. 885 (1985).

32. *See, e.g.,* BENJAMIN N. CARDOZO, THE NATURE OF THE JUDICIAL PROCESS 30–31, 33, 65–66, 112, 165–66 (1921); William N. Eskridge, Jr. & Philip P. Frickey, *Statutory Interpretation as Practical Reasoning*, 42 STAN. L. REV. 321, 353–54 (1990).

33. *See, e.g., McCreary County*, 125 S. Ct. at 2755–56 (Scalia, J., dissenting); *Van Orden*, 125 S. Ct. at 2865 (Thomas, J., dissenting).

34. *See* Paul Brest, *The Misconceived Quest for the Original Understanding*, 60 B.U. L. REV. 204 (1980); Jeffrey M. Shaman, *The Constitution, the Supreme Court, and Creativity*, 9 HASTINGS CONST. L.Q. 257; *see also* Larry Simon, *The Authority of the Framers of the Constitution: Can Originalist Interpretation Be Justified?* 73 CAL. L. REV. 1482 (1985).

35. *See generally* Ravitch, *supra* note 2 (suggesting that the Court's use of concepts such as neutrality is really a cover for decisions based on other grounds); Smith, *supra* note 2 (same).

36. U.S. 203 (1963).

37. School Dist. of Abington Township v. Schempp, 374 U.S. 203, 237–41 (1963) (Brennan, J., concurring) (footnotes and citations omitted).

38. *Compare Everson,* 330 U.S. 1; *McCollum,* 333 U.S. 203, *with McCollum,* 333 U.S. at 238 (Reed, J., dissenting).

39. *See, e.g.,* Furman v. Georgia, 408 U.S. 238 (1972) (Brennan, J., concurring in judgment) (examining framers' intent regarding the Eighth Amendment); Ker v. California, 374 U.S. 23, 47–51, 54 (1963) (Brennan, J., dissenting) (speaking of the intent of the framers regarding the Fourth Amendment).

40. *See generally* PHILIP BOBBITT, CONSTITUTIONAL FATE (Oxford 1984); PHILIP BOBBITT, CONSTITUTIONAL INTERPRETATION (Blackwell 1991).

41. Ravitch, *supra* note 2, at 531–44.

42. Bobbitt, *supra* note 40 (both books).

43. Ravitch, *supra* note 2; Smith *supra* note 2; STEVEN D. SMITH, FOREORDAINED FAILURE: THE QUEST FOR A CONSTITUTIONAL PRINCIPLE OF RELIGIOUS FREEDOM (Oxford 1995).

44. The use of neutrality and originalism is so pervasive that one could literally use a citation like "see generally Supreme Court religion clause jurisprudence 1947–Present." For the sake of expediency I would suggest seeing the various opinions in McCreary County v. ACLU of Kentucky, ___ U.S. ___, 125 S. Ct. 2722 (2005); Van Orden v. Perry, ___ U.S. ___, 125 S. Ct. 2854 (2005) (plurality opinion); Zelman v. Simmons-Harris, 536 U.S. 369 (2002); Abington Tp. v. Schempp, 374 U.S. 203 (1963).

45. *Id.* (all four cases).

46. *Id.; see also Everson,* 330 U.S. 1.

47. *Id.; see also* Lemon v. Kurtzman, 403 U.S. 602 (1971).

48. *See infra* chapters 2–8.

49. *Id.*

50. *McCollum,* 333 U.S. at 237–38 (Jackson, J., concurring).

51. *Id.*

52. Jacques Derrida is perhaps the most famous deconstructionist theorist, at least in the legal academy. For an example of his work, *see* Jacques Derrida, MARGINS OF PHILOSOPHY (Alan Bass trans., Univ. of Chic. Press 1982 from the French Marges de la Philosophie). For an interesting discussion of the commonalities and differences between Gadamer's philosophical hermeneutics and Derrida's deconstructionism, including an entertaining hypothetical dialogue between the two philosophers, *see* STEPHEN M. FELDMAN, AMERICAN LEGAL THOUGHT FROM PREMODERNISM TO POSTMODERNISM: AN INTELLECTUAL VOYAGE 33–38 (Oxford 2000).

53. A prime example of this was provided by a panelist at the Association of American Law Schools annual meeting a few years ago. I do not recall who the specific speaker was, but the panel dealt with law and interpretation. The speaker began his comments by attacking Gadamer, who was

not even the focus of his talk or the panel. The attack had nothing to do with Gadamer's actual philosophy and seemed to be more of a broad assertion that non-"objective" interpretive theory was
useless. Fortunately, Pierre Schlag, a well-regarded
theorist, was on the same panel and respectfully
addressed the ad hominem attack during his comments. Such ad hominem attacks on hermeneutic
theory are not uncommon in the legal academy despite the fact that the attackers are rarely all that
familiar with the theory as divorced from its use
by particular legal schools of thought. For a good
example of basic criticism of Gadamer, although
not crass criticism, see Michael S. Moore, *The Interpretive Turn in Modern Theory: A Turn for the
Worse?* 41 STAN. L. REV. 871, 923–27 (1989).
Moore writes: "Philosophical hermeneutics cannot
be the brand of interpretivism that any theoreti-
cian should want for her disciple—on pain of losing any discipline at all." *Id.* at 927. Of course,
this completely misses the point of Gadamer's primarily descriptive approach. The question is not a
what a theorist "should want," but rather how do
people interpret? The fact that one may not like
Gadamer's answer that there is no objective methodology for determining interpretive truth, or that
Gadamer's approach is inconvenient for those who
want correct or best answers, does not in any way
rebut Gadamer's arguments. In fact, it may prove
Gadamer's point because many who attack hermeneutic theory seem predisposed against philosophical hermeneutics based on their own theoretical
views and traditions.

54. Robin L. West, *Are There Nothing but Texts
in This Class? Interpreting the Interpretive Turns
in Legal Thought,* 76 CHI.-KENT L. REV. 1125,
1126–27 (2000).

55. *See* Feldman *supra* note 52.

56. Frank S. Ravitch, *Struggling with Text and
Context: A Hermeneutic Approach to Interpreting
and Realizing Law School Missions,* 74 ST. JOHN'S
L. REV. 731, 738–39 (2000).

57. *Id.* at 739.

58. *See infra* chapters 9 and 10.

59. For an interesting application of Pearce's tri-
adic semiotic theory in a legal context, *see* ROBIN
PAUL MALLOY, LAW AND MARKET ECONOMY
(Cambridge 2000).

60. HANS-GEORG GADAMER, TRUTH AND
METHOD (Joel Weinsheimer & Donald G. Marshall trans., Continuum, 2d rev. ed. 1989).

61. *Id.* at 259–64.

62. *Id.* at 265–71.

63. *Id.* at 265–307.

64. *Id.* at 360–61.

65. *Id.* at 302–07.

66. *Id.* at 266–77, 306–07, 374–75.

67. Bobbitt, CONSTITUTIONAL FATE, *supra* note
40.

68. Bobbitt, CONSTITUTIONAL INTERPRETATION,
supra note 40.

69. *Id.* at 12–13 (listing the "doctrinal" mode
of interpretation, which involves following precedent).

70. *See generally* Ravitch, *supra* note 2 (suggesting that the *Zelman* Court both ignored valid principles of stare decisis by mischaracterizing precedent and used that very precedent to support its illusory formal neutrality doctrine in the voucher
context).

71. Ravitch, *supra* note 56, at 735–41.

72. Bobbitt, CONSTITUTIONAL INTERPRETATION,
supra note 40, at 8–9.

73. *Id.; see generally id.*

74. *Id.* at 111–86.

75. *Id.* at 168–69.

76. *See generally id.*

77. *See infra* chapters 9 and 10.

78. *McCollum,* 333 U.S. at 237–38 (Jackson, J.,
concurring).

79. *See* Owen M. Fiss, *Objectivity and Interpretation,* 34 STAN. L. REV. 739, 744 (1982) ("The
idea of an objective interpretation does not require
that the interpretation be wholly determined by
some source external to the judge, but only that it
be constrained.").

NOTES TO CHAPTER 2

1. *See, e.g.,* STEVEN D. SMITH, FOREORDAINED
FAILURE: THE QUEST FOR A CONSTITUTIONAL
PRINCIPLE OF RELIGIOUS FREEDOM 96–97 (1995)
[hereinafter FOREORDAINED FAILURE] ("The foregoing discussion suggests that the quest for neutrality, despite its understandable appeal and the
tenacity with which it has been pursued, is an attempt to grasp at an illusion"); Alan E. Brownstein, *Interpreting the Religion Clauses in Terms of
Liberty, Equality, and Free Speech Values—A Critical Analysis of "Neutrality Theory" and Charitable Choice,* 13 NOTRE DAME J.L. ETHICS & PUB.
POL'Y 243, 246–56 (1999) ("In theory and practice, neutrality theory does not live up to its own
ideals. . . ."); Steven D. Smith, *Symbols, Perceptions, and Doctrinal Illusions: Establishment Neutrality and the "No Endorsement" Test,* 86 MICH.
L. REV. 266, 314 (1987) [hereinafter *Symbols, Perceptions, and Doctrinal Illusions*] (the "pervasive
commitment to neutrality has not yet generated
any clear and convincing account of what neutrality actually entails. It has become increasingly,
rather, that neutrality is a 'coat of many colors.' ");
id. at 316 ("our attempts to say what neutrality
means turn out to be indeterminate and deeply
ambiguous); *cf.* John T. Valauri, *The Concept of
Neutrality in Establishment Clause Doctrine,* 48
U. PITT. L. REV. 83, 92 (1986) ("The conceptual
complexity, formality, and ambiguity of neutrality
are interrelated and mutually reinforcing. They
make the concept abstract and incomplete").

2. *See, e.g.,* Douglas Laycock, *Formal, Substantive, and Disaggregated Neutrality Toward Religion,* 39 DEPAUL L. REV. 993, 1005 (1990) ("substantive neutrality requires a baseline from which
to measure encouragement and discouragement.
What state of affairs is the background norm from
which to judge whether religion has been encouraged or discouraged? This question also requires

judgment; there is no simple test that can be mechanically applied to yield sensible answers."); Larry Alexander, *Liberalism, Religion, and the Unity of Epistemology,* 30 SAN DIEGO L. REV. 763, 793 (1993) ("no neutral principle for selecting the baseline that defines neutrality has been established."); Michael A. Paulsen, *Religion, Equality, and the Constitution: An Equal Protection Approach to Establishment Clause Adjudication,* 61 NOTRE DAME L. REV. 311, 333 (1986) (" 'Neutrality,' like 'equality,' is a principle of relationship, not of content. A statement such as 'the state should be neutral' is completely vacuous; it says nothing about that with respect to which the state is supposed to be neutral."); *cf.* Steven D. Smith, *The Restoration of Tolerance,* 78 CAL. L. REV. 305, 319–24 (1990) (critiquing the argument that neutrality requires a baseline, and rejecting neutrality as an empty ideal).

3. Smith, FOREORDAINED FAILURE, *supra* note 1; Alexander, *supra* note 2; Paulsen, *supra* note 2; Smith, *Symbols, Perceptions, and Doctrinal Illusions, supra* note 1.

4. *See generally* Frank S. Ravitch, *A Funny Thing Happened on the Way to Neutrality: Broad Principles, Formalism, and the Establishment Clause,* 38 GA. L. REV. 489 (2004).

5. *Id.*

6. *See, e.g., Mitchell,* 530 U.S. at 809–811 (plurality opinion); *id.* at 877–884 (Souter, J., dissenting) (plurality relied on formal neutrality, and Justice Souter's dissent rejected formal neutrality in favor of a form of substantive neutrality that is not necessarily decisive); Sch. Dist. of Abington Tp. v. Schempp, 374 U.S. 203, 215, 222–27 (1963); *id.* at 311–13, 317 (Stewart, J., dissenting) (majority equating separation with neutrality and dissent suggesting that accommodation is consistent with neutrality, but coercion is not).

7. Smith, FOREORDAINED FAILURE, *supra* note 1, at 96–97; *See also* Smith, *Symbols, Perceptions, and Doctrinal Illusions, supra* note 1, at 314 (the "pervasive commitment to neutrality has not yet generated any clear and convincing account of what neutrality actually entails. It has become increasingly clear, rather, that neutrality is a 'coat of many colors' ").

8. *See generally,* Ravitch, *supra* note 4.

9. William P. Marshall, *"We Know It When We See It": The Supreme Court Establishment,* 59 S. CAL. L. REV. 495, 504 (1986) (advocating approach that is more focused on the symbolic impact of government action than on government involvement with, and support of, religion).

10. Of course, while the Court may have been trying to send the message that it was being balanced in its religion clause decisions, that message presumed that there is a way to be balanced in such cases, and of course many people disagreed that the Court was balanced. *See, e.g.,* FREDERICK MARK GEDICKS, THE RHETORIC OF CHURCH AND STATE: A CRITICAL ANALYSIS OF RELIGION CLAUSE JURISPRUDENCE 26–27 (1995); STEPHEN M. FELDMAN, PLEASE DON'T WISH ME A MERRY CHRIST-MAS: A CRITICAL HISTORY OF THE SEPARATION OF CHURCH AND STATE (1997).

11. Smith, *Symbols, Perceptions, and Doctrinal Illusions, supra* note 1, at 268, 325–31.

12. *Zelman,* 122 S. Ct. 2460; *Mitchell,* 530 U.S. 793 (plurality opinion).

13. In her concurring opinion in *Mitchell,* Justice O'Connor decried the central role of neutrality in the plurality's approach. *Mitchell,* 530 U.S. at 837 (O'Connor, J., concurring in the judgment) ("the plurality's treatment of neutrality comes close to assigning that factor singular importance in the future adjudication of Establishment Clause challenges to government school aid programs").

14. *See generally Zelman,* 122 S. Ct. 2460.

15. *Zelman,* 122 S. Ct. at 2484–85 (Stevens, J., dissenting); *id.* at 2485–86, 2490–97 (Souter, J., dissenting); *id.* at 2507–08 (Breyer, J., dissenting).

16. *Id.* at 2473.

17. *Id.* at 2467.

18. *Id.* at 2485 (Souter, J., dissenting).

19. *Id.* at 2484 (Stevens, J., dissenting).

20. *Zelman,* 122 S. Ct. 2460.

21. *Id.*

22. *Id.* at 2460.

23. *See* Ravitch, *supra* note 4, at 513–23; Ira C. Lupu and Robert W. Tuttle, *Zelman's Future: Vouchers, Sectarian Providers, and the Next Round of Constitutional Battles,* 78 NOTRE DAME L. REV. 917, 938 (2003).

24. *Zelman,* 122 S. Ct. 2460; Steven K. Green, *The Illusionary Aspect of "Private Choice" for Constitutional Analysis,* 38 WILLAMETTE L. REV. 549 (2002).

25. *See* Lemon v. Kurtzman, 403 U.S. 602, 612–13 (1971) (setting forth test based on earlier cases which required that government action have a secular purpose, a primary effect that neither advances nor inhibits religion, and that there can be no excessive entanglement between government and religion).

26. Michael W. McConnell, *Religious Freedom at a Crossroads,* 59 U. CHI. L. REV. 115, 127–34 (1992); Michael Stokes Paulsen, *Lemon Is Dead,* 43 CASE W. RES. L. REV. 795, 800–813 (1993).

27. Philip B. Kurland, *Of Church and State and the Supreme Court,* 29 U. CHI. L. REV. 1 (1961).

28. *Id.* at 2.

29. *Id.*

30. *Zelman,* 122 S. Ct. at 2467–68; *Mitchell,* 530 U.S. at 826–29 (plurality opinion); *cf. Good News Club,* 533 U.S. at 110–12, 114 (addressing viewpoint discrimination).

31. *Good News Club,* 533 U.S. at 118–20; *Mitchell,* 530 U.S. at 826–29 (plurality opinion).

32. *Smith,* 494 U.S. 872.

33. *See* Ravitch, *supra* note 4, at 498–523, 531–44.

34. S. Ct. 2460 (2002).

35. U.S. 98 (2001).

36. U.S. 872 (1990).

37. *Zelman,* 122 S. Ct. 2460.

38. *Good News Club,* 533 U.S. 98.

39. *Smith,* 494 U.S. 872.

40. Laycock, *supra* note 2, at 998; Smith, *Symbols, Perceptions, and Doctrinal Illusions, supra* note 1, at 313, 329, 331.

41. *Cf.* Frank S. Ravitch, *Can an Old Dog Learn New Tricks? A Nonfoundationalist Analysis of Richard Posner's The Problematics of Moral and Legal Theory,* 37 Tulsa L. Rev. 967, 971 (legal scholarship symposium) ("the social belief in 'natural' rights might be useful in a given context, even if they are not objectively natural and are actually contingent on context. . . .").

42. Walz v. Tax Comm., 397 U.S. 664, 669 (1970).

43. Douglas Laycock, *The Underlying Unity of Separation and Neutrality,* 46 Emory L.J. 43 (1997) (separation); Michael W. McConnell, *Accommodation of Religion,* 1985 Sup. Ct. Rev. 1, 3–6 (accommodation).

44. Smith, *Symbols, Perceptions, and Doctrinal Illusions, supra* note 1 (suggesting that it would be impossible to prove neutrality so the other principles could not be accurately defined by the neutrality ideal).

45. It is possible that concepts such as separation and accommodation might serve as baselines for neutrality, which requires the setting of baselines, see Laycock, *supra* note 2, at 996, 998, 1004–05, but there is no place from which one can prove that any such baseline is neutral. Smith, Foreordained Failure, *supra* note 1, at 96–97.

46. *See Zelman,* 122 S. Ct. 2460.

47. Laycock, *supra* note 2, at 1001–06; Laycock, *supra* note 43, at 68–73.

48. Hugh J. Breyer, *Laycock's Substantive Neutrality and Nuechterlein's Free Exercise Test: Implications of Their Convergence for the Religion Clauses,* 10 J.L. & Religion 467 (1994); Stephen V. Monsma, *Substantive Neutrality as a Basis for Free Exercise–No Establishment Common Ground,* 42 J. Church & State 13 (2000).

49. Perhaps the most eloquent plea for substantive neutrality in recent years has come form Justice Souter. *See Zelman,* 122 S. Ct. at 2490–92; *Mitchell,* 530 U.S. at 877–84 (Souter, J., dissenting); Liza Weiman Hanks, Note, *Justice Souter: Defining "Substantive Neutrality" in an Age of Religious Politics,* 48 Stan. L. Rev. 903 (1996).

50. This is not because of any flaw in Professor Laycock's reasoning, but rather a result of the epistemological claim inherent in any concept of neutrality. *See* Smith, Foreordained Failure, *supra* note 1, at 96–97. Laycock recognizes the epistemic problem with claims to neutrality and addresses the concern by pointing out that neutrality is a function of the baseline one sets for the concept. Laycock, *supra* note 2, at 994, 996, 1004–05. Yet, without some way to determine if a given baseline is neutral, the setting of such a baseline cannot make a concept neutral. Smith, *Restoration of Tolerance, supra* note 2, at 319–24.

51. Smith, *Restoration of Tolerance, supra* note 2, at 319–24.

52. Laycock, *supra* note 2, at 1001–02.

53. *Id.* at 994, 996, 1004–05.

54. *Cf.* Thomas S. Kuhn, The Structure of Scientific Revolutions (3d ed. 1996) (discussing paradigms in the sciences and asserting that there is no superparadigm to decide between conflicting paradigms).

55. Smith, *Restoration of Tolerance, supra* note 2, at 319–24.

56. This Hobson's choice may be reflective of a larger issue, namely, the possibility that cultural, legal, and political currents favor secularism and may place religious adherents at a disadvantage by inducing them to take part in the dominant secularized culture at the expense of their deeply held religious convictions. *See* Stephen L. Carter, The Culture of Disbelief: How American Law and Politics Trivialize Religious Devotion (1993).

57. *See Zelman,* 122 S. Ct 2484 (Stevens, J., dissenting); *id.* at 2485 (Souter, J., dissenting); Steven K. Green, *Of (Un)equal Jurisprudential Pedigree: Rectifying the Imbalance Between Neutrality and Separationism,* 43 B.C. L. Rev. 1111 (2002).

58. *Zelman,* 122 S. Ct. at 2494–97.

59. Smith, Foreordained Failure, *supra* note 1, at 96–97; Smith, *Symbols, Perceptions, and Doctrinal Illusions, supra* note 1, at 314.

60. Smith, *Symbols, Perceptions, and Doctrinal Illusions, supra* note 1, at 268, 325–31.

61. *See* Ravitch, *supra* note 4, at 544–58.

62. *See generally Zelman,* 122 S. Ct. 2460.

63. *See* Christopher L. Eisgruber & Lawrence G. Sager, *Equal Regard, in* Law & Religion: A Critical Anthology (Stephen M. Feldman ed., 2000); *cf.* Alan E. Brownstein, *Interpreting the Religion Clauses in Terms of Liberty, Equality, and Free Speech Values—A Critical Analysis of "Neutrality Theory" and Charitable Choice,* 13 Notre Dame J.L. Ethics & Pub. Pol'y 243, 246–56 (1999); *infra* at chapter 5.

64. Everson v. Bd. of Education, 330 U.S. 1 (1947); State of Illinois ex rel. McCollum v. Board of Ed., 333 U.S. 203 (1948); Sch. Dist. of Abington Tp. v. Schempp, 374 U.S. 203, 215, 222–27 (1963). The most prominent proponent of separation as neutrality is Justice Stevens. *Van Orden v. Perry,* 125 S. Ct. 2854, 2882–88 (Stevens, J., dissenting). Moreover, Justice Souter's substantive neutrality approach seems to reflect the separation as neutrality principle, although not by itself. *Zelman* at 2485 (Souter, J., dissenting).

65. *See generally Everson,* 330 U.S. 1.

66. *Id.*

67. *Id.* at 19 (Jackson, J., dissenting); *id.* at 29 (Rutledge, J., dissenting).

68. *Id.* at 20–21 (Jackson, J., dissenting).

69. *Everson,* 330 U.S. 4–6, 16–18.

70. Carl H. Esbeck, *The Establishment Clause as a Structural Restraint on Governmental Power,* 84 Iowa L. Rev. 1 (1998); Noah Feldman, *From Liberty to Equality: The Transformation of the Establishment Clause,* 90 Cal. L. Rev. 673, 679–80 (2002); Ira C. Lupu, *The Lingering Death of Separationism,* 62 Geo. Wash. L. Rev. 230 (1994); McConnell, *supra* note 43, at 14, 23–24.

71. Smith, *Symbols, Perceptions, and Doctrinal Illusions, supra* note 1, at 329–31. This is also reflected in the differences between the majority and dissenting opinions in *Zelman. See Zelman,* 122 S. Ct. 2460.

72. *Cf.* Kuhn, *supra* note 54 (making similar argument about the lack of a superparadigm in the sciences that would allow one to select between various contested scientific paradigms).

73. Laycock, *supra* note 2, at 994, 996, 1004–05.

74. The idea for the NSF hypothetical was sparked by the implications of *Zelman* in combination with *Witters* and *Zobrest,* in regard to a statement made in Dhananjai Shivakumar, *Neutrality and the Religion Clauses,* 33 HARV. C.R.-C.L. L. REV. 505, 544 (1998).

75. For an excellent discussion of the relationship, and differences, between creationism and intelligent design theory, *see* ROBERT T. PENNOCK, TOWER OF BABEL: THE EVIDENCE AGAINST THE NEW CREATIONISM (1999).

76. *Zelman,* 122 S. Ct. 2460; *Good News Club,* 533 U.S. at 117–20; *Mitchell,* 530 U.S. 793; *Zobrest,* 509 U.S. 1; *see also* Davey v. Locke, 299 F.3d 748 (9th Cir. 2002) (denial of funding to student wishing to pursue theology degree under broad funding program violates Free Exercise Clause and state interest in not funding religious instruction is not compelling after *Zelman*).

77. *Good News Club,* 533 U.S. at 117–20; *Rosenberger,* 515 U.S. at 835–37, 839, 842–46.

78. *Davey,* 299 F.3d at 752; *see also* Nat'l. Endowment for the Arts v. Finley, 524 U.S. 569 (1998); Rust v. Sullivan, 500 U.S. 173 (1999); Regan v. Taxation with Representation, 461 U.S. 540 (1983).

79. U.S. 569 (1998).

80. U.S. 819 (1995).

81. *Rosenberger,* 515 U.S. 819.

82. *Zelman* leaves this possibility open, especially when one considers it in connection with cases that have found programs that exclude religiously affected beneficiaries from government funds based on their religious perspectives to be unconstitutional. *Rosenberger,* 515 U.S. 819 (program that excluded proselytizing student publication from receiving funds because of its viewpoint violates the First Amendment); *Davey,* 299 F.3d 748 (denial of student wishing to pursue a theology degree under government program violates Free Exercise Clause). The fact that the program in question is a scientific program does not alter this under a formal neutrality/exclusion as hostility to religion approach, because scientific standards are simply one perspective under such an approach, and the exclusion of religious voices from the marketplace of ideas because they do not meet the secular standards would seemingly violate the formal neutrality approach. The fact that many in the secular community see the exclusion of such voices as obvious could be used to prove the point that religious views have been skewed out of the debate by massive government funding supporting the secu-

lar scientific view. The notion that the secular community may view a situation as obvious and fair, while a religious community may see discrimination and hostility in the same situation, is not new. *See, e.g.,* Gedicks, *supra* note 10, at 26–27 (the difference in perceptions of religion's place (private or public) between secular and religious discourse "explains why, all too often, religious organizations and individuals experience the Supreme Court's religion clause jurisprudence as oppressive and alienating at the same time that others sincerely believe it to be neutral").

83. *See* Ravitch, *supra* note 4, at 513–28. *Rosenberger,* 515 U.S. 819, and *Davey,* 299 F.3d 748, demonstrate that exclusion of religious viewpoints from a general program of funding violates the Constitution. Add to this *Zelman* and *Good News Club,* which would apparently allow access by religious groups to almost any government program or forum that is neutral on its face, *see* Ravitch, *supra* note 4, at 513–23, and it appears that religious entities and individuals have the potential right to access broad-ranging government programs and will be able to claim that exclusion is hostile to religion and unnecessary under the Establishment Clause if they are excluded based on their religious viewpoints or government preference for secular viewpoints.

84. Laycock, *supra* note 2, at 1003 ("Government routinely encourages and discourages all sorts of private behavior. Under substantive neutrality, these encouragements and discouragements are not to be applied to religion").

85. *Zelman,* 122 S. Ct. at 2466–68, 2473; *id.* at 2476–77 (O'Connor, J., concurring).

86. *Id.* at 2491 (Souter, J., dissenting).

87. *Id.* at 2465–66; *id.* at 2476 (O'Connor, J., concurring).

88. *Id.* at 2465.

89. *Id.* at 2465.

90. This is especially true since the Court rolled the entanglement prong of the *Lemon* test into the effects prong. *See* Agostini v. Felton, 521 U.S. 203 (1997).

91. *Zelman,* 122 S. Ct. at 2467, 2473.

92. *Mitchell,* 530 U.S. at 816 (plurality opinion).

93. *Id.; Zelman,* 122 S. Ct. at 2467–68.

94. *Zelman,* 122 S. Ct at 2473.

95. *Id.* at 2491 (Souter, J., dissenting).

96. *Id.* at 2486 ("verbal formalism").

97. *Id.* at 2473 (using term "true private choice").

98. *Id.* at 2491–93 (Souter, J., dissenting).

99. *See* Ravitch, *supra* note 4, at 502–13 (suggesting that neutrality is not appropriate as a central actuating principle under the Establishment Clause).

100. I am reminded of Alfred Kahn's famous juxtaposition of the term "recession" with the word "banana" (he later used "kumquat") after President Carter had asked advisers not to use the term "recession" (Kahn was a member of the Carter administration). Peter Carlson, *Yes, We*

Have No Banana, NEWARK STAR-LEDGER, February 11, 2001, at 1. Of course, the distinction between that brilliant and comical juxtaposition and the one suggested herein (aside from the latter not being brilliant) is that there was at least some "objective" definition of the term "recession" that economists agree upon, levels in certain economic indicators that mean we are in a recession. William Neikirk, *Economy Remains Largely Stagnant, Jobless Rate Up as Payrolls Show Second Straight Dip*, CHICAGO TRIBUNE, November 2, 2002, at 1 ("sustained decline of at least six months in gross domestic product, the total output of the economy's goods and services").

101. *See* Ravitch, *supra* note 4, at 502–13.

102. Smith, *Symbols, Perceptions, and Doctrinal Illusions*, *supra* note 1, at 325–31.

103. Laycock, *supra* note 2, at 1001–06.

104. *See* Ravitch, *supra* note 4, at 502–13.

105. Some would argue that is exactly what the Court did in *Mitchell* and *Zelman*. *See Mitchell,* 530 U.S. at 837 (O'Connor, J., concurring); *id.* at 899–900 (Souter, J., concurring); *Zelman,* 122 S. Ct. at 2486 (Souter, J., concurring).

106. *Zelman,* 122 S. Ct. at 2473.

107. This might be called "verbal neutrality" and contrasted with actual neutrality, that is, with provable neutrality if there is such a thing. Similarly, Justice Souter has used the term "verbal formalism" to describe the Court's approach. *Zelman,* 122 S. Ct. at 2486 (Souter, J., dissenting).

108. *See generally Zelman,* 122 S. Ct. 2460; *id.* at 2473 (O'Connor, J., concurring).

109. *Id.* at 2470–71 (majority opinion); *id.* at 2473–74 (O'Connor, J., concurring).

110. *Id.* at 2491 (Souter, J., dissenting).

111. *Cf.* Green, *supra* note 24 at 559–60 (suggesting that the market will favor more established faiths with existing schools over less established faiths, and that adherents of the former will have more options than adherents of the latter).

112. *But see* Laycock, *supra* note 2, at 1003 (secular programs should not be considered when determining whether government encourages or discourages religion simply because they are secular. The relevant comparison is between religious and antireligious government action).

113. *Zelman,* 122 S. Ct. at 2491–94 (Souter, J., concurring).

114. *Id.* at 2494–95 (Souter, J., dissenting).

115. *Id.* at 2464 (majority opinion). As Justice Souter points out in dissent, the exact statistic is 96.6 percent. *Id.* at 2494 (Souter, J., dissenting).

116. *Id.* at 2464 (majority opinion).

117. *Cf. Zelman,* 122 S. Ct. at 2495 (Souter, J., dissenting) (of the more than 3,700 participating voucher students, only 129 attended participating nonreligious private schools, and all such schools combined had a total of only 510 seats between kindergarten and eighth grade, which of course includes seats for their nonvoucher students).

118. *Zelman,* 122 S. Ct. at 2469–70; *see also* Joseph M. O'Keefe, S.J., *What Research Tells Us About the Contributions of Sectarian Schools*, 78 U. DET. MERCY L. REV. 425 n.1 (2001) ("According to the national center for educational statistics, nearly 80 percent of all private schools are sectarian . . .").

119. *Zelman,* 122 S. Ct. at 2473.

120. *Id.* at 2464–65.

121. *Id.* at 2470–71.

122. *Id.* at 2463.

123. This figure was obtained by comparing Justice O'Connor's figure of 3,637 students attending private religious schools under the voucher program, *Zelman,* 122 S. Ct. at 2473 (O'Connor, J., concurring), with the overall number of 75,000. The figure 4.85 percent would represent 3,637.5 out of 75,000 students.

124. The majority also mentions that suburban school districts could have participated in the program, but none chose to. *Id.* at 2463–64. There are significant financial disincentives for suburban districts wishing to participate in the program because the districts would only receive a per pupil amount equaling the voucher amount plus the state's normal contribution, but this would not cover the per pupil expenditures in such districts, since a significant amount of their funding comes from local property taxes. *Id.* at 2496 n.17 (Souter, J., dissenting).

125. *Id.* at 2464 (noting that admission to community schools is by lottery).

126. *Id.* at 2494–95 (Souter, J., dissenting).

127. The fact that children may be exempted from religious classes does not alter the sectarian messages and pedagogy that pervade (appropriately so) at many religious schools, or the possible discrimination that outsider children may face in such environments. *Cf.* FRANK S. RAVITCH, SCHOOL PRAYER AND DISCRIMINATION: THE CIVIL RIGHTS OF RELIGIOUS MINORITIES AND DISSENTERS 7–18 (Northeastern 1999) (discussing instances of religious discrimination and harassment aimed at religious minorities and dissenters which occurred in public schools that engaged in religious exercises in relatively homogeneous areas).

128. *Zelman,* 122 S. Ct. at 2473.

129. *Cf.* Church of the Lukumi Babalu Aye v. City of Hialeah, 508 U.S. 520 (1993) (law can be facially neutral yet not neutral in its object. The law in this case was designed to discriminate against a religious group).

130. *Zelman,* 122 S. Ct. at 2491–95.

131. Justice Souter suggests the constitutionality of such a program in his dissenting opinion in *Zelman,* but only if it provides a range of choices compatible with that in *Witters,* a highly unlikely and expensive possibility. *See Zelman,* 122 S. Ct. at 2496.

132. *See* Ravitch, *supra* note 4, at 544–73.

133. *Zobrest,* 509 U.S. 1.

134. *Witters,* 474 U.S. 481.

135. *See* Ravitch, *supra* note 4, at 544–73.

136. *Good News Club,* 533 U.S. 98, 114, 118–20.

137. Examples of these cases include *Rosenberger,* 515 U.S. 819; Lamb's Chapel v. Center

Moriches Union Free Sch. Dist., 508 U.S. 384 (1993); Bd. of Ed. of Westside Cmty. Schools v. Mergens, 496 U.S. 226 (1990); Widmar v. Vincent, 454 U.S. 263 (1981); *see also Capitol Square,* 515 U.S. 752 (viewpoint discrimination to deny access to traditional public forum based on religious message).

138. *Good News Club,* 533 U.S. at 106–07.

139. The school building includes students from kindergarten to twelfth grade. *Id.* at 118.

140. *Id.* at 114, 118–20.

141. *Id.* at 106–12.

142. *Id.* at 102, 108.

143. *Id.* at 108 (the district, however, disputed the scope of the forum).

144. *Id.* at 103–04.

145. N.Y. EDUC. LAW § 414 (McKinney 2000) (stating purposes for which schools may be opened for public use).

146. *Good News Club,* 533 U.S. at 103–04; *id.* at 137–39 (Souter, J., dissenting).

147. *Id.* at 107–10.

148. *Capitol Square,* 515 U.S. at 761; *see also* Church on the Rock v. City of Albuquerque, 84 F.3d 1273, 1279 (10th Cir. 1996) ("Content-based restrictions are subject to strict scrutiny. Viewpoint-based restrictions receive even more critical judicial treatment.").

149. *Id.*

150. *Rosenberger,* 515 U.S. at 829–30.

151. *Good News Club,* 533 U.S. at 112–13.

152. Bartnicki v. Vopper, 532 U.S. 514, 544 (2001) (Rehnquist, J., dissenting) (implying discrimination based on viewpoint is subject to strict scrutiny); *Church on the Rock,* 84 F.3d at 1279 ("Content-based restrictions are subject to strict scrutiny. Viewpoint-based restrictions receive even more critical judicial treatment."). The fact that the Court in *Good News Club* refused to decide whether viewpoint discrimination might be justified in order to prevent violations of the Establishment Clause in rare circumstances at least leaves the question open. *Good News Club,* 533 U.S. at 112–13.

153. *Good News Club,* 533 U.S. at 113–16; *id.* at 137–39 (Souter, J., dissenting).

154. *Id.* at 118–20.

155. The mission of the club is reflected in the format of the club's meetings as described by Justice Souter in his dissenting opinion. *Id.* at 137–39 (Souter, J., dissenting).

156. *Id.* at 111–12, 114, 118–20.

157. *Id.* at 118–20.

158. *Id.* at 106–12.

159. This is certainly implicit in *Good News Club. Id.* at 112–20.

160. *Id.*

161. *Id.*

162. *Cf.* Alexander T. Aleinikoff, *A Case for Race Consciousness,* 91 COLUM. L. REV. 1061, 1087–88 (1991) ("Recognizing race validates the lives and experiences of those who have been burdened because of their race. White racism has made 'blackness' a relevant category in our soci-

ety"); Frank S. Ravitch, *Creating Chaos in the Name of Consistency: Affirmative Action and the Odd Legacy of Adarand Constructors, Inc. v. Pena,* 101 DICK. L. REV. 281, 292–93 (1997) ("to treat legislation aimed at remedying the effects of past or present discrimination directed at racial minorities and legislation meant to discriminate against those minorities as the same, one must completely divorce the legislation from its historical context and turn the debate into an ahistorical analysis of racial categorization."); David A. Strauss, *The Myth of Colorblindness,* 1986 SUP. CT. REV. 99, 105–06 (race-neutral policies "give weight" to disabilities that racism has genuinely created for African Americans).

163. *See* Daniel O. Conkle, *The Path of American Religious Liberty: From the Original Theology to Formal Neutrality and an Uncertain Future,* 75 IND. L. J. 1, 25 (2000) ("the doctrine of formal neutrality implies that religion is neither distinct nor distinctly important. Indeed, it implies that religion is virtually an irrelevancy, to be treated under the Constitution in the same way that race is treated under the Constitution").

164. *Id.*

165. *Cf.* Green, *supra* note 24, at 559–60 (suggesting that vouchers will favor groups with larger numbers and established schools over those with fewer numbers and lower support for sectarian schools).

166. *Smith,* 494 U.S. at 874.

167. *Id.*

168. *Id.*

169. *See* Respondents' Brief at 1–5, Employment Div. v. Smith, 485 U.S. 660 (1988) (Nos. 86-946, 86-947), 1987 WL 880316; Garrett Epps, *To an Unknown God: The Hidden History of* Employment Division v. Smith, 30 ARIZ. ST. L.J. 953, 962–63, 981–85 (1998).

170. Garrett Epps, *What We Talk About When We Talk About Free Exercise,* 30 ARIZ. ST. L.J. 563, 583 (1998) ("An uncontroverted part of the record was the relentless opposition by the people religion to the use of peyote outside the ritual context, and to the use of other drugs and alcohol for any reason whatsoever."); *see also* Employment Div. v. Smith, 494 U.S. 872, 913–16 (1990) (Blackmun, J., dissenting).

171. *See generally Smith,* 494 U.S. 872.

172. *Id.*

173. *Id.*

174. U.S. 398 (1963).

175. *Id.*

176. *Id.* at 406; *see also* Douglas Laycock, *The Remnants of Free Exercise,* 1990 Sup. Ct. Rev. 1, 50 (1990) ("The other point in the Court's explanation of its unemployment compensation cases is secular exemptions. If the state grants exemptions from its law for secular reasons, then it must grant comparable exemptions for religious reasons. . . . In general, the allowance of any exemption is substantial evidence that religious exemptions would not threaten the statutory scheme.").

177. U.S. 205 (1972).

178. *Id.*

179. *Id.* at 209–12, 216–18, 222–27, 235–36.

180. Wisconsin v. Yoder, 406 U.S. 205, 241–42 (1972) (Douglas, J., dissenting); Stephen M. Feldman, *Religious Minorities and the First Amendment: The History, the Doctrine, and the Future*, 6 U. Pa. J. Const. L. 222, 252–56 (2003) (noting that *Yoder* "illustrates the importance of Christianity for a successful free exercise exemption claim"); *see also* Richard J. Arneson & Ian Shapiro, *Democratic Autonomy and Religious Freedom: A Critique of* Wisconsin v. Yoder, *in* Political Order 365–68 (Ian Shapiro & Russell Hardin eds., 1996); Ira C. Lupu, *Reconstructing the Establishment Clause: The Case Against Discretionary Accommodation of Religion*, 140 U. Pa. L. Rev. 555, 563 n.17 (1991).

181. *See* Garrett Epps, *To an Unknown God: The Hidden History of* Employment Division v. Smith, 30 Ariz. St. L.J. 953, 1015 (1998) ("[A]ll the parties were shocked at how the Court had decided [*Smith*]. Most observers, both at the time and later, have concluded that . . . the Court rewrote the entire jurisprudence of the Free Exercise Clause. . . ."); *see also id.* at 956–57 nn.11–12 (citing many legal and journalistic commentators criticizing *Smith* soon after it was decided).

182. *See* Brief for Petitioners, Employment Div. v. Smith, 494 U.S. 872 (1990) (No. 88-1213), 1989 WL 1126846; Garrett Epps, *To an Unknown God: The Hidden History of* Employment Division v. Smith, 30 Ariz. St. L.J. 953, 990, 1010–15 (1998). This was also confirmed in a conversation I had with former Oregon attorney general Dave Frohnmayer in Kyoto, Japan, in 2001, when we both spoke at a forum addressing the free exercise of religion at Doshisha University, where Frohnmayer was speaking as the president of the University of Oregon and I was a Fulbright Scholar at the Faculty of Law at Doshisha University.

183. *Id.*

184. *See infra* notes 193–94, and accompanying text.

185. In fact, no non-Christian has ever won a Free Exercise Clause exemption case before the U.S. Supreme Court, and even most Christians have lost such cases. Mark Tushnet, *"Of Church and State and the Supreme Court": Kurland Revisited*, 1989 S. Ct. Rev. 373, 381 (1989).

186. *See, e.g.,* Goldman v. Weinberger, 475 U.S. 503 (1986) (military setting); O'Lone v. Estate of Shabazz, 482 U.S. 342 (1987) (prison setting).

187. Bowen v. Roy, 476 U.S. 693 (1986).

188. United States v. Lee, 455 U.S. 252 (1982).

189. Lower court cases went both ways after *Sherbert* and *Yoder*, and while many denied the claimant's exemptions, a number did not. *See, e.g.,* Dayton Christian Schs., Inc. v. Ohio Civil Rights Comm'n, 766 F.2d 932 (6th Cir. 1985) (school's free exercise rights violated by application of civil rights laws); McCurry v. Tesch, 738 F.2d 271 (8th Cir. 1984) (enforcement of state order against operation of church school in violation of state law

infringed church's free exercise rights); *Warner v. Graham*, 675 F. Supp. 1171 (D.N.D. 1987) (Free Exercise Clause violated where plaintiff lost her job because of sacramental peyote use); United States v. Lewis, 638 F. Supp. 573 (W.D. Mich. 1986) (rule requiring government to consent to waiver of a jury trial violated defendants' free exercise rights); United States v. Abeyta, 632 F. Supp. 1301 (D.N.M. 1986) (Bald Eagle Protection Act violated defendant's free exercise rights); Equal Employment Opportunity Comm'n v. Fremont Christian Sch., 609 F. Supp. 344 (N.D. Calif. 1984) (same); Congregation Beth Yitzchok of Rockland, Inc. v. Town of Ramapo, 593 F. Supp. 655 (S.D.N.Y. 1984) (regulations interfering with congregation's operation of its nursery school violated free exercise rights); Chapman v. Pickett, 491 F. Supp. 967 (C.D. Ill. 1980) (free exercise rights of Black Muslim prisoner were violated by his punishment for refusal to follow order to handle pork); Geller v. Sec'y of Def., 423 F. Supp. 16 (D.D.C. 1976) (regulation denying Jewish chaplain right to wear facial hair violated his free exercise rights); Lincoln v. True, 408 F. Supp. 22 (W.D. Ky. 1975) (denial of unemployment compensation to claimant who terminated employment for religious reasons infringed her free exercise rights); Am. Friends Serv. Comm. v. United States, 368 F. Supp. 1176 (E.D. Pa. 1973) (tax withholding statute violates plaintiffs' free exercise rights); Nicholson v. Bd of Comm'rs, 338 F. Supp. 48 (N.D. Ala. 1972) (statutory oath required of applicant for admission to state bar infringed on applicant's free exercise rights).

190. *Smith,* 494 U.S. at 883–84.

191. *Id.* at 874–75, 878.

192. *Id.* at 881–82.

193. *Id.*

194. Frederick Mark Gedicks, The Rhetoric of Church and State 98–99 (1995); John Thomas Bannon, Jr., *The Legality of the Religious Use of Peyote by the Native American Church: A Commentary on the Free Exercise, Equal Protection, and Establishment Issues Raised by the* Peyote Way Church of God *Case,* 22 Am. Indian L. Rev. 475, 484 (1998); Christopher L. Eisgruber & Lawrence G. Sager, *Why the Religious Freedom Restoration Act Is Unconstitutional*, 69 N.Y.U. L. Rev. 437, 446–47 (1994); Lino A. Graglia, *Church of the Lukumi Babalu Aye: Of Animal Sacrifice and Religious Persecution*, 85 Geo. L.J. 1, 16 (1996); Marci A. Hamilton, *The Religious Freedom Restoration Act: Letting the Fox into the Henhouse Under Cover of Section 5 of the Fourteenth Amendment*, 16 Cardozo L. Rev. 357, 385 n.101 (1994); Ira C. Lupu, *The Lingering Death of Separationism*, 62 Geo. Wash. L. Rev. 230, 237 (1993); Robert W. Tuttle, *How Firm a Foundation? Protecting the Religious Land Uses After Boerne*, 68 Geo. Wash. L. Rev. 861, 871–72 (2000).

195. *Id.*

196. *See infra* chapters 4, 7, 9, and 10.

197. *See generally Smith,* 494 U.S. 872.

198. *Id.* at 891 (O'Connor, J., concurring in the judgment); *id.* at 907 (Blackmun, J., dissenting).
199. *Id.* at 890.
200. *See generally id.; id.* at 886 n.3.
201. *Id.* at 891 (O'Connor, J., concurring in the judgment); *id.* at 907 (Blackmun, J., dissenting).

NOTES TO CHAPTER 3

1. *See, e.g.,* Mitchell v. Helms, 530 U.S. 793, 827–28 (2000) (plurality opinion) (suggesting that the dissent "seemingly . . . reserve[s] special hostility for those who take their religion seriously"— apparently because the dissent did not apply formal neutrality—but without explaining further why this is hostility); Rosenberger v. Rector & Visitors of the Univ. of Va., 515 U.S. 819, 845–46 (1995) (explaining that the viewpoint discrimination under the facts of the case "would risk fostering a pervasive bias or hostility to religion," without explaining how viewpoint discrimination based on an erroneous interpretation of the Establishment Clause, but not on antagonism toward religion, would risk fostering hostility as opposed to bias against religion); Tex. Monthly, Inc. v. Bullock, 489 U.S. 1, 9 (1989) (noting that "government may not be overtly hostile to religion," without explaining what would constitute such hostility).

2. *Mitchell,* 530 U.S. at 827–28 (plurality opinion); *Rosenberger,* 515 U.S. at 845–46; *cf.* Bd. of Educ. of Westside Cmty. Schs. v. Mergens ex rel. Mergens, 496 U.S. 226, 248 (1990) (plurality opinion) ("[I]f a State refused to let religious groups use facilities open to others, then it would demonstrate not neutrality but hostility toward religion."). *But see* Locke v. Davey, 124 S. Ct. 1307, 1313–14 (2004) (holding that it is not hostile to religion to deny funding for training as a minister under a generally applicable funding program).

3. *See* Zelman v. Simmons-Harris, 536 U.S. 639 (2002) (upholding a voucher program in which more than 96 percent of tuition vouchers went to religious schools, where the bulk of the seats were available to voucher students, because the program was facially neutral and allowed parents to "choose" where to send their children); *Mitchell,* 530 U.S. at 793 (plurality opinion) (holding that facial neutrality is the primary test for judging the constitutionality of a government program through which equipment was lent to schools, including religious schools); Employment Div. v. Smith, 494 U.S. 872 (1990) (holding that exemptions to laws of "general applicability" are not mandated by the Free Exercise Clause). *But see* Santa Fe Indep. Sch. Dist. v. Doe, 530 U.S. 290 (2000) (applying the less formalistic endorsement, coercion, and Lemon tests to hold prayer at public high school football games unconstitutional).

4. *See, e.g.,* Frank S. Ravitch, *A Funny Thing Happened on the Way to Neutrality: Broad Principles, Formalism, and the Establishment Clause,* 38 GA. L. Rev. 489, 490–513 (2004) (criticizing the Court's shift to a formalistic neutrality approach in

Establishment Clause cases and asserting that the Court utterly fails to explain how its approach is neutral or how neutrality can exist in religion clause disputes).

5. 530 U.S. 793 (2000).
6. I have argued that it is not. *See generally* Ravitch, *supra* note 4.
7. 124 S. Ct. 1307 (2004).
8. I would suggest that in some contexts they are. For a discussion of this debate, *see, e.g.,* PHILIP HAMBURGER, SEPARATION OF CHURCH AND STATE (2002) (discussing the history of separation and suggesting that separationism has historically been connected to hostility toward religion); LEONARD W. LEVY, THE ESTABLISHMENT CLAUSE: RELIGION AND THE FIRST AMENDMENT (Univ. N.C. Press, rev. ed. 1994) (discussing the history of separation and its role in protecting religion and religious freedom); Douglas Laycock, *The Many Meanings of Separation,* 70 U. CHI. L. REV. 1667 (2003) (reviewing Hamburger's book and suggesting that Hamburger oversimplifies the justifications for separation)); *see also* Steven K. Green, *Of (Un)Equal Jurisprudential Pedigree: Rectifying the Imbalance Between Neutrality and Separationism,* 43 B.C. L. REV. 1111, 1117–25 (2002) (addressing the relationship between neutrality and separation and further addressing various views of separation).

9. *See, e.g.,* Rosenberger v. Rector & Visitors of the Univ. of Va., 515 U.S. 819, 845–46 (1995) (ruling that a university cannot deny funding to a religious student newspaper if it allows other non-school-sponsored student groups and publications access to such funding); Bd. of Educ. of Westside Cmty. Schs. v. Mergens ex rel. Mergens, 496 U.S. 226, 248 (1990) (plurality opinion) (upholding the Equal Access Act, which requires that public secondary schools give religious, political, and other groups access to meet at school facilities if other non-curriculum-related student groups are given access).

10. *See, e.g., Mitchell,* 530 U.S. at 827–28 (suggesting that the exclusion of religious schools from a government program that provided loaned equipment to qualifying schools is hostile to religion).

11. Formal neutrality requires that there be facial neutrality of government action—the government cannot intentionally favor or discriminate against religion or a specific religion. In the context of government aid—financial or otherwise—there must also be private choice, which requires that the aid flows literally or figuratively through the hands of private individuals before reaching a religious institution or organization. *See* Zelman v. Simmons-Harris, 536 U.S. 639, 649–53 (2002).

12. Ravitch, *supra* note 4, at 498–513; *see also* STEVEN D. SMITH, FOREORDAINED FAILURE: THE QUEST FOR A CONSTITUTIONAL PRINCIPLE OF RELIGIOUS FREEDOM 96 (1995) [hereinafter Smith, FOREORDAINED FAILURE] ("The foregoing discussion suggests that the quest for neutrality, despite its understandable appeal and the tenacity with

which it has been pursued, is an attempt to grasp at an illusion."); Steven D. Smith, *Symbols, Perceptions, and Doctrinal Illusions: Establishment Neutrality and the "No Endorsement" Test*, 86 MICH. L. REV. 266, 316 (1987) ("[O]ur attempts to say what neutrality means turn out to be indeterminate and deeply ambiguous.").

13. Ravitch, *supra* note 4, at 498–513 (suggesting that the concept of neutrality makes an inherent universal claim); cf. Smith, FORFORDAINED FAILURE, *supra* note 12, at 97 ("The impossibility of a truly 'neutral' theory of religious freedom is analogous to the impossibility, recognized by modern philosophers, of finding some outside Archimedean point . . . from which to look down on and describe reality.").

14. This has been reflected in a great deal of scholarship that has suggested that liberalism (or secularism) is hostile to religion when it attempts to keep public discourse and public life primarily secular. *See, e.g.*, Edward McGlynn Gaffney, Jr., *Hostility to Religion, American Style*, 42 DEPAUL L. REV. 263, 268–70, 298, 300–03 (1992); Frederick Mark Gedicks, *Public Life and Hostility to Religion*, 78 VA. L. REV. 671, 671–74, 678–86, 693–96 (1992). I agree with these authors that a pervasive favoring of secular principles in all public contexts can be biased against (some would say for) religion, but while such bias may be unconstitutional in some circumstances, it is not generally based on hostility. *See* Frank S. Ravitch, *The Supreme Court's Rhetorical Hostility: What Is "Hostile" to Religion Under the Establishment Clause?* 2004 BYU L. REV.1031 (2004) (symposium issue).

15. *See, e.g.*, Sch. Dist. of Abington Tp. v. Schempp, 374 U.S. 203, 225 (1963) ("We agree of course that the State may not establish a 'religion of secularism' in the sense of affirmatively opposing or showing hostility to religion. . . .").

16. Of course, the same could be said of the Court's earlier definitions, but it is the potency of the concept when combined with formal neutrality that makes the current Court's experimentation with the concept troubling. Ravitch, *supra* note 14.

17. Ravitch, *supra* note 4, at 493–94; *see also* Steven D. Smith, *The Restoration of Tolerance*, 78 CAL. L. REV. 305, 319–24 (1990) (critiquing the argument that neutrality requires a baseline and rejecting neutrality as an empty ideal).

18. 530 U.S. 793 (2000).

19. *Id.* at 827–28 (plurality opinion). The plurality later noted the abominable, but sadly effective, anti-Catholic influence on the opposition to funding sectarian schools from the late 1800s to more recent times—a true example of hostility toward religion (or a specific religion). *Id.* at 828–29 (plurality opinion). For further discussion of this animus, *see infra* notes 61–71 and accompanying text.

20. *Id.* at 827–28 (plurality opinion).

21. For an interesting, but highly critical, discussion of the history and evolution of separationist doctrine, *see* Hamburger, *supra* note 8.

22. S. Ct. 1307 (2004).

23. *Id.* at 1309.

24. *Id.* at 1312.

25. *Id.* at 1310.

26. *Id.* at 1311–12, 1315.

27. *Id.* at 1313–14.

28. *Id.* at 1313.

29. *Id.* at 1314–15. It is interesting that Justice Scalia's dissenting opinion in Locke, which Justice Thomas joins, accuses the state of discriminating against religion, *id.* at 1319–20 (Scalia, J., dissenting), but does not use the term "hostility" in a context relevant to this article. Justice Scalia does use the term in an unrelated context. *See id.* at 1316 (Scalia, J., dissenting) ("One can concede the Framers' hostility to funding the clergy specifically. . . ."). Justice Scalia is clear that such discrimination need not be the product of animus in order to be problematic. *Id.* at 1318–20 (Scalia, J., dissenting). This might simply be a result of the parameters of the Locke case itself, or it could reflect an intentional decision to use more precise concepts in addressing the disadvantaging of religion or religious perspectives. Focusing on discrimination rather than hostility would be a positive step because it is possible to engage in disparate treatment based on establishment or other concerns without being hostile toward religion. *See* Ravitch, *supra* note 14. Yet both Justices Scalia and Thomas were members of the *Mitchell* plurality and have used the ill-defined concept of hostility elsewhere, so it is unlikely that Justice Scalia's dissenting opinion in Locke signals an intent to abandon the hostility concept in other contexts.

30. *Locke*, 124 S. Ct. 1307.

31. *See* Ravitch, *supra* note 14, at 1033.

32. U.S. 98 (2001) (ruling that a Christian group focused on children in an elementary school must be given access to a school building for meetings if other non-curriculum-related student groups are given access).

33. 515 U.S. 819 (1995) (holding that a university cannot deny funding to a religious student newspaper if it allows other non-school-sponsored student groups and publications access to such funding).

34. *See, e.g.*, Lamb's Chapel v. Ctr. Moriches Union Free Sch. Dist., 508 U.S. 384 (1993) (holding that the exclusion of a church from using school facilities at night to show a film was unconstitutional); Widmar v. Vincent, 454 U.S. 263 (1981) (ruling that a religious student group is entitled to use university facilities that are open to other student groups).

35. *Good News Club*, 533 U.S. at 106–07 (applying a free speech argument developed in the secondary and postsecondary education context to prohibit the exclusion of an elementary-school religious club from a common school building that included the elementary school); Rosenberger, 515 U.S. at 829–30 (applying the public-forum argument developed in the government property context to a government funding program that provided funding for student publications).

36. *Good News Club,* 533 U.S. at 106–07; *Rosenberger,* 515 U.S. at 829–30.

37. 496 U.S. 226 (1990).

38. *Id.* at 248 (plurality opinion).

39. 435 U.S. 618 (1978).

40. *Mergens,* 496 U.S. at 248 (plurality opinion) (internal quotation marks omitted) (quoting *McDaniel,* 435 U.S. at 641 (Brennan, J., concurring in the judgment)).

41. I would add that even though excluding the group may not have been hostile, it could, and should, be found unconstitutional regardless of the Equal Access Act. The reason for this lies in the Free Speech Clause, however. If government creates a public or limited public forum and denies access to religious groups while allowing other groups to meet, government places religion at an unfair disadvantage in the marketplace of ideas. *See generally* Lamb's Chapel v. Ctr. Moriches Union Free Sch. Dist., 508 U.S. 384 (1993) (holding that a school district could not make its building available to groups discussing family issues from a variety of perspectives and deny access only to those wishing to discuss such issues from a religious perspective). As I have argued elsewhere, however, there are important reasons for limiting this analysis to the equal access context. Ravitch, *supra* note 4, at 524, 526–28, 530–31, 570–71.

42. Compare the Court's analysis of effects in Zelman v. Simmons-Harris, 536 U.S. 639 (2002), with the plurality's use of hostility in Mitchell v. Helms, 530 U.S. 793, 827–28 (2000) (plurality opinion). *But see* Locke v. Davey, 124 S. Ct. 1307, 1313–14 (2004) (holding the denial of state funding to a student pursuing a devotional-theology degree constitutional, even under a formally neutral program, but limiting the holding to training in devotional theology).

43. *See, e.g., Zelman,* 536 U.S. 639; *see id.* at 687–88, 695–708 (Souter, J., dissenting) (suggesting that the Court glossed over the impact of the voucher program, which could not have been upheld if the Court had seriously looked at its effects); *see also* Ravitch, *supra* note 4, at 513–16, 520–23 (suggesting that the *Zelman* Court has taken any serious analysis of the effects of government programs out of the "effects test").

44. *See* Ravitch, *supra* note 4, at 513–23 (suggesting that the impact of the program upheld in *Zelman* was to provide a substantial benefit to religion, especially to larger sects with established religious schools or the means of, and interest in, establishing such schools).

45. Implicit in the Court's holding in *Zelman* is the possibility that the neutrality principle will be violated if religious organizations or individuals are denied access to open government funding programs, even if the reason for the denial is a concern that religious entities will receive a disproportionate benefit if such access is granted. *But see* Locke, 124 S. Ct. 1307 (holding that a state has the ability to deny access to funding for training as a minister under an otherwise available government scholarship program).

46. This is apparently what a plurality of the court did in *Mitchell,* 530 U.S. at 827–28 (2000) (plurality opinion).

47. The biggest concerns may be (1) fidelity to constitutional values, which until recently had a more separationist bent, *see* Good News Club v. Milford Cent. Sch., 533 U.S. 98, 102–05 (2001); *id.* at 131–34 (Stevens, J., dissenting) (noting that when a school district denied access to a religious club due to concerns that the club would engage in religious instruction and proselytization, the district's motivation seemed to be compliance with state law and Establishment Clause concerns); and (2) an intent to protect religion from the "impurity" of government, a concern that some have traced to Roger Williams, *see* Levy, *supra* note 8, at 183–85.

48. Everson v. Bd. of Educ., 330 U.S. 1, 11 (1947) (holding that religious liberty can best be achieved by "a government . . . stripped of all power to tax, to support, or otherwise to assist any or all religions, or to interfere with the beliefs of any religious individual or group"); *see also* Illinois ex rel. McCollum v. Bd. of Educ., 333 U.S. 203, 211–12 (1948) (holding the same); Levy, *supra* note 8, at 183–85 (noting the same).

49. *See* Ravitch, *supra* note 14.

50. *See, e.g.,* Zelman v. Simmons-Harris, 536 U.S. 639 (2002) (upholding a city voucher program that ultimately sent millions of dollars in tuition to local religious schools—94.6% of voucher students attended religious schools—and such schools were primarily of only one or two denominations).

51. *See* Rosenberger v. Rector & Visitors of the Univ. of Va., 515 U.S. 819 (1995). *But see* Locke v. Davey, 124 S. Ct. 1307 (2004) (suggesting that an exception to this approach exists when a state denies funding for training as a minister, but not clarifying whether the exception goes beyond such limited circumstances).

52. Ravitch, *supra* note 14, at 1033, 1037–38.

53. *See* Lemon v. Kurtzman, 403 U.S. 602 (1971) (developing a test for Establishment Clause cases based heavily on separationist principles); *McCollum,* 333 U.S. at 211 (using Thomas Jefferson's metaphor of "a wall of separation between church and state" to interpret the Establishment Clause); *Everson,* 330 U.S. at 16.

54. *See, e.g.,* Mitchell v. Helms, 530 U.S. 793, 827–28 (2000) (plurality opinion) (holding that treating religion differently in the context of government aid programs manifests hostility toward religion); Rosenberger, 515 U.S. at 829 (denying government funds to a student newspaper under a generally open funding program because the paper's proselytizing message is viewpoint discrimination, and Establishment Clause concerns are not adequate to justify such viewpoint discrimination).

55. *See* Richard John Neuhaus, The Naked Public Square: Religion and Democracy in America (1984); Michael W. McConnell, *Religious Freedom at a Crossroads,* 59 U. Chi. L. Rev. 115, 124–25 (1992); *see also* Gedicks, *supra* note

14, at 671, 674, 693–94 (addressing hostility toward religion in U.S. Supreme Court opinions and American public life).

56. For a good example of an older case suggesting this, *see* Zorach v. Clauson, 343 U.S. 306 (1952). For a good example of a newer case suggesting the same, *see* Mitchell, 530 U.S. at 793 (plurality opinion).

57. *See, e.g.,* Douglas Laycock, *Formal, Substantive, and Disaggregated Neutrality Toward Religion,* 39 DePaul L. Rev. 993, 1001–02 (1990) ("[T]he religion clauses require government to minimize the extent to which it either encourages or discourages religious belief or disbelief, practice or nonpractice, observance or nonobservance. . . . But I must elaborate on what I mean by minimizing encouragement and discouragement. I mean that religion is to be left as wholly to private choice as anything can be. It should proceed as unaffected by government as possible." (footnote omitted)); Ravitch, *supra* note 4, at 544–49 (arguing that religion should be neither facilitated nor discouraged by government).

58. *See* Ravitch, *supra* note 14, at 1040–41.

59. The Oxford Desk Dictionary, American Edition 271 (Laurence Urdang ed. 1995).

60. *Id.*

61. Ravitch, *supra* note 14, at 1040–41.

62. *Id.* at 1041–42.

63. 508 U.S. 520 (1993).

64. *Id.* at 524–28.

65. *Id.*

66. *Id. passim.*

67. *See* Zorach v. Clauson, 343 U.S. 306, 314 (1952) ("[W]e find no constitutional requirement which makes it necessary for government to be hostile to religion and to throw its weight against efforts to widen the effective scope of religious influence.").

68. 530 U.S. 793, 828–29 (2000) (plurality opinion); *see also* Hamburger, *supra* note 8, at 321–28, 335–42 (explaining that both before and after Senator Blaine's failed attempt to amend the U.S. Constitution to prohibit any government funding of religious schools, there was a strong movement, heavily influenced by anti-Catholic animus, that agreed with Senator Blaine's proposal).

69. *See generally* Hamburger, *supra* note 8 (recounting the evolution of the early separationist movement and the activities of groups such as the anti-Catholic nativists).

70. *Id.*

71. *See* Lloyd P. Jorgenson, The State and the Non-Public School 1825–1925, at 83–85 (1987); Frank S. Ravitch, School Prayer and Discrimination: The Civil Rights of Religious Minorities and Dissenters 5 (Northeastern 1999).

72. This can be seen in any number of articles defending the value of separationism. *See, e.g.,* Green, *supra* note 8.

73. *See* Mitchell, 530 U.S. at 912–13 (Souter, J., dissenting).

74. Locke v. Davey, 124 S. Ct. 1307, 1314 n.7 (2004).

75. *Id.* at 1313–14.

76. *See* Stephen L. Carter, The Culture of Disbelief: How American Law and Politics Trivialize Religious Devotion 106–23 (1993); Gedicks, *supra* note 14, at 674, 678–82, 693–96 (connecting the distinction between public and private aspects of religion in cases and society at large to the broader liberal tradition). *See generally* Neuhaus, *supra* note 55.

77. *See* Gaffney, *supra* note 14, at 302 (noting that leading separationist Leo Pfeffer was not "in any real sense hostile to religion" and that in fact Pfeffer "is a devout Jew who is convinced that religion will thrive—even that it can only thrive—when it does not enjoy the benefit of government subsidies").

78. *See* Ravitch, *supra* note 14, at 1040–41.

79. Ravitch, *supra* note 4, at 544–73.

80. Compare Zelman v. Simmons-Harris, 536 U.S. 639 (2002) (upholding a voucher program in which 94.6 percent of voucher funds went to religious schools that represented only a few denominations), with Mitchell v. Helms, 530 U.S. 793 (2000) (plurality opinion) (holding that exclusion of religious schools from a general government program supporting the loan of educational equipment because the religious schools are "pervasively sectarian" reflects hostility toward religion and is unconstitutional), and Rosenberger v. Rector & Visitors of the Univ. of Va., 515 U.S. 819 (1995) (suggesting that the exclusion of a religious student newspaper from a general funding program would disfavor religious viewpoints and is therefore unconstitutional).

81. This is consistent with the approach taken by some scholars. *See, e.g.,* Neuhaus, *supra* note 55.

82. *Mitchell,* 530 U.S. 793 (2000) (plurality opinion).

NOTES TO CHAPTER 4

1. *See* Perry O. Chrisman, *Confessions of a Baptist Lawyer,* 27 Tex. Tech L. Rev. 1041 (1996) (arguing that "[i]n no area has the religious right more confused or abused the perception of the law than in the concepts of religious liberty based on the First Amendment protection"); John H. Garvey, *Free Exercise and the Values of Religious Liberty,* 18 Conn. L. Rev. 779, 783–86 (1986) (recognizing difficulties in defining religious liberty); Donald A. Giannella, *Religious Liberty, Nonestablishment, and Doctrinal Development,* 80 Harv. L. Rev. 1381, 1383 (1967) (same); Daniel R. Heimbach, *Contrasting Views of Religious Liberty: Clarifying the Relationship Between Responsible Government and the Freedom of Religion,* 11 J.L. & Religion 715 (1995) ("One's views on religious liberty . . . affect the way one understands relations of morality and law, of ethics and human government, and tensions that arise between the moral purposes of government and moral limita-

tions that should restrain the state's use of coercive power."); Ira C. Lupu, *Where Rights Begin: The Problem of Burdens on the Free Exercise of Religion*, 102 HARV. L. REV. 933, 971 982–83 (1989) (recognizing that there are "competing theories of religious liberty"). *See generally* RELIGIOUS LIBERTY IN WESTERN THOUGHT (Noel B. Reynolds & W. Cole Durham, Jr. eds., 1996) (tracing historical developments of concepts of religious liberty).

2. *See* Noah Feldman, *The Intellectual Origins of the Establishment Clause*, 77 N.Y.U. L. REV. 346, 384–85 (2002) (asserting that "the history of the idea of liberty of conscience" reveals that early Americans "shared a basic theory of religious liberty and drew on the same sources and Lockean ideas to express their views").

3. *See supra* note 1; Frank S. Ravitch, *A Funny Thing Happened on the Way to Neutrality: Broad Principles, Formalism, and the Establishment Clause*, 38 GA. L. REV. 489, 542 (2004) (primarily addressing neutrality, but also discussing liberty).

4. *See, e.g.,* Jonathan C. Lipson, *On Balance: Religious Liberty and Third-Party Harms*, 84 MINN. L. REV. 589, 593 (2000) (recognizing that "balancing the rights of religious actors and third parties reflects the two competing anxieties that have historically defined the boundaries of our religious liberty jurisprudence"); Josh Schopf, *Religious Activity and Proselytization in the Workplace: The Murky Line Between Healthy Expression and Unlawful Harrassment [sic]*, 31 COLUM. J.L. & SOC. PROBS. 39, 49 (1997) (explaining how courts balance the competing liberty interests of litigants); Jennifer Ann Drobac, Note, *For the Sake of the Children: Court Consideration of Religion in Child Custody Cases*, 50 STAN. L. REV. 1609, 1642 (1998) (observing that where parents' religious practices endanger children, courts "must balance the conflicting interests") (citing Osier v. Osier, 410 A.2d 1027, 1030 (Me. 1980)).

5. For examples and discussion of situations where such claims conflict under the Free Exercise Clause, *see* Lipson, *supra* note 4; Drobac, *supra* note 4.

6. *See, e.g.,* Patrick M. Garry, *The Institutional Side of Religious Liberty: A New Model of the Establishment Clause*, 2004 UTAH L. REV. 1155, 1163 (2004) ("The Free Exercise Clause defines a fundamental individual liberty. . . . The Establishment Clause, on the other hand, simply provides a negative check on certain governmental powers and functions."); Douglas Laycock, *The Supreme Court and Religious Liberty*, 40 CATH. LAW. 25, 25 (2000) (highlighting "the most promising arguments for lawyers asserting religious liberty claims," and giving "extra attention to free exercise, where recent developments are most subject to misunderstanding").

7. *See, e.g.,* NOAH FELDMAN, DIVIDED BY GOD: AMERICA'S CHURCH-STATE PROBLEM — AND WHAT WE SHOULD DO ABOUT IT (Farrar, Straus and Giroux 2005); Michael W. McConnell, *Religious Freedom at a Crossroads*, 59 U. CHI. L. REV. 115 (1992).

8. The equal access cases (cases involving access by religious groups to government property on the same terms as other non-government-related groups) are a good example of the concept of liberty being used helpfully in the Establishment Clause context, but of course, the liberty involved in those cases was both religious liberty and freedom of speech. Good News Club v. Milford Central Schools, 533 U.S. 98 (2001); Lamb's Chapel v. Center Moriches Union Free Sch. Dist., 508 U.S. 384 (1993); Widmar v. Vincent, 454 U.S. 263 (1981).

9. *See supra* note 1; *see also* Douglas Laycock, *Religious Liberty as Liberty*, 7 J. CONTEMP. LEGAL ISSUES 313, 313–14 (1996).

10. *See generally* McConnell, *supra* note 7.

11. *Cf. id.*

12. *See infra* chapters 9 and 10.

13. *See, e.g.,* McConnell, *supra* note 7; Michael W. McConnell, *Why Is Religious Liberty the "First Freedom"?* 21 CARDOZO L. REV. 1243 (2000); Michael W. McConnell, *Free Exercise Revisionism and the Smith Decision*, 57 U. CHI. L. REV. 1109 (1990); Michael W. McConnell, *The Origins and Historical Understanding of Free Exercise of Religion*, 103 HARV. L. REV. 1409 (1990).

14. McConnell, *supra* note 7, at 138–40; *cf.* McConnell, *Free Exercise Revisionism, supra* note 13, at 1152–53.

15. McConnell, *Free Exercise Revisionism, supra* note 13, at 1128, 1152–53.

16. Employment Division v. Smith, 494 U.S. 872 (1990).

17. *Id.*

18. *Id.* at 890.

19. Ravitch, *supra* note 3, at 542.

20. *See* Noah Feldman, *From Liberty to Equality: The Transformation of the Establishment Clause*, 90 Cal. L. Rev. 673 (2002); *cf.* Feldman, DIVIDED BY GOD, *supra* note 7.

21. *Id.*

22. Feldman, DIVIDED BY GOD, *supra* note 7, at 9–14.

23. *See supra* notes 10–15 and accompanying text; STEPHEN L. CARTER, THE CULTURE OF DISBELIEF: HOW AMERICAN LAW AND POLITICS TRIVIALIZE RELIGIOUS DEVOTION (Anchor Books 1993).

24. A significant amount of scholarship suggests fostering religious liberty is the purpose of the religion clauses making similar arguments. A complete discussion of each of these sources is far beyond the scope of this chapter. The references to Professors McConnell and Carter are illustrative of this broader literature.

25. Feldman, *From Liberty to Equality, supra* note 20; DIVIDED BY GOD, *supra* note 7.

26. Feldman, *From Liberty to Equality, supra* note 20, at 718–30.

27. *See generally id.*

28. *Id.* at 680–84.

29. *See supra* chapter 1; *infra* chapter 6.

30. James Madison, *The Federalist No. 10*, THE FEDERALIST PAPERS (Clinton Rossiter, ed., Mentor Books 1961).

31. Here I am suggesting that if one rejects Feldman's historical arguments, there is not much of a basis for the dichotomy between liberty and equality. They may complement as well as conflict with each other, and they may both be valuable and legitimate modes of religion clause interpretation.

32. Imagine a graduation prayer case where a student is selected by the school (or even by a class vote) to deliver a prayer at the ceremony. As has been the tradition, the student delivers a highly sectarian prayer. The bulk of the students, staff, and family at the ceremony are from the same or similar denominations as the student delivering the prayer (they are all "values Evangelicals). A few students, staff, and family members find the prayer offensive because it suggests that they will go to hell for not believing in Jesus (although this is not directly mentioned) and because it is a vocal reminder at an important government-sponsored event of their outsider status within the community, which they experience in day-to-day life without the force of government to remind them (these are secularists and minority religious folks). Put to the side the question of whether this prayer is constitutional (it is not), and consider the competing liberty of conscience claims. Feldman would suggest that this is not a problem because the symbolic religious event does not seriously violate the outsiders' liberty of conscience unless it involves legal (as opposed to psychological) coercion, and because allowing such religious symbolism as part of a compromise between legal secularists and values Evangelicals makes sense. Feldman *supra* note 7, at 235–44. Yet the outsiders may certainly experience a profound violation of their liberty of conscience. *See* Santa Fe Indep. Sch. Dist. v Doe, 530 U.S. 290 (2000); Lee v. Weisman, 505 U.S. 577 (1992); *see also* FRANK S. RAVITCH, SCHOOL PRAYER AND DISCRIMINATION: THE CIVIL RIGHTS OF RELIGIOUS MINORITIES AND DISSENTERS (Northeastern 1999) (demonstrating that such situations may also lead to overt discrimination against religious minorities and dissenters). At the same time, as Feldman explains, the majority may argue that it has the right to express itself religiously and that any limitation on this right would also violate liberty of conscience. *Lee,* 505 U.S. at 645–46 (Scalia, J., dissenting); Feldman, *supra* note 7, at 186–219, 235–44.

33. Feldman *supra* note 7.

34. *Id.* at 244–51.

35. *Id.*

36. *See* William M. Ball, *Law and Religion in America: The New Picture,* 16 CATH. LAW. 3, 3–4 (1970); Allen C. Brownfeld, *The Constitutional Intent Concerning Matters of Church and State,* 5 WM. & MARY L. REV. 174, 183–99 (1964); Steven K. Green, *Justice David Josiah Brewer and the "Christian Nation" Maxim,* 63 ALB. L. REV. 427, 449 (1999).

37. *See, e.g.,* Brownfeld, *supra* note 36, at 179 (noting that "Madison opposed the incorporation by the Federal government of religious institutions").

38. Steven H. Shiffrin, *The Pluralistic Foundations of the Religion Clauses,* 90 CORNELL L. REV. 9, 12 (2004).

39. Alan E. Brownstein, *Interpreting the Religion Clauses in Terms of Liberty, Equality, and Free Speech Values—A Critical Analysis of "Neutrality Theory" and Charitable Choice,* 13 NOTRE DAME J. L. ETHICS & PUB. POL'Y 243, 256–57 (1999).

40. *See* Feldman, *supra* note 20.

41. Even though Feldman does not claim to be a hard originalist, his approach has no more force than other historically grounded approaches. One may accept it on the force of his arguments, but as will be suggested in chapters 9 and 10 both his broad acceptance of public religious exercises and broad rejection of government funding to religion even in circumstances where that funding may not facilitate religion lead me to reject his conclusions. One can learn a lot from reading Feldman's work, but one cannot solve the interpretive difficulties raised under the religion clauses so easily.

42. HANS-GEORG GADAMER, TRUTH AND METHOD 259–67 (Joel Weinsheimer & Donald G. Marshall trans., Continuum, 2d rev. ed. 1989).

43. *Id.*

44. *Smith,* 494 U.S. 872; William P. Marshall, *In Defense of* Smith *and Free Exercise Revisionism,* 58 U. CHI. L. REV. 308, 319–28 (1991) (arguing that "[t]he free exercise exemption . . . offends Establishment Clause principles"); *see also* Marci A. Hamilton, GOD VS. THE GAVEL: RELIGION AND THE RULE OF LAW 276–79 (Cambridge 2005) (using a separationist argument to support broader argument that mandatory Free Exercise Clause exemptions can cause harm to individuals or society by putting religious entities and individuals above the law, and generally arguing against such exemptions).

45. Brownstein, *supra* note 39.

46. *See* Abington School District v. Schempp, 374 U.S. 203, 226 (1963) (The Free Exercise Clause has "never meant that a majority could use the machinery of the State to practice its beliefs").

47. *See* PHILIP HAMBURGER, SEPARATION OF CHURCH AND STATE 485 (2002).

48. Feldman *supra* note 7, at 186–219, 235–44, 251; *see also* Thomas C. Berg, 82 WASH. U. L.Q. 919, 981 (2004) (noting that "the right to engage in private religious expression in public settings may be essential for" some religious groups).

49. Church of the Lukumi Babalu Aye v. City of Hialeah, 508 U.S. 520 (1993) (intentional discrimination and religious gerrymandering by city aimed at religious group based on that group's practice of animal sacrifice).

50. *See* Suzanne Last Stone, *Cultural Pluralism, Nationalism, and Universal Rights,* 21 CARDOZO L. REV. 1211, 1215 (2000) ("[C]lassical liberalism implies that equal citizenship rights reside in the individual rather than in . . . groups.").

51. *See* McConnell, *Free Exercise Revisionism, supra* note 13, at 1114–16.

52. *Abington Township,* 374 U.S. at 226.

53. *Id.* at 312–13 (Stewart, J., dissenting); *see also Lee*, 505 U.S. at 645–46 (Scalia, J., dissenting).

54. *Id.*

55. City of Boerne v. Flores, 521 U.S. 507 (1997); Lyng v. Northwest Indian Cemetery Protective Association, 485 U.S. 439 (1988).

56. *Id.*

57. *Boerne*, 521 U.S. 507.

58. *Santa Fe Indep. Sch. Dist. v. Doe*, 530 U.S. 290 (2000); *Abington Township*, 374 U.S. 203.

NOTES TO CHAPTER 5

1. Timothy L. Hall, *Religion, Equality, and Difference*, 65 TEMP. L. REV. 1, 6–7 (1992).

2. Employment Division v. Smith, 494 U.S. 872 (1990).

3. Zelman v. Simmons-Harris, 536 U.S. 639 (2002).

4. NOAH FELDMAN, DIVIDED BY GOD: AMERICA'S CHURCH-STATE PROBLEM — AND WHAT WE SHOULD DO ABOUT IT (Farrar, Straus and Giroux 2005); Noah Feldman, *From Liberty to Equality: The Transformation of the Establishment Clause*, 90 Cal. L. Rev. 673 (2002).

5. *See supra* chapter 4.

6. *See* Feldman, *From Liberty to Equality, supra* note 4.

7. *See* Hall, *supra* note 1; Steven H. Shiffrin, *The Pluralistic Foundations of the Religion Clauses*, 90 CORNELL L. REV. 9 (2004); Alan E. Brownstein, *Interpreting the Religion Clauses in Terms of Liberty, Equality, and Free Speech Values — A Critical Analysis of "Neutrality Theory" and Charitable Choice*, 13 NOTRE DAME J. L. ETHICS & PUB. POL'Y 243 (1999).

8. Feldman, *From Liberty to Equality, supra* note 4.

9. Brownstein, *supra* note 7 (acknowledging and criticizing this trend); *see also* Walz v. Tax Comm'n, 397 U.S. 664 (1970) (Harlan, J., concurring) (stating that "[n]eutrality in its application requires an equal protection mode of analysis"); Welsh v. United States, 398 U.S. 333 (1970) (Harlan, J., concurring in result) (same).

10. Christopher L. Eisgruber and Lawrence G. Sager, *The Vulnerability of Conscience: The Constitutional Basis for Protecting Religious Conduct*, 61 U. CHI. L. REV. 1245 (1994).

11. *See* Brownstein *supra* note 7.

12. *See* Shiffrin, *supra* note 7.

13. *See* note 4 *supra*, and accompanying text; *see also supra* chapter 3.

14. *Id.*

15. Feldman, *From Liberty to Equality, supra* note 4, at 718–30.

16. *See* Shiffrin *supra* note 7 (arguing that equality and liberty are both important concepts in religion clause interpretation); Brownstein *supra* note 7 (same).

17. *See supra* chapter 1 and chapter 4.

18. *See generally* Feldman, DIVIDED BY GOD, *supra* note 4; Feldman, *From Liberty to Equality supra* note 4.

19. Helvering v. Hallock, 309 U.S. 106 (1940) (stating, per Frankfurter, J., that "stare decisis is a principle of policy and not a mechanical formula of adherence to the latest decision, however recent and questionable, when such adherence involves collision with a prior doctrine more embracing in its scope, intrinsically sounder, and verified by experience").

20. Feldman, DIVIDED BY GOD, *supra* note 4; Feldman, *From Liberty to Equality, supra* note 4.

21. *See supra* at Chapter Four.

22. *See* PHILIP HAMBURGER, SEPARATION OF CHURCH AND STATE 485 (2002); Akhil Reed Amar, THE BILL OF RIGHTS: CREATION AND RECONSTRUCTION (Yale 1998).

23. *Van Orden v. Perry*, 125 S. Ct. 2854, 2864–66 (2005) (Thomas, J., concurring); *Zelman v. Simmons-Harris*, 536 U.S. 639, 677–80, 683–84 (2002) (Thomas, J., concurring).

24. Feldman, DIVIDED BY GOD, *supra* note 4, at 173.

25. *See supra* at chapter 1.

26. H. Jefferson Powell, *The Original Understanding of Original Intent*, 98 HARV. L. REV. 885 (1985).

27. *See supra* note 9, and accompanying text.

28. *See, e.g., Zelman*, 536 U.S. 639 (school vouchers); Good News Club v. Milford Central School, 533 U.S. 98 (2001) (access by evangelical children's group to central school that included elementary school); Rosenberger v. Rector & Visitors of Univ. of Va., 515 U.S. 819 (1995) (access to public funding for student-run evangelical newspaper at public university); *Smith*, 494 U.S. 872 (denying mandatory exemptions to generally applicable laws under Free Exercise Clause).

29. *See* Martha Chamallas, *The Architecture of Bias: Deep Structures in Tort Law*, 146 U. PA. L. REV. 463, 464 (1998) (observing that in many areas of the law, formal equality "bears little connection to gender and race equity as measured by real-world standards"); Nancy E. Dowd, Kenneth B. Nunn & Jane E. Pendergast, *Diversity Matters: Race, Gender, and Ethnicity in Legal Education*, 15 U. FLA. J.L. & PUB. POL'Y 11, 15 & nn.30–32 (2003) (stating that formal equality has been criticized "as not only masking and reinscribing inequality, but sometimes providing new tools for those who have benefitted from gender, race, and class privilege to sustain privilege, rather than promote equality.") Citing, Ira C. Lupu, *Reconstructing the Establishment Clause: The Case Against Discretionary Accommodation of Religion*, 140 U. PA. L. REV. 555, 596 (1991) (noting that arguments may be made that "regimes of formal equality in the fields of race and gender formally privilege no one").

30. *See supra* chapter 2; Frank S. Ravitch, *A Funny Thing Happened on the Way to Neutrality: Broad Principles, Formalism, and the Establishment Clause*, 38 GA. L. REV. 489, 542 (2004) (pri-

marily addressing neutrality, but also discussing equality).

31. *Rosenberger*, 515 U.S. 819 (treating evangelical student newspaper that engaged in significant proselytizing and sectarianism the same as all other student newspapers and student groups for purposes of distribution of university funding at public university).

32. *Smith*, 494 U.S. 872 (denying mandatory exemptions under Free Exercise Clause when exemption is claimed under law of "general applicability" regardless of impact of such laws on specific religious entities or individuals).

33. *Cf.* Robin West, *Is American Constitutionalism Possible?* 4-SPG WIDENER L. SYMP. J. 1, 4 (1999) (stating that, ideally, equality requires "that when a state acts, it must treat similarly situated groups similarly, and differently situated groups differently"); Reed v. Reed, 404 U.S. 71, 75–77 (1971) (holding that the government must treat similarly situated groups similarly and differently situated groups differently).

34. *Smith* makes this abundantly clear. *Smith*, 494 U.S. 872.

35. *See infra* chapters 9 and 10.

36. *See* Paul N. Cox, *An Interpretation and (Partial) Defense of Legal Formalism,* 36 IND. L. REV. 57, 75 (2003) (acknowledging that "[i]t might . . . be said that formalists ignore or de-emphasize facts in service of conceptual order").

37. Justin Brookman, Note, *The Constitutionality of the Good Friday Holiday,* 73 N.Y.U. L. REV. 193, 210–11 & 110 (1998) (affirming that "courts have always been especially suspicious of laws which treat members of different religious groups differently").

38. *Cf.* Timothy P. Terrell, *Flatlaw: An Essay on the Dimensions of Legal Reasoning and the Development of Fundamental Normative Principles,* 72 CAL. L. REV. 288, 330 n.146 (1984) ("To achieve substantive equality, one may have to treat people who are in different situations differently; to give, for example, prerogatives to disfavored groups. Differential treatment of this kind *represents a departure from the ideal of formal equality. . . .*") (emphasis added).

39. This morphing of formal equality should not come as a surprise when it occurs because formalism frequently leads to fitting square pegs into round holes, and courts sometimes attempt to change either the peg or the hole to allow a cleaner fit. Ravitch, *supra* note 30, at 495 (suggesting that formalistic tests are frequently contorted to fit new situations or they function like a "bull in china shop").

40. Shiffrin, *supra* note 7; Ravitch, *supra* note 30; Eisgruber & Sager, *supra* note 10; Brownstein, *supra* note 7.

41. Eisgruber & Sager, *supra* note 10, at 1289–90.

42. Mitchell v. Helms, 500 U.S. 793, 867 (2000) (Souter, J., dissenting); Zelman, 536 U.S. 639, 686 (Souter, J., dissenting); Douglas Laycock, *Formal,*

Substantive, and Disaggregated Neutrality Toward Religion, 39 DEPAUL L. REV. 993, 1005 (1990).

43. *See supra* chapter 2, Ravitch, *supra* note 30.

44. *See* Eisgruber and Sager, *supra* note 10.

45. *Id.*

46. *Id.* at 1254–67.

47. *Id.* at 1260.

48. *Id.* at 1260–70.

49. *Id.* at 1260–70, 1282–84.

50. *Id.* at 1282–1301.

51. *Id.* at 1282–84.

52. *Id.* at 1284–91.

53. *Id.* at 1282–1301.

54. *Id.*

55. *Id.*

56. *See generally id.*

57. *Id.* at 1254–84.

58. *See* Michael W. McConnell, *Why Is Religious Liberty the "First Freedom"?* 21 CARDOZO L. REV. 1243 (2000); Michael W. McConnell, *The Origins and Historical Understanding of Free Exercise of Religion,* 103 HARV. L. REV. 1409 (1990); Laycock, *supra* note 42; Frank S. Ravitch, *Religious Objects as Legal Subjects,* 40 WAKE FOREST L. REV. 1011 (2005); Shiffrin *supra* note 7.

59. *Compare* Eisgruber and Sager, *supra* note 10, *with* Feldman, DIVIDED BY GOD, *supra* note 4; Feldman, *From Liberty to Equality, supra* note 4.

60. Eisgruber and Sager, *supra* note 10, at 1282–1301.

61. *Id.; see also* chapter 1, *supra* notes 50–64, and accompanying text.

62. *See generally* Eisgruber and Sager, *supra* note 10.

63. Brownstein, *supra* note 7.

64. *Id.*

65. Eisgruber and Sager, *supra* note 10, at 1285–86.

66. Brownstein, *supra* note 7, at 259–60.

67. *Id.* at 268–78.

68. *See generally* Brownstein, *supra* note 7; Alan E. Brownstein, *Evaluating School Voucher Programs Through a Liberty, Equality, and Free Speech Matrix,* 31 CONN. L. REV. 871, 886–88.

69. *See* Alan E. Brownstein, *Harmonizing the Heavenly and Earthly Spheres: The Fragmentation and Synthesis of Religion, Equality, and Speech in the Constitution,* 51 OHIO ST. L.J. 89 (1990).

70. Brownstein, *supra* note 7, at 257–58.

71. *Id.* at 260–65.

72. *Id.* at 261–62.

73. *Id.* at 259–60.

74. Although the rejection of disparate impact as a basis for an equal protection claim based on race, Washington v. Davis, 426 U.S. 229 (1976), is highly controversial because such laws may have adverse impact based on race due to demographic and economic factors connected to race and the history of racial discrimination.

75. Brownstein, *supra* note 7, at 262–64.

76. *Id.* at 264.

77. Shiffrin, *supra* note 7.

78. *Id.* at 15.

79. *Id.* at 62–63.
80. *Id.* at 42–47.
81. *Id.* at 13–15.
82. *Id.* at 64–79.
83. *Id.* at 39.
84. *Id.*
85. *Id.* at 63–64, 82–87.
86. *See generally id.*
87. *Id.* at 27–28, 39–40, 64, 82–83.
88. *Id.* at 24, 37–39.
89. FREDERICK MARK GEDICKS, THE RHETORIC OF CHURCH AND STATE: A CRITICAL ANALYSIS OF RELIGION CLAUSE JURISPRUDENCE 26–43 (Duke 1995); *see also* STEPHEN L. CARTER, THE CULTURE OF DISBELIEF: HOW AMERICAN LAW AND POLITICS TRIVIALIZE RELIGIOUS DEVOTION (Anchor 1993).
90. *See* Feldman, DIVIDED BY GOD, *supra* note 4; Feldman, *From Liberty to Equality, supra* note 4.
91. *See* Shiffrin, *supra* note 7.
92. *See, e.g.,* Gedicks, *supra* note 89; Carter, *supra* note 89.
93. Eisgruber and Sager, *supra* note 10, at 1254.
94. *E.g.,* Patrick M. Garry, *The Institutional Side of Religious Liberty: A New Model of the Establishment Clause,* 2004 UTAH L. REV. 1155, 1177–78 (2004).
95. *See supra* chapter 1, at notes 50–64, and accompanying text.
96. Law and society can be viewed from many vantage points, and from a nonfoundationalist perspective one can assert that various schools of thought provide different views of the mountain that is law and society. Some views may be more useful or supportable in particular contexts, but one must grapple with these various views of the mountain if one wants to interact with the mountain and how others engage the mountain. *Cf.* Frank S. Ravitch, *Can an Old Dog Learn New Tricks? A Nonfoundationalist Analysis of Richard Posner's The Problematics of Moral and Legal Theory,* 37 TULSA L. REV. 967, 971 (legal scholarship symposium) ("the social belief in 'natural' rights [or other views of law] might be useful in a given context, even if they are not objectively natural [or objective] and are actually contingent on context. . . .").
97. *See supra* chapter 1, at notes 50–64, and accompanying text.
98. *Cf.* Frank S. Ravitch, *Struggling with Text and Context: A Hermeneutic Approach to Interpreting and Realizing Law School Missions,* 74 ST. JOHN'S L. REV. 731, 735–36, 739–40 (2000).
99. *See, e.g., Smith,* 494 U.S. 872 (Native American Church members can be denied unemployment benefits if terminated for ritual use of peyote); Lyng v. Northwest Indian Cemetery Protective Association, 485 U.S. 439 (1988) (denying request to protect sacred native American ritual sites from government project); O'Lone v. Estate of Shabazz, 482 U.S. 342 (1987) (Muslim prisoner can be prevented from attending religious services at prison when on work detail outside prison even if prisoner has no choice but to be on work detail); Goldman v. Weinberger, 475 U.S. 503 (1986) (Or-

thodox Jewish military psychologist can be required to remove yarmulka in indoor military settings despite serious religious objections); Bowen v. Roy, 476 U.S. 693 (1986) (Native American denied request for daughter not to have social security number, despite serious religious concerns); United States v. Lee, 455 U.S. 252 (1982) (Amish employer must pay social security tax despite religious objection).
100. *See* Brownstein, *supra* note 7; Shiffrin *supra,* note 7.
101. Eisgruber and Sager, *supra* note 10, at 1254–77.
102. *See supra* chapter 2, at notes 55–63.
103. *See supra* chapter 2, Ravitch, *supra* note 30.
104. *See infra* at chapters 9 and 10.
105. *Id.*; Shiffrin, *supra* note 7.

NOTES TO CHAPTER 6

1. *See* Frank S. Ravitch, *A Funny Thing Happened on the Way to Neutrality: Broad Principles, Formalism, and the Establishment Clause,* 38 GA. L. REV. 489, 498–513, 539–44 (2004); *supra* chapters 4 and 5.
2. Ravitch, *supra* note 1, at 533–39; *see also* Marci A. Hamilton, *"Separation": From Epithet to Constitutional Norm,* 88 VA. L. REV. 1433, 1442–43 (2002) (reviewing PHILIP HAMBURGER, SEPARATION OF CHURCH AND STATE (2002)) (acknowledging that "there are degrees of separation, and any one political participant could mean one or another connotation of the term"); *see also* Ralph D. Mawdsley, *Access by Religious Community Organizations to Public Schools: A Degree of Separation Analysis,* 193 EDUC. L. REP. 633 (2005).
3. Ravitch, *supra* note 1, at 533–37.
4. *See, e.g.,* Steven G. Gey, *Why Is Religion Special? Reconsidering the Accommodation of Religion Under the Religion Clauses of the First Amendment,* 52 U. PITT. L. REV. 75, 97 (1990) (arguing that "[t]he internal contradictions between the values of separation and accommodation . . . make the continued dominance of the separation value in establishment clause doctrine highly uncertain").
5. U.S. 1 (1947).
6. *Id.* at 16, 18.
7. *Id.* at 17–18.
8. *Id.* at 18 (Jackson, J., dissenting); *id.* at 28 (Rutledge, J., dissenting).
9. *Id.*
10. *See generally Everson,* 330 U.S. 1.
11. U.S. 203 (1948).
12. *See id.* at 210–12 (describing concept of neutrality in context of strict separationist argument without expressly using term "neutrality").
13. *See, e.g.,* Santa Fe Indep. Sch. Dist. v. Doe, 530 U.S. 290 (2000); Edwards v. Aguilard, 482 U.S. 578 (1987); Wallace v. Jaffree, 472 U.S. 38 (1985); Lemon v. Kurtzman, 403 U.S. 602 (1971); Abington Tp. v. Schempp, 374 U.S. 203 (1963).

14. *See, e.g.,* Thomas C. Berg, *Slouching Towards Secularism: A Comment on* Kiryas Joel School District v. Grumet, 44 EMORY L.J. 433, 442 (1995) ("[M]aintaining church/state separation or religious liberty requires treating religion quite differently from other activities, a result inconsistent with equal treatment. . . . [S]eparationist efforts to shelter [government] from religious influence . . . are bound to push religion into a smaller and smaller corner of public life, violating both religious liberty and the equal status of religion with other ideas.").

15. *See* Richard Albert, *American Separationism and Liberal Democracy: The Establishment Clause in Historical and Comparative Perspective,* 88 MARQ. L. REV. 867, 902 (2005) (arguing that separationism "was based neither on philosophical truth nor the pursuit of an objective ideal, but instead represents a practical inevitability of its time").

16. *See* ALEXIS DE TOCQUEVILLE, DEMOCRACY IN AMERICA 295 (J. P. Mayer ed., George Lawrence trans., Anchor Books, Doubleday & Co. 1969) (1835) (commenting that Americans "all attributed the peaceful dominion of religion in their country mainly to the separation of church and state"). *See generally* Aristide Tessitore, *Alexis de Tocqueville on the Natural State of Religion in the Age of Democracy,* 64 J. POL. 1137 (2002).

17. Steven H. Shiffrin, *The Pluralistic Foundations of the Religion Clauses,* 90 CORNELL L. REV. 9, 48–54 (2004).

18. Ravitch *supra* note 1; STEVEN D. SMITH, FOREORDAINED FAILURE: THE QUEST FOR A CONSTITUTIONAL PRINCIPLE OF RELIGIOUS FREEDOM (Oxford 1995).

19. *See, e.g.,* Kitzmiller v. Dover Area Schools, 400 F. Supp.2d 707 (M.D. Pa. 2005) (school district cannot endorse intelligent design theory as science).

20. *Cf.* Ravitch, *supra* note 1, at 509–13 (suggesting that ID theorists or creation scientists may argue that secular scientific theory is placed at an advantage over religiously based theories).

21. *Kitzmiller,* 400 F.Sup.2d 707.

22. *Everson,* 330 U.S. 1.

23. *McCollum,* 333 U.S. 203, 238 (Reed, J., dissenting).

24. *See* chapter 1, *supra.*

25. *See* Van Orden v. Perry, ___ U.S. ___, 125 S. Ct. 2854 (2005) (plurality opinion); Lynch v. Donnelly, 465 U.S. 668 (1984); Marsh v. Chambers, 463 U.S. 783 (1983).

26. *Lynch,* 465 U.S. 688.

27. PHILIP HAMBURGER, SEPARATION OF CHURCH AND STATE (Harvard 2002) (addressing role of anti-Catholicism in separationist history).

28. *See id.* (providing history of anti-Catholicism in the United States); HAROLD E. QUINLEY & CHARLES Y. GLOCK, ANTI-SEMITISM IN AMERICA (1979) (discussing anti-Semitism); Thomas C. Berg, *Anti-Catholicism and Modern Church-State Relations,* 33 LOY. U. CHI. L.J. 121, 121 (2001) (discussing "societal attitudes toward Roman Catholicism"); Michael N. Dobkowski, *American Anti-Semitism: A Reinterpretation,* 29 AM. Q. 166 (1977) (discussing anti-Semitism); Elijah L. Milne, *Blaine Amendments and Polygamy Laws: The Constitutionality of Anti-Polygamy Laws Targeting Religion,* 28 W. NEW ENG. L. REV. 257 (2006) (discussing anti-Mormonism); Keith E. Sealing, *Polygamists Out of the Closet: Statutory and State Constitutional Prohibitions Against Polygamy Are Unconstitutional Under the Free Exercise Clause,* 17 GA. ST. U. L. REV. 691 (2001) (same).

29. Plessy v. Ferguson, 163 U.S. 537 (1896).

30. *E.g.,* Ingraham v. Wright, 430 U.S. 651, 659–65 (1977) (upholding corporal punishment in public schools in part because of its long tradition).

31. *E.g.,* Bradwell v. Illinois, 83 U.S. 130, 141 (1872) ("[T]he civil law, as well as nature herself, has always recognized a wide difference in the respective spheres and destinies of man and woman. . . . The natural and proper timidity and delicacy which belongs to the female sex evidently unfits it for many of the occupations of civil life.").

32. *See, e.g.,* Reed v. Reed, 404 U.S. 71, 76 (1971) (invalidating legislation that gave "a mandatory preference to members of either sex over members of the other"); Brown v. Bd. of Educ., 347 U.S. 483 (1954) (prohibiting segregation in public schools).

33. *See* Steven K. Green, *Federalism and the Establishment Clause: A Reassessment,* 38 CREIGHTON L. REV. 761, 796 (2005) [hereinafter Green, *Federalism*] ("The framers used terms and phrases familiar to the late eighteenth century, and frequently employed rhetoric that was intentionally vague or duplicitious [*sic*]. . . . Therefore, the precise meanings of recorded statements may be ambiguous at best."); Steven K. Green, *Of Misnomers and Misinformation,* 46-JUN FED. LAW. 38, 38 (1999) (noting that "[t]he originalist approach elevates the significance of isolated statements—usually taken out of context and laden with 18th century terminology and biases—over the more general themes and aspirations of the period and subsequent developments in understandings and attitudes toward constitutional rights"); *see also* Derek H. Davis & Matthew McMearty, *America's "Forsaken Roots": The Use and Abuse of Founders' Quotations,* 47 J. CHURCH & ST. 449 (2005) (correcting some popular misquotes and misinterpretations).

34. *See* JOHN H. ELY, DEMOCRACY AND DISTRUST 60–63 (1980); *see also* Adam B. Wolf, *Fundamentally Flawed: Tradition and Fundamental Rights,* 57 U. MIAMI L. REV. 101 (2002).

35. *See supra* chapter 1.

36. *Compare Everson,* 330 U.S. at 28 (Rutledge, J., dissenting), *with McCollum,* 333 U.S. at 238 (Reed, J., dissenting).

37. *Zelman,* 536 U.S. at 717 (Breyer, J., dissenting); *see also* Steven K. Green, *The Legal Argument Against Private School Choice,* 62 U. CIN. L. REV. 37, 50 (1993) (arguing that the potential to

"spark religious discord" was "a factor of great concern to the Framers").

38. NOAH FELDMAN, DIVIDED BY GOD: AMERICA'S CHURCH-STATE PROBLEM — AND WHAT WE SHOULD DO ABOUT IT (Farrar, Straus and Giroux 2005).

39. *Id.*; Frederick Mark Gedicks, THE RHETORIC OF CHURCH AND STATE: A CRITICAL ANALYSIS OF RELIGION CLAUSE JURISPRUDENCE (Duke 1995).

40. *See* Hamburger, *supra* note 27.

41. McCreary County v. ACLU of Kentucky, ___ U.S. ___, 125 S. Ct. 2722 (2005); Van Orden v. Perry, ___ U.S. ___, 125 S. Ct. 2854 (2005) (plurality opinion).

42. *McCreary,* 125 S. Ct. 2722; *Van Orden* 125 S. Ct. at 2873 (Stevens, J., dissenting); *id.* at 2892 (Souter, J., dissenting).

43. *McCreary,* 125 S. Ct. at 2748 (Scalia, J., dissenting).

44. *Van Orden,* 125 S. Ct. 2854 (plurality opinion).

45. *Id.* at 2868 (Breyer, J., concurring in the judgment).

46. *McCreary,* 125 S. Ct. 2722; *id.* at 2746 (O'Connor, J., concurring); *Van Orden,* 125 S. Ct. at 2873 (Stevens, J., dissenting); *id.* at 2892 (Souter, J., dissenting).

47. *See, e.g., Zelman,* 536 U.S. at 717 (Breyer, J., dissenting); Steven K. Green, *The Legal Argument Against Private School Choice,* 62 U. CHI. L. REV. 37, 50 (1993) (arguing that the potential to "spark religious discord" was "a factor of great concern to the Framers").

48. *See, e.g., Everson,* 330 U.S. 1; *McCollum,* 333 U.S. 203.

49. Cass R. Sunstein, *Five Theses on Originalism,* 19 HARV. J.L. & PUB. POL'Y 311, 313–15 (1996).

50. *Id.; Zelman,* 536 U.S. at 717 (Breyer, J., dissenting).

51. *See, e.g.,* Lynch v. Donnelly, 465 U.S. 668, 673 (1984); Gillette v. United States, 401 U.S. 437, 451 (1971); Illinois *ex rel.* McCollum v. Bd. of Educ., 333 U.S. 203, 213 (1948).

52. *See supra* chapter 1.

53. *See supra* note 47.

54. *Id.;* Lee v. Weisman, 505 U.S. 577, 587–88 (1992); Lemon v. Kurtzman, 403 U.S. 602, 623 (1971).

55. Gedicks, *supra* note 39, at 26–43; *see also* STEPHEN L. CARTER, THE CULTURE OF DISBELIEF: HOW AMERICAN LAW AND POLITICS TRIVIALIZE RELIGIOUS DEVOTION (Anchor 1993).

56. Hamburger, *supra* note 27.

57. Ravitch, *supra* note 1, at 533–37.

58. Feldman, *supra* note 38; Noah Feldman, *From Liberty to Equality: The Transformation of the Establishment Clause,* 90 Cal. L. Rev. 673 (2002).

59. *Id.; see also supra* at chapters 4 and 5.

60. Feldman, DIVIDED BY GOD, *supra* note 38; Hamburger, *supra* note 27; Feldman, *From Liberty to Equality supra* note 58.

61. *Id.*

62. Douglas Laycock, *Formal, Substantive, and Disaggregated Neutrality Toward Religion,* 39 DEPAUL L. REV. 993 (1990).

63. Feldman, DIVIDED BY GOD, *supra* note 38; Feldman, *From Liberty to Equality supra* note 58.

64. STEPHEN M. FELDMAN, AMERICAN LEGAL THOUGHT FROM PREMODERNISM TO POSTMODERNISM: AN INTELLECTUAL VOYAGE (Oxford 2000) (addressing shift from premodernism to modernism in twentieth-century legal and social thought).

65. U.S. 306 (1952).

66. Carter *supra* note 55; JAMES DAVISON HUNTER, CULTURE WARS: THE STRUGGLE TO DEFINE AMERICA (Basic Books 1991).

67. Ravitch, *supra* note 1, at 508.

68. *See* ROBERT WUTHNOW, AMERICA AND THE CHALLENGES OF RELIGIOUS DIVERSITY (2005) (arguing that America has become a more religiously diverse nation); Mary Beth Collins, 85 B.U. L. REV. 53, 60–61 (2005) (observing that "[w]e live in an increasingly mobile society in an era of rapidly escalating globalization"); James Davison Hunter, *Pluralism: Past and Present,* 8 J. L. & RELIGION 273, 273–75 (1990) (explaining the changing demographics of religion in the United States). *But see* Alison Stein Wellner, *The Mobility Myth,* 37 REASON 30 (2006) (arguing that the idea that Americans are increasingly "on the move" is a myth).

69. *See generally* WILLIAM R. HUTCHISON, RELIGIOUS PLURALISM IN AMERICA: THE CONTENTIOUS HISTORY OF A FOUNDING IDEAL (2003) (writing about progressive stages of religious diversity in the United States).

70. Gedicks, *supra* note 39, at 26–43; Carter, *supra* note 55.

71. *See* William P. Marshall, *Remembering the Values of Separatism and State Funding of Religious Organizations (Charitable Choice): To Aid Is Not Necessarily to Protect,* 18 J.L. & POL. 479, 480–81 (2002) ("[T]here never has been an absolute boundary between church and state in the United States. . . . [Constitutional law] never has demanded an absolute separation between church and state."); Michael W. McConnell, *The Selective Funding Problem: Abortions and Religious Schools,* 104 HARV. L. REV. 989, 1027 (1991) ("[T]he suggestion that religious organizations must categorically be barred from participation in all government-funded programs must be rejected. Although favored by the so-called 'strict separationists,' this has never been the rule in establishment clause cases and has been rejected by the Supreme Court in every case in which it has been seriously advanced.") (citations omitted).

72. The equal access cases do not concern many separationists because of the free speech principles that underlie them, assuming the forums are applied in an equal fashion and not one that favors religion. Lamb's Chapel v. Center Moriches Union Free Sch. Dist., 508 U.S. 384 (1993); Widmar v. Vincent, 454 U.S. 263 (1981). Good News Club v.

Milford Central Schools, 533 U.S. 98 (2001), may be an example of an equal access case that challenges separationist sensibilities. *See id.* at 130 (Stevens, J., dissenting); *id.* at 134 (Souter, J., dissenting)

73.*See, e.g.,* McCreary, 125 S. Ct. at 2748 (Scalia, J., dissenting); Lee v Weisman, 505 U.S. 577, 631 (1992) (Scalia, J., dissenting).

74. Ravitch, *supra* note 1, at 566–71; Frank S. Ravitch, *Religious Objects as Legal Subjects,* 40 WAKE FOREST L. REV. 1011, 1071–84 (2005).

75. Ravitch, *supra* note 1, at 523–31, 566–71; Ravitch, *supra* note 75, at 1071–84.

76. *See supra* chapter 5; Feldman, *supra* note 58.

77. Mitchell v. Helms, 530 U.S. 793, 828–29 (2000) (plurality opinion); Hamburger, *supra* note 27.

78. *See* Frank S. Ravitch, *The Supreme Court's Rhetorical Hostility: What Is "Hostile" to Religion Under the Establishment Clause?* 2004 BYU L. REV. 1031, 1043–47 (2004) (symposium) (suggesting that there may be a number of reasons for separationist doctrine, but anti-Catholicism was clearly a motivating factor for some justices in the early decisions even if that reason is no longer motivating separationists on the Court).

79. *See* the various opinions in *Abington Tp.,* 374 U.S. 203; Engel v. Vitale, 370 U.S. 421 (1962); *Zorach,* 343 U.S. 306.

80. *Mitchell,* 530 U.S. 793, 828–29 (plurality opinion); *cf.* Hamburger, *supra* note 27.

81. *See, e.g.,* Everson, 330 U.S. 1; *McCollum,* 333 U.S. 203; *Engel,* 370 U.S. 421; *Abington Tp.,* 374 U.S. 203.

82. *See supra* chapter 1; *McCollum,* 333 U.S. at 238 (Reed, J., dissenting).

83. *See supra* chapter 1; Cass R. Sunstein, *Five Theses on Originalism,* 19 HARV. J.L. & PUB. POL'Y 311, 313–15 (1996).

84. *See Everson,* 330 U.S. at 28 (Rutledge, J., dissenting); EDWIN S. GAUSTAD, SWORN ON THE ALTAR OF GOD: A RELIGIOUS BIOGRAPHY OF THOMAS JEFFERSON 198–200, 207–09, 226–28 (Eerdmans 1996).

85. *See supra* chapter 1.

86. See Gaustad, *supra* note 84; LEONARD W. LEVY, THE ESTABLISHMENT CLAUSE: RELIGION AND THE FIRST AMENDMENT (Macmillan 1986).

87. *Id.*

88. *See* Sunstein, *supra* note 83, at 313–15 (explaining concept of soft originalism and how it connects to the broad, rather than specific, intent of the framers).

89. *Id.* (explaining that soft originalism may not always be decisive, but that broad principles can be applied to new and different circumstances).

90. If religious entities are forced to compete with each other or with nonreligious entities for scarce resources, the potential for divisiveness and conflict (that would not be as strong absent the government funding) will increase. *Zelman,* 536 U.S. at 717 (Breyer, J., dissenting).

91. *See* FRANK S. RAVITCH, SCHOOL PRAYER

AND DISCRIMINATION: THE CIVIL RIGHTS OF RELIGIOUS MINORITIES AND DISSENTERS 92–96 (Northeastern 1999).

92. Roger Williams, *Mr. Cotton's Letter Lately Printed, Examined and Answered* (1644), *repr. in* 3 THE COMPLETE WRITINGS OF ROGER WILLIAMS 392 (Russell & Russell 1963).

93. *Id.*

94. *Zelman,* 536 U.S. at 684 (Stevens, J., dissenting); *id.* at 686 (Souter, J., dissenting); *id.* at 717 (Breyer, J., dissenting).

95. *See supra* note 16.

96. Hamburger, *supra* note 27.

97. *Zelman,* 536 U.S. at 717 (Breyer, J., dissenting).

98. *See, e.g.,* Ravitch, *supra* note 1 (suggesting this may be the result of some voucher programs); Church of the Lukumi Babalu Aye v. City of Hialeah, 508 U.S. 520 (1993) (religious gerrymandering of locally unpopular religious group unconstitutional).

99. This goes beyond the famous quotation from Matthew, *see* Matthew 22:21, because some faiths that benefit from such favoritism may be forced to meet government regulations that are troublesome from a theological perspective in order to get the funding, and the tenets of some faiths may be violated if the funding scheme results in discrimination against others.

100. For a discussion of the influence of legal realism on judging by a contemporary of the justices on the early separationist Courts, *see* Jerome Frank, *What Courts Do in Fact,* 26 U. ILL. L. REV. 645 (1932).

101. *McCollum,* 333 U.S. at 237–38 (Jackson, J., concurring).

102. *Id.*

103. *Compare* Richard Rorty, CONSEQUENCES OF PRAGMATISM (Minnesota 1982), *with* Richard A. Posner, THE PROBLEMATICS OF MORAL AND LEGAL THEORY (Harvard 1999).

104. *See supra* chapter 1; Frank S. Ravitch, *Can an Old Dog Learn New Tricks? A Nonfoundationalist Analysis of Richard Posner's The Problematics of Moral and Legal Theory,* 37 TULSA L. REV. 967 (2002) (legal scholarship symposium); Frank S. Ravitch, *Struggling with Text and Context: A Hermeneutic Approach to Interpreting and Realizing Law School Missions,* 74 ST. JOHN'S L. REV. 731, 738–39 (2000) (symposium).

105. *McCollum,* 333 U.S. at 237–38 (Jackson, J., concurring).

106. *Id.; see also* discussion of philosophical hermeneutics *supra* chapter 1 and *infra* chapter 9.

NOTES TO CHAPTER 7

1. Robert L. Cord, *Church-State Separation: Restoring the "No Preference" Doctrine of the First Amendment,* 9 HARV. J.L. & PUB. POL'Y 129 (1986) (supporting nonpreferentialism); Rodney K. Smith, *Nonpreferentialism in Establishment Clause Analysis: A Response to Professor Laycock,* 65 ST. JOHN'S L. REV. 245 (1991) (discussing

nonpreferentialism in response to Professor Douglas Laycock's repudiation of the concept).

2. McCreary County v. ACLU of Kentucky, ___ U.S. ___, 125 S. Ct. 2722, 2748 (2005) (Scalia, J., dissenting) (arguing that monotheism may be promoted by government in the religious symbolism context, but not directly in the funding context).

3. I may be seen as such an accommodationist, *see* Frank S. Ravitch, *A Funny Thing Happened on the Way to Neutrality: Broad Principles, Formalism, and the Establishment Clause,* 38 GA. L. REV. 489, 537–73 (2004), although my views under the Establishment Clause are not free of accommodationist concepts. *See infra* chapters 9 and 10; *see also* Douglas Laycock, *The Underlying Unity of Separation and Neutrality,* 46 EMORY L. J. 43 (1997); Douglas Laycock, *Formal, Substantive, and Disaggregated Neutrality Toward Religion,* 39 DEPAUL L. REV. 993 (1990).

4. Thomas C. Berg, *The Voluntary Principle and Church Autonomy, Then and Now,* 2004 B.Y.U. L. REV. 1593 (2004); Thomas C. Berg, *Religion Clause Anti-Theories,* 72 NOTRE DAME L. REV. 693 (1997).

5. Mild accommodationism may often be free exercise accommodationism in the Establishment Clause context. *See supra* note 3, and accompanying text.

6. *See infra* chapters 9 and 10.

7. Justice Breyer may be such an accommodationist. *See, e.g.,* Van Orden v. Perry, ___ U.S. ___, 125 S. Ct. 2854, 2868 (2005) (Breyer, J., concurring in the judgment); Good News Club v. Milford Central Schools, 533 U.S. 98, 127 (2001) (Breyer, J., concurring in part).

8. *See supra* sources cited in notes 1–7.

9. Michael W. McConnell, *Accommodation of Religion: An Update and a Response to the Critics,* 60 GEO. WASH. L. REV. 685 (1992); Michael W. McConnell, *Accommodation of Religion,* 1985 SUP. CT. REV. 1 (1985).

10. Douglas Laycock, *Formal, Substantive, and Disaggregated Neutrality Toward Religion,* 39 DEPAUL L. REV. 993 (1990).

11. *See supra* chapters 4 and 5.

12. Church of Lukumi Babalu Aye v. City of Hialeah, 508 U.S. 520 (1993).

13. *See, e.g.,* Sherbert v. Verner, 374 U.S. 398 (1963) (setting forth the compelling interest test for exemptions under the Free Exercise Clause).

14. *Id.*

15. *See* Patrick M. Garry, *The Institutional Side of Religious Liberty: A New Model of the Establishment Clause,* 2004 UTAH L. REV. 1155, 1171 (2004) (contending that "if free exercise requires accommodation, the Establishment Clause cannot deny it"); Calvin Massey, *The Political Marketplace of Religion,* 57 HASTINGS L.J. 1, 51 (2005) (observing that "the Free Exercise Clause requires some accommodations of religion and the Establishment Clause prohibits other accommodations"); *see also* Lynch v. Donnelly, 465 U.S. 668, 710 (1984) (Brennan, J., dissenting) ("The Free Exercise Clause . . . does not necessarily compel

the government to provide . . . accommodation, but neither is the Establishment Clause offended by such a step."). *But see* Michael W. McConnell, *Accommodation of Religion: An Update and a Response to the Critics,* 60 GEO. WASH. L. REV. 685, 695 (1992) (arguing for accommodation under both Free Exercise Clause and Establishment Clause).

16. *See* Michael W. McConnell, *The Origins and Historical Understanding of Free Exercise of Religion,* 103 HARV. L. REV. 1409, 1414–16 (1990).

17. *See* RICHARD HOFSTADTER, THE AMERICAN POLITICAL TRADITION AND THE MEN WHO MADE IT 4–5 (1948).

18. *See, e.g.,* Cass R. Sunstein, *Five Theses on Originalism,* 19 HARV. J.L. & PUB. POL'Y 311, 313–15 (1996) (explaining concept of "soft originalism).

19. *See supra* chapter 1.

20. *See* McConnell, *supra* note 9.

21. *See* Frederick Mark Gedicks, *An Unfirm Foundation: The Regrettable Indefensibility of Religious Exemptions,* 20 U. ARK. LITTLE ROCK L.J. 555, 556, 558–60 (1998); Timothy L. Hall, *Omnibus Protections of Religious Liberty and the Establishment Clause,* 21 CARDOZO L. REV. 539, 545 (1999); Douglas Laycock, *Religious Liberty as Liberty,* 7 J. CONTEMP. LEGAL ISSUES 313, 314 (1996); Michael W. McConnell, *Accommodation of Religion: An Update and Response to the Critics,* 60 GEO. WASH. L. REV. 685, 717 (1992); Stephen Pepper, *Conflicting Paradigms of Religious Liberty,* 1993 BYU L. REV. 7, 12 (1993).

22. *See* McConnell, *supra* note 9; *see also* Michael W. McConnell, *Why Is Religious Liberty the "First Freedom"?* 21 CARDOZO L. REV. 1243 (2000); Michael W. McConnell, *Religious Freedom at a Crossroads,* 59 U. CHI. L. REV. 115 (1992); Michael W. McConnell, *Free Exercise Revisionism and the Smith Decision,* 57 U. CHI. L. REV. 1109 (1990); Michael W. McConnell, *The Origins and Historical Understanding of Free Exercise of Religion,* 103 HARV. L. REV. 1409 (1990).

23. McConnell, *Religious Freedom at a Crossroads, supra* note 22, at 115–16.

24. *See* McConnell, *supra* note 9.

25. Frank S. Ravitch, *A Funny Thing Happened on the Way to Neutrality: Broad Principles, Formalism, and the Establishment Clause,* 38 GA. L. REV. 489, 542 (2004); Jesse Choper, *The Rise and Decline of the Constitutional Protection of Religious Liberty,* 70 NEB. L. REV. 651, 685 (1991); John H. Garvey, *Freedom and Equality in the Religion Clauses,* 1981 SUP. CT. REV. 193 (1981).

26. *See, e.g.,* Douglas Laycock, *Religious Liberty as Liberty,* 7 J. CONTEMP. LEGAL ISSUES 313, 314–15 (1996); *see also* Frank S. Ravitch, *A Funny Thing Happened On the Way to Neutrality: Broad Principles, Formalism, and the Establishment Clause,* 38 GA. L. REV. 489, 540–41 (2004).

27. *See supra* chapter 4; *infra* chapter 9.

28. U.S. 872 (1990).

29. *Id.*

30. *Id.* at 890.

31. See McConnell, *supra* note 9; McConnell, *Free Exercise Revisionism, supra* note 22; McConnell, *Religious Freedom at a Crossroads, supra* note 22; Choper, *supra* note 25; Laycock, *supra* note 10; *see also* Ravitch, *supra* note 25, at 572–73.

32. Ravitch, *supra* note 25, at 542.

33. *See, e.g.,* Wallace v. Jaffree, 472 U.S. 38, 91–114 (1985) (Rehnquist, J., dissenting) (arguing that a textual and historical view of the religion clauses suggests that Establishment Clause was intended to prevent government from making religious preferences); ROBERT L. CORD, SEPARATION OF CHURCH AND STATE: HISTORICAL FACT AND CURRENT FICTION (1982) (defending benevolent neutrality on basis of textualism); LEONARD W. LEVY, THE ESTABLISHMENT CLAUSE: RELIGION AND THE FIRST AMENDMENT (1986) (defending strict scrutiny on basis of neutrality).

34. *Cf.* James J. Knicely, *"First Principles" and the Misplacement of the "Wall of Separation": Too Late in the Day for a Cure?* 52 DRAKE L. REV. 171, 188 (2004) (stating that two recent books are "indispensable reading for a complete understanding of . . . the original meaning of the Establishment Clause in light of its application by the United States Supreme Court") (referring to DANIEL L. DREISBACH, THOMAS JEFFERSON AND THE WALL OF SEPARATION BETWEEN CHURCH AND STATE (2002), and PHILIP HAMBURGER, SEPARATION OF CHURCH AND STATE (2002)).

35. *See* sources cited *supra* note 21.

36. *See, e.g.,* Bronx Household of Faith, v. Bd. of Educ., 226 F. Supp. 2d 401, 414 (2002); James R. Beattie, Jr., *Taking Liberalism and Religious Liberty Seriously: Shifting Our Notion of Toleration from Locke to Mill,* 43 CATH. LAW. 367, 390 (2004); Frank H. Easterbrook, *Levels of Generality in Constitutional Interpretation,* 59 U. CHI. L. REV. 349, 377 (1992); McConnell, *supra* note 16, at 1409 (1990), Tania Saison, *Restoring Obscurity: The Shortcomings of the Religious Freedom Restoration Act,* 28 COLUM. J.L. & SOC. PROBS. 653, 662 n.31 (1995).

37. *See* Michael J. Perry, *Religion, Politics, and the Constitution,* 7 J. CONTEMP. LEGAL ISSUES 407, 429 (1996) (observing that "the conventional range of reference of the word 'prohibit' is broad enough to accommodate either the accommodation position or the rejection of the position").

38. *See* Kathleen M. Sullivan, *Religion and Liberal Democracy,* 59 U. CHI. L. REV. 195, 205–06 (1992) ("[T]he right to free exercise of religion implies the right to free exercise of nonreligion. No one may be coerced into worship, any more than out of it. . . . Thus the Free Exercise Clause would forbid the state to coerce minority sects or atheists into contrary beliefs, even without the Establishment Clause.").

39. *Cf.* Alex Kozinski & Eugene Volokh, *A Penumbra Too Far,* 106 HARV. L. REV. 1639, 1641 (1993) (pointing out that "[t]here are a thousand and one plausible readings of the Establishment Clause," and that it may be difficult to distinguish between "a genuine advance in constitutional thinking from a flight of fancy").

40. *See* discussion of philosophical hermeneutics *supra* at chapter 1.

41. *See* McConnell, *supra* note 9 (accommodation); chapter 6 *supra* (separation).

42. *Cf.* Steven G. Gey, *Why Is Religion Special? Reconsidering the Accommodation of Religion Under the Religion Clauses of the First Amendment,* 52 U. PITT. L. REV. 75, 82 n.25 (1990) (opining that the Supreme Court's "search for the precise degree of separation and accommodation required by the Constitution amounts to a typical balancing test"); *see also* Richard H. Jones, *Concerning Secularists' Proposed Restrictions on the Role of Religion in American Politics,* 8 BYU J. PUB. L. 343, 353 (1994) (acknowledging by implication the lack of textual guidance by categorizing differing degrees of separationists and accommodationists).

43. *Smith,* 494 U.S. at 878–80, 884–89.

44. In fact, the *Smith* dissenters pointed out there were similar exemptions even to drug laws pre-*Smith* and there were no significant enforcement problems as a result of the compelling interest/mandatory exemption concept. *Smith,* 494 U.S. at 911–13, 916–18.

45. In the post-*Yoder* federal context the unfortunate reality was that the Court continually narrowed the range of cases where exemptions could be mandated. *See, e.g.,* Lyng v. Northwest Indian Cemetery Protective Association, 485 U.S. 439 (1988) (denying request to protect sacred Native American ritual sites from government project); O'Lone v. Estate of Shabazz, 482 U.S. 342 (1987) (Muslim prisoner can be prevented from attending religious services at prison when on work detail outside prison even if prisoner has no choice but to be on work detail); Goldman v. Weinberger, 475 U.S. 503 (1986) (Orthodox Jewish military psychologist can be required to remove yarmulka in indoor military settings despite serious religious objections); Bowen v. Roy, 476 U.S. 693 (1986) (Native American denied request for daughter not to have social security number, despite serious religious concerns); United States v. Lee, 455 U.S. 252 (1982) (Amish employer must pay social security tax despite religious objection).

46. McConnell, *Accommodation of Religion, supra* note 9, at 26 ("The purpose of a religious accommodation is to relieve the believer—where it is possible to do so without sacrificing significant civic or social interests—from the conflicting claims of religion and society.").

47. *See, e.g.,* Lyng v. Northwest Indian Cemetery Protective Association, 485 U.S. 439 (1988) (denying request to protect sacred Native American ritual sites from government project); O'Lone v. Estate of Shabazz, 482 U.S. 342 (1987) (Muslim prisoner can be prevented from attending religious services at prison when on work detail outside prison even if prisoner has no choice but to be on work detail); Goldman v. Weinberger, 475 U.S.

503 (1986) (Orthodox Jewish military psychologist can be required to remove yarmulka in indoor
military settings despite serious religious objections); Bowen v. Roy, 476 U.S. 693 (1986) (Native
American denied request for daughter not to have
social security number, despite serious religious
concerns); United States v. Lee, 455 U.S. 252
(1982) (Amish employer must pay social security
tax despite religious objection).

48. See supra at chapter 5; Steven H. Shiffrin,
The Pluralistic Foundations of the Religion
Clauses, 90 CORNELL L. REV. 9 (2004); Alan E.
Brownstein, Interpreting the Religion Clauses in
Terms of Liberty, Equality, and Free Speech Values
—A Critical Analysis of "Neutrality Theory" and
Charitable Choice, 13 NOTRE DAME J. L. ETHICS &
PUB. POL'Y 243 (1999).

49. See supra chapter 5; Christopher L. Eisgruber and Lawrence G. Sager, The Vulnerability of
Conscience: The Constitutional Basis for Protecting Religious Conduct, 61 U. CHI. L. REV. 1245
(1994).

50. Id.

51. Id.

52. See supra chapter 5; Shiffrin supra note 48;
Brownstein, supra note 48.

53. See, e.g., Eisgruber and Sager, supra note 49
(promoting concept of equal regard).

54. See infra chapters 9 and 10.

55. Id.

56. See supra chapter 2.

57. Id.; Smith, 494 U.S. 872.

58. See Brownstein, supra note 48, at 262–64.

59. Id.

60. See generally McConnell supra notes 9 and
22; Choper supra note 25.

61. See Employment Div. v. Smith, 494 U.S.
872, 890 (1990) ("It may fairly be said that leaving accommodation to the political process will
place at a relative disadvantage those religious
practices that are not widely engaged in. . . .");
Thomas C. Berg, The Permissible Scope of Legal
Limitations on the Freedom of Religion or Belief
in the United States, 19 EMORY INT'L L. REV.
1277, 1307 (2005) ("Legislative exemptions . . .
will give only partial protection to minority religions, since the legislative process itself tends to reflect majoritarian views.").

62. Smith, 494 U.S. at 878–80, 888–89.

63. See Werner Cohn, When the Constitution
Fails on Church and State: Two Case Studies, 6
RUTGERS J. L. & RELIGION 2 (2004) ("Those who
lean toward accommodation will put emphasis on
the Free Exercise clause; those leaning toward sep-
arationism will emphasize the Establishment
Clause."); Richard C. Schragger, The Role of the
Local in the Doctrine and Discourse of Religious
Liberty, 117 HARV. L. REV. 1810, 1833 (2004)
(noting that "[t]he separationist argument asserts
that accommodations are required by the Free Ex-
ercise Clause"); Gregory C. Sisk, Searching for the
Soul of Judicial Decisionmaking: An Empirical
Study of Religious Freedom Decisions, 65 OHIO
ST. L.J. 491, 508 (2004) (noting that strict separa-

tionists resist accommodationism under both the
Establishment Clause and the Free Exercise
Clause).

64. Cf. Alan E. Brownstein, Harmonizing the
Heavenly and Earthly Spheres: The Fragmentation
and Synthesis of Religion, Equality, and Speech in
the Constitution, 51 OHIO ST. L.J. 89, 89 (1990)
(stating that "both separation and accommodation
approaches fail" in the "attempt to reconcile mandated exemptions" under the Free Exercise Clause
with the Establishment Clause). But see Gey, supra
note 42, at 79 (arguing that the accommodation
principle be eliminated because "it has no place in
either establishment or free exercise clause jurisprudence").

65. See Brett G. Scharffs, The Autonomy of
Church and State, 2004 BYU L. REV. 1217, 1235
(2004) (noting that "the history of the Establishment Clause jurisprudence . . . has been a story of
the struggle for dominance between separationist
and accommodationist viewpoints").

66. See supra note 1 (addressing nonpreferentialism); Ravitch, supra note 25, at 532 (suggesting
that the Court's formal neutrality test may operate
as a form of de facto nonpreferentialism).

67. See, e.g., Good News Club v. Milford Central Schools, 533 U.S. 98 (2001); Lamb's Chapel v.
Center Moriches Union Free Sch. Dist., 508 U.S.
384 (1993); Widmar v. Vincent, 454 U.S. 263
(1981).

68. Id.

69. Good News Club, 533 U.S. 98; Lamb's
Chapel, 508 U.S. 384.

70. Id.

71. Id.

72. Id.

73. Equal Access Act, 20 U.S.C. §4071 et seq.

74. Id.

75. Good News Club, 533 U.S. 98.

76. Id.

77. Of course, the specific context of a given
equal access situation would be relevant to many
separationists.

78. U.S. 98 (2001).

79. Id.

80. Id.

81. See, e.g., Child Evangelism Fellowship of
Md., Inc., v. Montgomery County Pub. Schs., 373
F.3d 589 (4th Cir. 2004) (holding that allowing religious organizations to distribute flyers at school
does not likely violate the Establishment Clause);
Peck v. Upshur County Bd. of Educ., 155 F.3d 274,
279 (4th Cir. 1998) (holding that group may distribute Bibles to students during school day).

82. Good News Club, 533 U.S. at 127–29
(Breyer, J., concurring in part); Capitol Square Review and Advisory Bd. v. Pinette, 515 U.S. 753,
777 (1995) (O'Connor, J., concurring in part and
concurring in the judgment).

83. Good News Club, 533 U.S. at 130 (Stevens,
J., dissenting); id. at 134 (Souter, J., dissenting).

84. Good News Club, 533 U.S. 98.

85. Id.; see also Capitol Square, 515 U.S. at
761–62.

86. *Good News Club,* 533 U.S. at 134 (Souter, J., dissenting).

87. In fact, both *Good News Club,* 533 U.S. 98, and *Capitol Square,* 515 U.S. 753 (plurality opinion), openly address the issue this way, even if they do not expressly use accommodationist terminology.

88. Ravitch, *supra* note 25 at 527–28, 530–31, 570–71.

89. *See infra* at chapters 9 and 10.

90. U.S. 38 (1985).

91. Walter v. W. Va. Bd. of Educ., 610 F. Supp. 1169 (D.W. Va. 1985) (finding moment of silence law unconstitutional as applied).

92. The various opinions in *Wallace,* 472 U.S. 39, taken together demonstrate that moment of silence laws are generally constitutional so long as no religious favoritism is involved.

93. Ravitch, *supra* note 25, at 559–60.

94. *Cf. id.*

95. *See infra* chapter 10.

96. *See, e.g.,* Lee v. Weisman, 505 U.S. 577, 645–46 (1992) (Scalia, J., dissenting) (arguing that collective prayer may be important and beneficial).

97. The minyan is just one example of religious rules that may suggest that collective prayer is required or beneficial. One can pray without a minyan, but there are certain prayers that can only be said with a minyan.

98. Schools sometimes make space available to accommodate religious practices, but in the absence of an equal access argument schools would not be required to do so under the Free Exercise Clause. *Smith,* 494 U.S. 872.

99. *Id.*

100. *See Wallace,* 472 U.S. 38; *Walter,* 610 F. Supp. 1169; Ravitch *supra* note 25, at 560.

101. Ravitch, *supra* note 25, at 559–60.

102. Zelman v. Simmons-Harris, 536 U.S. 639 (2002).

103. *See supra* chapter 2; Ravitch, *supra* note 25, at 498–523.

104. Ravitch, *supra* note 25, at 513–23.

105. Zobrest v. Catalina Foothills Sch. Dist., 509 U.S. 1 (1993); Witters v. Washington Dept. of Serv. for the Blind, 474 U.S. 481 (1986); Ravitch, *supra* note 25, at 563–66.

106. *Id.*

107. *See infra* chapters 9 and 10; Ravitch, *supra* note 25, at 544–73.

108. *See supra* note 1.

109. *See* Douglas Laycock, *"Nonpreferential" Aid to Religion: A False Claim About Original Intent,* 27 Wm. & Mary L. Rev. 875 (1986).

110. *Id.*

111. Ravitch, *supra* note 25, at 532.

112. Agostini v. Felton, 521 U.S. 203 (1997); Aguilar v. Felton, 473 U.S. 402 (1985).

113. *Agostini,* 521 U.S. at 208–11.

114. *Id.* at 213–14.

115. *Agostini,* 521 U.S. 203.

116. *Zobrest,* 509 U.S. 1; *Witters,* 474 U.S. 481.

117. *Compare* Steven B. Epstein, *Rethinking the Constitutionality of Ceremonial Deism,* 96

Colum. L. Rev. 2083 (1996), *with* Daniel O. Conkle, *Toward a General Theory of the Establishment Clause,* 82 Nw. U. L. Rev. 1113 (1988).

118. This is essentially my definition, but it is similar to the definitions used by judges and scholars who have addressed the issue.

119. *But see* Epstein, *supra* note 117 (questioning some of these practices).

120. *See infra* chapters 8, 9, and 10.

121. *Cf.* Epstein, *supra* note 117 (addressing what has and has not been considered ceremonial deism by judges and scholars and creating a definition for ceremonial deism).

122. *See infra* chapter 8.

123. Lisa Shaw Roy, Essay, *The Establishment Clause and the Concept of Inclusion,* 83 Or. L. Rev. 1, 7 (2004).

124. *See* Conkle, *supra* note 117, at 1185 n.283.

125. *See, e.g.,* Marsh v. Chambers, 463 U.S. 783 (1983); Lisa Shaw Roy, *supra* note 123, at 7.

126. Considering the history of anti-Catholicism in the United States, it should come as no surprise that there is no long-standing tradition of the government display of crèches prior to the latter part of the twentieth century. For a discussion of the history of anti-Catholicism, *see* Philip Hamburger, Separation of Church and State (Harvard 2002).

127. Abington Tp., 374 U.S. at 303–04 (Brennan, J., concurring); *cf.* Lisa Shaw Roy, *supra* note 123.

128. Epstein, *supra* note 117.

129. Frederick Mark Gedicks, The Rhetoric of Church and State: A Critical Analysis of Religion Clause Jurisprudence (Duke 1995); Stephen L. Carter, The Culture of Disbelief: How American Law and Politics Trivialize Religious Devotion (Anchor 1993).

130. *Cf.* Ravitch, *supra* note 25, at 569 ("while the presidential lighting of the tree violates the facilitation test, it is a battle one might wisely abstain from engaging in.").

131. Epstein, *supra* note 117 (expanding notions of ceremonial deism may swallow much of the Establishment Clause).

132. *Id.* (suggesting an extremely narrow range of acceptable ceremonial deism).

133. Frank S. Ravitch, *Religious Objects as Legal Subjects,* 40 Wake Forest L. Rev. 1011 (2005); Ravitch, *supra* note 25, at 558–60.

134. *Id.*; Frank S. Ravitch, School Prayer and Discrimination: The Civil Rights of Religious Minorities and Dissenters (Northeastern 1999).

135. *See infra* chapter 8.

136. *Id.*; Ravitch, *supra* note 133.

137. *See infra* chapters 8, 9, and 10.

138. *See, e.g.,* Douglas Laycock, *Theology Scholarships, the Pledge of Allegiance, and Religious Liberty: Avoiding the Extremes but Missing the Liberty,* 118 Harv. L. Rev. 155 (2004) ("At some point, the Court must recognize either a substantive de minimis exception or a category of

cases where the harm to individuals is too slight to justify standing."); Lisa Shaw Roy, *The Establishment Clause and the Concept of Inclusion,* 83 OR. L. REV. 1, 45 (2004) (arguing that "the Establishment Clause should not be interpreted as requiring elimination of every religious message or practice"); Richard F. Suhrheinrich & T. Melindah Bush, *The Ohio Motto Survives the Establishment Clause,* 64 OHIO ST. L.J. 585 (2003); Keith Werhan, *Navigating the New Neutrality: School Vouchers, the Pledge, and the Limits of a Purposive Establishment Clause,* 41 BRANDEIS L.J. 603, 626–27 (2003) (arguing that issues regarding ceremonial deism "are not of sufficient magnitude to compel federal courts to invest their resources, as well as their credibility, in a project to root out these references from official discourse").

139. As will be seen in chapter 9, there is nothing wrong with pragmatic concerns figuring into the interpretive calculus, but it is better when those concerns are laid bare in the interpretive process rather than covered in the illusion of historicity that conflicts with similar cases.

140. Ravitch, *supra* note 133; Ravitch, *supra* note 134; *see also* Ravitch, *supra* note 25, at 558–60.

141. This is inherent in the nature of accommodation and is a separate question from whether the benefit to religion is greater than that given to other belief systems and whether the benefit is constitutionally appropriate.

142. *See infra* chapters 9 and 10.

143. Ravitch, *supra* note 133; Ravitch, *supra* note 134.

144. Abington Tp. v. Schempp, 373 U.S. 203, 312–13 (1963) (Stewart, J., dissenting); Engel v. Vitale, 370 U.S. 471, 445–46 (1962) (Stewart, J., dissenting).

145. *Id.*

146. *Id.; see also* Lee, 505 U.S. at 645–46 (Scalia, J., dissenting).

147. *Lee,* 505 U.S. at 645–46 (Scalia, J., dissenting); *cf. Santa Fe v. Doe,* 530 U.S. 290, 322–23 (2000) (Rehnquist, C.J., dissenting).

148. *See Santa Fe,* 530 U.S. 290; Ravitch, *supra* note 25, at 558–60.

149. *See infra* chapters 9 and 10.

150. *Id.; supra* chapter 4.

151. *See supra* note1.

152. *See infra* chapter 8; *see also* Frank S. Ravitch, *Religious Objects as Legal Subjects,* 40 WAKE FOREST L. REV. 1011, 1023–25, 1075–78 (2005).

153. *See generally* Ravitch, *supra* note 152.

NOTES TO CHAPTER 8

1. *See, e.g.,* Troy L. Booher, *Finding Religion for the First Amendment,* 38 J. MARSHALL L. REV. 469 (2004); Jesse Choper, *Defining "Religion" in the First Amendment,* 1982 U. ILL. L. REV. 579 (1982); George C. Freeman III, *The Misguided Search for the Constitutional Definition of "Religion,"* 71 GEO. L.J. 1519 (1983); Douglas Laycock, *Religious Liberty as Liberty,* 7 J. CONTEMP.

LEGAL ISSUES 313, 326 (1996); Lee J. Strang, *The Meaning of "Religion" in the First Amendment,* 40 DUQ. L. REV. 181 (2002). For a trenchant critique of attempts to define religion, see WINNIFRED FALLERS SULLIVAN, THE IMPOSSIBILITY OF RELIGIOUS FREEDOM (Princeton 2005).

2. *See, e.g.,* Arlin M. Adams & Charles J. Emmerich, *A Heritage of Religious Liberty,* 137 U. PA. L. REV. 1559, 1667 (1989); Abner S. Greene, *The Political Balance of the Religion Clauses,* 102 YALE L.J. 1611, 1635 (1993); *see also* Malnak v. Yogi, 592 F.2d 197, 210–13 (3d Cir. 1979) (Adams, J., concurring in result).

3. *See, e.g.,* Stephen L. Carter, *Reflections on the Separation of Church and State,* 44 ARIZ. L. REV. 293, 298–99 (2002) ("[E]ven if we grant the shaky proposition that the religion clause is actually two clauses, there is no plausible interpretation on which the word 'religion,' mentioned once and then marked with a pregnant 'thereof,' can mean two different things.").

4. *See, e.g.,* LAURENCE H. TRIBE, AMERICAN CONSTITUTIONAL LAW § 14-6, at 1181, 1887 (2d ed. 1988).

5. *See, e.g.,* George W. Dent, Jr., *Of God and Caesar: The Free Exercise Rights of Public School Students,* 43 CASE W. RES. L. REV. 707, 726 (1993).

6. *See, e.g.,* Stanley Ingber, *Religion or Ideology: A Needed Clarification of the Religion Clauses,* 41 STAN. L. REV. 233, 325 & nn.574–76 (1989).

7. *See* Welsh v. United States, 398 U.S. 333 (1970); United States v. Seeger, 380 U.S. 163 (1965).

8. *Welsh,* 398 U.S. at 336–38; *Seeger,* 380 U.S. at 164–69.

9. *See* Christopher B. Gilbert, *Harry Potter and the Curse of the First Amendment: Schools, Esoteric Religions, and the Christian Backlash,* 198 EDUC. L. REP. 399, 403 (2005) (observing that "the Supreme Court has not given us a working definition of 'religion'); Donna D. Page, Comment, *Veganism and Sincerely Held "Religious" Beliefs in the Workplace: No Protection Without Definition,* 7 U. PA. J. LAB. & EMP. L. 363, 364 & n.4 (2005) (noting that "the Supreme Court has never attempted to articulate a precise definition of 'religion' ").

10. *Welsh,* 398 U.S. 333; *Seeger,* 380 U.S. 163; *see also* Gillete v. United States, 401 U.S. 437 (1971); United States v. Ballard, 322 U.S. 78 (1944).

11. As will be explored later in this chapter, how does one determine the constitutionality of a religious symbol without addressing its religious nature or the constitutionality of an abstinence-only program under the Establishment Clause without addressing whether such a program is religious?

12. *See, e.g.,* Strang, *supra* note 1, at 183 (arguing that "religion in the First Amendment context . . . is at least theistic, and likely monotheistic").

13. *See, e.g.,* Dent, *supra* note 5, at 726.

14. For example, in Establishment Clause cases

such as Abington Tp. v. Schempp, 374 U.S. 203 (1963), and Free Exercise Clause cases such as Goldman v. Weinberger, 475 U.S. 503 (1986).

15. For a brief discussion of the unitary clause concept, *see* STEPHEN L. CARTER, THE CULTURE OF DISBELIEF: HOW AMERICAN LAW AND POLITICS TRIVIALIZE RELIGIOUS DEVOTION 117–18 (Anchor 1993).

16. *See, e.g.,* Strang, *supra* note 1, at 183 (stating that "religion" under the First Amendment has the following attributes: "theistic, . . . the Supreme Being to whom the belief system claims adherence requires the believer to do and refrain from doing certain things, and the belief system must profess a future state of rewards and punishment").

17. *See* Francis J. Beckwith, *Public Education, Religious Establishment, and the Challenge of Intelligent Design,* 17 NOTRE DAME J.L. ETHICS & PUB. POL'Y 461, 486 (2003); John C. Knechtle, *If We Don't Know What It Is, How Do We Know If It's Established?* 41 BRANDEIS L.J. 521, 528–29 (2003) (mentioning the single use of religion argument).

18. *Welsh,* 398 U.S. at 340, *Seeger,* 380 U.S. at 176.

19. *Seeger,* 380 U.S. at 174–75.

20. Lee J. Strang, *The Meaning of "Religion" in the First Amendment,* 40 DUQ. L. REV. 181, 202–10 (2002) (arguing for definition of religion based on original intent which would likely include deity focus, and arguing that arguments for broader definitions are only self-justifying).

21. Frank S. Ravitch, *Religious Objects as Legal Subjects,* 40 WAKE FOREST L. REV. 1011 (2005).

22. Knechtle, *supra* note 17, at 527–28.

23. While most of the cries of the establishment of secular humanism come from partisan religious or social commentators, some academics have also raised the argument. *See, e.g.,* Richard Collin Mangrum, *Shall We Sing? Shall We Sing Religious Music in Public Schools?* 38 CREIGHTON L. REV. 815, 850–53 (2005).

24. FRANK S. RAVITCH, SCHOOL PRAYER AND DISCRIMINATION: THE CIVIL RIGHTS OF RELIGIOUS MINORITIES AND DISSENTERS 153 n.21 (Northeastern 1999); Douglas Laycock, *Religious Liberty as Liberty,* 7 J. CONTEMP. LEGAL ISSUES 313, 328–29 (1996).

25. *Welsh,* 398 U.S. 333; *Seeger,* 380 U.S. 163.

26. *See* The American Humanist Association Web site, *at* http://www.americanhumanist.org.

27. Laycock, *supra* note 24, at 329.

28. *Id.* at 328–30.

29. "[Religion is] the sigh of the distressed creature, the soul of a heartless world, as it is also the spirit of a spiritless condition. It is the opium of the people." KARL MARX, ON RELIGION xx (Saul K. Padover ed. & trans., 1974); "Religion . . . is the opium of the people." KARL MARX, TOWARD THE CRITIQUE OF HEGEL'S PHILOSOPHY OF RIGHT, *in* KARL MARX & FRIEDRICH ENGELS, BASIC WRITINGS ON POLITICS AND PHILOSOPHY 262, 263 (Lewis S. Feuer ed., 1959).

30. Laycock, *supra* note 24.

31. *See* Web site listed at note 26, *supra.*

32. *But see* George W. Dent, Jr., *Secularism and the Supreme Court,* 1999 BYU L. REV. 1 (1999) (criticizing the Court's secularist approach and arguing for a new approach).

33. McCreary County v. ACLU of Kentucky, ___ U.S. ___, 125 S. Ct. 2722, 2746 (2005) (O'Connor, J., concurring).

34. *See* Roger Williams, *Mr. Cottons [sic] Letter Lately Printed, Examined and Answered* (1644), *reprinted in* 1 THE COMPLETE WRITINGS OF ROGER WILLIAMS 313, 392 (1963) (speaking of a wall of separation between religion and "the wilderness"); *see also* Kristin N. Wuerffel, Note, *Discrimination Among Rights? A Nation's Legislating a Hierarchy of Human Rights in the Context of International Human Rights Customary Law,* 33 VAL. U. L. REV. 369, 373 n.25 (1998) (noting that natural law, to which Thomas Aquinas subscribed, developed out of an effort to separate natural rights from religion) (citing Jerome J. Shestack, *The Jurisprudence of Human Rights, in* HUMAN RIGHTS IN INTERNATIONAL LAW 77–78, 81 (Theodor Meron ed., 1984)).

35. NOAH FELDMAN, DIVIDED BY GOD: AMERICA'S CHURCH-STATE PROBLEM — AND WHAT WE SHOULD DO ABOUT IT (Farrar, Straus and Giroux 2005); FREDERICK MARK GEDICKS, THE RHETORIC OF CHURCH AND STATE: A CRITICAL ANALYSIS OF RELIGION CLAUSE JURISPRUDENCE (Duke 1995); STEPHEN L. CARTER, THE CULTURE OF DISBELIEF: HOW AMERICAN LAW AND POLITICS TRIVIALIZE RELIGIOUS DEVOTION (Anchor 1993).

36. *Cf.* Frank S. Ravitch, *The Supreme Court's Rhetorical Hostility: What Is "Hostile" to Religion Under the Establishment Clause?* 2004 B.Y.U. L. REV.1031 (2004) (symposium issue) (following secular interests or attempting to uphold the Establishment Clause is not inherently hostile to religion).

37. *Welsh,* 398 U.S. 333; *Seeger,* 380 U.S. 163

38. *Welsh,* 398 U.S. at 336–38; *Seeger,* 380 U.S. at 164–69.

39. *See* description on Star Trek.com, *at* http://www.startrek.com/startrek/view/series/TOS/character/1115257.html.

40. William Marshall, *In Defense of Smith and Free Exercise Revisionism,* 58 U. CHI. L. REV. 308, 320 (1991); Ellis West, *The Case Against a Right to Religion-Based Exemptions,* 4 NOTRE DAME J.L. ETHICS & PUB. POL'Y 591, 600 (1990).

41. *See supra* chapters 1, 4, and 7; *infra* chapters 9 and 10.

42. *See* JESSE H. CHOPER, SECURING RELIGIOUS LIBERTY: PRINCIPLES FOR JUDICIAL INTERPRETATION OF THE RELIGION CLAUSES 62–63 (1995) (stating that "[t]here is an obvious relationship between the legal definition of religion and the shaping of substantive doctrine under the free exercise clause" and that "it is unlikely that an extremely broad definition of religion will be permitted to co-exist with an extremely generous protection of the claims that fall within that definition").

43. *See* Michael W. McConnell, *Accommoda-*

tion of Religion: An Update and a Response to the Critics, 60 GEO. WASH. L. REV. 685 (1992); Michael W. McConnell, *Accommodation of Religion*, 1985 SUP. CT. REV. 1 (1985).

44. *See* McCreary County v. ACLU of Kentucky, ___ U.S. ___, 125 S. Ct. 2722 (2005) (striking down courthouse displays including Ten Commandments where displays were created as a means to post the Commandments in the courthouses); Van Orden v. Perry, ___ U.S. ___, 125 S. Ct. 2854 (2005) (plurality opinion) (upholding display of Ten Commandments monument donated by the Fraternal Order of Eagles in 1961 on the grounds between the Texas state capitol and state supreme court building); Stone v. Graham, 449 U.S. 39 (1981) (per curiam) (striking down Kentucky statute that required the posting of the Ten Commandments on each public school classroom in the state); *see also* King v. Richmond County, 331 F.3d 1271 (11th Cir. 2003) (upholding use of small seal that included a depiction of the Ten Commandments, but not the text, along with other images); Glassroth v. Moore, 335 F.3d 1282 (11th Cir. 2003) (striking down display of large granite Ten Commandments monument placed in the rotunda of Alabama state courthouse in the middle of the night by former chief justice of the Alabama Supreme Court); Freethought Soc'y of Greater Philadelphia v. Chester County, 334 F.3d 247 (3d Cir. 2003) (upholding display of small Ten Commandments plaque on old entrance to county courthouse, where plaque was placed on the building in 1920 and old entrance where plaque was located was no longer in use); Adland v. Russ, 307 F.3d 471 (6th Cir. 2002) (striking down display of monument donated by the Fraternal Order of Eagles in 1961 on grounds of the state capitol); Books v. City of Elkhart, 235 F.3d 292 (7th Cir. 2000) (same for monument donated in 1958 and located on grounds of city municipal building).

45. *See, e.g.*, County of Allegheny v. ACLU, 492 U.S. 573 (1989) (striking down display of crèche on grand staircase of courthouse where crèche was not part of broader display); Lynch v. Donnelly, 465 U.S. 668 (1984) (upholding display of crèche by city of Pawtucket as part of broader seasonal display).

46. *See, e.g.*, Capitol Square Review Bd. v. Pinette, 515 U.S. 753 (1995) (upholding display of Latin cross by Ku Klux Klan on the grounds of state capitol because cross was displayed in public forum open to all kinds of speech); Separation of Church and State Comm. v. City of Eugene, 93 F.3d 617 (9th Cir. 1996) (striking down fifty-one-foot-tall Latin cross that was erected in city park, and which was designated a war memorial after the court struck down its display in an earlier decision); Ellis v. City of La Mesa, 990 F.2d 1518 (9th Cir. 1993) (striking down the display of two large Latin crosses in separate public parks and the use of a Latin cross in the city's official insignia under the no-preference clause of the California Constitution).

47. *See, e.g., Allegheny*, 492 U.S. 573 (upholding display of a menorah along with a large Christmas tree and a sign saluting liberty at city-county building).

48. *Id.*

49. *See infra* at Part B.3 (discussing this criticism and breaking it down into four broad critiques of the Court's religious symbolism jurisprudence).

50. *See, e.g.*, Alan Brownstein, *A Decent Respect for Religious Liberty and Religious Equality: Justice O'Connor's Interpretation of the Religion Clauses of the First Amendment*, 32 MCGEORGE L. REV. 837, 855–58 (2001) (criticizing the Court's minimization of the impact government display of religious objects can have on religious minorities); Laura Underkuffler-Freund, *The Separation of the Religious and the Secular: A Foundational Challenge to First Amendment Theory*, 36 WM. & MARY L. REV. 837, 871–72, 971–72 (1995) (criticizing the Court's desacralization of religious symbols); Kenneth L. Karst, *The First Amendment: The Politics of Religion and the Symbols of Government*, 27 HARV. C.R.-C.L. L. REV. 503 (1992) (criticizing the Court's minimization of the impact government display of religious objects can have on religious minorities); Timothy Zick, *Cross Burning, Cockfighting, and Symbolic Meaning: Toward a First Amendment Ethnography*, 45 WM. & MARY L. REV. 2261 (2004) (criticizing the Court's desacralization of religious symbols).

51. Justice Breyer recently made this point in regard to what he called "borderline" cases involving religious objects. Van Orden v. Perry, 125 S. Ct. 2854, 2869 (2005) (Breyer, J., concurring). This book suggests that none of the current legal tests are up to the task of adequately addressing the constitutionality of religious objects, but courts must address these objects nonetheless.

52. There have been several attempts to take Establishment Clause issues away from the federal courts by limiting their jurisdiction over cases involving such issues. *See, e.g.*, We The People Act, H.R. 3893, 108th Congress §3.1(A) (2004) (attempting to remove federal court jurisdiction—including Supreme Court jurisdiction—to hear "any claim involving the laws, regulations, or policies of any State or unit of local government relating to the free exercise or establishment of religion"); Religious Liberties Restoration Act, S. 1558, 108th Congress §3 (2003) (attempting to remove lower federal court jurisdiction to hear cases involving the display of the Ten Commandments, the use of the word "God" in the Pledge of Allegiance, and the motto "In God We Trust"). This article suggests such attempts are inadvisable because of the mischief that could be created if government were given free rein to use powerful religious objects without any judicial oversight. *See* Ravitch, *supra* note 21 (suggesting that religious objects are powerful symbols for believers and that these symbols are sometimes used by government entities to facilitate a given religion or religions).

53. The interpretive concerns raise questions im-

plicating semiotics and hermeneutics. Zick, *supra* note 50, at 2292–97, 2308–11, 2365–74; James B. Raskin, *Polling Establishment: Judicial Review, Democracy, and the Endorsement Theory of the Establishment Clause—Commentary on Measured Endorsement,* 60 MD. L. REV. 761, 770 (2001); Joel S. Jacobs, *Endorsement as "Adoptive Action": A Suggested Definition of, and an Argument for, Justice O'Connor's Establishment Clause Test,* 22 HASTINGS CONST. L.Q. 29, 42–43 (1994); Janet L. Dolgin, *Religious Symbols and the Establishment of a National "Religion,"* 39 MERCER L. REV. 495, 497–98 (1988).

54. I am grateful to Robin Malloy for using this terminology during a conversation we had about this project when we were planning a panel on semiotics and law for the 2004 Law, Culture and Humanities meeting.

55. Dolgin, *supra* note 53, at 497–98; William P. Marshall, *"We Know It When We See It": The Supreme Court Establishment,* 59 S. CAL. L. REV. 495, 533–34 (1986).

56. *See generally Allegheny,* 492 U.S. 573 (suggesting that the physical context of a display can affect its religious message for constitutional purposes); *Lynch,* 465 U.S. 668 (same).

57. For example, Janet L. Dolgin suggests that a secularized citizen who identifies as Christian, but is not practicing, may not perceive a crèche as a religious object. Dolgin, *supra* note 53, at 504.

58. Gadamerian hermeneutics (the philosophical hermeneutics of Hans-George Gadamer) provides an excellent framework for understanding this process. *See supra* chapter 1; HANS-GEORG GADAMER, TRUTH AND METHOD (Joel Weinsheimer & Donald G. Marshall trans., Continuum, 2d rev. ed. 1989); *see also* HANS-GEORGE GADAMER, PHILOSOPHICAL HERMENEUTICS (David E. Linge ed. & trans., 1976); HANS-GEORGE GADAMER, REASON IN THE AGE OF SCIENCE (Frederick G. Lawrence trans., 1981). In addition to Gadamer's work, a number of good books can serve as introductions to the subject. *See, e.g.,* JOSEF BLEICHER, CONTEMPORARY HERMENEUTICS: HERMENEUTICS AS METHOD, PHILOSOPHY AND CRITIQUE (1980); JEAN GRONDIN, INTRODUCTION TO PHILOSOPHICAL HERMENEUTICS (Joel Weinsheimer trans., 1994). Examples of sources addressing legal hermeneutics include LEGAL HERMENEUTICS: HISTORY, THEORY, AND PRACTICE (Gregory Leyh ed., 1992); William N. Eskridge, Jr., *Gadamer/Statutory Interpretation,* 90 COLUM. L. REV. 609 (1990); Francis J. Mootz, *The Ontological Basis of Legal Hermeneutics: A Proposed Model of Inquiry Based on the Work of Gadamer, Habermas, and Ricoeur,* 68 B.U. L. REV. 523 (1988); *see also Symposium on Philosophical Hermeneutics and Critical Legal Theory,* 76 CHI.-KENT L. REV. 719 (2000).

59. *McCollum,* 333 U.S. at 237–38 (Jackson, J., concurring).

60. *Allegheny,* 492 U.S. at 595–96, 598–600, 613–21.

61. *Cf.* GADAMER, TRUTH AND METHOD, *supra*

note 58, at 302–07 (explaining the concept of horizons in the interpretive process).

62. *Lynch,* 465 U.S. at 700–01, 708–09, 711–12 (Brennan, J., dissenting); *id.* at 727 (Blackmun, J., dissenting); *Allegheny,* 492 U.S. at 643–45 (Brennan, J., concurring in part and dissenting in part); *id.* at 651 (Stevens, J., concurring in part and dissenting in part).

63. *Allegheny,* 492 U.S. at 644–46 (Brennan, J., concurring in part and dissenting in part); *id.* at 651 (Stevens, J., concurring in part and dissenting in part); *Lynch,* 465 U.S. at 701 (Brennan, J., dissenting); *id.* at 727 (Blackmun, J., dissenting).

64. Zick, *supra* note 50, at 2309–11

65. *Id.;* I Paul TILLICH, SYSTEMATIC THEOLOGY 240 (1951).

66. Brownstein, *supra* note 50, at 855–57; Karst, *supra* note 50.

67. Tillich's definition of religious symbols would include an event, an act, a story, or an object. A. R. McGlashan, *Symbolization and Human Development: The Use of Symbols in Religion from the Perspective of Analytical Psychology,* 25 RELIGIOUS STUD. 501 (1989) (citing Tillich's DYNAMICS OF FAITH (1957)).

68. *Id.*

69. U.S. 668 (1984).

70. *Id.* at 685.

71. Tillich, *supra* note 64, at 240; CHARLES H. LONG, SIGNIFICATIONS: SIGNS, SYMBOLS, AND IMAGES IN THE INTERPRETATION OF RELIGION (The Davies Group 1999) at 2; McGlashan, *supra* note 67, at 501. Long's reference to the power of symbols and signs may at first seem to conflict with Tillich's rather clear distinction between symbols and signs, but in context it does not seem that Long's description is at odds with Tillich's. Regardless, both agree about the power of religious symbols, including religious objects.

72. Zick, *supra* note 50; CLIFFORD GEERTZ, THE INTERPRETATION OF CULTURES (Basic Books 1973).

73. *Van Orden,* 125 S. Ct. at 2861, 2864.

74. *See, e.g.,* Dolgin, *supra* note 53, at 504–05 (suggesting that the Court turned Christmas into a secularized, yet sectarian, religious event); Daan Braveman, *The Establishment Clause and the Course of Religious Neutrality,* 45 MD. L. REV. 352 (1986) (criticizing the Court's decision in *Lynch* as being essentially Christocentric, while also demeaning religion).

75. *See Lynch,* 465 U.S. at 688 (O'Connor, J., concurring) (setting forth endorsement test and demonstrating that the test is focused on the perception of endorsement).

76. This becomes apparent when one reads the majority opinion in *Lynch* and Justice O'Connor's concurrence. While the legal methodologies differed between the two opinions, the view of the religious object did not. *Compare Lynch,* 465 U.S. 668, *with id.* at 687 (O'Connor, J., concurring).

77. *Van Orden,* 125 S. Ct. at 2862–64 (plurality opinion).

78. *See Lynch,* 465 U.S. 668 (suggesting that

crèche could be desacralized by its context, even if it retains its religious meaning more generally).

79. *Van Orden,* 125 S. Ct. 2854; County of Allegheny v. ACLU of Greater Pittsburgh, 492 U.S. 573 (1989) (analyzing crèche on grand staircase of courthouse and a menorah displayed near a Christmas tree on the grounds of city-county building).

80. *Cf.* GADAMER, TRUTH AND METHOD, *supra* note 58, at 302–07 (discussing the concept of horizons and the role of text and interpreter in the interpretive process).

81. Eskridge, *supra* note 58, at 623–24.

82. *Cf. id.* (discussing the role of reflection in challenging one's preconceptions when one confronts a text).

83. GADAMER, TRUTH AND METHOD, *supra* note 58, at 302–07; Eskridge, *supra* note 58, at 620–24.

84. McGlashan, *supra* note 67 (referring to Tillich's definition of religious symbols).

85. TILLICH, *supra* note 64, at 240. Religious symbols include more than simply tangible objects. *Id.*

86. GEERTZ, *supra* note 72 at 89. For an excellent and detailed discussion of the relevance to law of Geertz's work in the symbolism area, including a reasonably detailed discussion of "sacred symbols," *see* Zick, *supra* note 50.

87. ABRAHAM JOSHUA HESCHEL, MAN'S QUEST FOR GOD 129 (1954).

88. Aaron L. Mackler, *Symbols, Reality, and God: Heschel's Rejection of a Tillichian Understanding of Religious Symbols,* 40 JUDAISM 290 (1991).

89. *Id.* at 290.

90. HESCHEL, *supra* note 87, at 139; Mackler, *supra* note 88, at 292.

91. Heschel shares important elements of Tillich's understanding of symbols. "'A real symbol is a visible object that represents something invisible; something present representing something absent,' which may make that thing (e.g., the Divine) present by partaking in its reality. Such a symbol, though powerful, is dangerous, for it may idolatrously be understood to be equivalent to the Divine." Mackler, *supra* note 88, at 292 (citing HESCHEL, *supra* note 87, at 139).

92. An excellent example of this would be church doctrine regarding relics and the connection between relics and God. JOHN A. HARDON, S.J., THE CATHOLIC CATECHISM: A CONTEMPORARY CATECHISM OF THE TEACHINGS OF THE CATHOLIC CHURCH 298–99 (Doubleday 1975) (quoting the Second Ecumenical Council Nicea regarding relics: "the honor paid to the image passes on to the one who is represented, so that the person who venerates an image venerates the living reality whom the image depicts," and also noting similar statements from the Second Vatican Council).

93. *Cf.* Marshall, *supra* note 55, at 513–14 (discussing Raymond Firth's definition of "symbol").

94. *Lynch* and *Allegheny* provide examples of this. In *Lynch,* the crèche was treated essentially as just another object in a broader holiday display that included a number of secularized objects associated with Christmas. In *Allegheny,* the menorah was treated as such because of its location near a Christmas tree—an arguably secularized religious object—and a sign saluting liberty, a totally secular object.

95. I derive this term from the notion of "pure symbols" in the free speech area. Calvin Massey defines pure symbols as "those in which the symbol's corporeal existence is necessarily fused with the message it conveys." Calvin R. Massey, *Pure Symbols and the First Amendment,* 17 HASTINGS CONST. L.Q. 369, 373 (1990); *see also* Howard M. Wasserman, *Symbolic Counter-Speech,* 12 WM. & MARY BILL OF RTS. J. 367 (2004) (interesting discussion of how the message in certain symbols invites reply through the use of those same symbols). Pure religious objects, like "pure symbols," signify through their corporeal existence a message regarding the infinite. For example, the display of a pure religious object in a museum may affect the relationship between government and that object for constitutional purposes, and may affect the message that object sends to some observers, its physical form still signifies the infinite and the divine. *See* Tillich, *supra* note 64.

96. Some religious objects or symbols may hold little meaning for one tradition within a religion but may for others. Thus, for example, a rosary would hold religious meaning for a Catholic, but not for most Protestants, even though both are part of the broader Christian tradition. An object need not be a powerful symbol for all traditions within a religion in order to be considered a pure religious object. It need only be so for one tradition (so long as it is recognized as being powerful for those within the tradition by some outside the tradition).

97. McGlashan, *supra* note 58, at 501; Tillich, *supra* note 57, at 240.

98. While these objects are not generally venerated or used in rituals, disputes over them have sometimes led to prayer and other religious ceremonies near the objects. A good example of this is provided by the situation resulting from the behavior of former Alabama Supreme Court justice Roy Moore. People regularly prayed near the Ten Commandments monument he installed in the state courthouse building. Glassroth v. Moore, 335 F.3d 1282, 1286, 1291 (11th Cir. 2003).

99. *Lynch,* 465 U.S. at 700–01, 708–09, 711–12 (Brennan, J., dissenting); *id.* at 727 (Blackmun, J., dissenting); Zick, *supra* note 50, at 2309–10, 2371.

100. STEPHEN CARTER, THE CULTURE OF DISBELIEF 189 (1993) (suggesting that the Court in *Stone* overlooked the possibility that the Commandments might "inculcate some of the admittedly spiritual but not necessarily religious values with which many of the Commandments are concerned").

101. The latter types of objects have a closer

connection between their corporeal existence and the meaning they signify. *See* Massey, *supra* note 95, at 373. Or, put differently, they symbolize the infinite or the divine, while secularized religious objects do not necessarily do so. *See* Tillich, *supra* note 64, at 240. Multifaceted objects fall somewhere in between, as the term suggests, but they do evoke greater signification of the infinite or divine than secularized religious objects would.

102. U.S. 668 (1984).

103. U.S. 573 (1989).

104. *Id.* at 587, 614.

105. U.S. 39 (1981) (per curiam).

106. U.S. ___, 125 S. Ct. 2722 (2005) (plurality opinion).

107. U.S. ___, 125 S. Ct. 2854 (2005).

108. U.S. 753 (1995).

109. A surprising number of cases have involved government display of crosses, for example, Buono v. Norton, 371 F.3d 543 (9th Cir. 2004); Carpenter v. City & County of San Francisco, 93 F.3d 627 (9th Cir. 1996); Separation of Church and State Comm. v. City of Eugene, 93 F.3d 617 (9th Cir. 1996); Ellis v. City of La Mesa, 990 F.2d 1518 (9th Cir. 1993); Murray v. City of Austin, 947 F.2d 147 (5th Cir. 1991); Harris v. City of Zion, 927 F.2d 1401 (7th Cir. 1991); Mendelson v. City of St. Cloud, 719 F. Supp. 1065 (M.D. Fla. 1989); Jewish War Veterans of the United States v. United States, 695 F. Supp. 1 (D.D.C. 1987); ACLU v. City of St. Charles, 622 F. Supp. 1542 (N.D. Ill. 1985); Eugene Sand & Gravel, Inc. v. City of Eugene, 558 P.2d 338 (1976) (en banc); Lowe v. City of Eugene, 463 P.2d 360 (1969) (en banc); *see also* Paulsen v. City of San Diego, 294 F.3d 1124 (9th Cir. 2002) (involving sale of public land on which large Latin cross stood under circumstances that raised constitutional concerns under state "establishment clause"); Gonzales v. North Township, 4 F.3d 1412 (7th Cir. 1993) (involving crucifix).

110. Lynch v. Donnelly, 465 U.S. 668 (1984).

111. *Id.* at 671–72.

112. *Id.* at 678–85, 687.

113. U.S. 783 (1983).

114. *Lynch,* 465 U.S. at 674–78, 682, 686–87.

115. *Id.* at 671.

116. *Id.* at 679–83, 685–86.

117. *Id.* at 687; Steven D. Smith, *Separation and the "Secular": Reconstructing the Disestablishment Decision,* 67 TEX. L. REV. 955, 1002–03 (1989) (some critics of the decision misunderstand the majority's secularization position; that position did not result from a conclusion that the crèche lost its religious meaning because of its placement, but rather the majority employed a broad notion of the secular and found that the religious symbol served a secular purpose in the context involved).

118. *Lynch,* 465 U.S. at 679–85, 687.

119. *Id.* at 685. This passage is discussed in much greater detail *supra.*

120. *Id.* at 683–85.

121. *Id.* at 687 (O'Connor, J., concurring).

122. *See infra* Part B.3 (discussing scholarly criticism of the Court's religious symbolism cases, in-cluding criticism of Justice O'Connor's application of the endorsement test).

123. For example, in the Court's first religious symbolism case after *Lynch,* the Court applied the endorsement test, County of Allegheny v. ACLU, 492 U.S. 573 (1989), and the test has been applied in numerous religious symbolism cases by lower courts.

124. *Lynch,* 465 U.S. at 687–88 (O'Connor, J., concurring).

125. *Id.* at 690 (O'Connor, J., concurring).

126. *See, e.g.,* Steven D. Smith, *Symbols, Perception, and Doctrinal Illusions: Establishment Neutrality and the "No Endorsement" Test,* 86 MICH. L. REV. 266, 291–95 (1987) (arguing that the reasonable observer standard under the endorsement test creates several problems, including offending "the central principle of Justice O'Connor's own test," by favoring the majority perspective); March D. Coleman, Comment, *The Angel Tree Project,* 58 U. PITT. L. REV. 475, 489 (1997) (arguing that there are problems with Justice O'Connor's reasonable observer standard because it ignores the perspectives of "actual perceptions of real citizens"). *Cf.* Marshall, *supra* note 55, at 536–37 (the "objective" reasonable observer standard in Justice O'Connor's application of the endorsement test is likely to actually end up reflecting the subjective views of the judge(s) applying it).

127. *Id.* at 726 (Blackmun, J., dissenting); *id.* at 700–01 and n.6 (Brennan, J., dissenting).

128. *Id.* at 691 (O'Connor, J., concurring).

129. *Id.* at 692 (O'Connor, J., concurring).

130. *Id.* at 687 (O'Connor, J., concurring).

131. *Id.* at 692–93 (O'Connor, J., concurring).

132. *Id.* at 694 (Brennan, J., dissenting).

133. *Id.* at 726 (Blackmun, J., dissenting).

134. *Id.* at 697–714 (Brennan, J., dissenting); *id.* at 626–27 (Blackmun, J., dissenting).

135. *Id.* at 697, 700–02 (Brennan, J., dissenting).

136. *Id.*

137. *Id.* at 708–09 (Brennan, J., dissenting); *id.* at 726–27 (Blackmun, J., dissenting).

138. County of Allegheny v. ACLU, 492 U.S. 573 (1989).

139. *Id.* at 592–94.

140. *Id.* at 598–600.

141. *Id.* at 580–81, 598–600.

142. *Id.* at 580.

143. *Id.* at 598–602.

144. *Id.* at 601.

145. *Id.* at 598–601.

146. *See generally Allegheny,* 492 U.S. 598; *Lynch,* 465 U.S. 668.

147. *See* Smith, *supra* note 117.

148. U.S. 753 (1995).

149. *Id.* at 758.

150. *Id.* at 758, 761.

151. *Id.* at 761.

152. *Id.* at 761–62.

153. *Id.* at 762–70.

154. *Id.* at 765–770.

155. *Capitol Square,* 515 U.S. 753.

156. F.3d 617 (9th Cir. 1996).
157. *Id.* at 618–20.
158. *Id.* at 618.
159. *Id.* at 620.
160. *Allegheny,* 492 U.S. 573.
161. *Id.* at 587. Although the menorah was owned by Chabad, it was "stored, erected, and removed each year by the city." *Id.*
162. *Id.* at 582.
163. *Id.* at 583–85.
164. *Id.* at 582–87.
165. *Id.* at 617–20.
166. *Id.* at 619–20.
167. *Id.* at 617–20.
168. *Id.* at 635–36 (O'Connor, J., concurring in part and concurring in the judgment).
169. *Id.* at 637 (Brennan, J., concurring in part and dissenting in part); *id.* at 646 (Stevens, J., concurring in part and dissenting in part).
170. *Id.* at 643–45 (Brennan, J., concurring in part and dissenting in part).
171. *Id.* at 638–41 (Brennan, J., concurring in part and dissenting in part).
172. *Id.* at 643–44 (Brennan, J., concurring in part and dissenting in part).
173. *Id.* at 650–51 (Stevens, J., concurring in part and dissenting in part).
174. *Id.* at 644–46 (Brennan, J., concurring in part and dissenting in part); *id.* at 650–52 (Stevens, J., concurring in part and dissenting in part).
175. U.S. 39 (1981) (per curiam).
176. *Id.* at 39 n.1.
177. *Id.* at 39–43.
178. *Id.* at 41.
179. *Id.* at 40–43.
180. *Lynch,* 465 U.S. 668; *Allegheny,* 492 U.S. 573; *supra.*
181. McCreary County v. ACLU of Kentucky, ___ U.S. ___, 125 S. Ct. 2722 (2005); Van Orden v. Perry, ___ U.S. ___, 125 S. Ct. 2854 (2005) (plurality opinion).
182. U.S. ___, 125 S. Ct. 2722 (2005).
183. *Id.* at 2728.
184. *Id.* at 2729.
185. *Id.* at 2739.
186. *Id.* at 2730–31.
187. *Id.* at 2730–31, 2739–41.
188. *Id.* at 2739–41.
189. *Id.* at 2722.
190. *Id.* at 2732.
191. *Id.* at 2732–42.
192. *Id.* at 2733.
193. *Id.*
194. *Id.* at 2734.
195. *Id.* at 2732–34.
196. *Id.* at 2734–37.
197. *Id.* at 2737–38.
198. *Id.*
199. *Id.* at 2738–39.
200. *Id.*
201. *Id.* at 2739.
202. *Id.*
203. *Id.* at 2739–40.
204. *Id.* at 2741.

205. *Id.* at 2739–41.
206. *Id.* at 2740–41.
207. *Id.* at 2742–43.
208. *Id.* at 2743–45.
209. *Id.*
210. *Id.* at 2746 (O'Connor, J., concurring).
211. *Id.*
212. *Id.* at 2746–47.
213. *Id.* at 2748 (Scalia, J., dissenting).
214. *Id.*
215. *Id.* at 2748–53.
216. Justice Souter, of course, while acknowledging these problems, goes on to rely on originalist arguments himself. *Id.* at 2743–45 (majority opinion).
217. *Id.* at 2757–63 (Scalia, J., dissenting).
218. *Id.* at 2759–63.
219. *Id.*
220. U.S. ___, 125 S. Ct. 2854 (2005) (plurality opinion).
221. Regents of Univ. of Cal. v. Bakke, 438 U.S. 265 (1978).
222. *Id.*
223. Van Orden, 125 S. Ct. at 2868 (Breyer, J., concurring in the judgment).
224. *Id.* at 2858 (plurality opinion).
225. *Id.*
226. *Id.* at 2858, 2864 n.11.
227. *Id.* at 2859.
228. *Id.* at 2861–64.
229. *Id.* at 2861.
230. *Id.* at 2862–63.
231. *Stone,* 449 U.S. 39 (per curiam).
232. *Van Orden,* 125 S. Ct. at 2863–64 (plurality opinion).
233. *Id.* at 2861, 2864.
234. *Id.* at 2864.
235. *See generally id.*
236. *Id.* (Thomas, J., concurring).
237. *Id.* at 2865.
238. *Id.* at 2866–67.
239. *Id.* at 2865–68.
240. Elk Grove Unified School Dist. v. Newdow, 542 U.S. 1 (2004).
241. *Van Orden,* 125 S. Ct. at 2866–67 (Thomas, J., concurring).
242. *Id.* at 2867.
243. *Id.*
244. *Id.* at 2869 (Breyer, J., concurring in the judgment).
245. *Id.*
246. *Id.*
247. *Id.* at 2868–69.
248. *Id.* at 2871.
249. *Id.* at 2868, 2871.
250. *Id.* at 2871.
251. *Id.* at 2869–70.
252. *Id.* at 2869–71.
253. *See id.* (analyzing context of display to determine the message it sends).
254. *Id.* at 2873 (Stevens, J., dissenting).
255. *Id.* at 2874–82.
256. *Id.*
257. *Id.*

258. *Id.* at 2874–75.

259. *Id.* at 2882–90.

260. *Id.* at 2886–87.

261. *Id.* at 2873–90.

262. *Id.* at 2892 (Souter, J., dissenting).

263. *Id.* at 2893.

264. *Id.*

265. *Id.* at 2895.

266. *Id.* at 2893–94.

267. *Id.* at 2895–96.

268. *Id.* at 2896–97.

269. King v. Richmond County, 331 F.3d 1271 (11th Cir. 2003) (upholding use of small seal that included a depiction of the Ten Commandments, but not the text, along with other images); Glassroth v. Moore, 335 F.3d 1282 (11th Cir. 2003) (striking down display of large granite Ten Commandments monument placed in the rotunda of Alabama state courthouse in the middle of the night by former chief justice of the Alabama Supreme Court); Freethought Soc'y of Greater Philadelphia v. Chester County, 334 F.3d 247 (3d Cir. 2003) (upholding display of small Ten Commandments plaque on old entrance to county courthouse, where plaque was placed on the building in 1920 and old entrance where plaque was located was no longer in use); Adland v. Russ, 307 F.3d 471 (6th Cir. 2002) (striking down display of monument donated by the Fraternal Order of Eagles in 1961 on grounds of the state capitol); Books v. City of Elkhart, 235 F.3d 292 (7th Cir. 2000) (same for monument donated in 1958 and located on grounds of city municipal building).

270. *Id.* (all cases); *see also* Frank S. Ravitch, *Religious Objects as Legal Subjects*, 40 WAKE FOREST L. REV. 1011 (2005).

271. *See generally Lynch*, 465 U.S. 668; *Allegheny*, 492 U.S. 573.

272. *Allegheny*, 492 U.S. at 639 (Brennan, J., concurring in part and dissenting in part).

273. *See* Smith, *supra* note 124, at 314 (questioning efficacy of the endorsement test).

274. Zick, *supra* note 50 (criticizing the Court's desacralization of religious symbols); Underkuffler-Freund, *supra* note 50, at 871–72, 971–72 (same).

275. Smith, *supra* note 117, at 1002–03.

276. *Allegheny*, 492 U.S. at 620; *Lynch*, 465 U.S. at 679–81.

277. Van Orden v. Perry, ___ U.S. ___, 125 S. Ct. 2854 (2005) (plurality opinion).

278. Zick, *supra* note 50, at 2368–74; Jessie Hill, *Putting Religious Symbolism in Context: A Linguistic Critique of the Endorsement Test* (manuscript on file with author; paper has been submitted for publication).

279. *Lynch*, 465 U.S. at 685.

280. Zick, *supra* note 50, at 2368–74; Dolgin, *supra* note 53, at 504–05 (1988); Hill, *supra* note 278.

281. *See, e.g.,* Karst, *supra* note 50 (criticizing the Court's minimization of the impact government display of religious objects can have on religious minorities); Brownstein, *supra* note 50, at 855–58 (same).

282. *Cf.* Carter, *supra* note 35, at 94–95 (pointing out religious nature of the display of religious objects and the ridiculousness of treating them as though they are not religious in book addressing the issue of cultural dominance of secular values in America).

283. *See* Smith, *supra* note 117; Zick, *supra* note 50; Dolgin, *supra* note 53.

284. Coleman, *supra* note 124, at 489 (arguing that there are problems with Justice O'Connor's reasonable observer standard because it ignores the perspectives of "actual perceptions of real citizens.").

285. Neil R. Feigenson, *Political Standing and Governmental Endorsement of Religion: An Alternative to Current Establishment Clause Doctrine*, 40 DEPAUL L. REV. 53, 87–88 (1990).

286. U.S. 753 (1995).

287. *Id.* at 778–80 (O'Connor, J., concurring in part and concurring in the judgment); *id.* at 799–800 (Stevens, J., dissenting).

288. *Id.* at 778–80 (O'Connor, J., concurring in part and concurring in the judgment).

289. Feigenson, *supra* note 285; Dolgin, *supra* note 53.

290. *Van Orden*, 125 S. Ct. 2854 (plurality opinion); *Lynch*, 465 U.S. 668; *Marsh* v. Chambers, 463 U.S. 783 (1983).

291. *See* STEPHEN M. FELDMAN, PLEASE DON'T WISH ME A MERRY CHRISTMAS: A CRITICAL HISTORY OF THE SEPARATION OF CHURCH AND STATE (1997) (discussing perceptions of Christian dominance in American history and the difference between insider and outsider views regarding religion in public life).

292. *Id.*

293. Frank S. Ravitch, *A Funny Thing Happened on the Way to Neutrality: Broad Principles, Formalism, and the Establishment Clause*, 38 GA. L. REV. 489, 568–70 (2004).

294. *Id.*

295. *Id.*

296. *Id.*

297. *Id.* at 569.

298. Zick, *supra* note 50, at 2367–74; Matthew Paul Kammerer, Note, *County of Allegheny v. A.C.L.U.: Perpetuating the Setting Factor Myth*, 21 U. TOL. L. REV. 933 (1990).

299. Ravitch, *supra* note 293, at 568–70.

300. *See generally* Kammerer, *supra* note 298 (criticizing the use of physical context in the Court's analysis of religious objects).

301. The Court in *Lynch* relied heavily on this thematic context to uphold the display of the crèche in that case. *Lynch*, 465 U.S. at 680–81, 685–86.

302. Kammerer, *supra* note 298.

303. *See generally Lynch*, 465 U.S. 668 (suggesting long-standing tradition in the United States supports constitutionality of city's display of crèche); *Marsh*, 463 U.S 783 (same for legislative prayer).

304. *Compare Marsh*, 463 U.S. 783 (upholding "traditional" practice of legislative prayer), *with*

Lee v. Weisman, 505 U.S. 577 (1992) (striking down practice of prayer at public secondary school graduations).

305. *Lynch,* 465 U.S. 668 (upholding display of crèche by city).

306. Ravitch, *supra* note 293.

307. Zick, *supra* note 50, at 2365–66; Feigenson, *supra* note 285, at 84–86; Dolgin, *supra* note 53, at 497–98.

308. Zick, *supra* note 50, at 2367–74.

309. In both *Lynch* and *Allegheny,* the Court attempted to find a meaning for the religious objects involved based on their context. *Allegheny,* 492 U.S. 573; *Lynch,* 465 U.S. 668.

310. *See* Ravitch, *supra* note 21.

311. Dolgin, *supra* note 53, at 497–98.

312. Zick, *supra* note 50, at 2367–74.

313. Ravitch, *supra* note 21, at 1067–68.

314. Illinois *ex rel.* McCollum v. Bd. of Educ., 333 U.S. 203, 238 (1948) (Jackson, J., concurring).

315. *See supra* chapter 1.

316. See Frank S. Ravitch, *Struggling with Text and Context: A Hermeneutic Approach to Interpreting and Realizing Law School Missions,* 74 St. John's L. Rev. 731, 734–44 (2000) (discussing process of interpretation in Gadamerian theory).

317. *See* Ravitch, *supra* note 21.

318. Brooks v. City of Oak Ridge, 222 F.3d 259 (6th Cir. 2000).

319. *Cf.* Brown v. Hot, Sexy and Safer Productions, Inc., 68 F.3d 525 (1st Cir. 1995) (parents' challenge to children's compulsory attendance at a sexually charged AIDS awareness assembly under Free Exercise Clause and a number of other constitutional provisions unsuccessful primarily because the challenge was after the fact and in regard to a onetime event).

320. Gary J. Simson and Erika A. Sussman, *Keeping the Sex in Sex Education: The First Amendment's Religion Clauses and the Sex Education Debate,* 9 S. Cal. Rev. of L. & Women's Studies 265 (2000).

321. Doe v. Beaumont Indep. School Dist., 240 F.3d 462 (5th Cir. 2001) en banc, on remand, Oxford v. Beaumont Indep. School Dist., 224 F. Supp.2d 1099 (E.D. Texas 2002).

322. *Id.*

323. Simson and Sussman, *supra* note 320.

324. *Id.* at 268–70, 283–91.

325. *Id.* at 286–90.

326. *Id.* at 290.

327. Patricia Illingworth and Timothy Murphy, *In Our Best Interest: Meeting Moral Duties to Lesbian, Gay, and Bisexual Adolescent Students,* 35 J. of Social Philosophy 198 (2004).

328. *Cf.* Julie Jones, *Money, Sex, and the Religious Right: A Constitutional Analysis of Federally Funded Abstinence-Only-Until-Marriage Sexuality Education,* 35 Creighton L. Rev. 1075, 1084, 1094–95, 1105 (2002) (addressing organizations and interests that promote abstinence-only education).

329. Simson and Sussman, *supra* note 320, at 283–91.

330. *Cf.* John Copeland Nagle, *Playing Noah,* 82 Minn. L. Rev. 1171, 1242–43 (1998) (using the example of some legislators' reliance on the story of Noah to support an endangered species law to demonstrate that religious motivation does not inherently invalidate a law under the Establishment Clause). This is, of course, consistent with the long line of cases that suggest religion must be a primary motivation for a law in order to run afoul of the Establishment Clause based only on that motivation itself.

331. *See generally* McCreary County v. ACLU, 125 S. Ct. 2722 (2005) (addressing secular purpose analysis in context of Ten Commandments display by county lacking a valid secular purpose); Board of Educ. v. Mergens, 496 U.S. 226, 248–49 (1990) (upholding Equal Access Act despite evidence that some legislators may have had religious motivations in supporting it).

332. By focusing on the purpose of the government actions, courts focus on motivations of government actors and sometimes on the structure of the government action. This is often a step removed from exploration of the question whether the government action itself constitutes religion regardless of the motivation for the act (although such motivation may be useful in analyzing the government action, it is not by itself determinative).

333. U.S. 490, 560 (1989) (Stevens, J., concurring in part and dissenting in part).

334. *Id.* at 562–63.

335. *Id.* at 566–69.

336. *See, e.g.,* Stephen L. Carter, The Culture of Disbelief (1993); Kent Greenawalt, Private Consciences and Public Reasons (1995); Michael J. Perry, Religion in Politics: Constitutional and Moral Perspectives (1997); John Rawls, Political Liberalism (1993); Ronald F. Thiemann, Religion in Public Life: A Dilemma for Democracy (1996); Robert Audi, *The Place of Religious Argument in a Free and Democratic Society,* 30 San Diego L. Rev. 677 (1993); Christopher L. Eisgruber, *Madison's Wager: Religious Liberty in the Constitutional Order,* 89 Nw. U. L. Rev. 347 (1995); Lawrence Solum, *Constructing an Ideal of Public Reason,* 30 San Diego L. Rev. 729 (1993).

337. *Id.* (all); *see also* James P. Madigan, *The Idea of Public Reason Resuscitated,* 10 Wm. & Mary Bill Rts. J. 719 (2002).

338. *See* Carter, *supra* note 336.

339. *See* Madigan, *supra* note 337.

340. *See infra* at chapter 10; *cf.* Perry, *supra* note 336.

341. Simson and Sussman, *supra* note 320, at 284–91.

342. Jones, *supra* note 328, at 1084, 1094–95, 1105 (2002).

343. Simson and Sussman, *supra* note 320, at 284–91.

344. *Cf. Webster,* 492 U.S. at 566–69 (Stevens,

J., concurring in part and dissenting in part) (making similar arguments in regard to preamble to Missouri law involving reproductive rights).

345. Simson and Sussman, *supra* note 320, at 293–97.

346. Santa Fe Indep. Sch. Dist. v. Doe, 530 U.S. 290 (2000).

347. McCreary County v. ACLU, 125 S. Ct. 2722 (2005) (addressing divisiveness of Ten Commandments display among other issues).

348. Simson and Sussman, *supra* note 320, at 293–97.

349. *Id.*

350. Lee v. Weisman, 505 U.S. 577 (1992).

351. *Id.* at 593–94.

352. School Dist. of Abington Tp. v. Schempp, 373 U.S. 203, 221 (1963) (The Establishment Clause, unlike the Free Exercise Clause, does not depend upon any showing of direct governmental compulsion and is violated by the enactment of laws that establish an official religion whether those laws operate directly to coerce nonobserving individuals or not.).

353. Simson and Sussman, *supra* note 320, at 283–97.

354. *Id.* at 271–73 (using term "opt-out," but concluding that such exemptions are not mandated by the Free Exercise Clause).

355. *Id.* at 273; Employment Div. v. Smith, 494 U.S. 872, 890 (1990).

356. U.S. 872 (1990).

357. *Id.* at 881–82.

358. U.S. 205 (1972). See the *Smith* Court's treatment of *Yoder. Smith,* 494 U.S. at 881–82, 881 n.1.

359. U.S. 624 (1943).

360. Church of the Lukumi Babalu Aye, Inc. v. City of Hialeah, 508 U.S. 520, 566–67 (1993) (Souter, J., concurring).

361. *See* discussion of Braunfeld v. Brown, 366 U.S. 599 (1961) (plurality opinion) in the various opinions in Sherbert v. Verner, 374 U.S. 398 (1963); *see also* Michael W. McConnell, *Free Exercise Revisionism and the Smith Decision,* 57 U. CHI. L. REV. 1109, 1121–22 (1990); Joanne C. Brant, *Taking the Supreme Court at Its Word: The Implications for RFRA and Separation of Powers,* 56 MONT. L. REV. 5, 30 (1995).

362. *Cf.* William L. Esser IV, Note, *Religious Hybrids in the Lower Courts: Free Exercise Plus or Constitutional Smoke Screen?* 74 NOTRE DAME L. REV. 211 (1998).

363. *Smith,* 494 U.S. at 881 n.1.

364. *Id.*; Michael W. McConnell, *Free Exercise Revisionism and the Smith Decision,* 57 U. CHI. L. REV. 1109, 1121–22 (1990).

365. *Id.* at 1121–22 (1990).

366. *Smith,* 494 U.S. 881–82.

367. Hazelwood School Dist. v. Kuhlmeier, 484 U.S. 260 (1988).

368. Thomas v. Anchorage Equal Rights Commission, 165 F.3d 693, 703 (9th Cir. 1999); Vandiver v. Hardin County Bd. of Education, 925 F.2d 927, 933 (6th Cir. 1991); Hicks v. Halifax County Bd. of Education, 93 F. Supp.2d 649, 662–63 (E.D. N.C. 1999); *but see* Kissinger v. Bd. of Trustees, 5 F.3d 177, 180 (6th Cir. 1993) (refusing to apply strict scrutiny to a hybrid rights claim without further guidelines from the Supreme Court).

369. *Id.*

370. Frazee v. Illinois Dept. of Emp. Sec., 489 U.S. 829 (1989) (Free Exercise Clause protects an employee who refused to work on Sunday based on his belief that it was the Lord's day, even though he did not belong to established sect or church).

371. *Cf. Hicks,* 93 F. Supp.2d at 657–63 (explaining that only credible hybrid claims should allow for hybrid rights analysis, but suggesting that core parental religious beliefs and values can support applying hybrid rights analysis).

372. *See* Swanson v. Guthrie Indep. School Dist., 135 F.3d 694 (10th Cir. 1998) (stating that compelling interest test may apply to proper hybrid rights claims, but rejecting parental argument that parental right to have home-schooled children enroll in public school classes part-time despite state funding formula that would not compensate schools for part-time attendance was not adequate to support a hybrid rights claim).

373. These arguments would parallel the type of findings that the *Yoder* Court used to support its decision. *Yoder,* 406 U.S. 205 (1972).

374. Such a showing may be akin to the Amish showing in *Yoder* that their community has a high employment rate, strong work ethic, and low rates of various social problems. *Id.*

375. *See* Simson and Sussman, *supra* note 320, at 273–79 (suggesting that such arguments should be successful).

376. *Swanson,* 135 F.3d 694, 699–700.

377. Thomas C. Berg, *Religious Liberty in America at the End of the Century,* 16 J.L. & RELIGION 187, 202–04 (2001).

378. *Id.*

379. *See, e.g.,* Chaplinsky v. New Hampshire, 315 U.S. 568, 571 (1942) ("[W]e cannot conceive that cursing a public officer is the exercise of religion in any sense of the term."); Reynolds v. United States, 98 U.S. 145, 165 (1878) (stating that "it is impossible to believe that the constitutional guaranty of religious freedom was intended to" permit Mormon polygamy).

380. *See generally* William Herbrechtsmeier, *Buddhism and the Definition of Religion: One More Time,* 32 J. SCI. STUDY RELIGION 1 (1993) (discussing differing views of religion in Buddhism).

381. *See generally* AHMAD ABDULLAH SALAMAH, SHIA & SUNNI PERSPECTIVES ON ISLAM: AN OBJECTIVE COMPARISON OF THE SHIA AND SUNNI DOCTRINES BASED ON THE HOLY QURAN AND HADITH (1991) (discussing the differences between Sunni and Shiite Islam).

382. *See generally* R. Milton Winter, *Division & Reunion in the Presbyterian Church, U.S.: A Mississippi Retrospective,* 78 J. PRESBYTERIAN HIST.

67 (2000) (discussing schisms and controversies in Presbyterianism).

383. *See infra* chapters 9 and 10; *supra* chapter 7.

NOTES TO CHAPTER 9

1. STEVEN D. SMITH, FOREORDAINED FAILURE: THE QUEST FOR A CONSTITUTIONAL PRINCIPLE OF RELIGIOUS FREEDOM (Oxford 1995).

2. *Id.*; Steven D. Smith, *Symbols, Perceptions, and Doctrinal Illusions: Establishment Neutrality and the "No Endorsement" Test,* 86 MICH. L. REV. 266 (1987).

3. *See, e.g., id.*; Frank S. Ravitch, *A Funny Thing Happened on the Way to Neutrality: Broad Principles, Formalism, and the Establishment Clause,* 38 GA. L. REV. 489 (2004).

4. PHILIP BOBBITT, CONSTITUTIONAL FATE (Oxford 1984); PHILIP BOBBITT, CONSTITUTIONAL INTERPRETATION (Blackwell 1991).

5. Bobbitt, CONSTITUTIONAL INTERPRETATION, *supra* note 4.

6. *Id.*

7. *Id.*

8. *Id.; see also* Ravitch, *supra* note 3 (making this argument regarding neutrality).

9. Bobbitt, CONSTITUTIONAL INTERPRETATION, *supra* note 4.

10. *Id.* at 11–22

11. *Id.*

12. *Id.* at 168.

13. *See generally id.*

14. *Id.* at 111–17.

15. *See generally id.* at Book III.

16. This should not even need to be said, but the normative focus of much legal scholarship has often proceeded without an adequate descriptive of what is being analyzed. How can one begin to effect normative change if one's approach has not accounted for the interpretive realities of the system in which it will function?

17. Bobbitt's modalities function in a similar way. *See* Bobbitt, CONSTITUTIONAL FATE, *supra* note 4.

18. Each of the modes proposed herein could fit within one of Bobbitt's six modalities. Bobbitt, CONSTITUTIONAL INTERPRETATION, *supra* note 4, at 11–22.

19. *Id.*

20. *Id.* at Book III.

21. Concepts such as textual, historical, doctrinal, and structural interpretation are well established in the realm of constitutional interpretation. Bobbitt's concern is more with the way in which these interpretive modes, and the others he sets forth, are understood in the interpretive process. *See generally id.*

22. Smith, *supra* note 2, at 268, 325–31.

23. McCreary County v. ACLU of Kentucky, ___ U.S. ___, 125 S. Ct. 2722, 2748 (2005) (Scalia, J., dissenting).

24. *See* Ronald Dworkin, JUSTICE IN ROBES (Belknap 2006); RONALD DWORKIN, FREEDOM'S LAW: THE MORAL READING OF THE AMERICAN CONSTITUTION (Harvard 1996).

25. ANTONIN SCALIA, A MATTER OF INTERPRETATION (Princeton 1997).

26. Robert H. Bork, TEMPTING OF AMERICA (Free Press 1989).

27. *See* Dworkin, *supra* note 24.

28. *See supra* notes 25–27, and sources cited therein.

29. *See* Dworkin, *supra* note 24; Bork, *supra* note 26.

30. *See* the discussion of philosophical hermeneutics *supra* chapter 1; Bobbit, CONSTITUTIONAL INTERPRETATION, *supra* note 4, at Book III.

31. *Id.* (both sources).

32. *See* Ravitch, *supra* note 3, at 531–44.

33. Bobbitt, CONSTITUTIONAL INTERPRETATION, *supra* note 4, at 22, 157–62, 168.

34. *Id.* at 22, 163–70.

35. *See* discussion of philosophical hermeneutics, *supra* chapter 1.

36. Ravitch, *supra* note 3, at 531–44; William P. Marshall, *"We Know It When We See It": The Supreme Court Establishment,* 59 S. CAL. L. REV. 495, 500 (1986).

37. This contextual use of the separation concept is consistent with Supreme Court jurisprudence over the last two decades.

38. *Compare Zelman,* 122 S. Ct. 2460 (upholding voucher program where bulk of the money flowing to private school hands went to religious schools), *with* Santa Fe Independent School Dist. v Doe, 530 U.S. 290 (2000) (finding prayer at high school football games unconstitutional, where games are school sponsored and the district drafted and implemented "student-initiated" prayer policy).

39. U.S. 520 (1993).

40. Michael W. McConnell, *Accommodation of Religion,* 1985 SUP. CT. REV. 1 (1985) (exploring connection between accommodation and the broad concept of liberty).

41. *Id.* at 24–27.

42. *Id.*

43. *Id.* at 29–32; *Waltz,* 397 U.S. at 673.

44. Ravitch, *supra* note 3.

45. *See supra* chapter 5.

46. McConnell, *supra* note 40, at 24–27.

47. *See, e.g.,* Good News Club v. Milford Central Schools, 533 U.S. 98 (2001); Lamb's Chapel v. Center Moriches Union Free Sch. Dist., 508 U.S. 384 (1993); Widmar v. Vincent, 454 U.S. 263 (1981).

48. *See supra* chapters 4, 7, and 8.

49. *See generally* McConnell, *supra* note 40.

50. *Id.; see also* Michael W. McConnell, *Accommodation of Religion: An Update and a Response to the Critics,* 60 GEO. WASH. L. REV. 685 (1992).

51. *See, e.g.,* Cass R. Sunstein, *Five Theses on Originalism,* 19 HARV. J.L. & PUB. POL'Y 311, 313–15 (1996).

52. *See supra* chapter 5.

53. *See, e.g.,* Douglas Laycock, *Formal, Sub-*

stantive, and Disaggregated Neutrality Toward Religion, 39 DePaul L. Rev. 993 (1990) ("We can agree on the principle of neutrality without having agreed on anything at all").

54. Cf. id. at 996 (" . . . equality is an insufficient concept." "Claims about equality, or neutrality, always require further specification: equality with respect to what classification, for what purpose, in what sense, and to what extent?").

55. Zelman, 122 S. Ct. 2485 (Souter, J., dissenting); Steven K. Green, The Illusionary Aspect of "Private Choice" for Constitutional Analysis, 38 Willamette L. Rev. 549, 558–60 (2002).

56. See supra chapter 5.

57. See generally Ravitch, supra note 3.

58. See supra chapter 5.

59. See Sunstein, supra note 51, at 313–15.

60. All sides of the debate seem to agree that at the very least the Establishment Clause prohibits a religious entity from controlling government (although there may be some disagreement about what level of government between those who support incorporation of the Establishment Clause and those who do not).

61. Zelman, 536 U.S. at 717 (Breyer, J., dissenting); see also Steven K. Green, The Legal Argument Against Private School Choice, 62 U. Chi. L. Rev. 37, 50 (1993) (arguing that the potential to "spark religious discord" was "a factor of great concern to the Framers").

62. See Philip Hamburger, Separation of Church and State (Harvard 2002).

63. See Sunstein, supra note 51, at 315 (acknowledging that soft originalism will rarely be adequate by itself to interpret the Constitution in specific contexts).

64. Id. at 311–13; supra chapter 1.

65. See supra chapter 1.

66. See supra at note 63.

67. See supra at chapter 6 (in context of separationism); chapter 7 (context of accommodationism).

68. Bobbitt, Constitutional Interpretation, supra note 4, at 17–20.

69. Id.

70. Id. Of course, pragmatic concerns are still bound by the inherent constraint in the interpretive process. See discussion of philosophical hermeneutics, supra at chapter 1.

71. Again this is constrained by the interpretive process, and one should never forget Justice Jackson's warning in this regard. See supra chapter 1; McCollum, 333 U.S. at 237–38 (Jackson, J., concurring).

72. Id.; see infra chapter 10.

73. McCollum, 333 U.S. at 237–38 (Jackson, J., concurring).

74. See supra chapters 1 and 2.

75. Id.; Ravitch, supra at note 3; Smith, supra at note 1.

76. The classic Lemon test, see Lemon, 403 U.S. 602, was modified in Agostini v. Felton, 521 U.S. 203, 222–23 (1997) (folding the entanglement prong of Lemon into the "effects" prong, and

changing the Court's earlier focus on divisiveness as an element of entanglement).

77. Lynch, 465 U.S. at 690 (O'Connor, J., concurring); Wallace v. Jaffree, 472 U.S. 38, 56 (1985).

78. Lee v. Weisman, 505 U.S. 577 (1992).

79. Marsh v. Chambers, 463 U.S. 783 (1983).

80. Zelman, 122 S. Ct. 2460.

81. Justice O'Connor's perplexing application of the endorsement test is a prime example of the importance of how one applies a test. The endorsement test has the potential to seriously address the impact of religious establishments, or alleged religious establishments, on religious minorities. Yet her application of that test in cases like Lynch and Allegheny does not necessarily bear out that potential. Kenneth Karst, Law's Promise, Law's Expression 149–60 (1993); Alan Brownstein, A Decent Respect for Religious Liberty and Religious Equality: Justice O'Connor's Interpretation of the Religion Clauses of the First Amendment, 32 McGeorge L. Rev. 837, 845–57 (2001)

82. Ravitch, supra note 3, at 531–44.

83. Cf. Laycock, supra note 53, at 1003–06, 1011–13, 1018.

1. Effects were a central element of the Lemon test. See Lemon, 403 U.S. at 612. Of course, as was explained earlier, see supra chapter 2, the Court seems to have moved away from any serious effects test, at least in the aid context. See also Stephen M. Feldman, Religious Minorities and the First Amendment: The History, The Doctrine, and the Future, 6 U. Pa. J. Const. L. 222, 261–66 (2003) (arguing that the Zelman Court essentially gutted the effects test in the aid context, and that the current doctrine will uphold programs that have the effect of providing substantial benefits to mainstream religions, but will not likely have a similar effect for programs that benefit religious minorities).

2. The outcome in Lemon itself was determined by the entanglement element of the test, and thus the Court did not reach the effects element. Lemon, 403 U.S. at 613–14.

3. Lynch, 465 U.S. at 691–94 (O'Connor, J., concurring) (discussing the relationship between the endorsement test and the effects prong of Lemon).

4. Zelman, 122 S. Ct. 2460; Mitchell, 530 U.S. 793 (plurality opinion).

5. "Facilitate" is defined as "to make easier; help bring about," Merriam-Webster Dictionary (New ed. 1994), and to ease a process, The Oxford Desk Dictionary 202 (American ed. 1995) ("ease (a process, etc.)").

6. Frank S. Ravitch, A Funny Thing Happened on the Way to Neutrality: Broad Principles, Formalism, and the Establishment Clause, 38 Ga. L. Rev. 489, 544–58 (2004).

7. As will be seen, this suggests that Zobrest,

509 U.S. 1, and *Witters,* 474 U.S. 481, were correctly decided.

8. Ravitch, *supra* note 6, at 544–58.

9. *Id.*

10. *Id.* at 533–37; *supra* at chapter 6.

11. *See supra* chapter 9; Ravitch, *supra* note 6, at 558–71.

12. Ravitch, *supra* note 6, at 544–58.

13. *Id.*

14. *Id.*

15. *Id.*

16. *Id.* at 544–71.

17. *Id.*

18. *Id.*

19. *See supra* chapters 4 and 7.

20. *See* Cass R. Sunstein, *Five Theses on Originalism,* 19 Harv. J.L. & Pub. Pol'y 311, 313–15 (1996).

21. *See, e.g.,* Frederick Mark Gedicks, The Rhetoric of Church and State: A Critical Analysis of Religion Clause Jurisprudence (Duke 1995); Stephen L. Carter, The Culture of Disbelief: How American Law and Politics Trivialize Religious Devotion (Anchor 1993).

22. *See supra* chapters 4 and 6.

23. Douglas Laycock, *Formal, Substantive, and Disaggregated Neutrality Toward Religion,* 39 De-Paul L. Rev. 993, 1001–02 (1990).

24. *See supra* chapter 9.

25. *See* Dickerson v. United States, 530 U.S. 428, 443 (2000) ("While stare decisis is not an inexorable command, particularly when we are interpreting the Constitution, even in constitutional cases, the doctrine carries such persuasive force that we have always required a departure from precedent to be supported by some special justification.") (citations and internal quotation marks omitted).

26. *See* Ravitch, *supra* note 6, at 531–44; *supra* chapter 1; *supra* chapter 2.

27. Ravitch, *supra* note 6, at 558–73; *infra* this chapter.

28. Laycock, *supra* note 23; *supra* chapter 2; Ravitch, *supra* note 6, at 504–08, 544–58.

29. The concept of relying on multiple and varied approaches to constitutional interpretation, however, is not new. Philip Bobbitt's modalities of constitutional interpretation are an example of an approach that relies on a variety of factors whose importance varies given the interpretive situation. *See* Philip Bobbitt, Constitutional Interpretation 11–22 (1991). Admittedly, Bobbitt's modalities operate more as interpretive devices than the narrow principles suggested herein, which must be actuated through the interpretive process. *Id.* at 22 ("The modalities of constitutional argument are the ways in which law statements in constitutional matters are assessed; standing alone they assert nothing about the world. But they need only stand alone to provide the means for making constitutional argument.").

30. This should come as no surprise given that the Court's doctrine has not been consistent over the years.

31. U.S. Const. amend. I.

32. A number of these issues are discussed *infra* this chapter; *see also* Ravitch, *supra* note 6, at 558–73.

33. Perhaps the best example of this is the Rehnquist Court's treatment of financial aid that flows to religious entities and Free Exercise Clause exemptions, on the one hand, and school prayer, on the other hand. *Compare Zelman,* 122 S. Ct. 2460 (using formal neutrality to uphold school vouchers), *Mitchell,* 530 U.S. 793 (plurality opinion) (using formal neutrality to uphold the lending of equipment to religious schools), *and* Employment Division v. Smith (using a formal neutrality-type argument to hold that there is no constitutional right to an exemption from a generally applicable law that burdens one's religious practice), *with Santa Fe Independent School District v. Doe,* 530 U.S. 290 (2000) (prayer at public school football games delivered by a student pursuant to a school policy that allowed students to elect speaker is unconstitutional).

34. *Compare Lee,* 505 U.S. at 591 ("The First Amendment protects speech and religion by quite different mechanisms. Speech is protected by ensuring its full expression even when the government participates. . . . The method for protecting freedom of worship and freedom of conscience in religious matters is quite the reverse. In religious debate or expression the government is not a prime participant, for the framers deemed religious establishment antithetical to the freedom of all."), *McCollum,* 333 U.S. at 212 (". . . the First Amendment rests upon the premise that both religion and government can best work to achieve their lofty aims if each is left free from the other within its respective sphere"), *and Everson,* 330 U.S. at 18 ("The First Amendment has erected a wall between church and state. That wall must be kept high and impregnable. We could not approve the slightest breach"), *with Zelman,* 122 S. Ct. 2460 (facially neutral school voucher program is constitutional where 96.6 percent of voucher students attend religious schools because a few secular private schools and a sizable number of public magnet and charter schools are available, thus giving parents "true private choice" in deciding that their children will attend the religious schools).

35. *See, e.g., Everson,* 330 U.S. at 18 ("The First Amendment has erected a wall between church and state."); *McCollum,* 333 U.S. a 212 (". . . the First Amendment rests upon the premise that both religion and government can best work to achieve their lofty aims if each is left free from the other within its respective sphere.").

36. *See, e.g., Everson,* 330 U.S. at 16 (". . . we must be careful, in protecting the citizens of New Jersey against state-established churches, to be sure that we do not inadvertently prohibit New Jersey from extending its general state law benefits to all its citizens without regard to their religious belief."); *id.* at 18 ("State power is no more to be used so as to handicap religions, than it is to favor them").

37. *See* Laycock, *supra* note 23, at 1001–02.

38. *Id.* at 1004 ("Absolute zero is no more attainable in encouragement and discouragement than in temperature. We can aspire only to minimize encouragement and discouragement.").

39. U.S. 329 (1975).

40. U.S. 229 (1977).

41. U.S. 402 (1985).

42. U.S. 388 (1983).

43. U.S. 639 (2002).

44. U.S. 589 (1988).

45. *See infra* this chapter; *see also* Ravitch, *supra* note 6, at 558–60.

46. Ravitch, *supra* note 6, at 566–71; Frank S. Ravitch, *Religious Objects as Legal Subjects,* 40 WAKE FOREST L. REV. 1011, 1071–84 (2005).

47. U.S. 783 (1983).

48. U.S. 668 (1984).

49. U.S. 573 (1989).

50. Justice O'Connor has defined endorsement as:

> In my concurrence in *Lynch,* I suggested a clarification of our Establishment Clause doctrine to reinforce the concept that the Establishment Clause "prohibits government from making adherence to a religion relevant in any way to a person's standing in the political community." The government violates this prohibition if it endorses or disapproves of religion. "Endorsement sends a message to nonadherents that they are outsiders, not full members of the political community, and an accompanying message to adherents that they are insiders, favored members of the political community." Disapproval of religion conveys the opposite message.

Allegheny, 492 U.S. at 625 (O'Connor, J., concurring in part and in the judgment).

51. McCreary County v. ACLU of Kentucky, ___ U.S. ___, 125 S. Ct. 2722 (2005).

52. Glassroth v. Moore, 335 F.3d 1282 (11th Cir. 2003) (Justice Moore installed a massive stone tablet of the Ten Commandments in a central location in the courthouse in the middle of the night without informing the other justices and with a film crew from Coral Ridge Ministries present to film the event).

53. *See* Ravitch, *supra* note 46, at 1071–84.

54. It is the state sponsorship or endorsement of a religion that facilitates religion, and coercion is simply a by-product of something that would be unconstitutional under the facilitation test even if there was no coercion. *See* Ravitch, *supra* note 6, at 558–60. However, in its coercion analysis, the *Lee* Court repeatedly engaged in analysis that would support a similar result under the facilitation test. *See, e.g., Lee,* 505 U.S. at 598 ("The prayer exercises in this case are especially improper because the State has in every practical sense compelled attendance and participation in an explicit religious exercise at an event of singular importance to every student, one the objecting student had no real alternative to avoid.").

55. *See* Ravitch, *supra* note 6, at 558–60.

56. *See, e.g.,* Lamb's Chapel v. Ctr. Moriches Union Free Sch. Dist., 508 U.S. 384, 398 (1993) (Scalia, J., concurring); Comm. for Pub. Educ. & Religious Liberty v. Nyquist, 413 U.S. 756, 662 (1973) (White, J., dissenting).

57. *See Nyquist,* 413, U.S. at 662 (White, J., dissenting) (criticizing *Lemon* as sacrificing "clarity and predictability for flexibility").

58. Lemon v. Kurtzman, 403 U.S. 602 (1971).

59. *See* the various opinions in Agostini v. Felton, 521 U.S. 203 (1997), and Mitchell v. Helms, 530 U.S. 793 (2000) (plurality opinion).

60. *See supra* notes 56–57, and accompanying text.

61. *See* Ravitch, *supra* note 6, at 544–58.

62. This seems clear given the reasoning in *Lemon. Lemon,* 403 U.S. 602, and the use of that reasoning in some later cases.

63. U.S. 203 (1997).

64. *See supra* chapter 2.

65. U.S. 668 (1984).

66. See the discussion between Justice O'Connor and Justice Stevens in Capitol Square Review and Advisory Bd. v. Pinette, 515 U.S. 753, 772 (1995) (O'Connor, J., concurring); *id.* at 798 (Stevens, J., dissenting).

67. *Id.*

68. Ravitch, *supra* note 46, at 1015–16, 1020–21.

69. *Id.* at 1020–21.

70. *Id.; supra* at chapter 1.

71. Ravitch, *supra* note 46, at 1071–84.

72. *Id.* at 1018–27, 1071–84.

73. Ravitch, *supra* note 46, at 1015–16, 1020–21.

74. *Capitol Square,* 515 U.S. at 798 (Stevens, J., dissenting).

75. Ravitch, *supra* note 6, at 544–58; Ravitch, *supra* note 46, at 1071–84.

76. U.S. 577 (1992).

77. *Id.*

78. In fact, in *Lee* itself, the Court phrased the coercion test this way: "It is beyond dispute that, at a minimum, the Constitution guarantees that government may not coerce anyone to support or participate in religion or its exercise, or otherwise act in a way which establishes a [state] religion or religious faith. . . ." *Lee,* 505 U.S. at 587.

79. *Id.* at 631 (Scalia, J., dissenting).

80. *Id.*

81. Ravitch, *supra* note 6, at 556.

82. *See, e.g.,* Zelman, 536 U.S. 639 (most recent case in a long line of aid cases not applying the coercion test).

83. The cases applying the tradition test make it the primary focus of the decisions. *See, e.g., Lynch,* 465 U.S. 668; *Marsh,* 463 U.S. 783.

84. *See also* Ravitch, *supra* note 6, at 558–71.

85. In this situation the test leads to results similar to those in *Santa Fe,* 530 U.S. 290, *Lee,* 505 U.S. 577, *Abington,* 374 U.S. 203, and *Engel,* 370 U.S. 421, but as will be seen, under somewhat different reasoning.

86. *See* Ravitch, *supra* note 6, at 558–60;

Frank S. Ravitch, School Prayer and Discrimination: The Civil Rights of Religious Minorities and Dissenters (Northeastern 1999).

87. This was exactly the claim made by the district in *Santa Fe*, 530 U.S. at 302.

88. *Id.* at 302–06.

89. F.3d 1313 (11th Cir. 2000), *cert. denied*, 533 U.S. 916 (2001).

90. *Santa Fe*, 530 U.S. at 302–04.

91. *Id.* at 302–06.

92. U.S. 421 (1962).

93. U.S. 203 (1963).

94. U.S. 577 (1992).

95. U.S. 290 (2000).

96. U.S. 783 (1983).

97. *Marsh*, 463 U.S. at 797 (Brennan, J., dissenting).

98. *Id.* at 797–98 (Brennan, J., dissenting).

99. *Id.* at 822–23 (Stevens, J., dissenting).

100. U.S. 38 (1985).

101. *Id.* at 86–87 (Burger, J., dissenting).

102. *Contra Wallace*, 472 U.S. 38 (such a policy is facially invalid if the legislature did not have a valid secular purpose in enacting the law).

103. *Id.* at 85–86, 89–90 (Burger, J., dissenting).

104. *See* Walter v. West Virginia Board of Education, 610 F. Supp. 1169 (W.D. Va. 1985).

105. *Zelman*, 122 S. Ct. 2460 (2002).

106. *See supra* chapter 2.

107. *Zelman*, 122 S. Ct. at 2464–65, 2470–71; *id.* at 2473, 2477–80 (O'Connor, J., concurring).

108. *Id.* at 2473 (O'Connor, J., concurring).

109. *Id.* at 2495 (Souter, J., dissenting).

110. *Id.* at 2485 (Souter, J., dissenting).

111. *Id.* at 2494–95 (Souter, J., dissenting).

112. *Cf.* Lee v. Weisman, 505 U.S. 577 (applying captive audience concept to graduation ceremony).

113. Joseph M. O'Keefe, S.J., *What Research Tells Us About the Contributions of Sectarian Schools*, 78 U. Det. Mercy L. Rev. 425 (2001).

114. *Zelman*, 122 S. Ct. at 2495 (Souter, J., dissenting).

115. *Id.* at 2474 (O'Connor, J., concurring); *id.* at 2493 (Souter, J., dissenting).

116. *Id.* at 2473 (O'Connor, J., concurring).

117. *Id.* at 2494 (Souter, J., dissenting).

118. *Id.* at 2464.

119. *Id.* at 2495.

120. U.S. 1 (1993).

121. *Id.* at 10.

122. *Witters*, 474 U.S. at 485–86, 488.

123. *See generally Zelman*, 122 S. Ct. 2460.

124. *See* Ravitch, *supra* note 6, at 513–23.

125. *Id.*; *see also supra* chapters 4 and 6.

126. *See* Ravitch, *supra* note 6, at 513–23; *see also supra* at chapter 4.

127. *See supra* chapter 6 (discussing soft originalism in the context of the separation mode); *see also* the discussion of soft originalism in chapters 1 and 9.

128. U.S. 1 (1993).

129. U.S. 481 (1986).

130. For example, in *Zobrest* the purpose was to accommodate the petitioner's disability pursuant to the Individuals With Disabilities Education Act, 20 U.S.C. §1400 *et seq. See Zobrest*, 509 U.S. at 3–4.

131. *Zobrest*, 509 U.S. at 10; *Witters*, 474 U.S. at 487.

132. *Cf. Zobrest*, 509 U.S. at 10 (benefits are distributed under the IDEA "without regard to the 'sectarian-non-sectarian, or public-nonpublic nature' of the school the child attends.").

133. *Zobrest*, 509 U.S. at 3, 13.

134. *Witters*, 474 U.S. at 488.

135. *See supra* chapter 2; Ravitch, *supra* note 6, at 513–23.

136. This would be similar to the situation in *Witters* and *Zobrest*. *See, e.g., Zobrest*, 509 U.S. at 10 (benefits distributed under the IDEA are constitutional because they are available "without regard to the 'sectarian-non-sectarian, or public-nonpublic nature' of the school the child attends."). Of course, the wide scope of the programs in those cases made any funding that did flow to religious institutions more diffuse, and thus the amount of funds that might flow to religious institutions would be less substantial than in a tuition voucher program like the one in *Zelman*. Even if the level of aid was more substantial, however, the wide range of both nonsectarian and sectarian options available in those programs would support the defense.

137. *Zobrest*, 509 U.S. 1 (1993); *Witters*, 474 U.S. 481 (1986).

138. Unlike the program in *Zelman*, the programs involved in *Zobrest* and *Witters* were large programs with a wide geographic scope, which included numerous schools, both sectarian and nonsectarian. *Id.*

139. *See generally Zobrest*, 509 U.S. 1; *Witters*, 474 U.S. 481.

140. *See, e.g., Zelman*, 122 S. Ct. 2460.

141. *See* Laycock, *supra* note 23, at 1001–02. It is worth noting that as a general matter state programs that provide tuition support for college would not violate the facilitation test because the range of choices available would include all public and private colleges within the state, thus enabling the private choice defense. Additionally, the amounts flowing to religious institutions under most such programs would be more akin to the situation in *Witters* and *Zobrest* than that in *Zelman*, although it might be greater than in the former cases.

142. F. Supp.2d 707 (M.D. Pa. 2005).

143. *Id.*

144. *Id.*

145. *Id.* at 716–23.

146. *Id.*

147. *Id.* at 735–46.

148. Thomas S. Kuhn, The Structure of Scientific Revolutions (3d ed. 1996) (discussing paradigms in the sciences and asserting that there

is no superparadigm to decide between conflicting paradigms). Of course, it is highly unlikely that Kuhn would support intelligent design theory.

149. *Kitzmiller,* 400 F. Supp.3d at 716–23, 735–46.

150. *Id.* at 735–46.

151. *Id.* at 716–23, 735–46.

152. Obviously, teaching a religious message to a captive audience is not necessary for the facilitation test to be violated. *See* Ravitch, *supra* note 6, at 544–58.

153. This was essentially the situation in *Kitzmiller. See Kitzmiller,* 400 F. Supp.3d 707.

154. *Id.*

155. *Id.*

156. *See supra* chapters 4, 5, and 9.

157. *See, e.g.,* Derek H. Davis, *Kansas Versus Darwin: Examining the History and Future of the Creationism-Evolution Controversy in American Public Schools,* 9-WTR KAN. J.L. & PUB. POL'Y 205, 219–21 (1999) (arguing that intelligent design may be taught objectively so as to not violate the Establishment Clause).

158. The various opinions in *Lynch,* 465 U.S. 668, and *Allegheny,* 492 U.S. 573, demonstrate the variety of approaches justices have used to analyze government displays of religious symbols.

159. The decisions in *Allegheny* and *Lynch* have been highly criticized. *See, e.g.,* Daan Braveman, *The Establishment Clause and the Course of Religious Neutrality,* 45 MD. L. REV. 352 (1986) (criticizing the Court's decision in *Lynch*); Michael W. McConnell, *Religious Freedom at a Crossroads,* 59 U. CHI. L. REV. 115, 126–27 (1992) (criticizing the decisions in both cases and suggesting that the results of the cases are "the worst of all possible outcomes").

160. *See* Braveman, *supra* note 158, at 368–69.

161. U.S. 668 (1984).

162. *See* Braveman, *supra* note 158, at 368–74.

163. Questions about why that painting was chosen would also be relevant—thus reintroducing a limited purpose analysis (to determine if the decision was made to favor a particular faith or religion generally). For example, consider the difference between a mural of the Ten Commandments exhibited as part of a broader display of art in a public art museum and the actions of the current chief justice of the Alabama Supreme Court. Justice Moore, who is known as the "Ten Commandments" judge, snuck a large stone engraving of the Ten Commandments into the Supreme Court building in the middle of the night without consulting his fellow justices. The large stone monument is displayed prominently in the courthouse, and the chief justice has refused to allow other displays to receive similarly prominent attention. Manuel Roig-Franzia, *Biblical Display in Court Rejected,* CHICAGO TRIBUNE, November 19, 2002, at 10.

164. It is important to note that a particular government action may violate the Establishment Clause, yet it may be unwise to challenge that action because it may do more damage than good to the cause of protecting against government establishments when the likely public response to the challenge is weighed against the benefits of bringing the claim. This may be particularly true in situations where the challenged practice is one of ceremonial deism. An example might be the recent challenge to the Pledge of Allegiance, where the Court had already approved exemptions in *Barnette. See* Nedow v. U.S. Congress, 292 F.3d 597 (9th Cir. 2002).

165. *Lynch,* 465 U.S. at 725–26 (Brennan, J., dissenting).

166. *Allegheny,* 492 U.S. at 597–98, 601–02, 605, 612–13; *id.* at 625–27 (O'Connor, J., concurring in part and concurring in the judgment); *id.* at 650–51 (Stevens, J., concurring in part and dissenting in part).

167. *Cf.* March D. Coleman, Comment, *The Angel Tree Project,* 58 U. PITT. L. REV. 475 (1997) ("Reasoned elaboration does little to ensure consistency under a standard governed by the 'reasonable observer'; one judge may see an endorsement when another judge sees neutrality").

168. *See Good News Club,* 533 U.S. 107–09, 118–20.

169. This is consistent with aspects of the Court's approach in *Good News Club,* 533 U.S. 98, and *Lamb's Chapel,* 508 U.S. 384.

170. *See Capitol Square,* 515 U.S. 753.

171. *See Good News Club,* 533 U.S. 134 (Souter, J., dissenting).

172. *Id.* at 118–20 (majority opinion).

173. Church of the Lukumi Babalu Aye v. City of Hialeah, 508 U.S. 520 (1993).

174. *See* Employment Division v. Smith, 494 U.S. 872 (1990).

175. *See supra* at chapter 5.

176. This was Justice O'Connor's position in *Smith. See Smith,* 494 U.S. 899–900 (O'Connor, J., concurring in the judgment).

177. *See, e.g.,* Lyng v. Northwest Indian Cemetery Protective Association, 485 U.S. 439 (1988) (denying request to protect sacred Native American ritual sites from government project); O'Lone v. Estate of Shabazz, 482 U.S. 342 (1987) (Muslim prisoner can be prevented from attending religious services at prison when on work detail outside prison even if prisoner has no choice but to be on work detail); Goldman v. Weinberger, 475 U.S. 503 (1986) (Orthodox Jewish military psychologist can be required to remove yarmulka in indoor military settings despite serious religious objections); Bowen v. Roy, 476 U.S. 693 (1986) (Native American denied request for daughter not to have social security number, despite serious religious concerns); United States v. Lee, 455 U.S. 252 (1982) (Amish employer must pay social security tax despite religious objection).

Index

Jackson, Justice, 3, 8–9, 11, 20, 85–86, 114, 139, 165
Jefferson, Thomas, 3, 81–82
Judaism, 30, 67, 75, 108

Kennedy, Justice, 129, 179
Kitzmiller v. Dover Area School Dist., 186–187
Kuhn, Thomas, 187
Kurland, Philip, 15–16

Laycock, Douglas, 15, 18–20, 24, 26, 70, 88, 167, 173, 186
Lee v. Weisman, 57, 179, 181
Legislative prayer, 180
Lemon test, 15, 24, 122–123, 126–127, 130, 146–147, 169, 177, 188
Lemon/Agostini test, 166, 188
Levy, Leonard, 3
Liberty, *passim*; and accommodationism, 48, 56, 58; and the Establishment Clause, 47–48, 55, 58; and exemptions to generally applicable laws, 48, 50–51, 56, 58; and the Free Exercise Clause, 47–48, 55–56, 58; and pragmatism, 57; and religious equality, 52–54, 58, 162–164; and originalism, 56–58; and separationism, 48, 50, 55–56, 58
Limited public forum. *See* Public forum doctrine
Lincoln, Abraham, 3
Locke v. Davey, 38, 40–41, 43, 45
Lynch v. Donnelly, 75, 115–116, 120–123, 130–131, 134–137, 139–140, 176, 178, 188–189
Lyng v. Northwest Indian Cemetery Protection Assoc., 57–58

Madison, James, 3, 52, 81
Majoritarian dominance critique, 135–136
Marsh v. Chambers, 120, 176, 181
Marshall, Justice, 123, 125
Marshall, William P., 14
McCollum, State of Illinois ex rel. v. Board of Ed., 2–3, 5, 8, 20, 73–74, 85
McConnell, Michael W., 50–52, 54–55, 90
McDaniel v. Paty, 41
Meek v. Pittenger, 175
Menorah, 113, 115, 118, 120, 125–126, 137
Mitchell v. Helms, 37–40, 43–45, 169
Moment of silence, 98–99
Monotheism, 107
Moore, Roy, 176

Mormons, 75
Mueller v. Allen, 175

Nat'l Endowment for the Arts v. Finley, 22–23
Native Americans, 32–33, 57–58
Nativity scene, 101, 112, 113, 115, 118, 120–121, 123–124, 135–138
Neutrality, *passim*; facial, 15, 25–26, 29, 36, 40, 67; formal, 13, 15–36, 34–35, 37–39, 46, 59, 62–64, 73, 166, 177; Free Exercise Clause, 13, 34–36, 49–50, 153, 155, 158; nonexistence, 13–36, 60, 62–64, 73; and separation, 13, 15, 72–74, 84, 133; substantive, 1, 13, 15, 18–20, 24, 26
Newdow, Michael, 131
Nonfoundationalism, 85
Nonpreferentialism, 6–7, 99–101
Nonpublic fora. *See* Public forum doctrine

O'Connor, Justice, 97, 110, 115, 121–122, 125, 129, 136–137, 178
Old Amish Order, 33
Originalism, 1–8, 13, 51–52, 57, 61–62, 74–78, 81–86, 89, 129, 153, 155, 157–158, 164–165, 171
Oz, 15

Parental rights, 34
Peirce, Charles Sanders, 9
Pervasively sectarian institutions, 39–40
Peyote, 32–33
Philosophical hermeneutics, 9–11, 85
Plato, 16
Posner, Judge Richard, 85
Powell, Jefferson H., 4, 130
Pragmatism, 8, 76–78, 82, 83–86, 163–166, 172, 188
Prayer. *See* Legislative prayer; Establishment clause, school prayer
Presbyterianism, 152
Private schools: aid to, 20–21; religious, 20–21, 25; vouchers (*see* Government aid to religion, vouchers)
Protestants, 45, 129, 133
Public forum doctrine, 23, 27, 30–32, 38, 41
Purpose. *See* Secular purpose

Rawls, John, 111
Reed, Justice, 3, 5, 74–75
Rehnquist, Justice, 84, 115–116, 129–130

About the Author

Frank S. Ravitch is Professor of Law at Michigan State University College of Law. He is the author of *School Prayer and Discrimination: The Civil Rights of Religious Minorities and Dissenters; Law and Religion, A Reader: Cases, Concepts, and Theory*; and, with Janis McDonald and Pamela Sumners, *Employment Discrimination Law.*